Du Bois's Dialectics

Du Bois's Dialectics

Black Radical Politics and the Reconstruction of Critical Social Theory

Reiland Rabaka

LEXINGTON BOOKS
A division of
ROWMAN & LITTLEFIELD PUBLISHERS, INC.
Lanham • Boulder • New York • Toronto • Plymouth, UK

LEXINGTON BOOKS

A division of Rowman & Littlefield Publishers, Inc.
A wholly owned subsidary of The Rowman & Littlefield Publishing Group, Inc.
4501 Forbes Boulevard, Suite 200
Lanham, MD 20706

Estover Road
Plymouth PL6 7PY
United Kingdom

British Library Cataloguing in Publication Information Available

Library of Congress Cataloging-in-Publication Data

Rabaka, Reiland, 1972–
  Du Bois's dialectics: Black radical politics and the reconstruction of critical social
theory / Reiland Rabaka.
     p. cm.
  Includes bibliographical references and index.
  1. Du Bois, W. E. B. (William Edward Burghardt), 1868–1963—Political and social
views. 2. African Americans—Politics and government. 3. Radicalism—United States.
4. Critical theory—United States. 5. Critical pedagogy—United States. 6. Religion and
sociology—United States. 7. African Americans—Reparations. 8. African Americans—
Study and teaching. I. Title. II. Title: DuBois's dialectics.
  E185.97.D73R323 2008
  303.48'4092—dc22

                                                                           2008024517

  ISBN: 978-0-7391-1957-0 (cloth: alk. paper)
  ISBN: 978-0-7391-1958-7 (pbk.: alk. paper)
  ISBN: 978-0-7391-3099-5 (electronic)

Printed in the United States of America

∞™ The paper used in this publication meets the minimum requirements of American
National Standard for Information Sciences—Permanence of Paper for Printed Library
Materials, ANSI/NISO Z39.48-1992.

For my brothers
Robert Dean Smith II and Dwight Randle Wellington Clewis

And, as with all of my work,
for my mother, grandmothers, and great aunt
Marilyn Jean Giles, Lizzie Mae Davis, Elva Rita Warren,
and Arcressia Charlene Connor

Nkosi Sikelel' iAfrika . . .

Contents

Preface and Acknowledgments

I think all theories are suspect, that the finest principles may have to be modified, or may even be pulverized by the demands of life, and that one must find, therefore, one's own moral center and move through the world hoping that this center will guide one aright.

—James Baldwin, *Notes of a Native Son*, 9

Black Studies/African American Studies/Africana Studies was born with the express purpose of *decolonizing the minds of people, especially black people*. Although much knowledge can be produced by writing histories and social scientific studies, no amount of information could get very far in the absence of minds unable to see or understand it. Important as empirical work has been and continues to be, without interpretation, even at the level of the methods used for organizing the research and gathering data, such work would be meaningless. The power of interpretation is such, however, that it, too, is embedded in a special type of interpretation or hermeneutic without which it, as well, would be meaningless. And that interpretation we call *theory*.

—Lewis R. Gordon and Jane Anna Gordon, *Not Only the Master's Tools*, x

Critical theory envisions philosophy not so much as an abstract or general engagement with questions of human existence; rather, it envisions a productive relationship between philosophy and other disciplines—for example, sociology, cultural studies, feminist theory, African American studies—and the use of this knowledge in projects to radically transform society.

—Angela Y. Davis, *African American Philosophers: 17 Conversations*, 22

It should be understood that it is by far the significance of Du Bois's protest and of his gradual alienation, rather than the solutions he proposed, that are instructive. For he was an intellectual in the purest sense of the word—a thinker whose obligation was to be dissatisfied continually with his own thoughts and those of others. . . . In the course of his long, turbulent career, then, W.E.B. Du Bois attempted virtually every possible solution to the problem of twentieth century racism—scholarship, propaganda, integration, cultural and economic separatism, politics, international communism, expatriation, third-world solidarity. First had come culture and education for elites; then the ballot for the masses; then economic democracy; and finally all these solutions in the service of global racial parity and economic justice.

—David Levering Lewi*s, W.E.B. Du Bois: The Fight for Equality and the American Century, 1919–1963*, 570–71

DU BOIS'S DIALECTICS AND THE AFRICANA TRADITION OF CRITICAL THEORY: DECONSTRUCTING AND RECONSTRUCTING THE MEANING OF "CRITICAL" IN CRITICAL THEORY

Although critical theory has long been associated with the Frankfurt School, and specifically the intellectual lives and legacies of Theodor Adorno, Walter Benjamin, Erich Fromm, Jurgen Habermas, Max Horkheimer, and Herbert Marcuse, the names and contributions of several other significant critical social theorists have been recently raised. In my previous book, *W.E.B. Du Bois and the Problems of the Twenty-First Century*, I accented and analyzed Du Bois's distinct contributions to radical politics and critical social theory. The present volume, *Du Bois's Dialectics: Black Radical Politics and the Reconstruction of Critical Social Theory*, is unprecedented in the fact that it offers the first extended treatment of Du Bois's contributions to what has been called "new critical theory." Du Bois, of course, remains the primary point of departure here but, in an extremely intellectually audacious move, his contributions to radical politics and critical social theory are brought into critical dialogue with a wide range of contemporary discursive developments, new theories and praxes: from philosophy of education, sociology of education, and critical pedagogy to reparations theory and revolutionary humanism; from philosophy of religion, sociology of religion, black liberation theology, and womanist theology to the politics and problematics of the infamous Du Bois-Washington debate. *Du Bois's Dialectics* builds bridges from Du Bois's contributions to classical critical theory to several contemporary intellectual-activist communities, connecting Du Bois and the Africana tradition of critical theory to a wide range of new social scientific research, radical political struggles, and revolutionary social movements.

Now, at this point many of my readers may be scratching their heads and/or wondering aloud about Du Bois's contributions to "new" or contemporary critical theory, but that curiosity and faint feeling of confoundedness is precisely why this book warrants critical engagement by intellectual-activists both within and without Africana Studies, interdisciplinary intellectual-activists who have deep and abiding commitments (à la Du Bois) to politically engaged scholarship, insurgent intellectualism, radical political praxes, and revolutionary democratic social transformation. Du Bois's dialectical thought and radical political legacy challenges the interpretations (or, rather, the misinterpretations) of those who constantly quarantine him to his early years. Here I feel compelled to reiterate, as I did in *Du Bois and the Problems of the Twenty-First Century*, that those contemporary critics who start and stop with Du Bois's early work, such as *The Philadelphia Negro*, *The Souls of Black Folk*, and "The Talented Tenth," do him a great and grave disservice when they praise or criticize these works as though he never wrote another word.

In essence, and this is the major artery of my argument on this issue, contemporary critics customarily intellectually assassinate Du Bois at thirty-five, the age at which he wrote his most famous work, *The Souls of Black Folk*. It is as if he did not live another sixty years and die as a much revered revolutionary Pan-Africanist at the ripe old age of ninety-five with the Pan-African socialist president of Ghana, Kwame Nkrumah, at his bedside. It is as if he was not numbered among the radical leaders of the New Negro Movement, or repeatedly acknowledged as an impresario of the Harlem Renaissance with both physical and metaphysical connections to the aesthetic and political lives and legacies of Langston Hughes, Countee Cullen, Claude McKay, Jessie Fauset, Alain Locke, Zora Neale Hurston, James Weldon Johnson, and A. Philip Randolph, to name only a few. It is as if Du Bois did not spearhead the Niagara Movement and put forward intellectual history-making criticisms of Booker T. Washington and his accommodationist philosophy. It is as if he did not go on to establish the NAACP, the first national civil rights organization in United States history, and edit one of the most popular periodicals in African American history, *The Crisis*. It is as if he was not an active member of the Socialist Party from 1911 to 1912, and controversially joined the Communist Party fifty years later in 1961. It is as if he did not undertake the first major work on the intersections and interconnections between race and class or, rather, racism, colonialism, and capitalism, from a race-conscious and racism-critical Marxist perspective, simultaneously inaugurating what Cedric Robinson, Manning Marable, Gerald Horne, and Robin D.G. Kelley, among others, call "black Marxism." It is as if Du Bois was not the esteemed guest of Mao Tse-tung in communist China, or Nikita Khrushchev in Soviet Russia. And, finally, it is as if his passport was not revoked by the U.S. government for half a decade and he was not harassed and ultimately jailed at eighty-two years of age for advocating peace, disarmament, and associating with communists and socialists. In his magisterial *Black Marxism*, Cedric Robinson (2000) wrote of the blatant neglect of Du Bois and his later radical and revolutionary discourse by black and white conservatives, liberals, and radicals:

> The opposition to Du Bois was grounded on deeper reservations: the recognition that his work had origins independent of the impulses of Western liberal and radical thought. Thus, when his contribution to the American historical tradition should have been celebrated by its historians and scholars, the reaction of the academy was often vilification and neglect. And when he should have been recognized as one of the deans of radical historiography—in his seventh decade he became one of the two most sophisticated Marxist theorists in America—the orthodox and "authorized" intellectuals accused him of Marxian heresies, racial chauvinism, and flawed conceptualization. . . . Du Bois committed himself to the development of a theory of history, which by its emphasis on mass action was both a critique of the ideologies of American socialist movements and a revision of Marx's theory of revolution and class struggle. . . . Du Bois was one of the first American theorists to sympathetically confront Marxist thought in critical and independent terms. (pp. 186, 196, 207)[1]

Indeed, I say again, it is intellectually disingenuous to quarantine our criticisms to the first thirty-five years of the life of an intellectual-activist who, not simply continued to contribute to radical politics and revolutionary social movements for another sixty years after he wrote *The Souls of Black Folk* and "The Talented Tenth," but who, as Manning Marable observed, left an intellectual and political legacy that ranks with and rivals those of Frederick Douglass and Martin Luther King, Jr. Marable (1986) decidedly declared the following:

> Only Frederick Douglass and Martin Luther King, Jr., equaled Du Bois's role in the social movement for civil rights in the United States. But, in other respects, Du Bois's diverse activities over nearly a century left a larger legacy. Du Bois was the "father of Pan-Africanism" and a central theoretician of African independence; the major social scientist, educator, critic, and political journalist of black America for two generations; and an important figure in the international movements for peace and socialism. (p. viii)

For over a decade my primary theoretical preoccupation has been to chart Du Bois's contributions to radical politics and critical social theory. Not only have I read and reread his early work—of course, *The Philadelphia Negro*,

The Souls of Black Folk, and "The Talented Tenth" among them—but, in order to coherently and comprehensively chronicle his disparate contributions to critical theory of contemporary society, I have turned time and time again to his other, some might even go so far to say "more obscure," albeit groundbreaking, scholarly books, such as *The Negro, Darkwater, The Gift of Black Folk, Black Reconstruction, Black Folk, Then and Now, Color and Democracy*, and *The World and Africa*, among others; his innumerable efforts at autobiography, for instance, *Darkwater, Dusk of Dawn, In Battle for Peace*, and *The Autobiography of W.E.B. Du Bois*; his edited volumes, specifically the Atlanta University studies; his editorship of and publications in periodicals, such as *The Moon, The Horizon, The Crisis*, and *Phylon*; his, literally, hundreds of critical essays and scholarly articles on a staggeringly wide range of topics; his public intellectualism, political activism, and participation in national and international radical and revolutionary social movements, such as Pan-Africanism, the Niagara Movement, the NAACP, the New Negro Movement, the Harlem Renaissance, the Civil Rights Movement, the Women's Liberation Movement, and the Peace Movement, among others; and his countless creative writings, which encompass novels, short stories, poetry, and plays.

In my doctoral dissertation I stumbled across one of the most amazing discoveries of my intellectual life: an inchoate Africana tradition of critical theory. From 1997 to 2007 my research and writings have accented the primary point of departure and paradigmatic figure of the Africana tradition of critical theory, W.E.B. Du Bois, but, I should quickly bellow, there are several other major theorists in this tradition, and it is to these theorists and their contributions that my subsequent book, *Africana Critical Theory: Reconstructing the Black Radical Tradition from W.E.B. Du Bois to Amilcar Cabral*, will be devoted. However, here in the present volume Du Bois's contributions to new critical theory are brought into critical dialogue with several of the new theories and praxes that distinguish contemporary critical theory from classical critical theory, and it concretely connects Africana Studies and the Africana tradition of critical theory with the wider (often unwieldy) world of radical politics and critical social theory.

In my previous book I noted that W.E.B. Du Bois inaugurated an extremely distinct style of critical theorizing that could complement and aid those contemporary critical theorists who are interested in reconstructing and renewing the "critical" in "critical theory" and refocus it on the modern and postmodern, as well as the colonial and neocolonial problems of the twenty-first century. Du Bois's critical theoretical discourse was not derived from that of the Frankfurt School and, as I demonstrated in my first book, *Du Bois and the Problems of the Twenty-First Century*, many of its major theoretic motifs were developed long before the Frankfurt School (i.e., *Institut für Sozial-forschung* [the Institute for Social Research]) was formed at the University of Frankfurt am Main in 1930. In point of fact, and to get to the meat of the matter, W.E.B. Du Bois, who provides the Africana tradition of critical theory with its primary point of departure, graduated from Harvard University with a Ph.D. in history in 1895, the very same year that the oldest member of the Frankfurt School of critical theory, Max Horkheimer, was born. Prior to graduating with a Ph.D. from Harvard, Du Bois, as is well-known, earned a bachelor's degree from Fisk University, where he studied German, Greek, Latin, classical literature, philosophy, ethics, chemistry, and physics; received a second bachelor's degree, *cum laude*, in philosophy, and a master's degree in history, both from Harvard; and earned a second master's degree and completed his doctoral studies, studying history, economics, politics, and political economy, at Friedrich Wilhelm University, now the University of Berlin, in Germany. Therefore he, literally, was *developing* and *doing* authentic interdisciplinary critical social theory either before the Frankfurt School critical theorists were born or, at the least, when they were toddlers. One need look no further, for instance, than his early, critical politico-sociological works, which helped to inaugurate American sociology and, especially, sociology of race, and his early interdisciplinary "social" and "community" studies of black life and culture with which he, of course, initiated Africana Studies: *The Suppression of the African Slave Trade to the United States of America, 1638-1870*, "The Conservation of Races," "Careers Open to College-Bred Negroes," *The Philadelphia Negro: A Social Study*, *The Atlanta University Publications* under his editorship, *The Souls of Black Folk*, "The Talented Tenth," and his early "social" and "community" studies posthumously published in *W.E.B. Du Bois on Sociology and the Black Community*, among others.

Du Bois's Dialectics: Black Radical Politics and the Reconstruction of Critical Social Theory seeks to sidestep the intellectual timidity of classical and much of contemporary critical theory by, not simply arguing that critical theory has been and remains *intellectually insular* and *epistemically exclusive*, but by moving beyond the deconstructive moment that so many non-white and non-male critical theorists seem to be caught in and boldly advancing the possibilities of a new, reconceived and reconstructed critical theory of contemporary society. For instance, beyond the evils of capitalism, the Africana tradition of critical theory engages and sincerely seeks solutions to the problems of racism, sexism, colonialism, heterosexism, Eurocentrism, religious intolerance, war, nuclear annihilation, ecological devastation, and animal extinction, among many others. Here it is important to emphasize that though conventional critical theory does at times critique many of the aforementioned, though certainly not all of the aforementioned, it has not and does not now claim to do so in the interest of folk of color, especially blacks, as well as whites. Usually conventional critical theory's discourse is unwittingly and clandestinely quarantined to the life-worlds and lived experiences of whites in capitalist countries, though it, of course, claims to be a "universal" and "global" theory of history, human liberation, and social transformation. This conundrum cuts to the core of the Africana tradition of critical theory and its efforts to rescue and rehabilitate the "best" of the black radical tradition.

REVISITING (AND REVISING) THE MEANING OF "RADICAL" IN BLACK RADICAL POLITICS

Invoking the black radical tradition in an epoch of war and religious rivalry, at a time when our war-torn world seems closer than ever before to that final fiery moment, may shock and awe many of my more conservative and (neo)liberal readers. However, I believe that it is important to humbly—albeit strongly—stress that this often-despised, routinely overlooked, and frequently unengaged tradition of radicalism has and continues to provide viable solutions to many of the problems confronting the contemporary world. Further, it is my belief that the enigmatic issues of the contemporary world are illuminated by black radicals in unique ways in which they are not by Marxists, feminists, pragmatists, existentialists, phenomenologists, hermeneuticists, deconstructionists, poststructuralists, postmodernists, postcolonialists, critical pedagogues, liberation theologians, and (neo)liberal social scientists, among others.

The black radical tradition is much more than a deconstructive response to white supremacy, European modernity, the African holocaust, racial enslavement, racial colonialism, and racist capitalism; and the theories and praxes produced by its practitioners should not be ghettoized and quarantined to "black folk" and/or "the black experience." The acclaimed African American philosopher Cornel West has persuasively argued in *Prophesy Deliverance!: An Afro-American Revolutionary Christianity* (1982) that Africans were central to, if not the unacknowledged motors inside of the monstrous machines of, European modernity and its aftermaths. Therefore, to truly comprehend the issues arising out of European modernity and, even more, the pastiche and pitfalls of postmodernity, a critical engagement of not simply "the black experience," but continental and diasporan African history, culture, and thought, and specifically the black radical tradition, is necessary.

European modernity globalized, among other things, white supremacy, and the black radical tradition has consistently countered it, often providing glowing and irrefutable examples of its abominations and inhumanity, among other contradictions. In this sense, then, the black radical tradition offers more than five hundred years of theory and praxis that could potentially aid contemporary continental and diasporan Africans, as well as other people of color and white "race traitors," in their efforts to rupture their relationships with, not simply white supremacy but, considering the historical discourses and ongoing developments in womanism, black feminism, black liberation theology, revolutionary black nationalism, black Marxism, African socialism, and revolutionary decolonization, among others, the ways in which white supremacy overlaps, interlocks, and intersects with sexism, capitalism, and colonialism. What is often overlooked, and what *Du Bois's Dialectics* critically accents, is the historical fact that there is an undeniable and inextricable relationship between European modernity and the African holocaust, racial enslavement, racial colonialism, and the rise and racist nature of capitalism. Moving far beyond, and actually going against, "conventional" (read: white supremacist) conceptions of European modernity, from the critical points of view of people of color, of non-white folk, it had the exact opposite effects as it did for Europe and Europeans.

Where we are told that European modernity bequeathed "radical" political breakthroughs with regard to the American Revolution of 1776 and the French Revolution of 1789, during this same period both the Americans and the French, among other European nations, participated in holocausts against, and the enslavement and colonization of various non-white folk, particularly Native Americans and Africans. Where it is said that European modernity ushered in new notions of empire, what is most often not said is that they erected their empires on the carnage and ruins of the nation-states, nay, even more, on the cultures and civilizations, on the sciences and technologies of various peoples of color. Where we are told time and time again that European modernity contributed the modern philosophical foundation for the arts and the sciences, no mention is made of the many millions of ways in which non-Europeans have not simply influenced and inspired European artists and scientists, but in many instances provided them with points of departure, the basic architecture, if you will, and the very tools through which they have built their modern haunted houses and postmodern plantations.

European modernity, and its postmodern interpretation, has always been and remains one long self-congratulatory and narcissistic narrative, which has at its heart a centuries-spanning celebration of Europe's Europeanization, Europe's "civilization" and Christianization, Europe's whitewashing of the entire dark, unenlightened, non-European world. Deeply embedded in the discourse of, and the discourse on, European modernity is a latent *Eurocentric intellectual insularity* and *Eurocentric epistemic exclusiveness* that has been universalized and normalized as a result of Europe's international imperialism. This means, then, that almost *all* modern and postmodern intellectual activity, whether by whites or non-whites, unless it is critically conscious of white supremacy, adheres to Eurocentric paradigms of intellectualism, "scholarly" research, radicalism and, even, revolution. Consequently, this conundrum, this riddle of modern and postmodern radicalism, has profoundly influenced and impacted the history of classical and contemporary thought in general, and the study of modern Africana intellectual history in particular. Therefore, even though Africana Studies, among other (re)emerging disciplines, has made many strong strides in developing deconstructive devices for the critique of Eurocentrism in the arts, sciences, and society at large, it has been woefully weak in self-reflexively putting forward reconstructive tools and theories that move beyond the critique of Eurocentrism and emphasize the importance of revisiting and revising, extending and expanding traditions of black radicalism and, equally important, traditions of revolutionary humanism. This is the major motif and main concern of the present volume, my little labor of love, if you will.

PRELUDE TO A CONCEPTUAL KISS:
AFRICANA CRITICAL THEORY

Much more than neo-black radicalism, *Africana critical theory* is a twenty-first century outgrowth of efforts aimed at accenting *the dialects of deconstruction and reconstruction*, and *the dialectics of domination and liberation* in classical and contemporary, continental and diasporan African life-worlds and lived experiences. Its major preoccupation is with synthesizing classical and contemporary black radical theory with black revolutionary praxis. Consequently, Africana Studies provides Africana critical theory with its philosophical foundation(s) and primary point(s) of departure because it moves beyond monodisciplinary approaches to Africana phenomena. More than any other intellectual arena, Africana Studies has consistently offered the black radical tradition its highest commendations and its most meticulous criticisms. It is, also, the academic discipline that most inspired Africana critical theory's unique method—"unique" especially when compared to other forms of critical theory that emerge from traditional disciplines—because Africana Studies is a *transdisciplinary discipline*—that is, *a discipline that transgresses, transcends, and transverses the academic boundaries and intellectual borders, the color lines and racial chasms, and the jingoism and gender injustice of traditional single phenomenon-focused disciplines, owing to the fact that at its best it poses problems and seeks solutions on behalf of Africana (and other struggling) people employing the theoretic innovations of both the social sciences and humanities, as well as the political breakthroughs of grassroots radical and revolutionary social movements*.[2]

"But," the critics of Africana critical theory have been quick to query, "Isn't 'critical theory' Eurocentric?" I usually respond speaking almost in a whisper so that they will know that I am sincere when I say gently but emphatically, "No." Then I go on, "Frankfurt School critical theory may be Eurocentric, but critical theory, in a general sense, is not Eurocentric. If we take that argument, the assertion that 'critical theory' is Eurocentric, to its logical conclusion, then, ultimately, we are saying that critical thinking, that deep theorizing, that philosophizing is Eurocentric. And, what is worse, we are saying this without really taking into critical consideration that most forms of philosophy or theorizing are interrelated and have roots in ancient or classical thought traditions and, most, if not all, Africana Studies scholars and students know that ancient African thought traditions, take Kemet or Egypt as an initial example, provided the very foundations upon which philosophy was built" (see Asante, 2000; Diop, 1974, 1987, 1991; Gordon, 2008; Karenga, 2004; Obenga, 1990, 1993; Ogunmodede, 2004; Onyewuenyi, 1993; Sumner, 1985; Wiredu, 2004).

Part of the problem, I surmise, has to do with the fact that frequently the only form of critical theory that most people have been exposed to is Frankfurt School critical theory. However, truth be told, there are many forms, many traditions, of critical theory.[3] What the critics of Africana critical theory fail to understand is that the body of literature that constitutes the Frankfurt School of critical theory is but one European group's efforts to identify what they understand to be the most pressing problems of their age and put forward viable solutions to those problems.[4] In a nutshell, this is what critical theory, in a general sense, entails; this is its basic method. That so many sophisticated theorists, in Africana Studies in specific, cannot seem to comprehend that *posing problems and searching for solutions* to those problems not only preceded the Frankfurt School but, especially in the Africana tradition of critical theory, raised questions and offered answers above and beyond the intellectual and ethical universe(s) of the Eurocentric tradition of critical theory, is truly astonishing and, it seems to me, symptomatic of their intense internalization of what Du Bois dubbed "double consciousness," and what I have identified as *intellectual historical amnesia* and *the diabolical dialectic of white intellectual superiority and black intellectual inferiority*.

Some of my critics have said, "Well, why are you calling your work 'critical theory,' then, if it is not Eurocentric? Why not call it something else?" Again, I calmly, almost quietly, respond, saying: Another element of critical theory that intellectually attracted me to it was its almost inherent emphasis on linking theory with praxis. Now, as I understand Africana histories, cultures, and struggles, we black folk have been connecting our words and deeds, our ideas and actions for quite some time, actually since ancient times. So, since this is, perhaps, one of the most popular intellectual and political terms designating *praxis-promoting theory* or *theory with practical intent*, then, I decided to employ it, as one of my mentors, Lucius Outlaw (2005), is fond of saying, "in the interests of black folk."

I have also pointed out to many of my critics that I am fairly fluent in Swahili and could have easily provided Africana critical theory with a Swahili name (*unafahamu?*), but my intention is to make my work accessible to as wide an audience as possible (across the "lines" of race, gender, class, sexual orientation, and religious affiliation), not simply to black academics and Africana Studies intellectual-activists nationally, but to the black masses, other people of color, and even authentic white anti-racists and white "race traitors" internationally. On several occasions I have pointed out the fallacy of attempting to dismiss Africana critical theory solely on the basis of nomenclature by observing that many of its critics continue to work in "disciplines," in "the academy," and "critique" and produce "theory." Even if we were to critically engage just one of these European language-based terms, say, "theory," it, too, is not free from Eurocentric baggage, as the cultural linguistic work of Cheikh Anta Diop (1974, 1978a, 1978b, 1987, 1991, 1996) and Theophile Obenga (1990, 1992, 1993, 1995) deftly demonstrates. For example, the etymology of the word "theory" is derived from the Greek word *theoria*, which means, "to view." There are correlations between *theoria* and another Greek word, *theos* or *theus* or *Zeus*, each of which means "God," and each of which goes far to demonstrate that for the Greeks—as it was with the ancient Egyptians—the theorist is supposed "to view" the world as God would. And, consequently, in seeing the world the way God would, the theorist is supposed to search for and see "the truth," and reveal "the truth" about the world.

I seriously doubt that Africana Studies scholars will suddenly stop calling their conceptual generations "theory" because it is derived from a Greek word and emerges from Greek history, Greek culture, and Greek mythology. Therefore, we must all keep in mind that the great bulk of our modern discourse has taken and is taking place in European colonial languages and in a white supremacist world, and that what we have to do for the foreseeable future is *Africanize* (or, in many instances, *re-Africanize*) anything that can be used in our efforts to continue and further develop *the dialectical process of revolutionary decolonization and revolutionary re-Africanization*. This means, then, that Africana critical theory is incomprehensible without a thorough and critical knowledge of Africana intellectual history, the history of Africana philosophy, and the controversial history of *anti-Eurocentric Africana appropriation and Africanization* of European, among other cultures and civilizations', languages, thoughts, and practices.

Therefore, those who quickly and uncritically claim that Africana critical theory is Eurocentric because they hold the historically and intellectually uninformed belief that "all critical theory is Eurocentric," not only misunderstand and misrepresent critical theory in a general sense, but they also put their internalized Eurocentrism, intellectual historical amnesia, ungroundedness in Africana intellectual history, and, perhaps even, their *anti-Africana conceptual generation*, on display. The critics of Africana critical theory seriously when they argue, often without undertaking a thorough investigation of Africana critical theory, that it is nothing other than Frankfurt School critical theory in blackface, or black Marcusean or black Habermasian critical social theory. As has been witnessed above, and as will be witnessed in the subsequent chapters of the present study, although several Africana critical social theorists (myself included) have been influenced by the Frankfurt School tradition of critical theory, it would be foolhardy and fallacious to assume that such influence functions as a prerequisite or, even more, as a "cause" as opposed to a unique paradigmatic opportunity that is actually more indicative of the Eurocentric colonization of intellectual history and the world of ideas. What is more, and as will be discussed in detail in the subsequent chapter, if any thought tradition or classical theorist serves as a progenitor and prerequisite for Africana critical theory, undoubtedly that honor should be bestowed on W.E.B. Du Bois and his discourse because he above and beyond all others prefigured and provided the primary paradigms and points of departure for the discourse and development of an Africana critical theory of contemporary society.

To take this a step further, even in its *anti-Eurocentric Africana appropriation and Africanization* of certain models and methods of the Frankfurt School or other European traditions of critical theory, Africana critical theory utilizes the revolutionary rationale and the revolutionary intellectual and political resources of its own tradition of critical theory as a *critical theoretical criteria*. In particular, and as will be discussed in detail in my forthcoming book, *Africana Critical Theory*, it is the words and wisdom of the Cape Verdean and Guinea-Bissaun revolutionary, Amilcar Cabral (1979), that has indelibly influenced Africana critical theory's emphasis on appropriation and Africanization, and especially when he wisely warned, "A people who free themselves from foreign domination will not be culturally free unless, without underestimating the importance of positive contributions from the oppressor's culture and other cultures, they return to the upwards paths of their own culture" (p. 143). To "return" to the "upwards paths of [our] own culture" would mean, at least in part, sidestepping racial and cultural essentialists' claims against, and narrow-minded nationalists' knee-jerk reactions to, everything European or non-African, and it would also mean making a critical and, even more, a dialectical distinction between the abominations and undeniable negatives of white supremacy and Eurocentrism, on the one hand, and the positives of European and other cultures' authentic contributions to progressive (or, rather, revolutionary) human culture and civilization, on the other hand.

Again, the Africana tradition of critical theory precedes the Eurocentric tradition of critical theory, and it takes classical Africana intellectual-activists, such as Du Bois and C.L.R. James as points of departure, not the Frankfurt School critical theorists. However, and I should emphasize this, Africana critical theory is not afraid to intellectually interrogate, critically dialogue with, and/or astutely appropriate theoretic breakthroughs contributed by the Frankfurt School and other traditions of critical theory if it can *Africanize* them and put them to critical use in our efforts to continue and further develop *the dialectical process of revolutionary decolonization and revolutionary re-Africanization.* It is, therefore, extremely intellectually insincere of the critics of Africana critical theory to harp on a handful of Eurocentric influences without critically grappling with and attempting to grasp *how* or *the ways in which* it seeks to *Africanize* and utilize aspects of Eurocentric theory and methods *against* the Europeanization process and, even further, I reiterate, in our efforts to continue and further develop *the dialectical process of revolutionary decolonization and revolutionary re-Africanization.* It is also extremely intellectually disingenuous on the part of the critics of Africana critical theory to hoot and holler about the inclusion of some carefully and critically selected insights from a couple of the critical theorists of the Frankfurt School without critically comprehending that *all* of the primary points of departure of Africana critical theory have been and continue to be drawn from classical and contemporary, continental and diasporan African intellectual-activists' life-worlds and lived experiences. In other words, to contend that European critical theorists were the initiators of critical theory, to place them as the "cause" and Africana critical theory and Africana critical theorists as the "effect" is, quite simply, to place the proverbial cart before the horse. It is to intellectually erase or, at the least, to render intellectually invisible, continental and diasporan Africans as *intellectual and political inventors and agents.* It is, as Anthony Bogues (2003) observed, "to study the thought of black thinkers as primarily derivative" and this, of course, only continues Europeanization and Eurocentric intellectual colonization, because Africana

thinkers, then, "are never credited with intellectual independence and originality" (p. 2).

DANCING WITH THE DIALECTIC:
DU BOIS'S DISCURSIVE PRACTICES

In several senses *Du Bois's Dialectics* picks up where *Du Bois and the Problems of the Twenty-First Century* left off and, therefore, should be seen as
something of a sequel and read in tandem with its predecessor. In *Du Bois and
the Problems of the Twenty-First Century*, I identified Du Bois's seminal and
most significant donations to the discourse and development of classical critical theory by undertaking extended analyses of his concepts of race, anti-
racism, and critical race theory; his critique of sexism, and particularly patriarchy; his anti-colonialism and (proto) postcolonial theory; and, his concept
of a race-centered and racism-conscious critique of capitalism and Marxism.
Du Bois's Dialectics deepens and further develops my argument and assertion
of Du Bois as a classical critical theorist by exploring the ways in which his
discourse not simply inaugurated the Africana tradition of critical theory, but
also crucially contributes to the reconstruction of critical theory and what has
been recently referred to as "new critical theory."

   Du Bois's Dialectics is not simply about Du Bois and the Africana tradition of critical theory, but also about what the many people who have contributed to my personal, professional, and political development have taught
me. W.E.B. Du Bois, as I will repeat throughout the text, represents a radical
political intellectual ancestor who provides me with several paradigms and
points of departure to explore Africana Studies' contributions to critical theory of contemporary society. Though his thought is the primary point of departure, the theories and praxes of many, many others have influenced and in-
formed my conceptions of radical politics and critical social theory. Each
chapter of this book bears the imprint of the diverse—though often discon-
nected—intellectual and political arenas and agendas I draw from and endeavor to establish critical dialogue with. As a consequence, the list of intellectuals, activists, archivists, institutions, and organizations to which I am
indebted is, indeed, enormous. Such being the case, I hope I may be forgiven
for deciding that the most appropriate way in which to acknowledge my sincere appreciation is simply to list them below without the protracted praise
each has so solemnly earned. My deepest gratitude and most heartfelt *asante
sana* (a thousand thanks) is offered, first and foremost, to my family: my
mother, Marilyn Giles; my grandmothers, Lizzie Mae Davis (deceased) and
Elva Rita Warren; my great aunt, Arcressia Charlene Connor; my older

brother and his wife, Robert Smith II and Karen Smith; my younger brother and his wife, Dwight Clewis and Terica Clewis; my nieces and nephews, Dominique Clewis, Robert Smith III, Ryan Smith, Kalyn Smith, Remington Smith; and, *the beautiful ones who are not yet born*; my father, Robert Smith I; my grandfather, Joseph Warren (deceased); and, my innumerable aunts, uncles, and cousins throughout the Americas, the Caribbean, and Africa.

An undertaking as ambitious as *Du Bois's Dialectics* would have been impossible without the assistance of colleagues and comrades, both far and wide. I express my earnest appreciation to the following fine folk, who each in their own special way contributed to the composition and completion of this book: Lucius Outlaw; Sonia Sanchez; Amiri Baraka; Rhonda Tankerson; De Reef Jamison; Lamya Al-Kharusi; Denise Lovett; Stacey Smith; Patrick DeWalt; Kimberly Marshall; Lewis Gordon; Anthony Lemelle; Andrew Smallwood; Katherine Bankole; Sigmund Washington; Ursula Lindqvist; Toroitich Chereno; Onye Ozuzu; Troy Barnes; April Sweeney; Nicole Barcliff; Elzie Billops; Adam Clark; Zachary Epps; La'Neice Littleton; Marissa Manriquez; Sara Bloom; Kelly Orians; Daisy Wiberg; Cali Harris; Kristine Lewis; Bakari Kitwana; Paget Henry; Joy James; Alan Sica; Alison Jaggar; Dwight McBride; Lawrie Balfour; Joseph DeMarco; Vincent Harding; Otis L. Scott; George Junne; Tracey Sands; James Massengale; Janette Klingner; Daniel Liston; Mpozi Tolbert (deceased); and, Vincent Woodard (deceased).

I cannot adequately convey the depth of my gratitude to the National Council for Black Studies (NCBS) for providing me with critical feedback and fora to deepen and develop my relationship with Du Bois. I have been presenting my research on Du Bois at NCBS's annual conferences from the time that I was an undergraduate student. I continue to be amazed at how patient some of the senior scholars have been and remain with my interpretation of Du Bois, not only as an architect of Africana Studies, but also—and, perhaps, more controversially—as a classical critical theorist. At the 2008 annual conference my book, *Du Bois and the Problems of the Twenty-First Century*, was awarded NCBS's most prestigious scholarly honor, the coveted W.E.B. Du Bois-Anna Julia Cooper Award. I put into print here what I sincerely said upon receiving the award, and that is that my research and writings are inspired by and, therefore, are a most modest reflection of the insurgent intellectual-activist spirit of the National Council for Black Studies, and it is my humble hope that my work will extend and expand the meaning and mission of Africana Studies. With my work I solemnly seek to make a contribution to revolutionary decolonization and revolutionary re-Africanization, as well as the decolonization and liberation of humanity as a whole.

Along with saying *nashukuru sana* (special thanks) to NCBS in general, I would be remiss not to single out several members whose key contributions and intellectual encouragement have made the present volume possible. I express my earnest appreciation to the following NCBS colleagues and comrades: Molefi Asante; Maulana Karenga; James Turner; Delores Aldridge; James Stewart; James Conyers; Charles Jones; Sundiata Cha-Jua; Perry Hall; Shirley Weber; Barbara Wheeler; Alfred Young; Bill Little (deceased); Munasha Furusa; Akinyele Umoja; Fred Hord; Terry Kershaw; Jeffrey Ogbar; Scot Brown; Alan Colon; Abdul Nanji; Christel Temple; Patricia Reid-Merritt; Kevin Cokley; Salim Faraji; Cecil Gray; Mark Christian; and, Ricky Jones. NCBS board member and Marcus Garvey scholar Ronald Stephens deserves extra special thanks for silently serving as one of the referees for my manuscript and providing several constructive criticisms. I honestly believe that it is a better book because of his comments and suggestions. He is, indeed, a rare intellectual-activist who sidesteps all pretensions to academic rank and seniority, and humbly shares his vast knowledge with any and all who would listen and learn. This book bears the marks of his immense erudition and acumen.

The faculty, staff, and students in the Department of Ethnic Studies and the Center for Studies of Ethnicity and Race in America (CSERA) at the University of Colorado at Boulder deserve special thanks for their patience and critical support. *Nashukuru sana* to our steadfast staff, especially Susan Armstrong and Sandra Lane, for always being there and lending a brother a helping hand. I am also deeply indebted to my colleagues and comrades who selflessly serve on the fine faculty in the Department of Ethnic Studies, each of whom have listened to me rant and rave about Du Bois and his critics over the last couple of years. I say *nashukuru sana*, therefore, to William King, Albert Ramirez, Arturo Aldama, Elisa Facio, Emma Perez, Daryl Maeda, Ken Orona, Deward Walker, Seema Sohi, William Takamatsu, Stewart Lawler, Linda Hogan, Patricia Kaurouma, Vivian Delgado, and Jose Lugo. William King, a former president of NCBS, and his lovely wife Carla welcomed me to Boulder with open arms, and we have shared many memorable meals filled with love-laced words, lots of laughter, and heated discussions and critical debates about everything from the state of Africana Studies to the aesthetic evolution of jazz and "soul music" (as opposed to "rhythm and blues"). Bill has been a model mentor, and I humbly hope that the best of my teaching and research reflect my profound respect for him and what he has shared with me over the last couple of years. Also, I say *asante sana* (a thousand thanks) to the incredibly insightful students who took my seminar on W.E.B. Du Bois at the University of Colorado at Boulder. This book has greatly benefited from the critical questions and eloquent answers they offered me (and Du Bois).

Several libraries, research centers, special collections, and archives hosted and helped me transform this book from a dream into a reality. I am indelibly indebted to the directors, research fellows, and staffs of the W.E.B. Du Bois Memorial Center for Pan-African Culture, Accra, Ghana; Africana Rare Books Room, Balme Library, University of Ghana, Legon; Institute of African Studies, Nnamdi Azikiwe Library, University of Nigeria, Nsukka; George Padmore Institute, London; Center of African Studies, School of Oriental and African Studies, University of London; Department of the Languages and Cultures of Africa, School of Oriental and African Studies, University of London; Center for Ethnic Minority Studies, School of Oriental and African Studies, University of London; American Studies Research Center, King's College London, University of London; Eccles Center for American Studies, British Library, London; African Studies Center, University of Oxford; Rothermere American Institute, University of Oxford; School of American and Canadian Studies, University of Nottingham; Center for American Studies, University of Leicester; Center of African Studies, University of Cambridge; Ferguson Center for African and Asian Studies, Open University; Center for African Studies, University of Leeds; Center of West African Studies, University of Birmingham; Center of African Studies, University of Edinburgh; W.E.B. Du Bois Papers, Department of Special Collections and University Archives, W.E.B. Du Bois Library, University of Massachusetts at Amherst; W.E.B. Du Bois Institute for African and African American Research, Harvard University; Arthur A. Houghton, Jr., Library, Harvard University; Center for African American Studies, Wesleyan University; Schomburg Center for Research in Black Culture, New York Public Library; Nicholas Murray Butler Library, Columbia University; John Henrik Clarke Africana Library, Africana Studies and Research Center, Cornell University; African American Collection, Hillman Library, University of Pittsburgh; Africana Research Center, Pennsylvania State University; Charles L. Blockson African American Collection, Temple University; Center for African American History and Culture, Temple University; Center for Africana Studies, University of Pennsylvania; Moorland-Spingarn Research Center, Howard University; African American Studies Research and Resource Center, George Mason University; John Hope Franklin Collection for African and African American Documentation, Rare Book, Manuscript, and Special Collections Library, Duke University; Carter G. Woodson Center for African American and African Studies, University of Virginia; Robert W. Woodruff Library, Atlanta University Center Archives; Manuscript Sources for African American History, Special Collections, Emory University; Fisk University Library, Fisk University; Amistad Research Center, Tulane University; Center for African and African American Studies, University of Texas at Austin; Center for African American Studies, University of Houston; St. Clair Drake Center for African and African American Studies, Roosevelt University; Center for African American and African Studies, University of Michigan; Neal-Marshall African American Cultural Center, Indiana University; African and African American Collection, University Library, University of California, Berkeley; Ralph J. Bunche Center for African American Studies, University of California, Los Angeles; Center for Black Studies, University of California, Santa Barbara; Blair-Caldwell African American Research Library, Denver Public Library; and, Center for African American Policy, University of Denver.

My astute editor, Julie Kirsch, and the Lexington Books editorial board deserve very special thanks (*nashukuru sana*) for seeing the potential in this book project and prodding me along during the many months it took me to revise the manuscript and prepare it for production. I would like to formally thank Julie, Jessica Bradfield, and Joseph Parry for the care and promptness with which they have handled my book projects, and for their patience with my extremely erratic (if not a bit eccentric) research and writing regimen, which in this instance took me to more than three dozen university and public libraries, archives, and research centers in Africa, Europe, and the United States. I am not by any means the easiest person to get in touch with when I am writing, but throughout the entire research and writing process they have calmly fielded my questions and coolly encouraged me to complete my book.

This book is lovingly dedicated to my brilliant brothers, Dwight Randle Wellington Clewis and Robert Dean Smith II, and, as with all of my work, it is also dedicated to my mother, Marilyn Giles; my grandmothers, Lizzie Mae Davis and Elva Rita Warren; and, my great aunt, Arcressia Charlene Connor—and they individually and collectively know the many millions of reasons why. My brothers, Robert and Randy, have always been there for me, and each in their own unique way has encouraged me to become the person that I am in the process of becoming. I do not now possess the proper command of the English language to express how very proud I am of them and their families. I witnessed their miraculous transformations from boyhood to manhood, and want them both to know that they are a very special source of inspiration for my lifework. I, therefore, humbly offer this book as a testament to what they have taught me, and to my unfaltering faith in them. Needless to say, though I shall say it anyway, *nakupenda sana*—I love them more than any words can express. I am, also, at a loss for words to express my love to and my most profound reverence for my mother, grandmothers, and great aunt. They reared and raised me, loved me and listened to me, berated and believed in me when so many others seemed not the least bit concerned whether I, literally, lived or died. Though my brothers and I grew up in a most acute abject poverty, it was my mother, grandmothers, and great aunt who constantly reminded us that our poverty did not automatically deny our human dignity. They double-dared us to dream but, even more, they encouraged us to humbly and diligently work toward turning our dreams into our realities. Though they could have discouraged me from pursuing higher education, since no one in our immediate family has ever attended a college or university, they instead encouraged and supported me. Why or how remains unbeknownst to me. I suppose this is love in its purest and most unadulterated form. So, once again, to them, I simply say, *nakupenda sana*—I love, admire, and adore them more any words can express. If, then, my gentle readers, any inspiration or insights are gathered from my journey through the jungles of radical politics and critical theory, I pray you will attribute them to the aforementioned. However, if (and when) you find foibles and intellectual idiosyncrasies, I humbly hope you will neither associate them with any of the forenamed nor, most especially, W.E.B. Du Bois. I, and I alone, am responsible for what herein is written. *Nkosi Sikelel' iAfrika. . . .*[5]

Reiland Rabaka
Boulder, Colorado
23 February 2008
W.E.B. Du Bois's 140th Birthday

NOTES

1. As early as his 1907 essay, "The Negro and Socialism," Du Bois detected and detailed deficiencies in the Marxist tradition which included, among other things, a silence on and/or an inattention to race, racism, and anti-racist struggle; racial colonialism and anti-colonial struggle; and the ways in which *both* capitalism and colonialism exacerbate not simply the economic exploitation of non-Europeans, but continues (both physical and psychological) colonization beyond the realm of political economy. Du Bois, therefore, laboring long and critically with Marxian theory and methodology, deconstructed it and developed his own original radical democratic socialist theory that simultaneously built on his pioneering work as a critical race theorist and radical anti-colonialist; called for the radical transformation of U.S. society and the power relations of the world; was deeply concerned about and committed to world peace and demanded disarmament; and advocated the liberation of all colonized, politically oppressed, and economically exploited persons. For further discussion, see Rabaka (2007a), especially chapter 4, "Du Bois's Critique of Capitalism, Critical Marxism, and Discourse on Democratic Socialism."

2. The literature on Africana Studies, which in its most comprehensive sense includes African, African American, Afro-American, Afro-Asian, Afro-European, Afro-Latino, Afro-Native American, Caribbean, Pan-African, Black British and, of course, Black Studies, is diverse and extensive. The most noteworthy overviews and critical analyses are Aldridge (1988), Aldridge and James (2007), Aldridge and Young (2000), Alkalimat (1986, 1990), R. Allen (1974), T. Anderson (1990), Anderson and

Stewart (2007), Asante (1990, 1998, 2003a, 2007a), Asante and Abarry (1996), Asante and Karenga (2006), Azevedo (2005), Bailey (1970), Baker, Diawara, and Lindeborg (1996), Ba Nikongo (1997), Barrett and Carey (2003), Bates, Mudimbe and O'Barr (1993), Blassingame (1973), Bobo and Michel (2000), Bobo, Hudley and Michel (2004), Butler (1981, 2000, 2001), Conyers (2003, 2005), Cortada (1974), Croutchett (1971), Daniels (1980, 1981), Davies, Gadsby, Peterson and Williams (2003), Fierce (1991), N.A. Ford (1973), Fossett and Tucker (1997), Frye (1978), Geggus (2002), Gordon and Gordon (2006a, 2006b), P. Hall (1999), Hare (1972, 1998), Harris, Hine, and McKay (1990), Hayes (2000), Holloway and Keppel (2007), Hudson-Weems (2004, 2007), Johnson and Henderson (2005), Johnson and Lynne (2002), Karenga (1988, 2001, 2002), R.D.G. Kelley (1997b), Kershaw (1989, 1992, 2003), Kilson (1973, 2000a), Kopano and Williams (2004), Marable (2000, 2005), Marable and Mullings (2000), Mazrui (1967, 1974, 1978, 1980, 1986, 1993, 2002a, 2002c, 2004), Mazrui, Okpewho and Davies (1999), Mercer (1994), Norment (2007a, 2007b), Prashad (2000, 2001), Robinson, Foster and Ogilvie (1969), Rojas (2007), Rooks (2006), J.B. Stewart (1976, 1979, 1981, 1992, 1996b, 2004), Stewart, Hare, Young and Aldridge (2003), Turner and McGann (1980), J. Turner (1984), Walton (1969), and Whitten and Torres (1998).

3. Several works, which fall under the rubric of what is currently being called "new critical theory," are already taking up the challenge of making critical theory speak to more than merely European, European American, patriarchal, and heterosexual crises, cultures, and sociopolitical problems. These works lucidly demonstrate that there are many forms and many traditions of critical theory. For further discussion, see Agger (1992b, 1993), Alcoff (2006), Alcoff and Mendieta (2000), Arisaka (2001), P.H. Collins (1998, 2000, 2005, 2006), Dussel (1985, 1995, 1996, 2003), Essed and Goldberg (2001), Fraser (1989), Hames-Garcia (2001), L. Harris (1999b), Huntington (2001), Jafri (2004), Mendieta (2003, 2007), Mignolo (2000, 2003, 2005), Outlaw (2005), Pulitano (2003), Rabaka (2007a, 2008a, 2009), L.C. Simpson (2003), Wilkerson and Paris (2001), and Willet (2001).

4. For further discussion of critical theory, or critical social theory, "in a general sense" and/or beyond the Frankfurt School's conception of critical theory, see Agger (1992b, 2006), J.C. Alexander (2001), Best (1995), Blackburn (1972), Crossley (2005), Dant (2003), Elliott (2003), Fraser (1989, 1997), How (2003), Lichtman (1993), Outlaw (2005), Pensky (2005), Peters, Olssen and Lankshear (2003), Rabaka (2006a, 2007a, 2009), L. Ray (1993), Rhoads (1991), Sica (1998), and J.B. Thompson (1990).

5. Translation: "God bless Africa" in Xhosa. Azania or South Africa's national anthem, _Nkosi Sikelel' iAfrika_, was composed in 1897 by Enoch Mankayi Sontonga, a Xhosa teacher and choirmaster at a Methodist mission school in Johannesburg. Since it was first sung in 1899 at the ordination of Reverend Boweni, a minister in the Methodist tradition, it has been adopted as the anthem of the African National Congress and the national anthem of both Tanzania and Zambia. Additionally, it was sung in Zimbabwe and Namibia during their respective struggles against racial colonialism. Most of Sontonga's songs were heart-wrenching odes, somewhere between the spirituals and the blues, often grappling with the human suffering and social misery

of black life under apartheid. Sontonga, a reportedly deeply religious man, is said to have repeatedly recited this prayer and taught it to his many pupils. The African National Congress continues to close its meetings with this song, and it has been reported that, upon his release from being unjustly imprisoned for twenty-seven years on Robben Island, Madiba Nelson Rolihlahla Mandela was so moved by the solemn singing of it that once elected the president of South Africa he declared Sontonga's grave a national monument and erected a memorial in his honor. Therefore, in my earnest effort to show my sincere solidarity with my known and unknown kith and kin throughout continental and diasporan Africa, I know of no better way to conclude this preface and begin my beloved book: *Nkosi Sikelel' iAfrika.*

Chapter One

Introduction: Du Bois, the Renewal of Black Radical Politics, and the Reconstruction of Critical Social Theory

William Edward Burghardt Du Bois was one of the finest historians ever developed in the United States. The writing of history, though, was but one of his achievements. Though excruciatingly shy, he combined statesmanship and political activism with scholarship. In this way he managed to influence the lives and thoughts of legions. And notwithstanding the rigors of research he found time to inaugurate the systematic development of Black Studies; to found and edit for more than twenty years, *The Crisis*, the most influential black political journal of its time; to command the intellectual leadership of the American black movement; to catalyze the development of Pan-Africanism; and at the end of his days, to assume a role of leadership in the post-World War II peace movement.

—Cedric J. Robinson, *Black Marxism:*
The Making of the Black Radical Tradition, 185

But in a way both modest and extraordinary, Du Bois was a maker of history. Although he sometimes raged, he achieved success through his long, slow influence on the thinkers of black America and their white sympathizers and allies. If the history of ideas in Afro-America is ever written, Du Bois should occupy the most conspicuous place. If—even more unlikely—the full history of the impact of blacks on the American mind is ever charted, his education of the whole nation will be seen as significant indeed. His works have not received the study they deserve, and his modest reputation now rests on grounds that he would not wholly appreciate. He is remembered for his strategy in controversies not always properly understood, and for slogans and concepts that inadequately represent the range of his mind. His words appear to support a variety of contradictory causes and, in common with great bodies of art and literature, are susceptible to such a large number of interpretations that the casual reader is sometimes bewildered. These inexact views of the man occur because Du Bois's vision was filtered through a variety of experiences possible only in America. He was a product of black and white, poverty and privilege, love and hate. He was of New England and the South, an alien and an American, a provincial and a cosmopolite, nationalist and communist, Victorian and modern. With the soul of a poet and the intellect of a scientist, he lived at least a double life, continually compelled to respond to the challenge of reconciling opposites. The essential rhythm of his mind was not so much a steady transition from one set of beliefs to another as a vibrant oscillation between extremes. . . . His politics swung between saturnine conservatism and radical optimism, his body between sensuousness and moral asceticism, his psyche between elation and gloom. To calm the terror inherent in this instability, he relied on a powerful reason that dominated his mind without always fully controlling it.

— Arnold Rampersad, *The Art and Imagination of W.E.B. Du Bois, 292*

Du Bois was not one to cling to a point of view if he felt that changing times had undermined it. . . . Du Bois constantly shaped and refined his views . . . despite or perhaps because of these refinements, the core of Du Bois's thought, his passion for socialism, peace, and equality, remained immutable throughout.

— Gerald Horne, *Black and Red: W.E.B. Du Bois and
the Afro-American Response to the Cold War, 1944-1963*, 7–8

By not ever writing a central theoretical statement clearly articulating his worldview and its meaning, Du Bois left his disciples to interpret the master in a variety of ways.

— Manning Marable, *Black Leadership*, 57

DU BOIS, AFRICANA STUDIES, AND THE RECONSTRUCTION OF CONTEMPORARY CRITICAL THEORY

Du Bois's Dialectics: Black Radical Politics and the Reconstruction of Critical Social Theory offers various (re)interpretations of Du Bois that analyze his thought for its contribution to the discourse and development of "new" or contemporary critical theory. Building on and going beyond the discourse of my first book, *W.E.B. Du Bois and the Problems of the Twenty-First Century*, which explored his long-disregarded contributions to classical critical theory, *Du Bois's Dialectics* engages Du Bois's radical politics and interdisciplinary innovations as a paradigm and point of departure for the reconstruction of contemporary critical theory. Du Bois's seminal and storied work as an intellectual-activist is shown to be of immense importance to contemporary critical theorists interested in intellectually overhauling the foundations of critical theory, making it more multicultural, transethnic, transgender, sexuality-sensitive, and non-Western European philosophy focused by placing it in dialogue with theory and phenomena it has heretofore woefully neglected.

As the overarching issues of racism, sexism, capitalism, and colonialism were intensely scrutinized in my previous study, this volume undertakes critical engagements with and ideological critiques of the ways in which each of the aforementioned impacts and influences education, religion, radical politics, and the politics of reparations and human rights in contemporary culture and society. It employs Du Bois as its critical theoretical point of departure and demonstrates his (and Africana Studies') connections and contributions to philosophy of education, sociology of education, and critical pedagogy; philosophy of religion, sociology of religion, womanist theology, and black liberation theology; radical politics, reparations theory, and revolutionary humanism; and, it offers the first critical theoretical treatment of the W.E.B. Du Bois–Booker T. Washington debate, which inimitably highlights Du Bois's transition from a bourgeois black liberal to a bona fide black radical and revolutionary democratic socialist.[1] Contemporary critical theory purportedly prides itself on bringing dialectical thought to bear on the most pressing social and political problems of the present age, *Du Bois's Dialectics* is distinguished from other works which seek to develop critical theories of contemporary society in light of its unprecedented utilization of Du Bois's dialectical thought and methods as its primary paradigms and points of departure, and its *epistemic openness* and sincere willingness to intellectually interrogate, critically dialogue with, and/or astutely appropriate the theoretic breakthroughs of other traditions of critical theory if it can *Africanize* them and put them to critical use in earnest efforts to further develop *the dialectical process of revolutionary decolonization and revolutionary re-Africanization*.

Where *Du Bois and the Problems of the Twenty-First Century* exhibited a preoccupation with the philosophical foundations and intellectual and political agendas of classical critical theory (demonstrating that many of the problems of the past remain problems in the present because many classical critical theorists quarantined their discourses along racial and gender lines), *Du Bois's Dialectics* is intellectually obsessed with contemporary critical theory (demonstrating that many contemporary critical theorists are unwittingly weakening the critical potency and radical potential of their theories by limiting their intellectual lenses to traditional, single-subject disciplines, Eurocentric and patriarchal theories, and monocultural or white, as opposed to multicultural and transethnic, neo-Marxist and anti-imperialist discourse). The Africana tradition of critical theory (i.e., *Africana critical theory*), as I envision and argue it, not only challenges white Marxist/Eurocentric critical theory to be more cognizant of the constantly intersecting nature of racism, sexism, capitalism and colonialism, but it does so by displaying an *epistemic openness* that generously draws from the work of often-overlooked black contributors to critical theoretical discourse—for example, Du Bois, C.L.R. James, George Padmore, Oliver Cox, Ella Baker, Malcolm X, Frantz Fanon, Amilcar Cabral, Walter Rodney, Audre Lorde, Angela Davis, bell hooks, Cornel West, Manning Marable, Patricia Hill Collins, and Lucius Outlaw, among others—who collectively emphasized the importance of avoiding obsessive economism, the power of ideology critique, the primacy of politics, the political economy of racism and sexism, the politics of education, the politics of religion, cultural criticism, and the need to constantly reconstruct radical politics and critical social theory to speak to the novel and special needs of "the new times," to borrow one of Stuart Hall's (1996) favorite phrases.[2]

As an early interdisciplinarian with undeniable socio-theoretical leanings and deep connections to the discourse(s) of Africana Studies, Du Bois offers Africana critical theory an ideal point of departure to present and develop its discourse. In this study I radically reinterpret Du Bois as a critical social theorist whose extensive theoretical legacy has been omitted from the history and discourse of both classical and contemporary critical theory. Part of this omission, I have a sneaky suspicion, has to do with what is perceived as Du Bois's theoretical eclecticism—that is, his contraction of both Africana and European theory believed to be antithetical by thinkers interior to both thought traditions. However, I demonstrate that claims such as these are not only false but fall flat when Du Bois's discourse is viewed from the epistemically open Africana critical theoretical framework, a framework that acutely emphasizes the purposes and intended outcomes of Africana intellectual-activists' appropriations and combinations. Africana critical theory, then, is not as concerned with *which* (or *whose*) theories Du Bois used, as much as it seeks to discover and learn from *how* or the ways in which he creatively connected and used them.

Du Bois has been hailed as a historian, sociologist, Marxist, Pan-Africanist, and political activist, but never as an early interdisciplinary social theorist with concrete political commitments, not simply to black liberation and racial justice, but to women's liberation, the poor masses and working classes, and colonized and hyper-racialized people of color worldwide. He has long been praised and criticized by legions of scholars who have interpreted and rigorously reinterpreted his work, often overlooking its deep critical theoretical dimensions. In this book Du Bois's multifarious and ever-evolving social theory is situated at the center and examined for its significance to contemporary radical political thought and revolutionary social movements.

Taking Du Bois as its primary point of departure, *Du Bois's Dialectics* identifies and analyzes several issues and key contributions that Du Bois and the Africana tradition of critical theory offers to those interested in redeveloping and radically revising contemporary critical social theory. With chapters on critical pedagogy and philosophy of education, sociology of religion and liberation theology, reparations theory, and the politics and problematics of the Du Bois–Washington debate, this volume builds bridges from Africana Studies to disparate discursive communities, connecting Du Bois and the Africana tradition of critical theory with a wide range of new social scientific research and radical political struggles. Additionally, this study offers social scientists and political radicals an entry point in which to explore Africana Studies and several of its discursive communities, their major concerns, and their contributions to critical theory of contemporary society.

In the American academy, amid the current intellectual trepidation and word-wizardry of many of the more noted black scholars, Du Bois's discourse on education, reparations, religion, civil rights, social justice, women's liberation, world peace, and democratic socialism exist furtively in the black intellectual imagination, stripped of its critical potency, and even mocked by black postmodernists (among many others) who argue that his thought is outdated or old-fashioned. However, for those of us with unquenchable commitments to continuing the fight for freedom, for those of us deeply disturbed by what is going on in our war-torn world, and for those of us who desperately search for solutions to our most pressing social problems, Du Bois's anti-imperial ideas and actions, which emphasize the evil interconnections of racism and capitalism, his increasing commitment(s) to gender justice, his radical political vision, and his theory of social change offer a much needed *Africana* alternative to and through the mazes of postmodernism, postcolonialism, postfeminism, and post-Marxism, among other contemporary conceptual distractions and disruptions. Along with other black radical figures, like Fannie Lou Hamer, Malcolm X, Frantz Fanon, Amilcar Cabral, Ella Baker, and C.L.R. James, the example of Du Bois can serve as a means of rethinking the possibilities of resistance to, and transformation of, the new (global) imperialisms of our age. His work cuts across several disciplines and, therefore, closes the chasm between Africana Studies and critical theory, constantly demanding that intellectuals not simply think deep thoughts, develop new theories, and theoretically support radical politics, but *be* and constantly *become* political activists, social organizers, and cultural workers, folk Antonio Gramsci referred to as "organic intellectuals" (see Gramsci, 1971, p. 3–23 and 2000, p. 300–22). In this sense, the studies gathered in this volume contribute not only to Africana Studies, but also to contemporary critical theoretical discourse across the disciplines, and radical political activism outside of (and sometimes even *against*) the academy.

Bearing in mind the book's main objective, to accent and assess Du Bois's (and Africana Studies') contributions to the renewal of radical politics and the reconstruction of critical social theory, it is not my intention to offer a definitive or even exhaustive treatment of his biography or life-work, which would seem rather redundant coming so quickly on the heels of David Levering Lewis's Pulitzer Prize–winning volumes (see D.L. Lewis, 1993, 2000). I am concerned here primarily, and almost exclusively, with Du Bois's critical theoretical and radical political legacy—that is, with the ways he constructed, deconstructed, and reconstructed theory and the aims, objectives, and outcomes of his theoretical applications and discursive practices. He consistently appropriated, revised and rejected disparate concepts, always integrating what he perceived to be the most radical (and later *revolutionary*) thought into his critical socio-theoretical discourse. His work in several senses, therefore, lends itself to the reconstruction of critical social theory because it provides a novel and long-neglected model and methodology to affect and chart social change and the contours of a new kind of critical theory of contemporary society.[3]

DU BOIS'S DIALECTICS AND THE CRISES OF CONTEMPORARY CRITICAL SOCIAL THEORY

For over a decade several critical social theorists, especially those in America (e.g., Angela Davis (1981, 1989, 1998a), Lucius Outlaw (1983a, 1983b, 1983c, 1983d, 1987, 1990, 1996a, 2005), Nancy Fraser (1989, 1991, 1997), Douglas Kellner (1990c, 1993, 1995), and James Marsh (1995, 1998, 1999, 2001)), have been issuing calls for "a more multicultural, race and gender focused, and broad[er]-based" critical theory (Kellner, 1995, p. 20). Unfortunately, however, few of their fellow critical theorists have taken their summons seriously. One of the glaring ironies and intellectual injustices of contemporary critical theory is that even with the academic popularity of feminism, postcolonialism and, more recently, critical race theory, the white *and* male dominated discourse(s) of critical theory have yet to develop meaningful and in-depth dialogues with these discursive communities. In the introduction to their ground-breaking volume, *New Critical Theory*, William Wilkerson and Jeffrey Paris (2001) admit, "The challenge to critical theorists to rethink their presuppositions according to the realities of non-European cultures and technologies remains the most underthematized aspect of critical theories new and old" (p. 8).

Part of the current crisis of critical theory has to do with its often-uncritical reliance on classical Marxist concepts and categories without sufficiently revising and synthesizing them with new, especially non-Marxian and non-European, theoretical and political developments. Classical Marxism privileged class and the proletariat as the agents of revolutionary social transformation, while unwittingly neglecting the interlocking nature of racism and sexism in capitalist (and colonial) societies. In "The Obsolescence of Marxism?" Douglas Kellner (1995) argues that it is "widely accepted that classical Marxism exaggerates the primacy of class and downplays the salience of gender and race. Clearly, oppression takes place in many more spheres than just the economic and the workplace, so a radical politics of the future should take account of gender and race as well as class" (p. 20). Notice that Kellner is not calling for a complete rejection of Marxism and class theory but coupling it, revising and synthesizing it with race and gender theory. Many black radicals and multicultural Marxists, I believe, would partially agree with Kellner when he writes,

> [W]e need to build on viable political and theoretical perspectives and resources of the past, and I would argue that Marxism continues to provide vital resources for radical theory and politics today. . . . In sum, I believe that we need new theoretical and political syntheses, drawing on the best of classical Enlightenment theory, Marxian theory, feminism, and other progressive theoretical and political currents of the present. Key aspects for such new syntheses, however, are found in the Marxian tradition, and those who prematurely abandon it are turning away from a tradition that has been valuable since Marx's day and will continue to be so in the foreseeable future. Consequently, Marxism is not yet obsolete. Rather, the Marxian theory continues to provide resources and stimulus for critical theory and radical politics in the present age. (p. 25–26)[4]

Kellner and Africana critical theory, however, part company when and where he gives a detailed discussion of the relevance of European derived and developed theories or, rather, Eurocentric theories—Enlightenment theory, Marxism, and feminism—and only alludes to the work of non-European theorists or, as he put it "*other* progressive theoretical and political currents" for renewing radical politics and critical theory in the present (my emphasis). To his credit, Kellner states, "Radical politics today should be more multicultural, race and gender focused, and broad-based than the original Marxian theory" (p. 20). But, he does not identify or critically engage the "other progressive theoretical and political currents" the way, and to the depth and detail to which he does a plethora of white male radical thinkers whose thought, he believes, contributes indelibly to the reconstruction of critical social theory.

Kellner is not alone in arguing for the continued importance of Marxism for contemporary radical politics and the reconstruction of critical social theory. In "Toward a New Critical Theory," James Marsh (2001) audaciously asserts, "A critical theory without Marx" is a "critical theory that is insufficiently critical" (p. 57). He further contends that

> I think we need a much fuller appropriation and use of Marx than is going on in either postmodernism or Habermasian critical theory. If capitalism is deeply pathological and unjust, as I think it is and as I have argued in all of my works, then we need the resources of what still remains the deepest and most comprehensive critique of capitalist political economy, that which occurs in the late Marx in the pages of the *Grundrisse*, *Capital*, and *Theories of Surplus Value,* a total of seven volumes that are more relevant than ever. For these reasons, I draw on Marx's theory of exploited labor in the workplace, his theory of tyranny, in which the economy and money impinge on noneconomic aspects of the lifeworld in a way that is absurd, his theory of a marginalized industrial reserve army, his theory of value and surplus value, and his account of substantive socialism. Capitalist pathology is not just colonization of lifeworld by system, although that is certainly an important part of such pathology, but includes exploitation, tyranny, domination, and marginalization as well. (p. 57)

As with Kellner's claims, Marsh is on point when he asserts the comprehensive character of Marx's critique of capitalism. Similar to Kellner, he warns contemporary critical theorists about the insularity of their discourse and even goes so far to say that "both modern and postmodern critical theory runs the risk of being idealistic in a bad sense, that is, insufficiently attentive to the task of interpreting, criticizing, and overcoming late capitalism in its racist, sexist, classist, and heterosexist aspects. We, modernists and postmodernists alike, need to get down to the job of social transformation" (p. 53). Now, after taking all this in, one of the first critical thoughts that passes through the mind of an anti-sexist critical social theorist of color is, how will radical politics and critical theory become "more multicultural, and race and gender focused," as Kellner contends, if it does not turn to the thought and texts of the most progressive race and gender theorists, some of whom happen to be radical theorists of color, particularly folk of African origin or descent, and some of whom are, of course, women, and women of color in specific?

According to Anthony Bogues (2003), in *Black Heretics, Black Prophets: Radical Political Intellectuals*, "In radical historical studies, when one excavates a different archive, alternative categories are opened up" (p. 86). To be sure, black radical theorists, such as Du Bois, C.L.R. James, Frantz Fanon, Amilcar Cabral and Angela Davis, "deployed Marxism, but in [their] hands the categories used to describe historical processes were wrought into something else" (p. 81). That "something else" which Marxian categories were shaped and molded into by these theorists was based on their critical understanding of continental and diasporan African history, culture, and struggle.

Africana history, culture, and struggle are the deeply disregarded "different archives" that black radicals work with and operate from. These archives are not only in many senses distinctly divergent from the archives of white Marxists, but embedded in them are recurring racial motifs that shade and color black radical politics and social theory. White Marxists' efforts to diminish and downplay racial domination and discrimination have made black radicals' marriage to Marxism a turbulent and very unhappy one. For example, in *From Class to Race: Essays in White Marxism and Black Radicalism*, the Caribbean philosopher Charles Mills (2003) maintains,

> Throughout the twentieth century, many people of color were attracted to Marxism because of its far-ranging historical perspective, its theoretical centering of oppression, and its promise of liberation. But many of these recruits would later become disillusioned, both with Marxist theory and the practice of actual (white) Marxist parties. The historical vision turned out to be Eurocentric; the specificities of their racial oppression were often not recognized but were dissolved into supposedly all encompassing class categories; and the liberation envisaged did not include as a necessary goal the dismantling of white supremacy in all its aspects. Cedric Robinson's pioneering *Black Marxism* (2000), first published in 1983, recounts the long-troubled history of left-wing black diasporic intellectuals (W.E.B. Du Bois, C.L.R. James, George Padmore, Richard Wright, Aimé Césaire) with "white Marxism," and it argues for the existence of a distinct "black radical political tradition" whose historic foci and concerns cannot be simply assimilated to mainstream white Marxist theory. So even if the origin of white supremacy is most plausibly explained within a historical materialist framework that locates it in imperialist European expansionism—as the product, ultimately, of class forces and bourgeois class interests—race as an international global structure then achieves an intersubjective reality whose dialectic cannot simply be reduced to a class dynamic. (p. xvi)

In other words, black radicals' issues with white Marxism often stem from the fact that they understand racism to be both economic *and* experiential. Racial oppression has more than merely an economic exploitative or class dimension that can coolly and calmly be conjectured by well-meaning white Marxist social scientists (see Goldberg, 1990, 1993, 1997, 2001; L. Harris, 1999b; Outlaw, 1996, 2005; C.J. Robinson, 2000). As I discussed in detail in my previous study on Du Bois, racism is motive, and white Marxists' attempts to reduce it to an outgrowth or offshoot of class struggle, or something internal to class conflict robs the racially oppressed of an opportunity to critically theorize their lived reality and a major determinant of their social identities.[5]

Many black radicals, especially black Marxists, are at pains to point out that their criticisms "should not be taken in the spirit of a complete repudiation of Marxism," since, they maintain, "a *modified* historical materialism might be able to carry out an adequate conceptualization of the significance of race" (C.W. Mills, 2003, p. xvi–xvii, original emphasis). But, the long-standing problem has been and remains white Marxists' unwillingness to critically grasp and grapple with the political economy of race and racism, in both capitalist and colonial societies, in their extension and expansion of Marxian concepts and categories. Black Marxists have historically exhibited an epistemic openness, one quite characteristic of Africana critical theory, to critical class theory in a way brazenly counter to white Marxists' almost universal unreceptiveness to, and gnarly neglect of, critical race theory.[6]

Critical race theory, which could be defined as anti-racist praxis-promoting theory critical of the ways in which white supremacy impacts institutions and individuals, has its origins in the works of several civil rights lawyers in the early 1980s. Often associated with the Critical Legal Studies (CLS) movement, which demonstrated in dizzying ways that law is neither neutral nor apolitical, critical race theory began by challenging the racial neutrality of the law (Crenshaw, Gotanda, Peller and Thomas, 1995; Delgado, 1995, 2007; Delgado and Stefancic 2001; Essed and Goldberg 2001; Goldberg, Musheno and Bower, 2001). Legal scholars of color, in complete agreement with the argument that law is non-neutral, criticized the mostly white male leaders of the CLS movement for failing to recognize and critically theorize the crucial role and continued relevance of *race* in social and political interactions and institutions. Their work was quickly recognized as *critical race theory*, and they themselves as *critical race theorists*. In recent years, the term critical race theory has become what Edward Said (1999, 2000) referred to as a "traveling theory," moving in and out of intellectual and political discursive communities far from its theoretical and intellectual origins, and, with each move, taking on new or multiple meanings and losing some of its original logic.

In this sense, then, I argue that critical race theory should not be thought of as an uncritical coupling of anti-racism with Marxism/critical class theory, or limited to the work of the last twenty-five years explicitly identified under the rubric of "critical race theory." Its intellectual history and political journey, like that of Du Bois, has been much more complicated than previously noted, especially when read against the backdrop of Africana intellectual history. Within the world of the African diaspora there has been and remains radical anti-racist thought on racial domination and discrimination (specifically white supremacy) that prefigures and provides a black point of departure for contemporary critical race theory. Here I am hinting at what could be called *classical* critical race theory, which is not now and has never been an outgrowth of Western Marxism or Frankfurt School critical theory and, in fact, was underway long before the birth of Karl Marx.[7]

Well ahead of Marxism and the Frankfurt School, as Du Bois's *Black Reconstruction* and C.L.R. James's *The Black Jacobins* eloquently illustrate, enslaved Africans developed critical anti-racist thought traditions in their efforts to topple white supremacy and cut capitalism and colonialism off at their knees (Du Bois, 1995c; C.L.R. James 1963). They sought solutions to social and political problems as passionately and radically as—indeed, even more passionately and radically than—the white European working-class, who, as Eric Williams (1966) observed in *Capitalism and Slavery*, profited from and were complicit in the very white supremacist and enslaving system dominating and discriminating against blacks and other non-whites (see also E.E. Williams, 1942, 1955, 1961, 1962, 1963, 1964, 1965, 1969, 1970, 1993). Usually critical theory is linked to modernity and the Enlightenment, and modernity is only thought of from a Eurocentric point of view—that is, in the aftermath of European imperial expansion around the globe, what it means to be modern translates into how well Europeans and non-Europeans emulate European *imperial* thought, culture, politics, etc. But, if one were to call into question Eurocentric and imperial conceptions of what it means to be "modern," then, the very "alternative categories" that Bogues discussed above, "are opened up," and contemporary critical theorists are able to observe, perhaps for the first time, first, that it was on the fringes of Europe's imperial free-for-all, in the imperial outposts in the colored world where racism and colonialism were naturalized, where modernity was conceived, and in some senses aborted, and, second, that many of modernity's most perplexing problems were initially put forward and keenly considered by non-European, racialized, and colonized indigenous intellectuals. Charles Mills (2003) writes poignantly of this paradox and oft ignored predicament, and his penetrating words are worth quoting at length:

> All the issues we now think of as defining critical theory's concerns were brought home to the racially subordinated, the colonized and enslaved, in the most intimate and brutal way: the human alienation, the instrumentalization and deformation of reason in the service of power, the critique of abstract individualism, the paradox of reconciling proclamations of humanism with mass murder, the need to harness normative theory to the practical task of human liberation. So if Marx's proletariat too often had to have proletarian consciousness "imputed" (in Georg Lukács infamous phrase) to them, and if the relation between Marxism and the actual working-class outlook was often more a matter of faith and hopeful counterfactuals than actuality (what the workers *would* think if only . . .), then oppositional ideas on race have shaped the consciousness of the racially subordinated for centuries. If white workers have been alienated from their product, then people of color, especially black slaves, have been alienated from their personhood; if Enlightenment reason has been complicit with bourgeois projects, then it has been even more thoroughly corrupted by its accommodation to white supremacy; if liberal individualism has not always taken white workers fully into account, then it has often excluded nonwhites

altogether; if it was a post-World War II challenge to explain how the "civilized"
Germany of Goethe and Beethoven could have carried out the Jewish and Ro-
mani Holocausts, then it is a far older challenge to explain how "civilized" Europe as a whole could have carried out the savage genocide of indigenous populations and the barbaric enslavement of millions; and finally, if Marx's
proletarians have been called upon to see and lose their chains (and have often
seemed quite well-adjusted to them), then people of color (Native American
populations, enslaved and later Jim Crowed Africans in the New World, the colonized) have historically had little difficulty in recognizing their oppression—
after all, the chains were often literal!—and in seeking to throw it off. So if the
ideal of fusing intellectual history with political practice has been the long-term
goal of critical class theory, it has been far more frequently realized in the nas-
cent critical race theory of the racially subordinated, whose oppression has been
more blatant and unmediated and for whom the urgency of their situation has
necessitated a direct connection between the normative and practical emancipation. (p. xviii)

Here in unequivocal and penetrating prose Mills hints at and brilliantly
highlights precisely what I have come to call *the Africana tradition of critical theory* or, more succinctly, *Africana critical theory*. What is more, his
work here helps to drive home the crucial fact that critical theories are not
simply a synthesis of radical politics and social theory, but also a combination of cultural criticism and historical theory. Each version of critical theory,
whether critical race theory or critical class theory, seeks to radically reinterpret and revise history in light of, for example, race and racism for critical
race theorists, or capitalism and class struggle for critical class theorists. In
order to thoroughly comprehend a given phenomenon, critical theorists believe that one must contextualize it within its historical context, testing and
teasing out tensions between the phenomenon and the cultural, social, political, economic, scientific, aesthetic, and religious, among other, institutions
and struggles of its epoch.

Mills makes the point that though white Marxists/critical class theorists
have repeatedly revisited the connection(s) between theory and praxis, more
often than not the "revolutions" their works spawned have been theoretical
and one-dimensional (obsessively focused on the critique of capitalism), as
opposed to practical and multidimensional (simultaneously critiquing both
capitalism *and* racism). Black radicals/critical race theorists, he observes,
have frequently been more successful at linking radical (anti-racist and anti-
capitalist) theory to liberation struggles and social movements because their
"oppression has been more blatant and unmediated," and because "their situation has necessitated a direct connection between the normative and practical emancipation." The "situation" that Mills is referring to is simultaneously
historical, social, political, and economic, not to mention deeply raced and

gendered. So, though critical race theorists and critical class theorists both have macro-sociohistorical concerns, in the end it all comes down to, not necessarily the way they shift and bend the critical theoretical method for their particular purposes, but *what* they shift and bend the critical theoretical method to address. For most white Marxists race and racism are nonentities, but for many black Marxists capitalism is utterly incomprehensible without connecting it to the rise of race, racism, racial violence, white supremacy, and racial colonialism. Hence, black radicals' constant creations of timelines and topographies of the political economy of race and racism in capitalist and colonial contexts, and emphasis on revising and advancing alternatives to Eurocentric historiography and Marxist historical materialism in light of white supremacist and European imperial concepts and ruling race narratives that render race and racism historically invisible, obsolete, or nonexistent.[8]

Where white Marxists/critical class theorists have a longstanding tradition of neglecting the political economy of race and racism in capitalist and colonial contexts, critical gender theorists, usually white Marxist-feminists, have coupled the critique of capitalism with the critique of sexism but, similar to many of their white male Marxist counterparts, critical gender theorists have consistently downplayed and diminished the salience and political economy of race and racism in capitalist and colonial contexts, unwittingly weakening efforts to radically reconstruct critical theory to speak to the special needs of contemporary society, which is not simply sexist and capitalist but racist and (neo)colonialist as well. For example, in "What's Critical About Critical Theory?: The Case of Habermas and Gender," feminist political philosopher Nancy Fraser (1991) asserts that "a critical social theory of capitalist societies needs gender-sensitive categories," which is to say that critical theory should move away from the "usual androcentric understanding" and ordering of things commonplace in orthodox Marxian theory (p. 371). It should, contrary to the critical theories of many members of the Frankfurt School, seriously engage the particularities of, and differences between, female and male domination and discrimination. For instance, as Jürgen Habermas writes "virtually nothing about gender" in *Theory of Communicative Action*, his much-touted magnum opus, Fraser correctly finds his critical theory seriously deficient (p. 358). By conducting a "gender-sensitive reading" of his social theory, Fraser reveals that "there are some major lacunae in Habermas's otherwise powerful and sophisticated model of the relations between public and private institutions in classical capitalism" (p. 370). For Fraser, when Habermas writes of the worker-citizen-soldier in his critique of the public and private spheres under capitalism, he lays bare some of the major weaknesses of his—and, in my opinion, many of the other members of the Frankfurt School's—critical theory: his failure to come to critical terms with "the gender subtext of the relations and arrangements he describes," and the fact that "feminine and masculine identity run like pink and blue threads through the areas of paid work, state administration and citizenship as well as through the domain of familial and sexual relations. This is to say that gender identity is lived out in all arenas of life" (p. 367, 370).[9]

In agreement with Fraser, I believe that "gender-sensitive readings" of, and radical changes in, "the very concepts of citizenship, childrearing and unpaid work," as well as "changes in the relationships among the domestic, official-economic, state and political-public spheres" are necessary (p. 371). However, my conception of critical theory also takes into consideration the *racial subtext* and argues for *race-sensitive readings* of power relations in the modern and postmodern moments. I am very excited about the prospects of developing "feminist," "gender sensitive" and/or, as I prefer, *critical women's liberation theory*. In other words, I am deeply devoted to (re)developing radical politics and critical social theory that acknowledges, in Fraser's fierce words: "We are, therefore, struggling for women's autonomy in the following special sense: a measure of collective control over the means of interpretation and communication sufficient to permit us to participate on a par with men in all types of social interaction, including political deliberation and decision-making" (p. 378).

What bothers me about Fraser's articulation of a feminist critical theory, however, is the limited scope of her social-theoretical framework. While she correctly takes Habermas—and, in many senses, the whole of the Frankfurt School tradition of critical theory—to task for the "gender-blindness" or, what I am wont to call, the *gender insensitivity* of his social-theoretical framework, like Habermas, Fraser fails to theorize some of the ways racism adds a different, perhaps deeper dimension to domination and discrimination in contemporary society. Put another way, I am highly perplexed by the *racial myopia*, that is, the racial blindness of a sophisticated feminist social theorist such as Fraser who, perhaps, utilizing the Frankfurt School critical-theoretical framework and philosophically following many of its male members, treats race, racism, anti-racist struggle, and critical race theory as incidental and, more to the point, tertiary to the critique of sexism (and particularly patriarchy) and capitalism.

Many theorists have explored sexism, and many theorists have explored racism, and a multitude of theorists (especially Marxists!) have critiqued capitalism. But, racism *and* sexism *and* capitalism (*and* colonialism, I might add), treated in a critical conjunctive manner—perhaps of the sort advocated by the "black lesbian feminist socialist mother of two, including one boy," Audre Lorde (1984, p. 14), and the kind of analysis that the black feminist sociologist Deborah King (1995) writes of in her classic essay, "Multiple Jeopardy, Multiple Consciousness: The Context of Black Feminist Ideology"—calls for a critical engagement of W.E.B. Du Bois as it does for no other.

What do we find when we turn to Du Bois's thought and texts?

In Du Bois's corpus we are undoubtedly, and perhaps unexpectedly for some, exposed to an arsenal of criticisms which challenge and seek to provide solutions to several of the major social and political problems of the nineteenth, twentieth and, I should like to be one of the first to add, twenty-first centuries. Though his thought covers a wide range of intellectual terrain, and ducks and dips into and out of various academic disciplines (e.g., history, sociology, philosophy, political science, economics, religion, education, and literature, among others), Du Bois, it can be said at this point with little or no fanfare, laid a foundation and provides a critical-theoretical framework for the renewal of radical politics and the reconstruction of critical social theory in the twenty-first century (see Rabaka, 2007a). All of his work, whether we turn to his novels, volumes of poetry, plays, autobiographies, cultural criticisms, histories, social studies, political treatises, or economic analyses, emanate from his conjunctive critiques of racism, sexism, capitalism, and colonialism, which continue to plague humanity and, therefore, remain on the radical political agenda.

Returning to Fraser and feminist critical theory, again, I feel compelled to reiterate that I utterly agree with her project when and where she argues that the worker-citizen-soldier in classical and contemporary Marxian traditions (of which Frankfurt School critical theory is a provocative and extremely important twentieth-century strand) is not androgynous or gender neutral but, in fact, dreadfully gendered, and thoroughly male-centered at that. Fraser's radical socialist-feminist theory resonates deeply with my articulation of an Africana critical theory of contemporary society when she accents some of the ways in which basic Marxian categories, such as "worker," "wage," "consumer," and "citizen,"—in her own words

> are not, in fact, strictly economic concepts. Rather, they have an implicit gender subtext and thus are "gender-economic" concepts. Likewise, the relevant concept of citizenship is not strictly a political concept; it has an implicit gender subtext and so, rather, is a "gender-political" concept. Thus, this analysis reveals the inadequacy of those critical theories that treat gender as incidental to politics and political economy. It highlights the need for a critical-theoretical categorical framework in which gender, politics and political economy are internally integrated. (Fraser, 1991, p. 371)

For Fraser, there are few, if any, gender-neutral concepts in Marxian theory. In fact, much of Marxism, as she avers above, is rather gender-specific and often only speaks to male struggles against economic exploitation, which is to say that Marxism, as it was originally conceived and propagated from Karl Marx through to Herbert Marcuse and the Western or Hegelian Marxist tradition, is one long theorization of working-class men's experience of, and class struggles against, the evils of capitalism (P. Anderson, 1976; Gottlieb, 1992; Kolakowski, 1978a, 1978b, 1978c; Jay, 1984). The trick, though, and one that has not gone unnoticed by Marxist feminists and socialist feminists, is that for a very long time many Marxists (many female Marxists notwithstanding) did not realize or critically take into consideration the simple fact that when they wrote or spoke of "workers," "wages," "citizens," and the like, their ideas and arguments were premised on a false gender neutrality that more often than not signified males and their gender-specific sociopolitical wishes and whims (see M. Barrett, 1980; Boxer and Quartaert, 1978; Braun, 1987; M.J. Buhle, 1981; Di Stephano, 1991, 2008; Eisenstein, 1979; A. Ferguson, 1986, 1998; K.E. Ferguson, 1980; Guettel, 1974; Hansen and Philipson, 1990; Hennessey and Ingraham, 1997; Holmstrom, 2002; Meulenbelt, 1984; Roberts and Mizuta, 1993; Rowbotham, 1973, 1979; Sargent, 1981; Slaughter and Kern, 1981).

In a patriarchal society, it is "normal," utterly "universal" for theorizing men to exclude the plight of women from their so-called "radical social theory," "theories of social change," and/or their "dialectical" discourses on domination and liberation (see Benhabib and Cornell, 1987). For male theorists to identify themselves and their discourses as patriarchal, male supremacist or masculinist, or to make mention of gender at all, is—from their patriarchal vantage point—superfluous because of the super-structural and supra-structural dynamics of patriarchy and the ways it plays itself out in male supremacist societies. Fraser is, indeed, on point when she suggests that what is needed is a closer, more critical "gender-sensitive reading" of classical and contemporary radical thought and praxis in order to develop a critical theory of contemporary society.

Africana critical theory of contemporary society, however, parts company with Fraser's feminist critical theory when it calls for "a critical-theoretical categorical framework in which gender, politics, and political economy are internally integrated" without so much as mentioning, let alone seriously engaging, the sociohistorical fact that race and racism as well have shaped the modern world and, therefore, should be included in any authentic critical theory of *contemporary* society. Contemporary society, as several self-described "feminists" and "womanists" of African descent have argued, is simultaneously sexist, racist, and classist—one need not think long about the various vicissitudes of contemporary capitalism and colonialism.[10] The task, then, of contemporary critical theory is to seek solutions to the problems of racism, sexism, capitalism, and colonialism, among other social and political problems as they arise.

In the classical Marxist tradition, and in most of the contemporary Marxist tradition, when Marxists theorize the plight of the "worker," they are not only writing about gender-specific workers, *male workers*, but also, as demonstrated in my previous study, racially specific workers, *white workers*. The terms that the Marxists use are neither gender- nor race-neutral terms. For instance, just as males are normative in a patriarchal society, so too are whites in a socio-historically white supremacist society. Again, it is superfluous to make mention of such matters as race and gender in a white- and male-supremacist society, because the white male worldview is always and ever thought and taught to be "neutral" and "universal." To put it plainly: In a white- *and* male-supremacist society, all are indoctrinated with the dominant ideology, which is inherently a hegemonic white male worldview. Moreover, the appeal of purportedly gender- and race-neutral terms—such as *worker*, *consumer*, and *citizen*—is that they often silently signify white males without actually overtly saying so. What this means, then, is that there are actually invisible pre-reflexive parenthetical adjectives clandestinely attached to these supposedly gender- and race-neutral terms: (white male) *worker*, (white male) *consumer*, and (white male) *citizen*.

Hence, had Fraser turned to Du Bois's discourse, she would have found not only a critical and analytical engagement of capitalism and sexism, but also one of the most sustained and sophisticated theorizations of race and racism, perhaps, in recent human history. She would, further, have been able to observe not simply the gendered subtext of the Marxian tradition, but also its racial (and racist) subtext, positing, as I intend to, the need for Marxists to critically note that their basic concepts and categories are race and gender specific (and supremacist), as well as political and economic. In other words, I am arguing, following the Eritrean philosopher Tsenay Serequeberhan (1994), that "political 'neutrality' in philosophy, as in most other things, is at best a 'harmless' naiveté, and at worst a pernicious subterfuge for hidden agendas" (p. 4). It is not enough, from the Africana critical theoretical perspective, for Fraser to highlight gender's import for radical political and economic analysis without, in the spirit of Du Bois and countless colored and colonized "others," stretching it to encompass the study of race, racism, critical race theory, and contemporary anti-racist struggle. Finally, in Du Bois's corpus, had Fraser turned to his critical thought, she would have also found an anti-colonial theory and discourse on decolonization that could have possibly helped her extend and expand her concept of the "inner colonization of the life-world," which she borrowed from Habermas, and "decolonization," which she—similar to almost the entire Frankfurt School tradition of critical theory—limits to life-worlds and lived experiences in capitalist countries (Fraser, 1989, p. 129–43, 161–87).[11]

Capitalism, it should be stated outright, does marginalize, exploit, and oppress women in ways markedly different from men, and especially in patriarchal

capitalist societies. However, and equally important, capitalism also perpetu-
ates and exacerbates racial domination and discrimination, especially in white-
supremacist, patriarchal, colonial, capitalist societies. This is a sociohistorical
fact that many white Marxist feminists and socialist feminists have long neglected, and also a fact to which Du Bois and a host of black women's liberation theorists have devoted a great deal of time and intellectual energy.
Though there is much more in Fraser's theory and feminist critiques of Frankfurt School critical theory that I find philosophically fascinating, for the purposes of the discussion at hand I have accentuated those aspects of Fraser's
arguments that help to highlight the distinctive features of Du Bois's interdisciplinary innovations and my articulation of an Africana critical theory of
contemporary society. But, really now, what is Africana critical theory, and
how does it relate to the renewal of radical politics and the reconstruction of
critical social theory in the twenty-first century?

UPPING THE ANTE: OPERATIONALIZING
AFRICANA CRITICAL THEORY AND
RENEWING BLACK RADICAL POLITICS

Africana critical theory is *theory critical of domination and discrimination in
classical and contemporary, continental and diasporan African life-worlds
and lived experiences*. It is a style of critical theorizing, inextricably linked to
progressive political practice(s) that highlights and accents black radicals'
and revolutionaries' answers to the key questions posed by the major forms
and forces of domination and discrimination that have historically and continue currently to shape and mold our modern/postmodern and/or neo-colo-
nial/postcolonial world. Africana critical theory involves not only the critique
of domination and discrimination, but also a deep commitment to human liberation and revolutionary social transformation.

Similar to other traditions of critical social theory, Africana critical theory
is concerned with thoroughly analyzing contemporary society "in light of its
used and unused or abused capabilities for improving the human [and deteri-
orating environmental] condition" (Marcuse, 1964, p. xlii; see also Rabaka,
2006a; Wilkerson and Paris, 2001). What distinguishes and helps to define
Africana critical theory is its emphasis on the often-overlooked continental
and diasporan African contributions to critical theory. It draws from critical
thought and philosophical traditions rooted in the realities of continental and
diasporan African history, culture, and struggle, which, in other words, is to
say that Africana critical theory inherently employs a methodological orientation that highlights and accents black radicalism and Africana philosophies,

as Leonard Harris (1983) said, "born of struggle."[12] And, if it need be said at this point, the black liberation struggle is simultaneously national and international, transgender and transgenerational and, therefore, requires multidimensional and multiperspectival theory in which to interpret and explain the various diverse phenomena, philosophical motifs, and social and political movements characteristic of—to use Fanon's famous phrase—*l'expérience vécue du Noir* ("the lived experience of the black"), that is, the reality of constantly wrestling simultaneously with racism, sexism, capitalism, and colonialism (Fanon, 2001; see also Gordon, Sharpley-Whiting and White, 1996; Weate, 2001).

Why, one may ask, focus on black radicals' and revolutionaries' theories of social change? An initial answer to this question takes us directly to Du Bois's dictum, in "The Conservation of Races," that people of African origin and descent "have a contribution to make to civilization and humanity" that their historic experiences of holocaust, enslavement, colonization, and segregation have long throttled and thwarted (1986c, p. 825). He maintained that, "[t]he methods which we evolved for opposing slavery and fighting prejudice are not to be forgotten, but learned for our own and others' instruction" (Du Bois, 1973, p. 144). Hence, Du Bois is suggesting that black liberation struggle(s)—that is, the combined continental and diasporan African fight(s) for freedom—may have much to contribute to critical theory, and his comments here also hit at the heart of one of the core concepts of critical theory, the *critique of domination and discrimination* (see Agger, 1992a; O'Neill, 1976; Rasmussen and Swindal, 2004).

From a methodological point of view, critical theory seeks to simultaneously (1) comprehend the established society; (2) criticize its contradictions and conflicts; and (3) create egalitarian (most often democratic socialist) alternatives (Morrow, 1994; Outlaw, 2005). The ultimate emphasis on the creation and offering of alternatives brings to the fore another core concept of critical theory, its *theory of liberation and social(ist) transformation* (Marcuse, 1968, 1969; Marsh, 1995, 1999; Ray, 1993).[13] The paradigms and points of departure for critical theorists vary depending on the theorists' race, gender, intellectual interests, and political persuasions. For instance, many European critical theorists turn to Hegel, Marx, Weber, Freud, and/or the Frankfurt School (Adorno, Benjamin, Fromm, Habermas, Horkheimer and Marcuse), among others, because they understand these thinkers' thoughts and texts to speak in special ways to modern and/or "postmodern" life-worlds and lived experiences (see Held, 1980; Jay, 1996; Kellner, 1989; Wiggerhaus, 1995). My work, Africana critical theory, utilizes the thought and texts of Africana intellectual ancestors as critical theoretical paradigms and points of departure because so much of their thought is not simply *problem posing* but

solution providing where the specific life-struggles of persons of African descent (or "black people") and other non-whites are concerned—human life-
struggles, it should be said with no hyperbolic and high-sounding words,
which European critical theorists (who are usually Eurocentric and often unwittingly white supremacist) have woefully neglected in their classical and
contemporary critical theoretical discourse, a discourse that ironically has
consistently congratulated itself on the universality of its interests, all the
while, for the most part, side-stepping the centrality of racism and colonialism within its own discursive communities and out in the wider world. Moreover, my conception of critical theory is critically preoccupied with classical
Africana thought traditions, not only because of the long unlearned lessons
they have to teach contemporary critical theorists about the dialectics of being simultaneously radically humanist and morally committed agents of a
specific nation or cultural group's liberation and social(ist) transformation,
but also because the ideas and ideals of continental and diasporan African intellectuals of the past indisputably prefigure and provide a foundation for
contemporary Africana Studies, and Africana philosophy in specific.[14] In fact,
in many ways, Africana critical theory, besides being grounded in and growing out of the discourse of Africana Studies, can be said to be an offshoot of
Africana philosophy, which according to the acclaimed African American
philosopher, Lucius Outlaw (1997), is

> a "gathering" notion under which to situate the articulations (writings, speeches,
> etc.), and traditions of the same, of Africans and peoples of African descent col-
> lectively, as well as the sub-discipline or field-forming, tradition-defining, tra-
> dition-organizing reconstructive efforts which are (to be) regarded as philoso-
> phy. However, "Africana philosophy" is to include, as well, the work of those
> persons who are neither African nor of African descent but who recognize the
> legitimacy and importance of the issues and endeavors that constitute the disci-
> plinary activities of African or [African Caribbean or] African American philos-
> ophy and contribute to the efforts—persons whose work justifies their being
> called "Africanists." Use of the qualifier "Africana" is consistent with the prac-
> tice of naming intellectual traditions and practices in terms of the national, geo-
> graphic, cultural, racial, and/or ethnic descriptor or identity of the persons who
> initiated and were/are the primary practitioners—and/or are the subjects and ob-
> jects—of the practices and traditions in question (e.g., "American," "British,"
> "French," "German," or "continental" philosophy). (p. 64)

Africana critical theory is distinguished from Africana philosophy by the
fact that critical theory cannot be situated within the world of conventional
academic disciplines and divisions of labor. It transverses and transgresses
boundaries between traditional disciplines and accents the interconnections
and intersections of philosophy, history, politics, economics, the arts, psy-

chology, and sociology, among other disciplines. Critical theory is contrasted with mainstream, monodisciplinary social theory through its multidisciplinary methodology and its efforts to develop a comprehensive dialectical theory of domination and liberation specific to the special needs of contemporary society (see Agger, 1998; Habermas, 1984, 1987a, 1988, 1989b; Outlaw, 1983a, 1983b, 1983c, 1983d; Rasmussen and Swindal, 2004; Wilkerson and Paris, 2001). Africana philosophy has a very different agenda, one that seems to me more meta-philosophical than philosophical at this point, because it entails theorizing on tradition and tradition construction more than tradition extension and expansion through the production of normative theory and critical pedagogical praxis aimed at application (i.e., immediate self and social transformation).[15]

The primary purpose of critical theory is to relate radical thought to revolutionary practice, which is to say that its focus—philosophical, social, and political—is always and ever the search for ethical alternatives and viable moral solutions to the most pressing problems of our present age. Critical theory is not about, or rather *should not* be about allegiance to intellectual ancestors and/or ancient schools of thought, but about using *all* (without regard to race, gender, class, sexual orientation, and/or religious affiliation) accumulated radical thought and revolutionary practices in the interest of human liberation and democratic social(ist) transformation. With this in mind, Cornel West's (1982) contentions concerning "Afro-American critical thought" offer an outline for the type of theorizing that Africana critical theory endeavors:

> The object of inquiry for Afro-American critical thought is the past and present, the doings and the sufferings of African people in the United States. Rather than a new scientific discipline or field of study, it is a genre of writing, a textuality, a mode of discourse that interprets, describes, and evaluates Afro-American life in order comprehensively to understand and effectively to transform it. It is not concerned with "foundations" or transcendental "grounds" but with how to build its language in such a way that the configuration of sentences and the constellation of paragraphs themselves create a textuality and distinctive discourse which are a material force for Afro-American freedom. (p. 15)

Though Africana critical theory encompasses and is concerned with much more than the life-worlds and lived experiences of "African people in the United States," West's comments here are helpful, as they give us a glimpse at the kind of connections critical theorists make in terms of their ideas having an impact and significant influence on society. Africana critical theory is not thought for thought's sake (as it often seems is the case with so much contemporary philosophy—Africana philosophy notwithstanding), but *thought for life and liberation's sake*. It is not only a style of writing which focuses

on radicalism and revolution, but a new way of *thinking* and *doing* revolution
that is based and constantly being built on the radicalisms and revolutions of
the past.

From West's frame of reference, "Afro-American philosophy expresses the
particular American variation of European modernity that Afro-Americans
helped shape in this country and must contend with in the future. While it
might be possible to articulate a competing Afro-American philosophy based
principally on African norms and notions, it is likely that the result would be
theoretically thin" (p. 24). Contrary to West's comments, Africana critical
theory represents and registers as that "possible articulat[ion] of a competing
[Africana] philosophy based principally [albeit, not exclusively] on African
norms and notions," and though he thinks that the results will be "theoretically thin," Africana critical theory—faithfully following Fanon (1965, 1967,
1968, 1969)—understands this risk to be part of the price the oppressed must
be willing to pay for their (intellectual, political, psychological, and physical)
freedom.[16] Intellectually audacious, especially considering the widespread
Eurocentrism and white supremacism of contemporary conceptual generation, Africana critical theory does not acquiesce or give priority and special
privilege to European history, culture, and thought. It turns to the long-over-
looked thought and texts of women and men of African descent who have developed and contributed radical thought and revolutionary practices that
could possibly aid us in our endeavors to continuously create a theory critical
of domination and discrimination in contemporary culture and society.

Above and beyond all of the aforementioned, Africana critical theory is
about offering alternatives to *what is* (domination and discrimination) by pro-
jecting possibilities of *what ought to be* and/or *what could be* (human liberation and revolutionary social transformation). It is not afraid, to put it as
plainly as possible, to critically engage and dialogue deeply with European
and/or other cultural groups' thought traditions. In fact, it often finds critical
cross-cultural dialogue necessary considering the historical conundrums and
current shared conditions and crises of the modern, almost completely multicultural world (see Goldberg, 1994; McLaren, 1997). Africana critical theory,
quite simply, does not privilege or give priority to European and/or other cultural groups' thought traditions since its philosophical foci and primary purpose revolves around the search for solutions to the most pressing social and
political problems in continental and diasporan African (among other non-
whites') life-worlds and lived experiences in the present age.

The conception(s) of critical theory that I articulate and elaborate in the following chapters, then, utterly agrees that Marx and Marxism have long provided the most comprehensive class analysis and critique of capitalist political economy. But, it finds Marxism shamefully deficient where the critique of

racism, sexism, and colonialism, among other issues, are concerned. For these reasons, Africana critical theory, in addition to Marx and Marxism, draws from black Marxism, philosophy of race, sociology of race, history of race, anthropology of race, geography of race, and critical race theory; black radical feminism, Marxist feminism, anti-racist feminism, feminist philosophy, male-feminism, and womanism; and Pan-Africanism, postcolonialism, African socialism, Fanonian philosophy, and decolonization theory, among others. As intimated earlier, Du Bois's discourse amazingly prefigures and provides a paradigm and point of departure for renewing radical politics and reconstructing critical theory because of its interdisciplinary innovations and emphasis on creating praxis-promoting social theory; theory that is simultaneously anti-racist, anti-sexist, anti-capitalist and anti-colonial, and theory that takes James Marsh (2001) very seriously when he asserts, "We also desperately need a critical theory of neoimperialism" (p. 57). With this in mind, this book documents and dialogues with Du Bois and Africana Studies' contributions to the creation of a critical theory of new forms of imperialism by undertaking ideological critiques of the ways in which neoimperialism has impacted and infected social, political, educational, and religious institutions and arrangements.

DISTORTING DU BOIS, DENYING (MONO)DISCIPLINARY DECADENCE

Because Du Bois is widely considered, as Cornel West (1996) contends, "the towering black scholar of the twentieth century" whose "prolific writings bespeak a level of genius unequaled among modern black intellectuals," he has been the target of polemics and many misinterpretations that have frequently distorted his discourse and obscured his corpus's contributions to critical social theory (p. 55). Interpretations of Du Bois are enormously varied and widespread throughout traditional and non-traditional disciplines. Previous books on him have neglected to present his complex and sometimes seemingly contradictory relationship to the wide range of theory he contracted and demonstrate how he constructed, deconstructed, and reconstructed theory in light of changing politico-economic and socio-cultural conditions.

Critics with various academic agendas and political programs have made many efforts to refute Du Bois and illustrate the inadequacies of his thought. Work in this vein has a tendency to elide the political and intellectual origins and inspirations of his ideas. These kinds of criticisms also often fail to discuss Du Bois's work in relation to the history of Africana thought and dialectically observe *how* and *which* limitations internal to his project, as well as historical obstacles, led Du Bois to constantly revise and redevelop his social and political theory and praxis. Moreover, many of the books and studies published in the last quarter of the twentieth century frequently focus on a specific stage of Du Bois's thought and, therefore, are often intellectually disingenuous as they practice a type of theoretical freeze-framing that Du Bois long and loudly opposed. Although there have been several watershed works in Du Bois studies that urbanely engage a stage of his project or an aspect of his intellectual-activist history, most interpretations have been deficient in their presentation of the broad range and reach of his social thought and political practices, especially the ways in which he synthesized history and philosophy with the social sciences.

This book moves beyond one-dimensional interpretations of Du Bois and analyzes in detail syntheses, ambiguities, and modifications in his thought by employing the Africana critical theoretical framework. This framework will allow me to trace the developments and revisions of his thought rather than reproduce the conventional flat-footed analyses that approach or, rather, *reproach* his work as though it were ideology or a completed thought-complex. Utilizing the Africana critical theoretical framework also enables me to chart both the conceptual ruptures and theoretical revolutions in Du Bois's thinking and emphasize the intellectual constants and long-held political positions at the core of his corpus.

In the spirit of his life-long advocacy of critical thought, I develop detailed discussions of Du Bois's work which address the success or failure of his efforts to provide new theories and praxes to help human beings understand and alter contemporary society. From this angle his work can be simultaneously evaluated based on the goals he himself set for it and based on the aims and objectives of developing an Africana critical theory of contemporary society. I observe how the tensions within his project(s) either hindered him from reformulating, and/or, as in many instances, helped him to rethink and redesign his increasingly *radical* politics and *critical* social theory. And, I also accent instances where Du Bois turns phenomena that initially presented serious theoretical and political obstacles into theoretical and political putty in his hands.

In my effort to illuminate the itinerary of Du Bois's thought as it passes through several stages of development that appropriate Africana and European ideas, I examine how his theory reaches, or fails to reach, the outcomes he initially envisioned. This method of closely reading his theory in light of its objectives enables me to perceive how Du Bois deepens and develops critical social theory, infusing it with elements from thought-traditions that engage issues and prioritize problems that critical theory (especially that of the Frankfurt School) has historically downplayed and diminished, if not outright ignored and omitted. Du Bois's contributions to philosophy, radical politics, and social theory, among other areas, enhance and extend critical theory of contemporary society by offering a compelling and comprehensive body of writings comparable in scope to the monumental work of Karl Marx, C.L.R. James, Antonio Gramsci, Frantz Fanon, Herbert Marcuse, and Amilcar Cabral.

Because Du Bois's work represents a series of responses to complex and quickly changing historical conditions and social crises, an adequate interpretation of his thought requires a creative combination of intellectual history, critical race theory, women's studies, hermeneutics, semiotics, polemics, epistemological investigation, philosophical exploration, social and political analysis, and critical evaluation of both its theoretical and political dimensions. Prior studies of Du Bois's thought have been vitiated by their failure to sufficiently situate his works within their multidimensional historical, political and intellectual milieux, and have failed to demonstrate how the diverse stages and works fit into his overarching intellectual history and constantly evolving political project. To overcome this problem I interpret Du Bois's writings in relation to their classical and our contemporary contexts and illustrate how history and various theoretical and practical questions and critiques point to the limitations of his theories and inspire (and sometimes incite) him to radically revise his positions. *Du Bois's Du Bois: Black Radical Politics and the Reconstruction of Critical Social Theory*, then, seeks to provide interpretations and criticisms of Du Bois's thought and texts in an effort to develop a discussion of his contributions to the reconstruction of critical theory and emphasize Africana Studies' gifts to modern movements geared toward human liberation and radical social transformation.

The next chapter engages four issues central to Du Bois's philosophy of education and critical pedagogy. First, I discuss Du Bois's development of a critical theory of history (as opposed to or contrasted with a conventional "philosophy of history") and its impact on his philosophy of education. Next, I examine Du Bois's philosophy of culture and the distinct style of cultural criticism he developed for its centrality to his philosophy of education and critical educational theory more generally. Third, I endeavor to objectively analyze some of the major deficiencies and limitations of Du Bois's philosophy of education by briefly contrasting his 1903 theory of the Talented Tenth with his 1948 revision of the Talented Tenth thesis into a more Marxist and/or democratic-socialist theory of "the Guiding Hundredth." Finally, I conclude commenting on the contributions Du Bois's philosophy of education and Africana critical pedagogy make to contemporary critical educational theory and praxis.

Chapter 3 elaborates on many of the issues raised at the end of chapter 2, specifically the controversy surrounding Du Bois's theory of the Talented

Tenth. It revisits the Du Bois–Washington debate and analyzes this infamous intellectual and crucial political moment for its import to Africana critical theory, African American social thought, and radical politics in the present age. After carefully and critically laying out each thinkers' key positions on African American social development and cultural survival at the turn of the twentieth century, I bring the best of Washington and Du Bois's discourse into dialogue with the social and political problems of the present age. A main objective of the chapter is to offer this historic debate and the diverse discourse it spawned as a model for (post)modern black political theory and social praxis. Central to this discussion are questions concerning black conservatism and black radicalism, the meaning and fundamental mission of black education, black intellectuals' social and political obligations to the black community, and racism's relationship to capitalism.

In chapter 4, I explore Du Bois's discourse on religion. I argue that his religious thought—being distinguished by its emphasis on Africana religiosity and spirituality, the relationship between and the political economy of religion and racism, and the ways oppressing and oppressed people use and/or abuse religion either as a form of social pacification or social protest—simultaneously deconstructs and reconstructs the conventional analytical categories of philosophy of religion, sociology of religion, and liberation theology. Du Bois's work in this area makes a profound contribution to contemporary critical theory in so far as it provides a paradigm that enables us to critique the ideological elements of religion while simultaneously accenting its more emancipatory aspects. His critical thought on religion, as will be observed of his critical social theory in general, is shown to be self-reflexive, constantly exhibiting the ability to revise and refine itself and, therefore, remains remarkably relevant for contemporary religious criticism.

Chapter 5 analyzes Du Bois's social, political, and economic thought for its contribution to the contemporary discourse and debates regarding reparations for continental and diasporan Africans, and particularly African Americans. Du Bois's pioneering work with the Pan-African movement and his efforts to argue for redress for anti-African racist wrongdoing and human rights abuses, by bringing the U.S. and other European imperial powers before the League of Nations and, later, the United Nations, register as clear-cut examples of some of the ways that his radical political thought contributes to modern reparations theory and the development of what I am calling *critical reparations theory*. The contention here is not that Du Bois put forward a systematic or sophisticated reparations argument, but that there is a sense in which his thinking at specific intervals in his oeuvre lays a philosophical foundation and provides paradigms for modern Africana reparations arguments and movements. One of the central tasks of this chapter, then, is to outline and develop

Du Bois's position(s) on reparations by taking a piecemeal approach to several of his seminal works on black social, political, and economic justice.

The concluding chapter engages Du Bois's oeuvre as an unfinished project of human liberation and radical social transformation. It points to some of the pitfalls and problematics of previous interpretations and criticisms of Du Bois and strongly stresses the necessity of future studies to examine his work as theory as opposed to (racial) ideology. I also make note of many of the remaining tasks for reconstructing critical theory of contemporary society and argue that henceforth it must be more multicultural, transethnic, transgender, sexuality sensitive, and have a broader base than classical and/or conventional critical theory. Contemporary critical theory, I contend, must initiate the arduous and intricate task of simultaneously and dialectically redeveloping and revising its classical philosophical foundation, move beyond its now inadequate and/or obsolete positions, and constantly synthesize itself with the most critical and cutting edge social an political theory available. Du Bois's discourse, I end the book asserting, offers an almost ideal source of and site for the radical reconstruction of critical theory and contemporary society.

NOTES

1. Indeed, it was the Du Bois-Washington debate that forced Du Bois to radically rethink his black bourgeois and reformist politics and, in many senses, inaugurate what Cedric Robinson (2000), among others, has dubbed "the black radical tradition" (see also D.C. Thomas, 2005). Since Du Bois's radical (and later revolutionary) politics remain one of the most misunderstood areas of his oeuvre, it is important at the outset to point to pertinent primary and secondary sources, which, as quiet as it is kept, are quite extensive. In terms of Du Bois's critical writings on radical politics, democratic socialism, and Marxism, which many Du Bois scholars have had a tendency to quickly pass over in order to get to his classic *Black Reconstruction*, see, for instance: "Socialist of the Path," "The Negro and Socialism," "The Economic Aspects of Race Prejudice," "The Economics of Negro Emancipation in the United States," "Socialism Is Too Narrow For Negroes," "A Field for Socialists," "Socialism and the Negro Problem," "The Problem of Problems," "Brothers, Come North," "Of Work and Wealth," "Of the Ruling of Men," "The Social Equality of Blacks and Whites," "Socialism and the Negro," "The Negro and Radical Thought," "Class Struggle," "Communists Boring into Negro Labor," "Russia, 1926," "The Denial of Economic Justice to Negroes," "The American Federation of Labor and the Negro," "The Negro and Communism," "Communists and the Color Line," "Socialism in England," "Karl Marx and the Negro," "Marxism and the Negro Problem," "The U.S. Will Come to Communism," "Where Do We Go From Here?: An Essay on the Negroes' Economic Plight," "The Present Economic Problem of the American Negro," "A Negro Nation Within the Nation," "Lifting from the Bottom," "A Social Program for Black and

White Americans," "A Program of Organization for Realizing Democracy in the United States by Securing to Americans of Negro Descent the Full Rights of Citizens," "My Evolving Program for Negro Freedom," "The Negro and Imperialism," "Behold the Land," "Socialism," "A Petition to the Human Rights Commission of the Social and Economic Council of the United Nations; and to the General Assembly of the United Nations; and to Several Delegations of the Member States of the United Nations," "There Must Come a Vast Social Change in the United States," "Address at the American Labor Party Election," "Negroes and the Crisis of Capitalism in the United States," "Colonialism and the Russian Revolution," "Ethiopia: State Socialism Under An Emperor," "The Stalin Era," "Socialism and Democracy," "Negroes and Socialism," "A Future for Pan-Africa: Freedom, Peace, Socialism," "The Future of All Africa Lies In Socialism," "The Negro and Socialism," "The Dream of Socialism," "The Vast Miracle of China Today," "Socialism and the American Negro," *Socialism Today*, "Whither Now and Why," and "Application for Membership in the Communist Party of the United States of America." My interpretation and reconstruction of Du Bois's concept(s) of democratic socialism and critique(s) of capitalism and Marxism derive, in part, from careful and critical investigation of these articles and essays (see these in anthologies of Du Bois 1965, 1970c, 1970d, 1971a, 1971b, 1985a, 1986a1, 1995a, 1996a). Influential secondary sources on Du Bois's democratic socialism include Horne (1986), Marable (1986), Moses (1978), A.L. Reed (1997), C.J. Robinson (2000), W.D. Wright (1985), and Yuan (1998). Similar to William Jeremiah Moses (1978, p. 138), who contends that Du Bois "became a socialist by gradual stages," Manning Marable (1986) argues:

> Du Bois's introduction to Marxism and socialism was extremely fragmentary. At Harvard, Marx's work was briefly discussed, "but only incidentally and as one whose doubtful theories had long since been refuted," Du Bois wrote later. "Socialism as dream of philanthropy or as will-o-wisp of hotheads was dismissed as unimportant." At [the University of] Berlin, Karl Marx was mentioned, only to point out how thoroughly his theses had been disproven; of his theory itself almost nothing was said." Only at Atlanta University did Du Bois begin to acquaint himself with writings by socialists and radical liberals. . . . In the second issue of the *Horizon*, in February 1908 [sic], Du Bois stated that he considered himself a "Socialist-of-the-Path." Du Bois had certain misgivings about the Socialist party, but still believed that "the socialist trend" represented the "one great hope of the Negro American." As the Socialist party acquired a mass following, Du Bois monitored its progress as an ally to the democratic struggles of blacks. In February 1908 [sic], Du Bois advised readers of the *Horizon* that "the only party today which treats Negroes as men, North and South, are the Socialists." (p. 89)

From the foregoing it seems clear that even Du Bois's early relationship with Marxism was critical, complex, and extremely complicated. Similar to the thought of many black radicals, Du Bois's radical ruminations cannot easily and one-dimensionally be characterized as Marxist or "black Marxist" because, as we will soon see, his thought routinely re-theorized Marxist/critical class theory by combining it with a critical race component, and by emphasizing racial strife within the working class. At times in Du

Bois's later discourse race simply was not as central as many black nationalist and other race-centered theorists would like. But, it would be difficult for these theorists to argue that race occupies a secondary or tertiary position in his critical socio-theoretical framework. Race and racism were consistent foci in his discourse, but as his thinking evolved, and he identified capitalism and sexism as oppressive systems that interlock with racism, each system was often simultaneously engaged (see Gilkes, 1996; Gillman and Weinbaum, 2004; J. A. James, 1997; Lemons, 2001; McKay, 1985, 1990; Rabaka, 2003d, 2004). It is the simultaneity (and, I should add, the interdisciplinary nature) of Du Bois's engagement of these interlocking oppressive systems that misleads many Du Bois scholars into arguing that in his later years he privileged class over race. This issue does not arise as much where Du Bois's discourse on colonialism is concerned because of the overt racially oppressive character of colonialism (hence, *racial colonialism*) in continental and diasporan African modernity (see Mostern, 2000; Rabaka, 2003c, 2005a).

2. I advance this book, then, as a continuation of the Africana Critical Theory (ACT) intellectual archaeology project, which was initiated with my doctoral dissertation, "Africana Critical Theory: From W.E.B. Du Bois and C.L.R. James's Discourse on Domination and Liberation to Frantz Fanon and Amilcar Cabral's Dialectics of Decolonization" (Rabaka, 2001). It need be noted at the outset, and in agreement with David Held (1980), "Critical theory, it should be emphasized, does *not* form a unity; it does not mean the same thing to all its adherents" (p. 14, original emphasis). For instance, Steven Best and Douglas Kellner (1991) employ the term "critical theory" in a general sense in their critique of postmodern theory, stating, "We are using 'critical theory' here in the general sense of critical social and cultural theory and not in the specific sense that refers to the critical theory of society developed by the Frankfurt School" (p. 33). Further, Raymond Morrow (1994) has forwarded that the term *critical theory* "has its origins in the work of a group of German scholars [of Jewish descent] (collectively referred to as the *Frankfurt School*) in the 1920s who used the term initially (*Kritische Theorie* in German) to designate a specific approach to interpreting Marxist theory. But the term has taken on new meanings in the interim and can be neither exclusively identified with the Marxist tradition from which it has become increasingly distinct nor reserved exclusively to the Frankfurt School, given extensive new variations outside the original German context" (p. 6). Finally, in his study of Marx, Foucault, and Habermas's philosophies of history and contributions to critical theory, Steven Best (1995) uses the term *critical theory* "in the most general sense, designating simply a critical social theory, that is, a social theory critical of present forms of domination, injustice, coercion, and inequality" (p. xvii). He, therefore, does not "limit the term to refer to only the Frankfurt School" (p. xvii). This means, then, that the term "critical theory," and the methods, presuppositions, and positions it has come to be associated with in the humanities and social sciences, (1) connotes and continues to exhibit an *epistemic openness* and style of radical cultural criticism that highlights and accents the historical alternatives and emancipatory possibilities of a specific age and/or sociocultural condition; (2) is not the exclusive domain of Marxists, neo-Marxists, post-Marxists, feminists, post-feminists,

poststructuralists, postmodernists, and/or Habermasians; and, (3) can be radically reinterpreted and redefined to identify and encompass *classical and contemporary, continental and diasporan African liberation theory and revolutionary praxis*. For a few of the more noteworthy histories of the Frankfurt School and their philosophical project and various sociopolitical programs, see Bernstein (1995), Bottomore (1985), Bubner (1988), Dews (1987), Freundlieb, Hudson and Rundell (2004), Friedman (1980), Geuss (1981), Held (1980), Ingram (1990), Jay (1996), Kellner (1989), Kohlenbach and Geuss (2005), T. McCarthy (1991), McCarthy and Hoy (1994), Mendieta (2007), Morrow (1994), Nealon and Irr (2002), O'Neill (1976), Pensky (2005), Rasmussen (1999), Rasmussen and Swindal (2004), Stirk (2000), J.B. Thompson (1990), Wiggerhaus (1995), and Wolin (1992, 1994, 1995, 2006). And, for further discussion of the Africana tradition of critical theory, see Rabaka (2002, 2003a, 2003b, 2003c, 2003d, 2003e, 2004, 2005a, 2006a, 2006b, 2006c, 2006d, 2007a, 2007b, 2008a, 2008b, 2009).

    3. For a more detailed discussion of Du Bois's life and work, see first and foremost his own adventures in autobiography: "The Celebration of My Twenty-fifth Birthday," *The Souls of Black Folk*, "Credo," "I Am Resolved," *Darkwater: Voices from Within the Veil*, "So the Girl Marries," "On Being Ashamed of Oneself: An Essay on Race Pride," *A Pageant in Seven Decades, 1868-1938, Dusk of Dawn: An Essay Toward an Autobiography of a Race Concept*, "My Evolving Program for Negro Freedom," "My Golden Wedding," "I Bury My Wife," "I Take My Stand," *In Battle for Peace: The Story of My 83rd Birthday*, "A Vista of Ninety Fruitful Years," "My Last Message to the World," "To an American Born Last Christmas Day," "Advice to a Great-Grandson," "A Negro Student at Harvard at the End of the Nineteenth Century," *W.E.B. Du Bois: A Recorded Autobiography*, and *The Autobiography of W.E.B. Du Bois: A Soliloquy on Viewing My Life from the Last Decade of Its First Century* (for these, please see Du Bois 1938, 1952, 1960a, 1968a, 1968b, 1969a, 1969b, 1970d, 1985a, 1997a). One should also consult his posthumously published, *Against Racism: Unpublished Essays, Papers, Addresses, 1887-1961*, and the three-volume collection of his correspondence, *The Correspondence of W.E.B. Du Bois, 1877-1963*, see Du Bois (1985a, 1997b, 1997c, 1997d). Also, helpful in this regard are several secondary sources which often reveal more about various trends and traditions in Africana social and political theory and praxis than they do Du Bois's intellectual development and biography. For example, see Broderick (1955, 1958a, 1958b, 1959, 1974), Cain (1990a), Chandler (1997), Clarke, Jackson, Kaiser, and O'Dell (1970), W. A. Davis (1974), DeMarco (1974), S. C. Drake (1986/87), W. A. Drake (1985), Drummer (1995), Durr (2001), V. P. Franklin (1995), Golden and Milikan (1966), Guzman (1961), Higbee (1995b), Karenga (2003), Katznelson (1999), Lester (1971), D. L. Lewis (1993, 2000), Logan (1971), Marable (1985a, 1986, 1996, 1998), J. B. Moore (1981), Moses (1975, 1978, 1993a, 1996, 1998), Outlaw (1992, 1995, 1996b), Rampersad (1990), A. L. Reed (1985, 1997), Rudwick (1956, 1960a, 1968, 1982a), Stuckey (1987), Sundquist (1993, 1996), Tuttle (1957, 1973), Tyner (1997), Walden (1966), 1977), R. Williams (2001), Wolters (2001), F. Woodard (1976), W.D. Wright (1985) and Zamir (1995, 2008).

4. Since its inception Marxism has been in crisis, but this does not negate the fact that it has historically and continues currently to provide one of, if not *the* most penetrating and provocative critiques of capitalism. In response to constant criticisms that Marxism has been falsified, Herbert Marcuse (1978b) may have put it best when he asserted in a 1978 BBC interview that

> [I] do not believe that the theory [Marxism], as such, has been falsified. What has happened is that some of the concepts of Marxian theory, as I said before, have had to be reexamined; but this is not something from outside brought into Marxist theory, it is something which Marxist theory itself, as an historical and dialectical theory, demands. It would be relatively easy for me to enumerate, or give you a catalogue of, those decisive concepts of Marx which have been corroborated by the development of capitalism; the concentration of economic power, the fusion of economic and political power, the increasing intervention of the state into the economy, the decline in the rate of profit, the need for engaging in a neo-imperialist policy in order to create markets and opportunity of enlarged accumulation of capital, and so on. This is a formidable catalogue — and it speaks a lot for Marxian theory . . . Marxian theory would be falsified when the conflict between our everincreasing social wealth and its destructive use were to be solved within the framework of Capitalism; when the poisoning of the life environment were to be eliminated; when capital could expand in a peaceful way; when the gap between rich and poor were being continuously reduced; when technical progress were to be made to serve the growth of human freedom — and all this, I repeat, within the framework of Capitalism. (pp. 72–73; see also Marcuse, 1967, 1978c, 1979a, 1979b)

Many black radicals, especially black Marxists, concede with their white Marxist counterparts that capitalism does not enhance but inhibits human life and liberation. However, in contradistinction to white Marxists, black Marxists also emphasize the political economy of race and racism and, often employing a reconstructed race-conscious and racism-critical historical materialist framework, point to the interconnections and parallel historical evolutions of racism and capitalism. As early as his 1907 essays, "Socialist of the Path" and "The Negro and Socialism," for instance, Du Bois (1985c) detected and detailed deficiencies in the Marxist tradition which included, among other things, a silence on and/or an inattention to race, racism, and anti-racist struggle; racial colonialism and anti-colonial struggle; and the ways in which *both* capitalism and colonialism exacerbate not simply the economic exploitation of non-Europeans, but continues (both physical and psychological) colonization beyond the realm of political economy. Du Bois, therefore, laboring long and critically with Marxian theory and methodology, deconstructed it and developed his own original radical democratic socialist theory that simultaneously built on his pioneering work as a (classical) critical race theorist and anti-colonialist; called for the radical transformation of U.S. society and the power relations of the world; was deeply concerned about and committed to world peace and demanded disarmament; and, advocated the liberation of all colonized, politically oppressed, and economically exploited persons. For further discussion, see Rabaka (2007a), especially chapter 4, "Du Bois's Critique of Capitalism, Critical Marxism, and Discourse on Democratic Socialism," as well as Horne (1986), Marable (1986), and C. J. Robinson (2000).

5. In terms of "black radicalism" and the "black radical tradition," I should observe at the outset that though it has been consistently discussed and heatedly debated over the years, few scholars have endeavored extended analytical studies in this area. Often a paragraph or, at most, a journal article or book chapter surfaces every now and then, but book-length studies that critically engage this tradition as a resource for radical politics and critical social theory have been and remain extremely rare. Consequently, I turned to a wide-range of sources to deconstruct and reconstruct the black radical tradition. Most helpful in this regard were Alkebulan (2007), Bogues (1983, 2003), Bush (1999), Cox (1948, 1959, 1962, 1964, 1976, 1987), Cruse (1965, 1967, 1969, 2002), Foley (2003), Foner (1976, 1977), Foner and Allen (1987), Foner and Lewis (1989), Foner and Shapiro (1991), Haines (1988), C.L.R.James (1963, 1992, 1994, 1995, 1996, 1999), J.A. James (1996a, 1997, 1999), W. James (1998), C. Johnson (2007), Joseph (2006a, 2006b), R. D. G. Kelley (1990, 1994, 1997a, 2002), Kornweibel (1998, 2002), Lazerow and Williams (2006), Lemelle and Kelley (1994), Marable (1983, 1985a, 1986, 1987, 1996, 2000, 2002, 2005, 2006), Meeks (1993, 1996, 2000), Meeks and Lindah (2001), C.W. Mills (2003), Moten (2003), Mullen (1999, 2004), Mullen and Smethurst (2003), Naison (1983), Ogbar (2004), Padmore (1931, 1936, 1942, 1945, 1946, 1949, 1953, 1956, 1972), Parascandola (2005), Pulido (2006), C.J. Robinson (1997, 2000), Schor (1977), Singh (2004), Springer (1999, 2005), Theoharis and Woodard (2003), Tyner (2006), West (1988b, 1993a, 1999), Wilmore (1983), K. Woodard (1999), and J. Woods (2004).

6. For further discussion of black radicals and black Marxists' ragged relationship with white Marxism and white Marxist party politics and movements, see Baraka (1966, 1970, 1971, 1972, 1984, 1994, 1995, 1997, 2000), Bogues (1983, 2003), Cox (1959, 1987), Cruse (1967, 2002), A.Y. Davis (1998a), Foner and Allen (1987), Grigsby (1987), Haywood (1934, 1948, 1978), Hennessey (1992), P. Henry (2000), C.L.R. James (1992, 1994, 1996), W. James (1998), R.D.G. Kelley (1990, 1994, 2002), Kornweibel (1998), Marable (1983, 1985a, 1987, 1996), Naison (1983), Outlaw (1983a, 1983b, 1987), Padmore (1945, 1956), Serequeberhan (1990), Sivanandan (1990), C.J. Robinson (2000), West (1988b, 1993a, 1999) and E.E. Williams (1993).

7. Traditionally "white supremacy" has been treated in race and racism discourse as *white domination of and white discrimination against non-whites*, and especially blacks. It is a term that often carries a primarily legal and political connotation, which has been claimed time and time again to be best exemplified by the historic events and contemporary effects of African holocaust, enslavement, and colonization; the "failure" of Reconstruction, the ritual of lynching, and the rise of Jim Crow segregation in the United States; and, white colonial and racial rule throughout Africa, and especially apartheid in South Africa (Cell, 1982; Dykstra, 1993; Fredrickson, 1981; A.W. Marx, 1998; Nolen, 1967; Shapiro, 1988; Schultz, 2005). Considering the fact that state-sanctioned segregation and black political disenfranchisement have seemed to come to an end, "white supremacy" is now seen as classical nomenclature which no longer refers to contemporary racial and social conditions. However, instead of being a relic of the past that refers to an odd or embarrassing moment in the United States and South Africa's (among many other racist nations and empires') march to-

ward a truly transethnic and multicultural democracy, it remains one of the most appropriate ways to characterize current racial national and international conditions (Dobratz and Shanks-Melie, 1997; Kaplan and Bjorgo, 1998; Massey and Denton, 1993; Nesbitt, 2004; Novick, 1995), which, in other words, is to say that white supremacy has been and remains central to modernity (and "postmodernity"), because "modernity" (especially in the sense that this term is being used in European and American academic and aesthetic discourse) reeks of racial domination and discrimination. It is an epoch (or aggregate of eras) which symbolizes not simply the invention of race, but the perfection of a particular species of *global* racism: white supremacy. Hence, modernity is not merely the moment of the invention of race, but more; as Theodore Allen (1994, 1997) argues in *The Invention of the White Race*, it served as an incubator for the invention of the white race and a peculiar pan-European imperialism predicated on the racial ruling, economic exploitation, cultural degradation and, at times, physical decimation of the life-worlds of non-whites. In "The Souls of White Folk," which was initially published in the *Independent* in 1910, then substantially revised and published in *Darkwater* (1920), Du Bois (1995a) stated, "Everything considered, the title to the universe claimed by White Folk is faulty" (p. 454). Long before the recent discourse on critical race theory and critical white studies, Du Bois called into question white superiority and white privilege, and the possibility of white racelessness and/or white racial neutrality and white universality. He was one of the first theorists to chart the changes in race relations from *de jure* to *de facto* forms of white supremacy, referring to it, as early as 1910, as "the new religion of whiteness" (p. 454; see also Rabaka, 2007b). Hence, the conception and critique of white supremacy that I develop here does not seek to sidestep socio-legal race discourse as much as it intends to supplement it with Du Bois and others' work in radical politics and critical social theory. One of the main reasons this supplemental approach to critical white studies and critical race theory is important is because typically legal studies of race confine theorists to particular national social and political arenas, which is problematic considering the fact that white supremacy is a global racist system (Bonilla-Silva, 2001, 2003; Bonilla-Silva and Doane, 2003; M. Christian, 2002, 2006; C.W. Mills, 1999, 2001). Du Bois (1995a) declared, "Whiteness is the ownership of the earth forever and ever, Amen!" (p. 454). Here he is sardonically hinting at the cardinal difference between white supremacy and most other forms of racism: its worldwide or global historical, cultural, social, political, legal, and economic influence and impact. White supremacy serves as the glue that connects and combines racism to colonialism, and racism to capitalism. It has also been illustrated that it exacerbates sexism by sexing racism and racing sexism, to put it unpretentiously. Thus, white supremacy as a global racism intersects and interconnects with sexism, and particularly patriarchy, as a global system that oppresses and denies women's human dignity and right to be humanly different from men, the ruling gender (A.Y. Davis, 1981, 1989; hooks, 1981, 1984, 1995, 2004a, 2004b; J.A. James, 1996a, 1999; Rabaka, 2003d, 2004, 2006c).

8. My interpretation of (white) Marxism here and throughout this chapter has been primarily drawn from several "Hegelian" or "Western" Marxist works, as well as a

few of the more philosophy-focused texts in Marxist studies, see P. Anderson (1976), Arnold (1990), Aronson (1995), P. Buhle (1991), Callari, Cullenberg and Biewener (1995), Castoriadis (1991, 1997), Gottlieb (1989, 1992), Gouldner (1980), Hindess (1993), Howard (1972, 1988), Howard and Klare (1972), Jacoby (1981), Jameson (1971, 1975, 1979a, 1979b, 1979c, 1990, 1991), Jay (1984), Kellner (1995), Kelly (1982), Kolakowski (1978a, 1978b, 1978c), Lenin (1975, 1987), Leonhard (1971), Lichtheim (1965, 1966), Marcuse (1960, 1967, 1970b, 2001, 2004), Marx (1964, 1968, 1971, 1974, 1975, 1994, 1996, 2002), Marx and Engels (1964, 1972, 1978, 1989), Nelson and Grossberg (1988), and Therborn (1996).

9. With regard to Frankfurt School critical theory, Erich Fromm and Herbert Marcuse incorporated aspects of what could loosely be termed "feminist theory" into their articulations of a critical theory of contemporary society. However, neither theorist was consistent nor ever fully developed a feminist and/or anti-sexist dimension of his respective theory of social change. Though Fromm's inchoate socialist-feminist thinking by far surpasses that of Marcuse prior to the 1960s, it is important to observe Marcuse's efforts in the last decade of his life to take a "feminist turn," if you will, and to merge Marxism with feminism, among other elements of 1960s radical social thought and political practice. See, for example, Fromm's "The Theory of Mother Right and Its Relevance for Social Psychology," "Sex and Character," "Man-Woman," and "The Significance of Mother Right for Today," and Marcuse's "Dear Angela," *Counterrevolution and Revolt*, and "Marxism and Feminism" (Fromm, 1947, 1955, 1970; Marcuse, 1971, 1972a, 1974). For critical commentary on these thinkers' pro-feminist thought, see P. Mills (1987), Funk (1982), and Kellner (1984, 1989, 1992). And, for further feminist critiques of classical and contemporary Frankfurt School–based critical theory, see Benhabib (1986, 1992), Fraser (1989, 1991), and Meehan (1995). More than by any other major Frankfurt School critical theorist—Theodor Adorno, Max Horkheimer, Walter Benjamin, and Jürgen Habermas—my conception of critical theory has been indelibly influenced by Herbert Marcuse, whose critical theory increasingly incorporated and openly exhibited the influence of Africana liberation theory (Martin Luther King, Jr., Malcolm X, Frantz Fanon and the Black Panthers), Latin American liberation theory (Che Guevara and Fidel Castro), and women's liberation theory (Rosa Luxemburg and Angela Davis) (see Marcuse, 1969, pp. 7, 46–47, 79–91, 1970a, pp. 82–108, and 1972a). Though Marcuse never dialogued with Africana, Latin American, and women's liberation theory with the depth and detail which he did European and European American (male) theory, and considering the fact that his approach to the life-worlds and lived experiences of people of color was thoroughly shot through with the accoutrements of Eurocentrism—Marcuse (1972a, pp. 9, 29) employed labels and language such as "backward capitalist countries" and "barbarian civilization[s]"—there may, yet and still, be much in his social thought that could be of use to Africana and other critical theorists of color (see Marcuse, 1964, 1965c, 1969, 1970a, 1970b, 1972a, 1973, 1978a, 1997a, 2001, 2004, 2007a, 2007b).

10. For Africana womanist, black feminist, and/or feminist discussions of the intersection and interconnections of race, gender, and class, see Awkward (2000), Bambara (1970), Bobo (2001), Butler and Walter (1991), Busby (1992), B. Christian

(1985, 1989, 1994), P.H. Collins (1993, 1998, 2000), A.Y. Davis (1981, 1989, 1998a), Dill (1979, 1983), Dove (1998a, 1998b), Guy-Sheftall (1990, 1995), hooks (1981, 1984, 1989, 1990, 1991, 1995, 2000a), Hudson-Weems (1995, 1997, 1998a, 1998b, 2000), Hull, Scott and Smith (1982), James and Busia (1993), J.A. James (1996a, 1996b, 1997, 1999), James and Sharpley-Whiting (2000), Lorde (1984, 1988, 1996, 2004), Marsh-Lockett (1997), Nnaemeka (1998), B. Smith (1983, 1998), Terborg-Penn, Harley, and Rushing (1987), Zack (1997, 2000), and Zack, Shrage and Sartwell (1998). Black feminist/womanist historians have also engaged the overlapping nature of race, gender, and class in the lives of women of African descent. A few of the most noteworthy major studies are: Giddings (1984), Hine (1990, 1996), Hine, King, and Reed (1995), Hine and Thompson (1998), J. Jones (1985), Noble (1978), and D.G. White (1999).

11. With regard to Du Bois's "male-feminism," "pro-feminist politics" "womanism," and/or, as I prefer, his women's liberation theory or anti-sexist critical social theory, I am specifically referring to the following: "A Woman," "The Work of Negro Women in Society," "The Woman," "The Black Mother," "Suffering Suffragettes," "Suffrage Workers," "Votes for Women," "Hail Columbia!," "The Burden of Black Women," "Woman Suffrage," "Votes for Women," "The Damnation of Women," "The Freedom of Womanhood," "So the Girl Marries," "The Vision of Phillis the Blessed: An Allegory of Negro American Literature in the Eighteenth and Nineteenth Centuries," "Sex and Racism," and "Greetings to Women." For above, see Du Bois 1980b, 1982a, 1982b, 1983a, 1983b, 1985a, 1986a, 1986g, 1995a, 1996a. I have also consulted several secondary sources, among them: B. Aptheker (1975), Balfour (2003), P.H. Collins (2000), Diggs (1974), Gilman and Weinbaum (2007), Gilkes (1996), Griffin (2000), J.A. James (1996b, 1997), Lemons (2001), Lucal (1996), McKay (1985, 1990), Pauley (2000), and Yellin (1973). Moreover, and to get to the meat of the matter, Nellie McKay, Gary Lemons, and Hazel Carby each bemoan the fact that there is a strong tendency among critics and theorists to read Du Bois primarily as a "race man" and downplay his contributions to "feminist" and/or "womanist" discourse. For example, in her essay, "The Souls of Black Women Folk in the Writings of W.E.B. Du Bois," McKay (1990) claims that Du Bois was one of very few black men who wrote "feminist autobiography": "More than any other black man in our history, his three autobiographies [*Darkwater*, *Dusk of Dawn*, and *The Autobiography of W.E.B. Du Bois*] demonstrate that black women have been central to the development of his intellectual thought" (pp. 229, 231). McKay, who is a literary theorist and critic, argues that one of the reasons that so many Du Bois scholars, among others, read him as a "race man" is because they often overlook his "more creative, less sociological works, where most of his thoughts on women and his own fundamental spirituality are expressed" (p. 230). "Few people, even those who have spent years reading and studying Du Bois," quips McKay, "know that he wrote five novels and published a volume of poetry" (p. 231). Furthermore, in "'When and Where [We] Enter': In Search of a Feminist Forefather—Reclaiming the Womanist Legacy of W.E.B. Du Bois," Lemons (2001) laments that Du Bois's "womanist activism remains to be fully claimed by contemporary black men, as he continues to be viewed primarily

as a 'race man'" (p. 72). What perplexes Lemons is the fact that the critics who elide and erase Du Bois's women's liberation work do not simply do Du Bois a disservice, but rob contemporary men, and men of African descent in particular, of an Africana male *anti-sexist* role model. According to Lemons, "not only" was Du Bois's "conception of anti-racist resistance feminist-inspired, his worldview was profoundly influenced by black women" (p. 73). And finally, in the first chapter of her book, *Race Men*, "The Souls of Black Men," Hazel Carby (1998) offers contemporary academics and political activists a deconstruction of Du Bois as "race man" that acknowledges that he "advocated equality for women and consistently supported feminist causes" (p. 12). Carby, who asserts that it is not her intention to claim that Du Bois was "a sexist male individual," is not, however, as concerned with Du Bois's "male-feminist" thought—though she gives it her customary critical feminist treatment—as with many black male intellectuals' erasure and omission of his feminist thought from their discourse on Du Bois and their obsessive concerns with "the reproduction of Race Men" (p. 12, 25). She states: "If, as intellectuals and as activists, we are committed, like Du Bois, to struggles for liberation and democratic egalitarianism, then surely it is not contradictory also to struggle to be critically aware of the ways in which *ideologies of gender* have undermined our egalitarian visions in the past and continue to do so in the present" (p. 12, my emphasis). Carby's caveat, like the cautions of McKay and Lemons, essentially asks that we be cognizant of not only the "ideologies of gender" in the present, but also the "ideologies of gender" of the past, and how this specific species of ideology may have and/or, more than likely, indeed did influence the ways our intellectual ancestors theorized about this or that issue. In other words, we must make ourselves and others critically conscious of sexist sentiment in both classical and contemporary Africana liberation theory and revolutionary praxes. My work here, then, registers as an effort to simultaneously deepen and develop the anti-sexist aspects of Africana critical theory, and an attempt to move beyond one-dimensional interpretations of Du Bois which downplay the multidimensionality of his thought and texts. It is important here to note that because of the richness and wide range and reach of Du Bois's thought, within Du Bois studies there are various research areas and agendas—for example, history, philosophy, social theory, politics, economics, aesthetics, religion, education, and so forth. Depending on one's intellectual orientation, academic training, and discipline of preference, his thought and texts may serve a multiplicity of purposes and may be approached from a wide array of discursive directions. Needless to say, my interpretations of Du Bois have been deeply influenced by my training in and trek through Africana studies, and specifically Africana philosophy, social theory, and radical politics. I think it most fitting to conclude here by noting that since she published "What's Critical About Critical Theory?: The Case of Habermas and Gender" (which was originally published in 1985), Fraser (1998) has critically engaged the discourse of critical race theory, especially in her breath-takingly brilliant essay, "Another Pragmatism: Alain Locke, Critical 'Race' Theory, and the Politics of Culture." Therefore, I want to make it clear that my criticisms of her conception of critical theory are specific to this particular essay and are not in anyway indicative of my, otherwise, profound intellectual admiration for and affinity to her work. Truth be told, she, too, has made her own unique contribution to my conception of Africana critical theory. Here, then, I have only raised my concerns about how her omission of critical race theory and the Africana tradition of critical theory—and Du Bois's anti-sexist, anti-racist, anti-colonial, and radical democratic socialist thought in specific—weakened her otherwise extremely erudite and astute articulation of a new critical theory of contemporary society.

12. Along with Africana Studies and more general critical social scientific research methods, Africana critical theory has also been deeply influenced by the monumental meta-methodological studies of Gunaratnam (2003), Sandoval (2000), and L.T. Smith (1999), which each seek to decolonize research methods and emphasize their importance in developing critical theories of white-supremacist, patriarchal, capitalist, and colonial societies. The influence of these works on Africana critical theory's methodological orientation cannot be overstated.

13. In his introduction to *One-Dimensional Man*, Herbert Marcuse (1964) argues that "[s]ocial theory is concerned with the historical alternatives which haunt the established society as subversive tendencies and forces" (pp. xliii–xliv). Part of the task of a critical theory of contemporary society, then, lies in its ability to critique society "in light of its used and unused or abused capabilities for improving the human condition" (p. xlii). When I write of "ethical," "historical," and/or "radical" alternatives here, I am advocating new modes of human existence and humane interaction predicated on practices rooted in the realities of our past, present, and hoped-for future. I am following in the footsteps of one of the great impresarios of the Black Arts movement, Larry Neal (1989), who taught us that one of the most urgent tasks of radical artists and intellectuals is to offer "visions of a liberated future." In offering *ethical alternatives* to the established order, critical theorists highlight and accent right and wrong thought and action, perhaps the single most important issue in the field of moral philosophy (Frey and Wellman, 2003; Lafollette, 1999, 2003; Singer, 1993; Sterba, 1998). The critique of racism, sexism, and colonialism register, or rather *should* register right alongside the critique of capitalism in critical theorists' conceptual universe(s), because part of the established order's ideology and, in particular, part of its political and economic agenda involves domination and discrimination based on race, gender, and capitalist and/or colonial class/caste. Anti-racist, anti-sexist, and anti-colonial thought, practices, and social movements help to provide *historical alternatives* that Marx's and Marxists' criticisms of capitalism, to date, have not been able to adequately translate into reality (Aronson, 1995; Best, 1995; Callari, Cullenberg and Biewener, 1995; Gottlieb, 1992; Nelson and Grossberg, 1988; Magnus and Cullenberg, 1995). In fact, many former and neo-Marxists openly acknowledge that "classical" Marxism privileged class and gave special priority to economic issues which enabled it to easily overlook and/or omit the multiple issues arising from the socio-historical realities of racism, sexism, and colonialism in modern history, culture, politics, and society (Agger, 1992b, 1998; A.Y. Davis, 1981, 1989, 1998a; Dussel, 1985, 1995, 1996; Ingram, 1990, 1995; Kellner, 1989, 1995; Kuhn and Wolpe, 1978; Marsh, 1995, 1999, 2001; Matustik, 1998; C.W. Mills, 1987, 1997, 1998, 2003; Nelson and Grossberg, 1988; Sargent, 1981; Vogel, 1983; Weinbaum, 1978; West, 1988b, 1993a). What I am calling for here, though, is not a neglect of class and the role that political economy plays in contemporary culture and society, but rather the

placing of critical class theory in dialogue and on equal theoretical terms with critical race theory, women's liberation theory, and postcolonial theory in order to develop a broader-based, multiperspectival, and polyvocal radical political theory of contemporary society. The sites and sources of oppression in contemporary culture and society are multiple and do not emerge from the economy and the crises of capitalism alone. New critical theory must take into consideration the long neglected or often-overlooked new and novel forces and forms of domination and discrimination. Africana critical theory, therefore, is an earnest effort aimed at chronicling continental and diasporan African radicals and revolutionaries' contributions to a reconstructed critical theory of contemporary society.

14. Here, and throughout the remainder of this section of the introduction, I draw heavily from the discourse of Africana hermeneutics, or Africana philosophy of interpretation, in an effort to emphasize the importance of culturally grounded inquiry and interpretation in Africana critical theory. As Okonda Okolo (1991) observed in his classic essay, "Tradition and Destiny: Horizons of an African Philosophical Hermeneutics," Africana hermeneutics, as with almost all hermeneutical endeavors, centers on the ideas of "Tradition and Destiny" and how successive generations interpret, explain, and embrace their historical, cultural, and intellectual heritage. In his own words,

> For our part, we want to test the resources but also the limits of our hermeneutical models and practices, by examining the two notions that encompass our interpretative efforts in an unconquerable circle—the notions of Tradition and Destiny. These notions simultaneously define the object, the subject, the horizons, and the limits of interpretation. To interpret is always to close the circle of the subject and the object. We cannot, however, make this circle our own if we do not lay it out beyond the thought of the subject and the object, toward a thinking of our horizons and the limits of our interpretation defined by the reality of our traditions and the ideality of our destiny. (p. 202)

Okolo, among other Africana hermeneutics, highlights the abstruse issues that arise in interpretative theory and praxis in our present social world and world of ideas. Historical and cultural experiences determine and, often subtly, define what we interpret and the way we interpret. If, for instance, Africana thought traditions are not known to, and not shared with, theorists and philosophers of African descent and other interested scholars, then they will assume there is no history of theory or philosophy in the African world (see L. Harris, 1983; Eze, 1997a; Lott and Pittman, 2003; Rabaka, 2009; Wiredu, 2004). These would-be Africana theorists will draw from another cultural group's schools of thought, because human existence, as the Africana philosophers of existence have pointed out, is nothing other than our constant confrontation with ontological issues and existential questions. What is more, the nature of theory, especially in the current postcolonial/postmodern period, is that it incessantly builds on other theories. In other words, a competent theorist must not only be familiar with the history and evolutionary character of theory, but the intellectual origins of theories—that is, with *who*, *where*, and *why* specific theories were created to describe and explain a particular subject and/or object. For further discussion of Africana hermeneutics, see Okere (1971, 1991), Outlaw (1974, 1983a, 1983c) and, of course, the seminal research and writings of Serequeberhan (1991, 1994, 1997, 1998, 2000, 2003, 2007).

15. Part of Africana philosophy's current meta-philosophical character has to due with both its critical and uncritical appropriation of several Western European philosophical concepts and categories. As more philosophers of African origin and descent receive training in and/or dialogue with Africana Studies theory and methodology, the basic notions and nature of Africana philosophy will undoubtedly change. Needless to say, Africana philosophy has an intellectual arena and engages issues that are often distinctly different from the phenomena that preoccupy and have long plagued Western European and European American philosophy. I am not criticizing the meta-philosophical motivations in the discourse of contemporary Africana philosophy as much as I am pleading with workers in the field to develop a "division of labor"—à la Du Bois's classic caveat(s) to continental and diasporan Africans in the face of white supremacy (see Du Bois, 1973, 2002). A move should be made away from "philosophizing on Africana philosophy" (i.e., meta-philosophy), and more Africana philosophical attention should be directed toward the cultural crises and social and political problems of the present age. In order to do this, Africana philosophers will have to turn to the advances of Africana Studies scholars working in history, cultural criticism, economics, politics, and social theory, among other areas. For a more detailed discussion of the nature and tasks of Africana philosophy, see Lucius Outlaw's groundbreaking, "Africana Philosophy" and "African, African American, Africana Philosophy" (Outlaw, 1996a, 1997). Also of immense importance and extremely influential with regard to my interpretation of Africana philosophy are Babbitt and Campbell (1999), R.H. Bell (2002), L.M. Brown (2004), Chukwu (2002), Coetzee and Roux (1998), English and Kalumba (1996), Eze (1997a, 1997b), Gordon (1997a, 1997b, 1998, 2000a, 2006a, 2006b, 2008), Gyekye (1995, 1996, 1997), L. Harris (1983), Hord and Lee (1995), Hountondji (1996), Imbo (1998), Kwame (1995), Locke (1983b, 1989, 1992), Lott (2002), Lott and Pittman (2003), Masolo (1994), C.W. Mills (1998), Mosley (1995), Mudimbe (1988, 1994), Pittman (1997), Scott and Franklin (2006), Serequeberhan (1991, 1994, 1997, 2000, 2007), Sumner and Wolde (2002), Waters and Conaway (2007), Wiredu (1980, 1995, 1996, 2004), R.A. Wright (1984), and Yancy (1998, 2004, 2005).

16. Fanon's four books—*Black Skin, White Masks*; *A Dying Colonialism*; *The Wretched of the Earth*; and *Toward the African Revolution*—reveal a critical theorist of extraordinary depth and exceptional insight, especially with regard to issues involving Europe's supposed white superiority and Africa's alleged black inferiority; racism, sexism, colonialism, and neocolonialism; revolutionary self-determination and revolutionary decolonization; the nature of revolutionary nationalism and its interconnections with revolutionary humanism; colonial violence and anti-colonial violence; national consciousness, national culture, and national liberation; the psychology of both the colonizer and the colonized; and, the prospects and problematics of a truly "postcolonial" African state. Fanon, the critical theorist who came to be called "the apostle of violence," "the prophet of a violent Third World revolution," "the prisoner of hate," and "the preacher of the gospel of the wretched of the earth," decidedly disagrees with Cornel West's contention concerning the prospects of an Africana

philosophy "based principally [albeit, not exclusively] on African norms and notions" (E. Hansen, 1977, p. 52; Macey, 2000, p. 2). Allow me to explain: David Macey (2000), perhaps, captured the ever-evolving posthumous life of Frantz Fanon best when he wrote at the dawn of the new century, "Over forty years after his death, Fanon remains a surprisingly enigmatic and elusive figure. Whether he should be regarded as 'Martiniquan,' 'Algerian,' 'French,' or simply 'Black' is not a question that can be decided easily. It is also a long-standing question" (p. 7). Undoubtedly, Fanon has profoundly influenced twentieth- and twenty-first century thinking about racism and colonialism, and whether his readers understand him to have been Caribbean, African, or French—or some synthesis of each of the foresaid—it is extremely important to emphasize that he desired, above all else, to be regarded quite simply as *human*, as a brother in the house of hard-working, humble humanity. However, as the Ethiopian philosopher Teodros Kiros (2004) readily reminds us, "We are the children of geography and history, born to a given race, a given region, at a particular time, in a particular place" (p. 217). Fanon, no matter how radically humanist, was not during his lifetime, and certainly is not now, immune to these inescapable facts—the facts, as he himself said, of his blackness. "An accomplished writer," Kiros contends, "Frantz Fanon is regarded by many as one of the greatest revolutionary thinkers of the twentieth century" (p. 217). He holds a special place in the hearts and minds of black radicals, revolutionary nationalists, and Pan-Africanists because, Kiros continues,

> He was a Pan-Africanist who did not divide Africa into north and south, and he made it his mission always to remind the Algerians of their Africanity, and other Africans of the Africanity of the north of the continent. His activities and writings were always guided by a Pan-African lodestar. (p. 216)

Fanon (1968), then, was not simply against the colonization of African people and the African continent, but he was also against the colonization of African thought, what he termed in *The Wretched of the Earth*, the "racialization of thought" (p. 212). I take Cornel West's assertion that he honestly believes that an Africana philosophy "based principally on African norms and notions" would, ultimately, be "theoretically thin" very seriously. Africana critical theory faithfully follows Fanon—an Africana philosophical figure that remains underengaged in West's discourse, which, if the truth be told, seems to be more and more preoccupied with critically commenting on European and European-American philosophers and their philosophies, all the while lucidly demonstrating the ways in which his (however "critical") thought is caught in an obsessive-compulsive deconstructive (albeit, yet and still, Eurocentric) moment and mode. After all of the smoke clears and all of the dust settles, Fanon's philosophy of freedom and discourse on revolutionary decolonization astutely enables Africana critical theorists to see that West actually practices a Manichaeanization or "racialization of thought," and Africana thought in specific, when he dismisses "African norms and notions" without, first and foremost, critically considering that he should, at the very least, reveal to his readers what he understands "African norms and notions" to be and *why* they are inappropriate for the development of *African* American or *Africana* philosophy. Secondly, West fails to take into account the ways in which he is, I believe unwittingly, creating a false dichotomy between continental and diasporan African thought traditions that contributes and helps to continue the "divide and conquer" colonization and Europeanization of Africana thought traditions. And, finally, here West's work does not bear in mind that the forms of European and European-American philosophy that he intensely espouses and critiques so passionately were all "theoretically thin" at one point or another, and that Africana philosophy would not be "theoretically thin" if more brilliant philosophers and critical thinkers like himself consciously contributed to it. This, I honestly believe, is one of Fanon's greatest challenges to Africana philosophers, and it is a challenge that, though I left philosophy for the wider world of critical theory long ago, I have very humbly accepted.

Chapter Two

Africana Critical Pedagogy: Du Bois's Philosophy of Education, Sociology of Education, Anthropology of Education, and Critical Educational Theory[1]

We must accept equality or die. What we must also do is to lay down a line of thought and action which will accomplish two things: the utter disappearance of color discrimination in American life and the preservation of African history and culture as a valuable contribution to modern civilization as it was to medieval and ancient civilization. To do this is not easy. It calls for intelligence, cooperation and careful planning. It would meet head on the baffling difficulties that face us today.

— W.E.B. Du Bois, *The Education of Black People:*
Ten Critiques, 1906–1960, 151

Negro children educated in integrated schools and northern colleges often know nothing of Negro history. Know nothing of Negro leadership and doubt if there ever have been leaders in Africa, the West Indies and the United States who equal white folk. Some are ashamed of themselves and their folk. They regard the study of Negro biography and the writing of Negro literature as a vain attempt to pretend that Negroes are really the equal of whites. That tends to be the point of view of those of our children who are educated in white schools. There are going to be schools which do not discriminate against colored people and the number is going to increase slowly in the present, but rapidly in the future until long before the year 2000, there will be no school segregation on the basis of race. The deficiency in knowledge of Negro history and culture, however, will remain and this danger must be met or else American Negroes will disappear. Their history and culture will be lost. Their connection with the rising African world will be impossible. What then can we do or should we try to do?

— W.E.B. Du Bois, *The Education of Black People:*
Ten Critiques, 1906–1960, 151–52

43

Everything can be explained to the people, on the single condition that you really want them to understand. . . . You will not be able to do all this unless you give the people some political education.

—Fanon, The Wretched of the Earth, 180, 189

INTRODUCTION: DU BOIS'S PHILOSOPHY OF EDUCATION AND AFRICANA CRITICAL PEDAGOGY

It is, perhaps, common knowledge at this point that W.E.B. Du Bois conceived of and characterized dialectics as what he termed "problems." In fact, it could be easily averred that Du Bois spent the sweep of his publishing life, an almost unfathomable eighty years (from 1883 to 1963), searching for solutions to problems, and not just "Negro" or black problems, but problems which plagued humanity as a whole. These "problems" varied in nature and nuance, but each emerged from the incontrovertible fact(s) of modern (and/or postmodern) imperialism—and specifically and especially as expressed and experienced in various forms of racism, sexism, capitalism and colonialism (Rabaka, 2007a). According to Du Bois, one of the most pressing problems confronting humanity, and people of color (in capitalist, communist, and colonial countries) in particular, is "the problem of education."

Education, for Du Bois, is "by derivation and in fact a drawing out of human powers," and it involves, or, at the least, education according to Du Bois *should* involve, essentially three things. First, education requires a critical knowledge of the past—that is, critical study of history, Africana as well as "world" history. Du Bois argued that *history*, as conventionally conceived in white-supremacist, capitalist, and colonialist contexts, was often an ideological ruse in the hands of the ruling race/class. He, therefore, developed a critical theory of history, a counter-history, if you will, that chronicled the hidden agenda of European imperial hegemony and Africana and other progressive peoples' resistance and radical social(ist) transformation efforts.

Second, education entails questions of culture, "cultural study"—as Du Bois (1973, p. 9, 28) put it long before Stuart Hall (1996) and his cultural studies colleagues—and critical cultural inquiry. History and culture go hand in hand, and to rob and reframe a people's history and culture from an oppressive point of view, or in the interest of imperialism, is to distort and deny that which is most human in each of us: our right to live decent and dignified lives, to walk unmolested in the world, and to develop (freely and to our fullest potential) our own unique contributions to the various traditions and heritages that constitute human culture and civilization. Lastly, Du Boisian education demands a critical understanding of present and future vital needs, the needs of not simply this or that specific cultural group, class, race, or gender, but humanity and our fragile ecology as a whole. This means, then, that the Du Boisian conception of education (as with the Du Boisian dialectic in general) is inherently and radically humanist, multicultural, and transethnic, and often uses history and culture as a basis to apprehend, interpret, and create critical consciousness concerning life- and world-threatening conflicts and contradictions. Considering Du Bois's definition of education—a process by which persons are taught to draw out and draw upon human powers and potentialities in the interest of radical (if not revolutionary) self and social transformation—this chapter takes as one of its central tasks an exploration of Du Bois's evolving philosophy of education and considers its import for contemporary critical educational theory and what I have termed *Africana critical pedagogy*.[2]

Africana critical pedagogy employs a critical theoretical framework and methodology, which is to say that it is inherently interdisciplinary and interested in relating theory to praxis, and education to radical self and social transformation (Giroux, 1983b; McLaren, Fischman, Sunker and Lankshear, 2005; McLaren and Giarelli, 1995; McLaren and Kincheloe, 2007). Similar to critical pedagogy in general, Africana critical pedagogy combines philosophy of education with radical politics, critical social theory, class analysis, and cultural criticism. It stresses the need for education that empowers and inspires individuals to struggle against (neo)imperialism in its many global and local manifestations and machinations. Following in the footsteps of the Brazilian radical educator and political activist, Paulo Freire, Africana critical pedagogy is a "pedagogy of the oppressed" that seeks to create and accessibly offer oppositional and alternative educational theories and praxes.[3] However, unlike much of the contemporary discourse of critical pedagogy, which has domesticated and academized the more radical aspects of Freire's philosophy of education (see McLaren and Leonard, 1993; McLaren and Lankshear, 1994; McLaren, Bahruth, Steiner and Krank, 2000; McLaren, 2000b), Africana critical pedagogy draws on the rich resources of Africana Studies, and the history of Africana revolutionary thought and practice in specific.

Critical pedagogy generally contracts the critical educational theory of Freire as its paradigm and point of departure, often coupling it with Western Marxism (especially Frankfurt School critical theory, Gramscism, and Althusserism), feminism, Deweyan pragmatism, poststructuralism, postmodernism, and British cultural studies (à la Stuart Hall), among others. Henry Giroux and Peter McLaren, two of the leading theorists of critical pedagogy, have both deepened and developed this discourse by placing it in dialogue with a wide range of theory and incorporating radical political elements into their work. Giroux, for instance, has produced several groundbreaking inter-disciplinary studies on youth culture, the media, teachers, and various kinds of politics and conflicts in educational institutions and intellectual cultures (see Giroux, 1988, 1991, 1992, 1993, 1994, 1996, 1997, 1998, 1999, 2000, 2001, 2002, 2003a, 2003b, 2004, 2005a, 2005b 2006a, 2006b, 2006c, 2006d, 2007). Moreover, McLaren has made his mark by highlighting how Freirian peda-gogical paradigms, critical multiculturalism, and revolutionary Marxism, es-pecially (Che) Guevarian guerrillaism and (Raya) Dunayevskayian Marxist-humanism, can aid in the reconstruction and radical democratization of contemporary education (see McLaren, 1995, 1997, 1998, 1999a, 2000a, 2002, 2005a, 2005b, 2006; McLaren and Farahmandur, 2005; McLaren, Fis-chman, Sunker, and Lankshear, 2005; McLaren, Hill, Cole and Rikowski, 2002; McLaren and Kincheloe, 2007). Indeed, the discourse of critical peda-gogy is exciting and inspiring; however, one of the contradictions of this dis-course is its consistent omission of Africana philosophy of education and the advances of black radical politics and Africana critical thought more generally.

In neglecting Africana educational thought and practice traditions, critical pedagogues are depriving themselves (and their students!) and impoverishing their theories. They are passing up an ideal opportunity to reconstruct critical pedagogy and complement it with a diverse array of alternative educational theories and practices that speak in special ways to a wide range of contem-porary (and crucial) didactic issues such as racism, sexism, heterosexism, colonialism, the racist nature of capitalism, multiculturalism, environmental-ism, political education, peace education, social ethics, social justice, and par-ticipatory democracy, among many others. What is more, in downplaying Africana educational discourse, contemporary critical pedagogues unwit-tingly diminish the critical multicultural component of their work, often pro-ducing reformist, (neo)liberal, and Eurocentric theories that resemble weak versions of traditional white-supremacist pedagogy (and ideology).

When and where black teaching theory is engaged, bell hooks, and specif-ically her magisterial *Teaching to Transgress* (1994a) and *Teaching Commu-nity* (2003a), frequently serve as the definitive embodiments of, and state-ments on, Africana educational thought. Along with hooks's work, the research and writings of the extremely adept African American pedagogue Gloria Ladson-Billings (1994, 2001, 2003, 2005a, 2005b) may also be in-voked when and where conventional critical pedagogues wish to practice *tex-tual tokenism*, but often her work, too, is treated in a superficial and single-minded manner—a monodimensional manner, it should be intensely emphasized, that routinely erodes its distinct contributions of the concepts of culturally relevant pedagogy, research in the public interest, and critical race theory in pedagogy (see also, Ladson-Billings and Fecho, 2003; Ladson-

Billings and Tate, 2006). This, thus, erases and gives many (would-be "critical") multiculturalists and pedagogues the impression that blacks have not created and constantly developed longstanding traditions of cultural education, political education, and counter-pedagogy. It also aids in forwarding the flat-footed (and subtle racist) thesis that two or three theorists of color can speak for all theorists and people of color. In saying this, I, of course, wish to take nothing away from the brilliance and brawn of hooks and Ladson-Billings's pedagogical breakthroughs, which have indelibly influenced my conception of Africana critical pedagogy. I only want (à la hooks and Ladson-Billings) to point to a couple of the problematics of contemporary critical pedagogy: its deep and undeniable connections to, and practices of, cultural hegemony, textual tokenism, conservative multiculturalism, neocolonialism, and (neo)liberal racism.

It should also be made clear that I am not accusing critical pedagogues of omitting Africana thinkers from their discourse *tout court*. On the contrary, one of the reasons I find critical pedagogy so promising is that it is one of the few contemporary discourses to emerge outside of Africana (and other ethnic) Studies circles that has consistently made reference to black radicals and other critics of color. The issue that I am raising here, though, is one that involves the degree to which critical pedagogues seriously and sincerely engage black radical politics and Africana philosophies of liberation. For example, mentioning Malcolm X, Frederick Douglass, or Frantz Fanon and quickly moving on does not demonstrate to contemporary critical educational theorists (or their students) how these intellectual-activists' ideas and actions offer oppositional and/or alternative pedagogical paradigms and practices. Invoking the names of Ella Baker, Audre Lorde, or Amilcar Cabral may earn critical pedagogues a couple of "cool" multicultural points with the white educational left, but it does little to demonstrate how these black socialist humanists helped to shape and mold unique anti-imperial pedagogical paradigms that were inextricable from the most radical political and revolutionary social movements of their times, and how their work continues to critically inform insurgent intellectual and radical political struggles in the present age.

Put another way, and taking a different literary tone, I am perplexed by critical pedagogues' unwillingness to dialectically dialogue with black radical politics and Africana critical thought traditions. I am highly bothered by their consistent reference to black thinkers without critically and carefully engaging the black thinkers' thoughts and the schools of thought (or thought-traditions) that provide a paradigm and educational foundation for black pedagogical praxis. Hence, the discourse of critical pedagogy is often intellectually disingenuous as it allows the names of Africana thinkers to appear as their critical discourse disappears. Thus, many critical pedagogues have an almost exclusively *nominal* relationship with Africana Studies—that is, they know when and where to drop an Africana thinker's name, as opposed to an Africana thinker's theory, to build their arguments and assume the accoutrements of multiculturalism, postmodernism, postcolonialism, post-Marxism, or postfeminism.

Africana critical pedagogy, being a cog in the overarching Africana critical theoretical wheel, is a corrective to conventional critical pedagogues' intellectual oversights as well as Africana intellectual invisibility throughout the academy. It emerges from an intellectual and political arena that few philosophers of education have taken seriously or studied thoroughly. In this sense, and much like the best of critical multicultural and critical pedagogical thought, Africana critical pedagogy explores uncharted theoretical terrains and disparate discourses for their contributions to contemporary consciousness-raising, radical politics, and democratic socialist movements. What distinguishes and helps to define Africana critical pedagogy, however, is its stress on Africana struggle and its emphasis on the often overlooked contributions of continental and diasporan African thought to critical pedagogical discourse. It draws from liberation thought and practices grounded in and growing out of the varied legacies of Africana history, culture, and struggle. Which is to say, Africana critical pedagogy inherently employs a critical theoretical and critical multicultural methodological orientation that enables it to accent Africana thought and "philosophies born of struggle" (L. Harris, 1983).

Taking a piecemeal approach to Africana philosophy of education and dropping the hallowed names of bell hooks or Stuart Hall here and there simply will not help radical educators think through the problematics and dialectics of critical pedagogical discourse as efficiently and/or eruditely as examining the wide range and whole history of classical and contemporary Africana educational theory and praxis. There simply are no substitutes, and we must immediately initiate archaeologies of this hidden intellectual history and the subjugated knowledge embedded in it. Unfortunately, almost the entire discourse of critical pedagogy is riddled with such false or faulty substitutions and decontextualizations; negations of critical pedagogical thought and practices that could contribute to, and I think are necessary for, the reconstruction of critical educational theory and the radical multicultural and social(ist) transformation of contemporary society.

Perusing conventional critical pedagogical discourse, one would think that persons of African origin and descent have little or no classical (not to mention contemporary) thought on education. Such simply is not so, and though there are countless classical Africana educational theorists that we could turn to (e.g., Anna Julia Cooper, Frederick Douglass, Ida B. Wells, Marcus Garvey, Mary McLeod Bethune, and Carter G. Woodson, among innumerable others), I believe Du Bois's articles and addresses collected in *The Education of Black People* (1973) and *Du Bois on Education* (2002) provide us with one of the best points of departure to explore Africana philosophy of education and establish Africana critical pedagogy.

In what follows I will, first, discuss Du Bois's development of a critical theory of history (as opposed to, or contrasted with a conventional "philosophy of history") and its impact on his "philosophy of education," as he characterized his educational thought as early as his classic 1906 address, "The Hampton Idea" (Du Bois, 1973, p. 11). Next, I examine Du Bois's philosophy of culture and the distinct style of cultural criticism he developed for its centrality to his philosophy of education and critical educational theory more generally. Third, I endeavor to objectively analyze some of the major deficiencies and limitations of Du Bois's philosophy of education by contrasting his 1903 theory of the Talented Tenth with his 1948 revision of the Talented Tenth thesis into a more Marxist and/or democratic socialist theory of "the Guiding Hundredth." Finally, I conclude commenting on the contributions Du Bois's philosophy of education and Africana critical pedagogy make to contemporary critical educational theory and praxis. Let us begin, then, by hitting at the heart of Du Bois's philosophy of education, his critical theory of history.

DU BOIS'S CRITICAL THEORY OF HISTORY AND THE PRODUCTION OF PRACTICAL KNOWLEDGE IN AFRICANA PHILOSOPHY OF EDUCATION

For Du Bois, Africana education—that is, the education of persons of African origin and descent and others about "the part which Africa has played in world history" (Du Bois, 1965)—"should be founded on a knowledge of the history of their people in Africa and in the United States [and other parts of the African diaspora], and their present condition[s]" (1973, p. 93). Du Bois's educational philosophy is distinguished in that it was one of (if not "the") first to maintain that "the whole cultural history of Africans in the world" should be taken into consideration when one is seeking to grasp and grapple with the "present condition[s]" of continental and diasporan Africans (Du Bois, 1973, p. 150). To begin, according to Du Bois, one needs to know about "the history of their people in Africa," "the slave trade and slavery," "abolition," and "the struggle for emancipation" (p. 150). Only after a careful and critical study of classical, colonial, and contemporary continental and diasporan African history did Du Bois deem an educator minimally prepared to proceed with the pedagogical process where continental and diasporan Africans are concerned.[4]

Knowledge of "the whole cultural history of Africans in the world" is a necessity in Du Bois's philosophy of education on account of the complexities and conundrums of the colonial, neocolonial, and, some would add, "post-colonial" Africana condition (see Eze, 1997b; Olaniyan, 1992, 2000; Quayson, 2000a, 2000b; Rabaka, 2003c, 2003e).[5] Africana education "starts from a different point" because continental and diasporan Africans' historicity—that is, their concrete historical and cultural experiences and actualities—have been and continue to be ones which require, and ofttimes demand, as Du Bois (1973) put it, "a different starting point" (p. 95).

Du Bois's demand for a different point of departure for Africana education rests on the realities of continental and diasporan Africans' situatedness in the modern world. In other words, he understood continental and diasporan Africans to be "facing a serious and difficult situation," one that was at once "baffling and contradictory," and "made all the more difficult for us because we are by blood and descent and popular opinion an integral part of that vast majority of mankind which is the Victim and not the Beneficiary of present conditions; which is today working at starvation wages and on a level of brute toil and without voice in its own government or education in its ignorance, for the benefit, the enormous profit, and the dazzling luxury of the white world" (p. 48, 75).

As the Eritrean philosopher Tsenay Serequeberhan (1994) has pointed out, "Philosophy, African or otherwise, is a critical and systematic interpretative exploration of our lived historico-cultural actuality"; it is a "critical and explorative engagement of one's own cultural specificity and lived historicalness" (p. 3, 23). This means, then, that Du Bois's philosophy of education is on point when and where it emphasizes "cultural specificity" and Africans' particular and peculiar historicity (Du Bois, 1973, p. 11). Du Bois's concept of culture and its connections to his educational thought will be the subject of the succeeding section. Therefore, I will sidestep direct discussions of culture here and focus primarily on how history is regarded by Du Bois, among other Africana educators, as the prime point of departure for interpretation and analysis where continental and diasporan African life-worlds and lived experiences are concerned.

Africana education, according to Du Bois, "cannot begin with history and lead to Negro history. It cannot start with sociology and end with Negro sociology" (p. 95). It "must be grounded in the condition and work of . . . black men [and women]" (p. 95), which is to say that Africana education, educators, and students "must start where we are and not where we wish to be" (p. 94).

Drawing parallels between African American education and European education, Du Bois argued that much in the same manner that education and educational institutions function in England, France, Spain, and Russia, they have a similar task and must play a comparable role in African American life. As he understood it, education and educational centers in the aforementioned countries used the history of the country and the culture of its people as aids in the socialization and acculturation of its citizens. Like education and educational centers elsewhere, Du Bois admonished Africana educators and educational institutions to utilize continental and diasporan African history and culture as their foundation and grounding point of departure. Employing the educational atmosphere in Spain as an initial example, Du Bois sternly stated,

> A university in Spain is not simply a university. It is a Spanish university. It is a university located in Spain. It uses the Spanish language. It starts with Spanish history and makes conditions in Spain the starting point of its teaching. Its education is for Spaniards, not for them as they may be or ought to be, but as they are with their present problems and disadvantages and opportunities. (p. 93)

Building on the above and bearing both historical and cultural context in mind, Du Bois then turned toward the French intellectual environment and contended with critical candor,

> In other words, the Spanish university is founded and ground in Spain, just as surely as a French university is French. There are some people who have difficulty in apprehending this very clear truth. They assume, for instance, that the French university is in a singular sense universal, and is based on a comprehension and inclusion of all mankind and of their problems. But it is not, and the assumption that it is arises simply because so much of French culture has been built into universal civilization. A French university is founded in France; it uses the French language and assumes a knowledge of French history. The present problems of the French people are its major problems and it becomes universal only so far as other peoples of the world comprehend and are at one with France in its mighty and beautiful history. (p. 93)

When and where education, educational institutions, and continental and diasporan Africans are concerned, Du Bois maintained that Africana education properly "begins with Negroes;" "uses that variety of the English idiom which they understand;" and "above all, it is founded, or it should be founded on a knowledge of the history of their people in Africa and in the United States, and their present condition" (p. 93). So, at first glance we could aver that Du Bois, similar to Frantz Fanon, understood that speaking a language meant much more than using a certain syntax, learning the lexicon, and mastering the morphology, but it meant "above all to assume a culture, to support

the weight of a civilization" (Fanon, 1967, p. 18).[6] Du Bois's emphasis on using "that variety of the English idiom which *they*"—meaning Africans in
North America or, rather, African Americans—"understand," also helps to
highlight his concerns with and commitment to the production of practical
knowledge expressed in language, whether written or spoken, that is accessible to Africana educators across disciplines, students, and laypeople alike. He
made it a point in both of the passages cited above to note that the language
employed for critical pedagogical purposes is always and ever the *lingua
franca*, or common language: Spanish in Spain, and French in France.[7]

Immediately after observing the importance of language in the learning
process, Du Bois turns toward history. In each instance it is the history of the
particular people, in their specific geographical, social, and political setting
that informs not only their pedagogical process, but also the very purpose and
life-principles of the people. Where Spanish education and educational institutions start "with Spanish history and make conditions in Spain the starting
point of its teaching," and where French education "assumes a knowledge of
French history" and makes the "present problems of the French people . . . its
major problems," so then, Du Bois (1973) definitively declared that

> starting with present conditions and using the facts and the knowledge of the
> present situation of American Negroes, the Negro university expands toward the
> possession and the conquest of all knowledge. It seeks from a beginning of the
> history of the Negro in America and in Africa to interpret all history; from a be-
> ginning of social development among Negro slaves and freedmen in America
> and Negro tribes and kingdoms in Africa, to interpret and understand the social
> development of all mankind in all ages. It seeks to reach modern science of mat-
> ter and life from the surroundings and habits and aptitudes of American Negroes
> and thus lead up to an understanding of life and matter in the universe.
>
> And this is a different program than a similar function would be in a white
> university, because it starts from a different point. It is a matter of beginnings
> and integrations of one group which sweep instinctive knowledge and inheri-
> tance and current reactions into a universal world of science, sociology, and art.
> In no other way can the American Negro college function. It cannot begin with
> history and lead to Negro history. It cannot start with sociology and end with
> Negro sociology. (p. 95)

It is the history of continental and diasporan Africans that is at the heart of
Du Bois's philosophy of education, and it is the harsh realities of that history
which demand a "different program" and require Africana education to "start
. . . from a different point." As with contemporary Africana studies theory and
research methods, Du Bois's prophetic pedagogy utilized Africana history
and culture, Africana thought, spiritual traditions, and value systems to "interpret and understand" "all history" and "all mankind in all ages."[8] For Du

Bois (1986a)—and the same may be said of many Pan-Africanists, black nationalists, artists of the Harlem Renaissance and the Black Arts Movement, Negritude theorists, and black feminists—Africana perspectives and points of view, Africana interpretations and explanations of the human experience (history) and the human condition (actuality) are viable and valid insofar as it is understood that "the Negro people, as a race, have a contribution to make to civilization and humanity, which no other race can make" (p. 825).

Each human group has its philosophy, which is to say that each group of human beings harbors a certain "habit of reflection" that helps them "interpret and understand" the world in which they live.[9] As the Ghanaian philosopher Kwasi Wiredu (1991) put it, "Any group of human beings will have to have some world outlook, that is, some general conceptions about the world in which they live and about themselves both as individuals and as members of society" (p. 87). In Du Bois's thinking, it is Africana "world outlook[s]," Africana conceptions of history, society, politics, economics, religion, and art, among other important issues, that have afforded and continue to offer continental and diasporan Africa's "contributions" to human culture and civilization. Indeed, for Du Bois (1986a) Africana people have a "great message . . . for humanity," and it is only through careful, critical, and concerted study of their history and culture that they (and ethically committed anti-imperial others) will be able to discover and recover, as well as extend and expand not only what it means to be black in a white-supremacist, capitalist, colonial world, but also, and perhaps more importantly, what it means to be human and deeply devoted to the search for social justice in the neocolonial/ (post)modern moment (p. 820).

DU BOIS'S PHILOSOPHY OF CULTURE AND CRITICAL EDUCATIONAL THEORY

Du Bois's philosophy of education involves not only reclamation of Africana historical memory in the interest of radically re-educating critical educators and students about Africa's creation of and contributions to civilization, but also a struggle over the meaning of culture and cultural meanings. In order to resist the imperial impulse, Africana and other oppressed people must do more than merely rediscover their long-hidden history. They also have to—as Amilcar Cabral (1973) succinctly put it—critically "return to the source" of their history, which is their culture, the specific or local thought and practice traditions that they have developed to sustain and enhance their life-worlds and lived experiences. For Du Bois, culture plays a special part in the critical consciousness-raising process (what Freire (1996a, p. 41–58) calls "conscientização") and its degradation helps to highlight the white-supremacist and

Eurocentric cultural hegemonic dimension of what is currently being vari-
ously called "globalization," "global capitalism," "transnational capitalism,"
and/or "corporate capitalism" (McLaren, 1998, 1999b, 2000, 2005a, 2005b;
McLaren and Farahmandur, 2005; McLaren, Hill, Cole and Rikowski, 2002).
Capitalism and racism, as with capitalism and sexism, are inextricable and
constantly influencing and exacerbating each other (Giroux, 1991, 1992,
1993; hooks, 2003a). They are interlocking oppressive systems that conceal a
kind of cultural racism deeply embedded in the language(s) and logic(s),
mores and twisted morals, institutions and individual imperial expressions of
the ruling race/class and its (neo)colonized colored lackeys. Concerning cultural racism and its ongoing effects on every aspect of the lives of the oppressed, Du Bois (1973) wrote,

> To kidnap a nation; to transplant it in a new land, to a new language, new cli-
> mate, new economic organization, a new religion and new moral customs; to do
> this is a tremendous wrenching of social adjustments; and when society is
> wrenched and torn and revolutionized, then, whether the group be white or
> black, or of this race or that, the results are bound to be far reaching. (p. 33)

Two of the many "far reaching" results of the African holocaust and
African enslavement have been historical amnesia and cultural dislocation. In
light of the fact that the preceding section was devoted to the role history
plays in Du Bois's philosophy of education, I will forego a discussion of historical amnesia here and focus instead on how Du Bois's concept of culture
informs his philosophy of education.[10] In the passage above, Du Bois observes that Africans were taken from Africa and coerced into a "new" culture
and, in point of fact, their (classical or "pre-colonial") culture was "wrenched
and torn and revolutionized." In the "new land," the diaspora—and often in
the "old land," Africa—Africans (or, "blacks," if you prefer) were "trained"
only "grudgingly and suspiciously," and often without "reference to what we
can be, but with sole reference to what somebody [else] wants us to be" (p.
9). Two of the "far reaching" results of this type of "training" was and continues to be cultural degradation and cultural dislocation.

Because continental and diasporan Africans' culture was and continues to
be "wrenched and torn and revolutionized," there is a decisive and dire need
to break with and go beyond the boundaries of the culture of the imperial established order (i.e., the white-supremacist, patriarchal, capitalist, colonial
world), and discover and recover those aspects of classical and traditional
African culture which, in Wiredu's words, "may hold some lessons of moral
significance for a more industrialized society" (p. 1991, p. 98). Looking at
this issue from the perspective of Du Bois's philosophy of education, we are
wont to ask a question that Du Bois (1973, p. 10) asked long ago: How can

we use "the accumulated wisdom of the world for the development of full human power" and to "raise the black race to its full humanity"? What bothered Du Bois was the fact that Africana contributions to "the accumulated wisdom of the world" were often either utterly left out of, or claimed by Europeans (or whites) in discussions of issues that he felt they had direct and practical bearing on. He was also perplexed by the fact that so many persons of African origin and descent knew few or "no norms" that were not "thoroughly shot through with [European imperial] ideals," and relied so heavily on European thought traditions, religious conceptions, and cultural values. Du Bois's critical comments are worth quoting at length:

> With few exceptions, we are all today "white folks' niggers." No, do not wince. I mean nothing insulting or derogatory, but this is a concrete designation which indicates that very very many colored folk: Japanese, Chinese, Indians, Negroes; and, of course, the vast majority of white folk; have been so enthused, oppressed, and suppressed by current white civilization that they think and judge everything by its terms. They have no norms that are not set in the nineteenth and twentieth centuries. They can conceive of no future world which is not dominated by present white nations and thoroughly shot through with their ideals, their method of government, their economic organization, their literature and their art; or in other words their throttling of democracy, their exploitation of labor, their industrial imperialism and their color hate. To broach before such persons any suggestion of radical change; any idea of intrusion, physical or spiritual, on the part of alien races is to bring down upon one's devoted head the most tremendous astonishment and contempt. (p. 123)

When persons of African origin and descent "think and judge everything by [their own] terms," they share the perspective or point of view of their particular people or cultural group with the wider world; they extend and expand what it means to be both African and human; they add to "the accumulated wisdom of the world;" and they take Du Bois (1986a) seriously when he said, "[I] believe that the Negro people, as a race, have a contribution to make to civilization and humanity, which no other race can make" (p. 825). In order to contribute to "civilization and humanity," Africana and other oppressed and anti-imperial people have to know not only *their* history, as was pointed out in the preceding section, but also *their* culture, which includes continental and diasporan traditions of critique, resistance, radical politics, and projects of multicultural and democratic social(ist) transformation. Without knowledge of cultural "norms" and "terms"—by which I take Du Bois to mean Africana views and values—prior to and in defiance of European imperial conquest and various forms of colonization, which continue well into the contemporary "postcolonial" period, black and other people of color are racistly rendered the very "cultural foundlings" and "social wards" that the acclaimed African American philosopher Alain Locke (1983a), and many members of the New Negro Movement and Harlem Renaissance perceptively prophesied, unrepentantly resented, and warily warned against (p. 247).[11]

The "radical change" that Du Bois is intimating above is *radical socio-cultural and politico-economic change*, which is one of the reasons he highlights not just "norms" and "terms," but also "ideals," "government," "economic organization," "literature," and "art." In the passage cited at the beginning of this section Du Bois noted that continental and diasporan Africans were not simply "kidnap[ped]" and "transplant[ed]" into a "new land," but that they were forced — which is why he used the term "kidnap[ped]" — to learn "a new language, new climate, new economic organization, a new religion and new moral customs." Though they were coerced into this "new" culture and various "new" societies, Africana people were still "separated and isolated" from the "new" established order (Du Bois, 1973, p. 122). It is this separation and isolation, along with the explicit domination of and discrimination against Africans and other people of color in both the "new" and "old" lands which compelled Du Bois to contend that blacks "form and long will form a perfectly definite group, not entirely segregated and isolated from our surroundings, but differentiated to such a degree that we have very largely a life and thought of our own. And it is this fact that we as scientists, and teachers and persons engaged in living, [and] earning a living, have got to take into account and make our major problem" (p. 121).

For Du Bois, blacks have "very largely a life and thought of [their] own," which in other words is to say that continental and diasporan Africans, as Wiredu made mention of above, "have some world outlook . . . some general conceptions about the world in which they live and about themselves both as individuals and as members [or non-members] of society," even in the midst and often in spite of the machinations and manipulations of the culture of the imperial established order. Du Bois understood blacks to be bound together not by biology, but by psychology, stating: "Biologically we are mingled of all conceivable elements, but race is psychology, not biology; and psychologically we are a unified race with one history, one red memory, and one revolt" (p. 100). In *Dusk of Dawn*, which was originally published in 1940, Du Bois (1986d) pointed out that it was blacks' collective experience of a "common disaster," their inheritance of the "social heritage of slavery," and their endurance of "discrimination and insult" that bound them together (p. 640). In fact, "this heritage binds together not simply the children of Africa, but extends through yellow Asia and into the South Seas" (p. 640).

Du Bois's concept of culture, similar to his concept of race, is predicated on experience, not biology or geography, and this is one of the reasons he stresses psychology and discrimination in his critical race theory. He stated clearly that "[t]here are certainly no biological races in the sense of people with large groups of unvarying inherited gifts and instincts thus set apart by nature as eternally separate," and "[w]e have seen the whole world reluctantly but surely approaching this truth" (Du Bois, 1973, p. 121). It was of minis- cule consequence to Du Bois what one called this group who *experienced* the "common disaster" of the African holocaust and collective racial "discrimi- nation and insult" at almost every turn in both the "new" and "old" lands, which is to say that Du Bois did not dive head first into semantics, and that he did not care whether one referred to continental and diasporan Africans as a "race" or a "distinct and unique cultural" group, because "separated and iso- lated as we are so largely, we form in America an integral group, call it by any name you will, and this fact in itself has its meaning, its worth and its values" (p. 122). It is the experience and endurance, then, of "the slave trade and slav- ery," "abolition" and "the struggle for emancipation"; of segregation, separa- tion, and isolation; and of contemporary "discrimination and insult" that pro- vided both the fuel and the fire for Du Bois's concept of culture. Speaking directly to Africans in the United States, Du Bois stated,

> We American Negroes are not simply Americans, or simply Negroes. We form a minority group in a great vast conglomerated land and a minority group which by reason of its efforts during the last two generations has made extraordinary and gratifying progress. But in the making of this progress, in the working to- gether of peoples belonging to this group, in the patterns of thinking which they have had to follow and the memories which they shared, they have built up a distinct and unique culture, a body of habit, thought and adjustment which they cannot escape because it is in the marrow of their bones and which they ought not to ignore because it is the only path to a successful future. (p. 143)

The experiences of African Americans have produced certain "patterns of thinking" and a "body of habit, thought and adjustment" that could and should be employed more frequently to address contemporary queries and crises, and not simply in the African world but in the world at large. How many contemporary questions could be answered if more people, of African descent and otherwise, were willing to acutely dialogue with Africana culture and civilization? Which contemporary problems does the Africana tradition of critical theory offer solutions to?

To dialogue deeply with Africana culture means, more than anything else, using it as a resource rather than as a quick reference. It means communicat- ing critically and becoming conversant with continental and diasporan thought and practice traditions that point to new passions and possibilities. This is what Du Bois meant above when he said, "it"—meaning, understanding

and grounding in Africana history and culture—"is the only path to a successful future" for African Americans. In so many words, he is intimating that
Africana and other progressive people should utilize the "patterns of thinking," "the memories they shared," the "distinct and unique culture," and the
"body of habit, thought and adjustment" of classical and contemporary, continental and diasporan Africa as a resource rather than as a superficial, politically correct, or curt multicultural reference.

Where Hegel infamously argued that Africa has no history and no real relevance for "civilized" (read: European imperial and bourgeois) history,
countless white supremacists of almost every political persuasion have
pygmyized Africana culture, contending that if indeed Africa (and its diaspora) does possess classical and contemporary culture it is "primitive" in
comparison to or, at the very least, derisively derived from European culture.
Du Bois defiantly countered these claims by documenting Africana contributions to human culture and civilization, and by developing an Africana philosophy of culture—that is, a philosophy of culture that is not only grounded
in and grows out of Africana conceptions of and contributions to the wider
world of human culture but also is an anti-racist counter-cultural praxis-promoting theory. This, thus, brings us to a discussion of Du Bois's answer to the
question: "What is a culture?"

> It is a careful Knowledge of the Past out of which the group as such has
> emerged: in our case a knowledge of African history and social development—
> one of the richest and most intriguing which the world has known. Our history
> in America, north, south and Caribbean, has been an extraordinary one which
> we must know to understand ourselves and our world. The experience through
> which our ancestors have gone for four hundred years is part of our bone and
> sinew whether we know it or not. The methods which we evolved for opposing
> slavery and fighting prejudice are not to be forgotten, but learned for our own
> and others' instruction. We must understand the differences in social problems
> between Africa, the West Indies, South and Central America, not only among the
> Negroes but those affecting Indians and other minority groups. Plans for the fu-
> ture of our group must be built on a base of our problems, our dreams and frus-
> trations; they cannot stem from empty air or successfully be based on the expe-
> riences of others alone. (1973, p. 143–44)

Beginning with "a careful Knowledge of the Past," both continental and diasporan, Du Bois's definition of culture takes a hard turn toward "experience"
and he states that the lived experiences of "our ancestors" are "part of our
bone and sinew whether we know it or not." In fact, "we must know" "[o]ur
history" in Africa, the Americas—for Du Bois this is North (the U.S. and
Canada), Central, and South America—and the Caribbean, in order to "un-

derstand ourselves and our world." So, besides being grounded historically in Africana lived experiences, Du Bois's concept of culture gravitates and grows toward an experiential and existential exploration and explanation of past and present Africana life-worlds and actualities. In other words, if indeed culture has to do with "a careful Knowledge of the Past out of which the group as such has emerged," the "Past" in Du Bois's thinking was much more than history, it was also inextricably connected to culture.

Culture is the thought, belief, and value systems and traditions that a people create, extend and expand to not only make sense of the world, but also to alter it in their own and others' anti-imperial interests. That is why Du Bois asserted above, "The methods which we evolved for opposing slavery and fighting prejudice are not to be forgotten, but learned for our own and others' instruction." Here he is suggesting that Africana liberation thought and practice in the face of and in the fight against "slavery" (domination) and "prejudice" (discrimination) could and should be instructional for Africana and other people struggling against imperialism. It is these and the other instructional elements of Africana liberation thought and practice that have the greatest import for contemporary critical educational theory and multicultural social(ist) transformation. Additionally, it is these same instructional elements that help to drive home Du Bois's contention that Africa and Africans have a "great message for the world."

The Malian philosopher, Lansana Keita (1991), contends that "[p]hilosophical thought, like any human product, derives its value according to its perceived usefulness," and that "the theoreticians of philosophy in an African context must attempt to construct a modern African philosophy with the notion that its formulation would be geared toward helping in the development of a modern African civilization" (p. 144, 147). Du Bois's philosophy of education, like Africana educational thought in general, is defined by and demands historical and cultural grounding because it understands that Africana history and culture have been and remain under attack and threatened by both omission and erasure within the intellectual circles and educational centers of the white-supremacist, patriarchal, capitalist, colonial world and, unfortunately, even in multicultural and critical pedagogical discourse. Without a "careful Knowledge of the Past out of which the group as such has emerged"—that is to say, without a careful and critical understanding of continental and diasporan African history and culture—Africana people at the dawn and well into the twenty-first century will more than likely remain plagued by many of the "problems" of the twentieth century (see Rabaka, 2007a). These problems, the Caribbean philosopher Lewis Gordon (1998) argues, are "amazingly embodied in the thought of W.E.B. Du Bois in the North [meaning, North America] and Frantz Fanon in the Caribbean" (p. 1).

For Gordon, Du Bois and Fanon help to highlight problems of identity, liberation, and "self-reflexive incompleteness." The problem of identity is compounded by the problem of the color-line, as Du Bois announced metaphorically at the dawn of the twentieth century in *The Souls of Black Folk*. But, the color-line is not now and has never been simply about the social construction of race and the harsh realities of racism. Much more, it is about categorizing and dividing human beings in adherence with white-supremacist, capitalist, colonial, social hierarchy. Indeed, the color-line at this point is an age-old imperial aggregate, a racist ruse created to conceal the constant construction and reconstruction of hegemonic borders based on denied humanity, dashed democratic dreams, bracketed identities, broken bodies, suppressed spirits, and grotesque global greed. As a metaphor, the color-line triggers and entraps all our anxieties about difference and deviance, and it exposes us to what the black, feminist, socialist, humanist Audre Lorde (1984) referred to as "the enemy's many faces," faces which are sometimes white and other times (oft times) non-white (p. 75). In our postmodern/postcolonial/postmarxist/postfeminist world, *who* we are is deeply bound up with *what* we are, or, at the least, what we are perceived to be. That is to say that at the heart of the problem of identity are not only existential but ontological questions, crucial questions concerning essence and being.[12]

With regard to the problem of liberation, questions concerning decolonization and revolutionary social(ist) transformation arise. In terms of Africana philosophy of liberation, the Haitian revolution, the African American struggle against slavocracy, sharecropping, peonage, and Jim and Jane Crow segregation, and the continental and diasporan Pan-African movements serve as modern points of departure for those in pursuit of answers to questions such as, in Cabral's words, "against [what and] whom are our people struggling?" (1979, p. 75) and in Serequeberhan's words, "What are the people of Africa trying to free themselves from and what are they trying to establish?" (1991, p. 12).

Finally, the problem of incompleteness is posed on account of the very historical experiences that Du Bois argued Africana and other struggling people are not being exposed to, but should be critically and morally made aware of on account of their instructional import and contribution to "the accumulated wisdom of the world." Another way of putting it is that the problem of incompleteness accents the fact that a bona fide philosophical anthropology is one that takes into consideration both the high points and horrors of human history, all the triumphs and tragedies of our transgressions, and based upon those events denies any essence, totality, or teleology outside of them. It engages our impulse to search and yearn for new modes and models of human existence and experience beyond ourselves and our societies as they currently exist.

Many of the problems of the past remain problems in the present, which is to say that, among other problems, problems of identity, liberation, and incompleteness continue to plague Africana and other oppressed people. Education in its best sense should expose continental and diasporan Africans not simply to their "distinct and unique" history and culture, but also to their problems and the historical circumstances and situations that imperially produced and neo-imperially perpetuate those problems. Also—and I should like to place special emphasis on this—education should expose Africana and other struggling people to ways in which they can solve their problems. As Du Bois put it above, "Plans for the future of our group must be built on a base of our problems, our dreams and frustrations; they cannot stem from empty air or successfully be based on the experiences of others alone." This means, then, that Du Bois's philosophy of education is ultimately directed at rescuing and reclaiming the denied humanity of Africana and other oppressed people by critiquing and combating domination and discrimination and extending and expanding the prospects and promises of critical multicultural and radical democratic social(ist) transformation.

FROM "TALENTED TENTH" TO "GUIDING HUNDREDTH": A FEW OF THE LIMITATIONS AND DEFICIENCIES OF DU BOIS'S DISCOURSE ON EDUCATION

Du Bois's arguments for historical and cultural grounding in, and a different point of departure for, Africana education are penetrating and often brilliant, but there is a sense in which his declarations are underdeveloped and inadequate so far as application and implication are concerned. Put another way, Du Bois's educational thought is a virtual treasure trove in theoretical terms—meaning, he engaged a multiplicity of educational issues over an extended period of time—but often gave few clues as to how and to whom his educational theory could and should be applied. This presents something of a paradox in Du Bois's educational thought, especially considering the fact that so much of it was geared toward the production of practical knowledge. However, Du Bois's pedagogical weakness is also, I believe, a source of his critical theoretical strength and stamina, and this conceptual conundrum ultimately points to the profundity and durability of the Du Boisian dialectic, his philosophy of education, and his overarching critical social theory.

It is precisely Du Bois's unrelenting refusal to offer concrete alternatives and solid solutions to pedagogical and pressing social problems that allows critical theorists from disparate disciplines and political organizations to contract and reconstruct his theory in contemporary contexts, thereby deepening and developing his radical humanist, critical multiculturalist, and democratic socialist project(s), which long transversed and transgressed the battery of borders built to protect imperial interests. He did not begin by bellowing against and aiming his critical theoretical weaponry at imperial educational practices, but believed in a form of liberal education that would eventually place social and political power in the hands of the black bourgeoisie. Du Bois's early thoughts on education are, as we will soon see, at best conservative and in direct and blatant contradiction to his later, more Marxist and increasingly internationalist philosophy of education. Instead of focusing on the seemingly schizophrenic nature of the history of his educational thought, a more meaningful and critical engagement of Du Bois's constantly evolving pedagogy demands that we do precisely what he advised his students and readers to do in his "Last Message to the World," where he humbly and lovingly stated,

> I have loved my work, I have loved people and my play, but always I have been uplifted by the thought that what I have done well will live long and justify my life; that what I have done ill or never finished can now be handed on to others for endless days to be finished, perhaps better than I could have done. (Du Bois, 1971b, p. 736)

Here a dying Du Bois openly asks us to learn from his mistakes and failures and build on and go beyond his intellectual and political contributions. In what follows I intend to honor his request and heed his last words by briefly discussing some of the limitations and deficiencies of his philosophy of education and provide an alternate critical educational theory grounded in and growing out of his educational thought and contemporary Africana pedagogical theory and praxis.

At first issue is the fact that Du Bois's early educational thought, specifically with regard to essays such as "The Talented Tenth," "The Hampton Idea," and to a certain extent "Galileo Galilei," placed Africana advancement squarely on the shoulders of the black intellectual elite (see Du Bois, 1973, 1986e, 2002). His thinking at this point did not in anyway associate upward mobility with the black masses and working classes and, in fact, in his infamous 1903 essay, "The Talented Tenth," he went so far as to query, "Was there ever a nation on God's fair earth civilized from the bottom upward?" Du Bois's emphatic answer to his rhetorical question was "Never; it is, ever was and ever will be from the top downward that culture filters. The Talented Tenth rises and pulls all that are worth saving up to their vantage ground" (1986a, p. 847).[13]

Besides exhibiting a virulent intellectual elitism that privileges black academics and professionals over the black masses and working classes, Du Bois's Talented Tenth theory proves impoverished and inadequate when one

reflects on the fact that most people of African descent have few if any opportunities to do the very "cultural study" which he asserts is such an integral
part of the Africana pedagogical process (1973, p. 28). Du Bois is caught in
a contradiction when one realizes, as he did much later (see Du Bois, 1996c),
that his philosophy of education is in no uncertain terms asking "teachers [to]
teach that which they have learned in no American school" (1973, p. 98),
which, in other words, is to say that Du Bois knew good and well—first, that
his philosophy of education was at loggerheads with Western European and
European American educational thought and practice, and, second, that his
philosophy of education did not ask, but *demand* Africana educators to go
above and beyond their training in Western European and European American history, culture, religion, politics, arts, and so on, and re-root themselves
and their constituencies in Africana history and culture, Africana thought, belief, and values systems and traditions.

Du Bois stated above that people of African descent are often educated
"grudgingly and suspiciously; trained not with reference to what we can be,
but with sole reference to what somebody [else] wants us to be" (p. 9). Even
in "The Talented Tenth" he argues unequivocally for "culture training" for
black "group leaders," "leaders of thought among Negroes," and black "educated thinkers" (1986e, p. 855). But here paradox presents itself immediately:
If, indeed, the Talented Tenth "rises and pulls all that are worth saving up to
their vantage ground," and if, as Du Bois intimated, the Talented Tenth are often educated "not with reference to what we can be, but with sole reference
to what somebody [else] wants us to be," then, the question quickly becomes
which or, more to the point, *whose* "vantage ground" will the Talented Tenth
be pulling the black masses up to? We could throw a third critical query in
here and ask *how* will the Talented Tenth pull the black masses up to their
"vantage ground" since, in Du Bois's words, "they have no traditions to fall
back upon, no long-established customs, no strong family ties, [and] no well-
defined social classes" (p. 852)?[14]

The "vantage ground" or worldview of the Talented Tenth is often that of
the imperial agents who educate them "grudgingly and suspiciously," which
is one of the reasons Du Bois declared above that "very very many colored
folk . . . can conceive of no future world which is not dominated by present
white nations and thoroughly shot through with their ideals, their method of
government, their economic organization, their literature and their art; or in
other words their throttling of democracy, their exploitation of labor, their industrial imperialism and their color hate." It is the very "vantage ground" of
the Talented Tenth which Du Bois would later argue is problematic and in
need of radical reconstruction by the "human power" of much more than the
black intelligentsia.

In 1948, forty-five years after his initial articulation of his Talented Tenth theory, Du Bois (1996c) delivered "The Talented Tenth Memorial Address," in which he sternly stated,

> When I came out of college into the world of work, I realized that it was quite possible that my plan of training a talented tenth might put in control and power, a group of selfish, self-indulgent, well-to-do men, whose basic interest in solving the Negro problem was personal; personal freedom and unhampered enjoyment and use of the world, without any real care, or certainly no arousing care, as to what became of the mass of American Negroes, or of the mass of any people. My Talented Tenth, I could see, might result in a sort of interracial free-for-all, with the devil taking the hindmost and the foremost taking anything they could lay hands on. (p. 162)

Besides sounding like the penetrating pronouncements of Fanon in *The Wretched of the Earth* concerning the "national bourgeoisie" or the "national middle class" in their greed and intense identification with and imitation of the culture of the colonizers, Du Bois's assertions above help to highlight a shift in his liberation and leadership thought from the black elite to the black masses. In his revised and reformulated Talented Tenth thesis, Du Bois not only stresses *struggle, sacrifice*, and *service* as prerequisites for black and global human progress, but he ultimately abandons the Talented Tenth thesis for "the doctrine of the 'Guiding Hundredth.'" Here, as Joy James pointed out in *Transcending the Talented Tenth*, Du Bois is attempting to simultaneously democratize and internationalize his philosophy of education and his black liberation and leadership theory (see James, 1997, p. 45–46).

It is not enough for the Talented Tenth to be talented, quipped Du Bois, but they must also be willing and able to *struggle, sacrifice*, and *serve*. What black and other oppressed and poverty-stricken people need is "honest," "unselfish, far-seeing leadership." Du Bois (1996c) put it this way: "We cannot have perfection. We have few saints. But we must have honest men [and women] or we die. We must have unselfish, far-seeing leadership or we fail" (p. 173). He learned from bitter experience that unless the Talented Tenth was composed of "men and women of character and almost fanatic devotion" to Africana and universal human liberation, then, "mass misery" and "the poor [which] need not always be with us" will become permanent parts of the human experience and condition (p. 161–62; see also C.F. Peterson, 2000, 2007; Rabaka, 2005b).

In revising and reformulating his Talented Tenth thesis into a theory of "the Guiding Hundredth," Du Bois (1996c) democratized and internationalized his black liberation and leadership thought, asserting that it must be based on "group leadership, not simply educated and self-sacrificing, but with a clear vision of present world conditions and dangers, and conducting American Negroes to alliance with culture groups in Europe, America, Asia and Africa, and looking toward a new world culture" (p. 168). Du Bois's theory of the "Guiding Hundredth," then, is predicated on a concept of collective leadership which harbors an openness to coalitions and alliances with other "culture groups," and which is geared toward the creation of "a new world culture."

Where his early articulation of the Talented Tenth theory limited itself to both the African American intelligentsia and problems endemic to and emanating from African Americans' particular and peculiar existential and ontological experiences in North America, Du Bois's evolving critical thought—and especially as embodied in his "Guiding Hundredth" thesis—took on a world historical tone which found the greatest promise and potential for radical social and global change, not in the heads of intellectuals and academics, but in the hearts and hands of "men and women of character"—regardless of their race, culture, class, and/or occupation. For Du Bois, character became the greatest gauge of radical political potential, and this is one of the reasons he repeatedly wrote of "great moral leaders," "prophets and reformers," "honest men" and "unselfish, far-seeing leadership" in "The Talented Tenth Memorial Address" (p. 162, 173). In the face of his early black bourgeois pedagogical pronouncements, Du Bois now came to realize that education and ability were not panaceas for the problems plaguing people of African descent. In his own weighted words,

> My Talented Tenth must be more than talented, and work not simply as individuals. Its passport to leadership was not alone learning but expert knowledge of modern economics as it affected American Negroes; and in addition to this and fundamental, would be its willingness to sacrifice and plan for such economic revolution in industry and just distribution of wealth, as would make the rise of our group possible. (p. 163)

In the final analysis, education and ability must be coupled with character and radical democratic socialism, and in Du Bois's evolving critical social theory this involves not simply the black intelligentsia, but also the black masses' and the global working classes' "almost fanatic devotion" to cultural and "economic revolution;" "the ideal of plain living and high thinking, in defiance of American noise, waste and display; the rehabilitation of the indispensable family group;" and the eradication of the "wholesale neglect of invaluable human resources" (p. 175, 177). The Talented Tenth, thus, was conceived and christened by Du Bois, long given his best blessings, and then, without a lot of brouhaha and brandishing of theoretical weaponry, laid to rest in an act of *intellectual infanticide*. There is a sense in which "The Talented Tenth Memorial Address" simultaneously serves as an epitaph for one of Du

Bois's infamous theoretic failures and an exciting announcement that he was not afraid to conceptually begin again, revising and reconstructing his leadership and liberation thought in light of increasing African American professional and intellectual elitism, a growing black bourgeoisie shamelessly and pretentiously grounded in European imperial culture and, perhaps most importantly, his deep and abiding interests in coupling his philosophy of education and critical race theory with Marxist critiques of capitalism, critical class theory, and radical democratic socialism.[15]

Education, liberation, and leadership are not the exclusive domain of the ruling race, gender, and/or class; they are vital human needs just as food, clothing, and shelter are human necessities. But, without critical education and liberation thought that speaks to the specificities of Africana and other subjugated souls' life-worlds and lived experiences, ongoing hardships and unspeakable hurts, long-held utopian hopes, and deep-seated radical democratic desires, then all oppressed and (neo)colonized people have are abstract and empty inquiries into Eurocentric notions of "justice," "freedom," "democracy," "liberation," "peace," and, perhaps most importantly, what it means to be "human." Capitalist, colonial, and/or global imperial "democracy" is a deformation of democracy that enables the ruling race, gender, and/or class to put the premium on *what* the oppressed are fighting for and *how* they fight for what they are fighting for. Africana education must not simply expose and introduce us and tyrannized others to Africana history and culture, Africana thought, belief, and value systems and traditions, but it must also aid us in our efforts to engage, explore, and ethically alter the world in our own and other downtrodden and dispossessed peoples' anti-imperial interests. What I am calling for here is nothing short of a critical multiculturalist, radical humanist, and revolutionary democratic socialist transgression and transcendence of Eurocentric-ideological-imperial education, socialization, and globalization.

CONCLUSION: DU BOIS, CRITICAL EDUCATIONAL THEORY, AND AFRICANA CRITICAL PEDAGOGY

Du Bois serves as an ideal point of departure for contemporary Africana philosophy of education when and where he asserts that Africana people "have a contribution to make to civilization and humanity, which no other race can make," and in so far as he stresses the necessity and importance of Africana education beginning with and being rooted in, Africa—its people and problems, its history and culture, its thought, belief, and value systems and traditions—and ever-expanding "toward the possession and the conquest of all knowledge." Du Bois also poses a paradigm for critical pedagogy, particularly in terms of recent efforts geared toward de-domesticating and reconstructing it to reflect criticisms of its inattention to racism, sexism, radical politics, and revolutionary democratic socialist transformation. For example, critical pedagogues frequently reproach racism, but very rarely systematically analyze it and incorporate philosophy of race, sociology of race, and, especially, critical race theory into their educational theory (Dixson and Rousseau, 2006; Parker, Deyhle and Villenas, 1999). Such a synthesis, one of critical pedagogy and critical race theory, has precedent in Du Bois's philosophy of education and the history of Africana critical educational theory in general. What Du Bois's educational thought and Africana critical pedagogy urges conventional critical pedagogues to do is broaden their critical theoretical base by making it more multicultural and expanding the range of pedagogical (and social and political) problems to which they seek solutions.

Freire's philosophy of education has long served as the fountainhead and foundation for critical pedagogy, but the politics of postmodernism and/or postmodern politics have downplayed and diminished its inherent radical humanism and promotion of revolutionary democratic socialist projects. Postmodern pedagogues have pointed out that Freire's formulations often raise important issues but do not adequately provide the necessary philosophical foundation for putting forward more progressive and programmatic alternatives to the (mostly European, modernist, and masculinist) pedagogical perspectives he criticizes. For instance, Freire provides few concrete (as opposed to abstract) accounts of ways in which critical educators progress from critical thought to critical practice, self-consciously demanding that their critical pedagogical discourse constantly translate into and support radical politics and critical multicultural democratic socialist movements. However, I should obstinately observe, Freire's pedagogical pronouncements are often purposely universal, and this gives them their intellectual and political potency (much like Du Bois's educational thought) such that they can be conscripted by progressive educators to criticize and to counterpoint imperial pedagogical practices worldwide.

Indeed, many of the postmodern pedagogues may have misread Freire's philosophy of education, but perhaps part of the confusion is due to the fact that there has been a mounting debate amongst Freirean critical pedagogues as to how best to interpret and apply his radical pedagogy and radical politics. However, and this must be made clear, even before postmodernism taunted and tantalized pedagogues lost in the theoretical labyrinths of the last couple of decades, Freirean critical pedagogy failed to adequately engage race and racism, and the same should be said of its silence regarding gender and sexism (hooks, 2003a; Luke, 1996; Luke and Gore, 1992). McLaren (2000b) makes the following point: "The legacy of racism left by the New World European oppressor—that Blacks and Latino/as are simply a species of inferior invertebrates—was harshly condemned but never systematically analyzed by Freire. And while Freire was a vociferous critic of racism and sexism, he did not, as Kathleen Weiler points out, sufficiently problematize his conceptualization of liberation and the oppressed in terms of his own male experience" (p. 14; see Weiler, 1994, 2001).

Unfortunately in all of the recent theoretical wrangling amongst Freireans, few have indexed the important deficiencies that could be developed were they to do as Freire admonished them to before the massive heart attack that claimed his life: "Reinvent me," Freire said somberly. In one of his last works he wrote, "The progressive educator must always be moving out on his or her own, continually reinventing me and reinventing what it means to be democratic in his or her own specific cultural and historical contexts" (quoted in McLaren, 2000b, p. 14). What I am advocating here is a "reinvention" and radical reconstruction of critical pedagogy, a return to its theoretical roots, if you will, and also a theoretical branching out that will bring it into dialogue with critical race theory, anti-racist radical feminism, revolutionary democratic socialism, and the discourse on revolutionary decolonization.

Almost unanimously regarded as the preeminent philosopher of race of the twentieth century, Du Bois and his anti-racist philosophy of education helps to fill one of the major theoretical lacunae of Freire's philosophy of education and, therefore, a yawning intellectual chasm in contemporary critical pedagogy. Where Freire's work is weak when it comes to the critique of racism and sexism, Du Bois's educational discourse is particularly powerful and distinguished by its emphasis on anti-racism and gender justice. For instance, though many read him as an archetypal "race man," according to Joy James (1997) in *Transcending the Talented Tenth*, Du Bois actually practiced "a politics remarkably progressive for his time and ours" (p. 36).[16] James notes, "Du Bois confronted race, class, and gender oppression while maintaining conceptual and political linkages between the struggles to end racism, sexism, and war" (p. 36–37). His critical socio-theoretical framework was dynamic and constantly integrated diverse components of African American liberation and critical race theory; anti-colonial and decolonization theory; women's liberation and feminist theory; peace, disarmament, and radical democratic theory; and, the Marxist critique of capitalism and revolutionary democratic socialist theory, among others (Rabaka, 2007a).

In "The Souls of Black Women Folk in the Writings of W.E.B. Du Bois," acclaimed African American feminist literary theorist Nellie McKay (1990) contends, "At a time when black male writers concentrated their efforts on the social, economic, and educational advancement of black men as the 'leaders' of the race, Du Bois is something of an anomaly in his recognition that black women were equal partners in the struggle to claim the human dignity all black people were seeking" (p. 236). Moreover, in *Daughters of Sorrow: Attitudes Toward Black Women, 1880–1920*, Beverly Guy-Sheftall (1990) maintains that Du Bois was not only one of "the most passionate defenders of black women," but also one of the "most outspoken [male-] feminists" in African American history and, more generally, American history (p. 13). In fact, in Guy-Sheftall's opinion, Du Bois "devote[d] his life's work to the emancipation of blacks *and* women" (p. 161, emphasis in original).[17]

In *W.E.B. Du Bois: Black Radical Democrat*, Manning Marable (1986) echoes Guy-Sheftall's observations, declaring, "Like [Frederick] Douglass, Du Bois was probably the most advanced male leader of his era on the question of gender inequality" and woman suffrage, though he was deeply "troubled by the racism within the white women's movement" (p. 85). Particularly perplexing for Du Bois was the white women's movement's inattention to, and perpetuation of, racism or, more specifically, white supremacy. For instance, Du Bois was bothered by the racial politics of the National American Woman Suffrage Association (NAWSA), whose president, Carrie Chapman Catt, asserted that democratic rights had been granted to black men "with possibly ill-advised haste," producing "[p]erilous conditions" in U.S. society, as it introduced "into the body politic vast numbers of irresponsible citizens." Belle Kearney, the Mississippi suffragist leader, practiced an even more overtly racist politics by advocating that white women's enfranchisement would guarantee, among other things, an "immediate and [more] durable white supremacy" (quoted in Marable, 1986, p. 85; see also Bhavnani, 2001; Blee, 1991, 2002; Breines, 2006; Caraway, 1991; Ferber, 2004; Newman, 1999; Roth, 2003; Twine and Blee, 2001; Ware, 1992). Du Bois (1995a), in characteristic fashion, shot back, "Every argument for Negro suffrage is an argument for woman's suffrage; every argument for woman's suffrage is an argument for Negro suffrage; both are great movements in democracy" (p. 298).

In terms of developing critical educational theory, and Africana critical pedagogy in particular, what I am most interested in here is how Du Bois maintained, as James put it above, "conceptual and political linkages" between various anti-racist, anti-sexist, anti-colonial, and anti-capitalist thought traditions and sociopolitical movements. Unlike most of the critics in the Frankfurt School tradition of critical theory and Freirean critical pedagogues, Du Bois did not downplay racial and gender domination and discrimination. On the contrary, he placed the critique of sexism and racism right alongside Marxism and its critique of capitalism. In tune with the thinking of many Marxist feminists and socialist feminists, Du Bois was critical of both capitalism and patriarchy. He understood women, in general, to have great potential as agents of social transformation because of their simultaneous experience of, and resistance efforts against, capitalist and sexist oppression. However, similar to contemporary Africana anti-sexist critical social theorists—both black feminists and womanists—Du Bois understood women of African descent, in particular, to have even greater potential as agents of radical social change on account of their simultaneous experience of, and revolutionary praxis against racism, sexism, and economic exploitation, whether under capitalism or colonialism (Guy-Sheftall, 1995; hooks, 1981, 1984, 1995; Hudson-Weems, 1995, 1997, 2004; James and Sharpley-Whiting, 2000; Nnaemeka, 1998; Rabaka 2003d, 2004). Du Bois's critical socio-theoretical framework, therefore, has immense import for the discussion at hand so far as it provides critical educational theory and Africana critical pedagogy with a paradigm and point of departure for developing a multiperspectival social theory that is simultaneously critical of racism, sexism, capitalism, and colonialism.

Though there is much more in Du Bois's educational thought that warrants our critical attention, I believe that the major issues—issues of historical and cultural grounding, intellectual elitism, pedagogical discursive development, and the relationship between critical pedagogical theory and radical political praxis—have been adequately addressed. Therefore, despite the conundrums of, and contradictions in, his philosophy of education, I believe that Du Bois was one of the most important critical pedagogues of the late nineteenth and twentieth centuries, and that his life-work harbors an unrivaled relevance and crucial significance for Africana, critical multicultural, feminist, womanist, democratic socialist, and radical humanist philosophers of education attempting to grasp and grapple with the problems of the twenty-first century.

In conclusion, then, it could be said that as Du Bois came to see character, cultural grounding, anti-imperial ethics, and radical resistance as the cornerstones of Africana education and leadership, he grew increasingly critical of Africana educators and leaders, and, ironically, his own antecedent thought on Africana education and leadership. Perhaps there is no better example of this than his epoch-initiating and black world of ideas-shaking debate with Booker T. Washington. The Du Bois–Washington debate is relevant with regard to contemporary radical politics and critical social theory insofar as it puts the self-reflexive nature of Du Bois's critical social theory in bold relief, placing his development of the Du Boisian dialectic, his discursive practices of ideology critique, and his ever-evolving social and political philosophy in plain view. What is more, the Du Bois-Washington debate provides a widely known—albeit usually misinterpreted for (post)modern purposes—historic example of the often overlooked fact that Africana critical thought is not simply preoccupied with the critique of white supremacy or anti-black racism, but has long been deeply concerned with developing dialectical thought on the connections between white supremacy and capitalism, *and* the black bourgeoisie and capitalism. Thus, we enter that theater of the absurd where Washington and Du Bois waged one of the greatest fights in Africana intellectual history.

NOTES

1. This chapter evolved from a paper originally entitled "W.E.B. Du Bois, the Problem of Education, and the Politics of Critical Pedagogy," which was delivered as the W.E.B. Du Bois Distinguished Lecture at California State University, Dominguez Hills, February 20, 2002. It was subsequently substantially revised and presented as "W.E.B. Du Bois's Philosophy of Education: Issues and Implications for Postmodern and Postcolonial Critical Pedagogical Praxis" at the National Council for Black Studies 26th Annual International Conference, San Diego, California, March 24–27, 2002. An early version of this chapter was published as "W.E.B. Du Bois's Evolving Africana Philosophy of Education" in the *Journal of Black Studies* 33, 4 (2003), 399–449. I am deeply indebted to Kristine Lewis and Patrick DeWalt for their friendship and critical comments on and highly constructive criticisms of my thoughts on philosophy of education, sociology of education, anthropology of education, critical educational theory, and critical pedagogy. Kristine's spirited and incessant questions concerning Africana critical theory and its implications for contemporary education inspired me to deepen and develop my conceptions of Du Bois's philosophy of education and the history of Africana educational thought and practice. This chapter, therefore, is humbly dedicated to her because "she came out in front when I was hiding," as Donny Hathaway sings in one of our favorite songs. In serving as the chair of Patrick's doctoral dissertation committee, I should humbly say that he has probably shared with me and taught me more than I have him about the need for stronger connections and more critical dialogue between Africana Studies and education. Therefore, this chapter is also dedicated to him and, it is hoped, will stand as a testament to my unfaltering faith in him and his lifework.

2. For a more detailed discussion of Du Bois's life and work, see first and foremost Du Bois's own adventures in autobiography, Du Bois (1938, 1952, 1968a, 1968b, 1969a, 1969b, 1970d, 1985a, 1997a). Also helpful in this regard are several secondary sources which often reveal more about various trends and traditions in Africana social and political theory and praxis than they do Du Bois's intellectual development and biography. See, for example, Anderson and Zuberi (2000), W.L. Andrews (1985), Aptheker (1948, 1949, 1966, 1981, 1982, 1983, 1989, 1990), Bell, Grosholz, and Stewart (1996), Broderick (1955, 1958a, 1958b, 1959, 1974), Byerman (1978, 1994), Cain (1990a, 1993), Chandler (1997), Clarke, Jackson, Kraiser, and O'Dell (1970), W.A. Davis (1974), DeMarco (1974), S.C. Drake (1985), W.A. Drake (1986–1987), Drummer (1995), Durr (2001), Fontenot (2001), V.P. Franklin (1995), Golden (1966), Guzman (1961), Higbee (1995b), Horne (1986), Juguo (2001), Katznelson (1999),

D.L. Lewis (1993, 2000), Logan (1971), Marable (1985a, 1986, 1996, 1998), J.B. Moore (1981), Moses (1975, 1978b, 1993a, 1996, 1998), Rampersad (1990), A.L. Reed (1985, 1997), Rudwick (1956, 1960a, 1968, 1982a), Stuckey (1987), Sundquist (1993, 1996), Tuttle (1957, 1973), Tyner (1997), Walden (1966), 1977), West (1989, 1996), R. Williams (2001), Wolters (2001), F. Woodard (1976), W.D. Wright (1985), Yuan (2000), and Zamir (1995, 2008). For critical investigations into Du Bois's educational thought in specific, and for examples of the types of texts I consulted in the construction of my arguments throughout this chapter, see Derrick P. Alridge (1997, 1999a, 1999b, 2003, 2008), Bridges (1973), Burks (1997), Dennis (1977), Glascoe (1996), Goldstein (1972), Greco (1984), A. Johnson (1976), Mielke (1977), Moore (1996), Neal (1984), Nwankwo (1989), Oatts (2003, 2006), Okoro (1982), E.C. Smith (1975), Sumpter (1973), and N. Warren (1984). In terms of primary source material with regard to Du Bois's philosophy of education, I have consulted and concentrated on his articles and addresses collected in *The Education of Black People: Ten Critiques, 1906–1960*, edited by Herbert Aptheker, and *Du Bois on Education*, edited by Eugene F. Provenzo, Jr., see Du Bois (1973, 2002).

3. My interpretation of Freire's radical politics and critical pedagogy has been culled from my systematic consultation of the following primary sources: Freire (1975, 1976, 1978, 1985, 1987, 1989, 1993, 1994, 1996a, 1996b, 1997, 1998a, 1998b, 2000, 2004, 2005, 2007) as well as, Freire and Fraser (1997). Freire influence on the discourse and development of Africana critical pedagogy cannot be overstated.

4. This interpretation of Du Bois's critical theory of history, as well as my general argument here, derives in part from careful and critical investigation of primary sources in which Du Bois developed and detailed his radical historiographical method, see Du Bois (1930a, 1930b, 1939, 1945, 1965, 1970a, 1970b, 1995c, 2001), and several seminal secondary sources which either critically engage Du Bois's theory of history or his historiographical method. See Blight (1994), Broderick (1958c, 1959), Byerman (1994), Gilkes (1996), Gooding-Williams (1987), Gregg (1998), Guzman (1961), Hansberry (1970), Harding (1970), Higbee (1995a), Lash (1957), D.L. Lewis (1993, 2000), Monteiro (2000), Moses (1975, 1978, 1993a, 1996, 1998), Rampersad (1989), A.L. Reed (1997), C.J. Robinson (1977, 2000), Rudwick (1968), Schrager (1996), Siemerling (2001), Speck (1974), J.B. Stewart (1996a), Stuckey (1987, 1994), Walden (1963a), S.J. Walker (1975), Wesley (1965), and R. Williams (1983).

5. The Nigerian philosopher, Emmanuel Eze (1997b), argues that "post" should be employed as a prefix insofar as colonialism is concerned, "only as far as the lived actuality of the peoples and lands formerly occupied by European imperial powers can suggest, or confirm, in some meaningful ways, the sense of that word, the 'post' of the (post)colonial" (p. 341). In light of the fact that many, if not most, of the formerly colonized countries remain under some mutated and/or (post)modern form of colonialism, Amilcar Cabral's assertions concerning *classical colonialism* as "direct domination," and *neocolonialism* as "indirect domination" help to highlight and accent a bitter and brutal truth: We—meaning African and other oppressed peoples—are not in a *post*colonial period, which is to say that we are not in a period *after* colonialism, when and where we understand colonialism as Cabral (1972, 1973, 1979) did, as in-

terlocking systems of racial and gender domination and discrimination and economic exploitation. In fact, at this point it seems safe to say that we are actually in a transitional stage/state between a now-aging colonial era and an emerging postcolonial epoch that remains to be adequately charted and changed based on our most moral and audacious anti-imperial aspirations. I elaborate on how Du Bois's anti-colonial theory critically deconstructs the discourse of postcolonialism in greater detail in "'Deliberately Using the Word *Colonial* in a Much Broader Sense': W.E.B. Du Bois's Concept of 'Semi-Colonialism' as Critique of and Contribution to Postcolonialism" (see Rabaka, 2003c).

6. Fanon's work, especially "The Negro and Language" in *Black Skin, White Masks*, helps to highlight the existential-linguistic dynamics and dimensions of the colonized being educated or, rather *miseducated*, in colonial languages. To begin, he noted that along with the racist-colonial-capitalist church and its colonial missionary endeavors, the educational systems in colonial countries serve the interests of the colonizers and *not* the colonized. In the colonial school system, as they learn the language of the white colonizers, colonized black children are simultaneously indoctrinated into the Eurocentric-imperial ideological world where various words impart the Eurocentric-imperial ideological value judgments associated with the antonyms "black" and "white." Fanon (1967) prodded us to critically consider the matter: "Is not whiteness in symbols always ascribed in French [and in English, we could add] to Justice, Truth, Virginity? . . . The black man is the symbol of Evil and Ugliness. . . . *In Europe, the black man is the symbol of Evil*" (p. 180, 188, original emphasis). Notice Fanon's shift of tone and timbre here. He goes from questioning to contending white-supremacist constructions of blackness. Then, with his customary critical candor, he went one step further:

> The torturer is the black man, Satan is black, one talks of shadows, when one is dirty one is black—whether one is thinking of physical dirtiness or of moral dirtiness. It would be astonishing, if the trouble were taken to bring them all together, to see the vast number of expressions that make the black man the equivalent of sin. In Europe, whether concretely or symbolically, the black man stands for the bad side of the character. As long as one cannot understand this fact, one is doomed to talk in circles about the "black problem." Blackness, darkness, shadow, shades, night, the labyrinths of the earth, abysmal depths, blacken someone's reputation. . . . In Europe, that is to say, in every civilized and civilizing country, the Negro is the symbol of sin. The archetype of the lowest values is represented by the Negro. (p. 189)

This means, then, that blacks—especially young, impressionable school children—in white-supremacist colonial countries are not educated about continental and diasporan Africa, but indoctrinated into the many millions of ways in which "blackness," or "the Negro" represents the "archetype of the lowest values." Because they are children, much passes unnoticed and they begin to employ Eurocentric-imperial expressions, proverbs, and parables with greater and greater frequency. In other words, they ultimately identify with what they are in the process of learning, and this is when and where their internalization of white-supremacist, patriarchal, capitalist, colonial ideologies influence their frames of reference and worldviews. Consequently, the colonized black school children look at other blacks through this insidious Eurocentric-imperial lens and, then, the black existential trauma and tragedy of their own "blackness" in a white-supremacist, anti-black, racist world is bemoaned when they come to the anxiety-filled and agonizing realization that they are not white, and therefore they are not free to do as they please, but, unbeknownst to themselves up until this black existential moment, they are black and colonized and, consequently, they must do as the white-supremacist, anti-black, racist colonists wish. Fanon argued that for the colonized the mastery of the colonizer's language was a prerequisite for what little advancement is available to them in the colonial society, and that their indigenous language is all but banned in the context of the colonial society: from receipts to road signs, hospitals to transportation information, education to employment in the colonial administration, everything is written and spoken in the colonizer's language in colonial society. Therefore, the colonized who do not have the opportunity to learn the colonizer's language literally become strangers in their own country. In speaking of this situation in his own colonized country, Fanon (1967) put it this way:

> The Negro of the Antilles will be proportionately whiter—that is, he will come closer to being a real human being—in direct ratio to his mastery of the French language. . . . A man who has a language consequently possesses the world expressed and implied by that language. What we are getting at becomes plain: Mastery of language affords remarkable power. . . . Every colonized people—in other words, every people in whose soul an inferiority complex has been created by the death and burial of its local cultural originality—finds itself face to face with the language of the civilizing nation; that is, with the culture of the mother country. The colonized is elevated above his jungle status in proportion to his adoption of the mother country's cultural standards. He becomes whiter as he renounces his blackness, his jungle" (p. 18).

Du Bois's emphasis on language in his philosophy of education and sociology of education, therefore, demonstrates that his dialectic, in several senses, prefigures Fanon's and, in addition, makes a major contribution to the discourse on decolonization. For further discussion of the sociology of language, sociolinguistics, cultural linguistics, black linguistics and ebonics, especially as they concern African and African American education, please see Alexandre (1972), M. Andrews (1973), Asante (1969, 1972, 1973, 2005b), Asante and Gudykunst (1989), Asante and Rich (1970), Asante and Robb (1971), Dillard (1975), L.J. Green (2002), W.S. Hall (1975), Haskins (1993), J.E. Holloway (1991, 1997), Kautzsch (2002), Labov (1972), Lanehart (2001), Makoni (2003), Mawasha (1982), Mazrui (1975, 1998), Poplack (2000, 2001), Rickford (1987, 1999, 2000), Rickford, Mufwene, Bailey, and Baugh (1998), Smitherman (1975, 1986, 2000), Sutcliffe and Wong (1986), and Wolfram (2002).

    7. According to the African American feminist bell hooks (1984), radical pedagogues must develop the ability to "'translate' ideas to an audience that varies in age, sex, ethnicity, [and] degree of literacy" (p. 111). Though she was writing directly to "feminist educators" and "feminist scholars" when she wrote this, I understand hooks's theory of "translation" techniques and textual practices to have great import

for Africana, multicultural, and other educators and scholars as well, both female and male. She writes, "All too often educators, especially university professors, fear their work will not be valued by other academics if it is presented in a way that makes it accessible to a wider audience. If these educators thought of rendering their work in a number of different styles, 'translations,' they would be able to satisfy arbitrary academic standards while making their work available to masses of people" (p. 111). It hits a chord that resonates profoundly with Du Bois's theory of the production of practical knowledge. In advocating that Africana educators use "that variety of the English idiom which [their constituencies] understand," Du Bois is in no small way charging and challenging Africana educators and scholars to develop the ability to "'translate' ideas to an audience that varies in age, sex, ethnicity, [and] degree of literacy," and "render . . . their work in a number of different styles, 'translations'." The production of practical knowledge, then, is predicated upon *the production of easily accessible knowledge*. And, knowledge that has the ability to be accessed with ease often offers *attractive ethical and emancipatory alternatives* to both the oppressed and their oppressors (see Fanon, 1965, 1967, 1968, 1969; Freire, 1985, 1989, 1993, 1994, 1996a, 1997, 1998a, 2005, 2007). Also by bell hooks, and extremely informative with regard to the development of Africana critical pedagogy, are her books on contemporary teaching theory and pedagogical praxis: *Teaching to Transgress: Education as the Practice of Freedom* (1994a) and *Teaching Communities: A Pedagogy of Hope* (2003a).

8. For further discussion of Africana Studies theory and research methods, see Aldridge and James (2007), Aldridge and Young (2000), T. Anderson (1990), Asante and Karenga (2006), Azevedo (2005), Ba Nikongo (1997), Bates, Mudimbe and O'Barr (1993), Bobo and Michel (2000), Bobo, Hudley and Michel (2004), Conyers (2003, 2005), Fossett and Tucker (1997), Gordon and Gordon (2006a, 2006b), Hudson-Weems (2004, 2007), Johnson and Henderson (2005), Johnson and Lynne (2002), Karenga (1988, 2001, 2002), Kershaw (1989, 1992, 2003), Kopano and Williams (2004), Marable (2000, 2005), Norment (2007a, 2007b), Rojas (2007), Rooks (2006), and J.B. Stewart (1979, 1992, 2004).

9. My conception of "philosophy" has been deeply influenced by contemporary critical debates and discursive formations and formulations of Africana philosophy. See Appiah (1992), Coetzee and Abraham (1998), English and Kalumba (1996), Eze (1997a, 1997b), Gordon (1997a, 1997b, 2000a), Gbadegesin (1991a), Gyekye (1995, 1996, 1997), L. Harris (1983), Hord and Lee (1995), Hountondji (1996), Imbo (1998), Kwame (1995), Lott (2002), Lott and Pittman (2003), Masolo (1994), Mosley (1995), Mudimbe (1988, 1994), Outlaw (1996a, 1997), Pittman (1997), Serequeberhan (1991, 1994, 2000, 2003, 2007), West (1982, 1988a, 1993a, 1999), Wiredu (1980, 1996, 2004), R.A. Wright (1984), and Yancy (1998, 2004, 2005).

10. This interpretation of Du Bois's concept of culture, as well as my general argument here, derives in part from critical investigation and interrogation of primary sources in which Du Bois develops and details his theory of culture. See Du Bois (1930a, 1939, 1945, 1965, 1968b, 1969a, 1970a, 1978, 1996b, 1997a), and several seminal secondary sources which critically engage Du Bois's cultural thought. See Anderson and Zuberi (2000), Andrews (1985), Aptheker (1981, 1983, 1990), Baber

(1992), Baker (1972), Beavers (2000), Bell (1985, 1996), Bell, Grosholz and Stewart (1996), R.A. Berman (1997), Chandler (1997), Clarke, Jackson, Kaiser and O'Dell (1970), Darsey (1998), W.A. Davis (1974), Durr (2001), Green and Smith (1983), Grosholz (1996), Harrison (1992), Higbee (1995a), Holt (1990, 1998), Kaiser (1970), Lott (1997, 2000, 2001), Lucal (1996), Magubane (1987), Marable (1985a, 1998), E.P. Mitchell (1993), Moses (1990, 1996), O'Dell (1970), Ofari (1970), Outlaw (1995, 2000), Paynter (1992), Pollard (1993), Posnock (1995, 1997, 1998), Rutledge (2001), Schneider (1998), Schrager (1996), J.B. Stewart (1984, 1996a), Stuckey (1987), Sundquist (1993), E. Wright (2001), and Zamir (1995, 2008). To date, one of the best analyses of Du Bois's concept of culture is Bernard Boxill's often overlooked theoretical gem, "Du Bois and Fanon on Culture." See Boxill (1977-78). My analysis of Du Bois's concept of culture and argument for its impact on and implications for not simply his philosophy of education, but also his liberation and leadership thought, is culled in part from Boxill's stringent investigation into and stress on the connections between Du Bois's concept of culture and his ideas concerning persons of African origin and descent's "common history," "common experience," "common destiny," "common ancestors," and "common status" (Boxill, 1977–1978, p. 331–32). Also by Boxill (1996), and both informative and instructive in this regard, is his essay "Du Bois on Cultural Pluralism," which recasts many of the analyses and arguments he made twenty years prior in "Du Bois and Fanon on Culture." For a controversial critique of Du Bois's thought concerning race and culture, see Anthony Appiah's "The Uncompleted Argument: Du Bois and the Illusion of Race," see Appiah (1995); this essay, which was originally published in *Critical Inquiry* in 1985, was revised, retitled and reprinted as "Illusions of Race," in Appiah's *In My Father's House: Africa in the Philosophy of Culture*. See Appiah (1992, p. 28–46). For a hard-hitting critique of Appiah's criticisms of Du Bois's concept of culture and philosophy of race, see Lucius Outlaw's "'Conserve' Races?: In Defense of W.E.B. DuBois." See Outlaw (1996b). And for a vociferous yet not vicious critique of Du Bois, Appiah and Outlaw's discourse and debates on race and culture, see Robert Gooding-Williams's "Outlaw, Appiah, and Du Bois 'The Conservation of Races." See Gooding-Williams (1996). Gooding-Williams (1987, 1991, 1991–1992) also offers critical commentary on Du Bois and Cornel West's (mis)interpretation of Du Bois in his essays "Philosophy of History and Social Critique in *The Souls of Black Folk*" and "Evading Narrative Myth, Evading Prophetic Pragmatism: A Review of Cornel West's *The American Evasion of Philosophy*." Lucius Outlaw (2001), in "Cornel West on W.E.B. Du Bois," has also taken issue with West's interpretation of Du Bois, though his opposition to "West's Du Bois" differs greatly from that of Gooding-Williams because Gooding-Williams's critique is directed at West's "W.E.B. Du Bois: The Jamesian Organic Intellectual," and Outlaw's at West's "Black Strivings in a Twilight Civilization." See West (1989, 1996).

    11. For a sampling of and critical introduction to Alain Locke's philosophy of culture, see L. Harris (1999a), Linnemann (1982), Locke (1983b, 1989, 1992), and Washington (1986, 1994). On the New Negro movement, see Locke (1968), and for a few of the more noteworthy books about and anthologies on the Harlem Renais-

sance, see Huggins (1971, 1995), Hutchinson (1995, 2007), D.L. Lewis (1989, 1994), Vincent (1973), and Watson (1995).

12. The Caribbean political philosopher, Charles Mills, gives a good discussion of the ocularcentric and somatic syndrome in Western European and European American thought and behavior in his book, *The Racial Contract* (1997). Perception plays a big part in racial categorization and classification, and the way persons of African descent and other people of color are seen has curiously become—in the Eurocentric mind-set—just as important as the way people of color actually are, or exist, or experience life and the world in which they live. In other words, I am hinting at the issue that Fanon (1967, p. 111–23) exposed in *Black Skins, White Masks* when he recollected how "the black body" is seen, or sometimes not seen because it is different from the white/Western European somatic norm, a norm as Mills (1997, p. 53) points out, that is almost at every instance predicated on the white male body. For contemporary critical reflections on Fanon's conception of invisibility and anonymity where the black body in a white world is concerned, see Lewis Gordon's "The Black and the Body Politic: Fanon's Existential Phenomenological Critique of Psychoanalysis," in Gordon, Sharpley-Whiting, and White (1996, p. 74–83), and his "Existential Dynamics of Theorizing Black Invisibility," in Gordon (1997a, p. 69–80). Du Bois's discussion of invisibility and anonymity where the black body in a white-supremacist, patriarchal, capitalist, colonial world is concerned emerges when and where he writes of race, deploys the metaphor of "the veil," and develops his concept of "double consciousness," which is also to say that Du Bois deals with these themes throughout his *oeuvre*, and specifically and especially in his major scholarly, autobiographical, and fiction writings. For the key primary sources, see Du Bois (1938, 1939, 1945, 1952, 1965, 1968a, 1968b, 1969a, 1970b, 1985a, 1995c, 1996b, 1997a), and for a sampling of some of the major secondary sources, see Adell (1994), E. Allen (1992), Baber (1992), Beavers (2000), B.W. Bell (1996), Blau and Brown (2001), L.D. Bobo (2000), Bruce (1992, 1995), Byerman (1978, 1981, 1994), Castronovo (2000), Chaffee (1956), Dennis (1996b), V.P. Franklin (1995), Gates (1996), Gilroy (1993a), Gipson (1971), Gooding-Williams (1994), Gordon (2000a, 2000b), Grosholz (1996), Harding (1970), Higbee (1995a), Holt (1990, 1998), G. Jones (1997), Juguo (2001), Kostelanetz (1985), Krell (2000), M. Lee (1999), Lemert (1994), Lincoln (1993), Liss (1998), Lott (1997, 2000, 2001), Lucal (1996), Magubane (1987), Makang (1993), Marable (1985a, 1985b), Marshall (1994), Meade (1987), Meier (1959, 1963), E.P. Mitchell (1993), Mizruchi (1996), Moses (1975, 1990, 1993b), Mostern (1996), Moss (1975), Newsome (1971), D. Peterson (1994), Pollard (1993), Posnock (1997, 1998), Quainoo (1993), Rampersad (1989, 1990, 1996a), Rawls (2000), A.L. Reed (1992, 1997), Rutledge (2001), Schrager (1996), Sequeberhan (2000), Siemerling (2001), Stepto (1985), J.B. Stewart (1983), Stuckey (1987, 1994), Sundquist (1993, 1996), Taylor (1971), Travis (1996), Velikova (2000), Watts (1995, 2001), West (1996), Wiatrowski-Phillips (1995), and Zamir (1994, 1995, 2008).

13. On the origins of the concept of "the Talented Tenth" and Du Bois's essay by that name, see Higginbotham (1993) and Lewis (1993), and for critiques of Du Bois's use of the concept and his essay, see Broderick (1959), Bulmer (1995), Cain (1993),

Carter (1998), DeMarco (1983), Dennis (1977, 1996a), Drake (1985), Drummer (1995), Gates and West (1996), Gatewood (1994), Green (1977), J.A. James (1997, 2000), Killian (1999), Kilson (2000b), Marable (1986), Meier (1959, 1963), A.L. Reed (1997), Rudwick (1956, 1960a, 1968, 1982a), E.C. Smith (1975), Travis (1996), Tyner (1997), and Zamir (1994, 1995).

14. In "W.E.B. Du Bois and 'The Talented Tenth'," acclaimed African American literary theorist Henry Louis Gates, Jr., (1996, p. 129) argues that Du Bois "overstates the case" when he writes "they"—meaning "the Talented Tenth"—"have no traditions to fall back upon, no long-established customs, no strong family ties, [and] no well-defined social classes," because he, Du Bois, is "attempting to persuade even the most skeptical or hostile racist, by appearing to accept the racist premise that the Negro people need social leadership more than most groups" on account of the African holocaust and African Americans' subsequent enslavement and experience and endurance of peonage, share-cropping, lynching, and Jim and Jane Crow segregation. Gates, I will concede, correctly contends that Du Bois's leadership thought at this point parallels many of the positions of the "pathological" sociological school of thought most evident in the thought and texts of Robert Parks—a claim and/or connection which Jessica Marshall (1994) also makes in her doctoral dissertation, "'Counsels of Despair': W.E.B. Du Bois, Robert E. Parks, and the Establishment of American Race Sociology." But, there is a sense in which, I believe, Gates is too quick to call Du Bois's thought "pathological" without fully exploring—first, Du Bois's use of this part of his argument as a rhetorical device, and second, the social, political, and intellectual context in which Du Bois's essay, "The Talented Tenth," was written and published. At first issue, it could be said that Gates overlooks the fact that though *The Souls of Black Folk* was written for and directed at a broad public audience, both black and white, fairly knowledgeable of and sympathetic to "the plight of the Negro"—the essays collected in *The Souls of Black Folk*, according to David Levering Lewis (1993, p. 265–96), were culled from pieces Du Bois had published in the popular press, magazines, and journals such as *The Independent, The Nation, The Southern Workman, Harper's Weekly, World's Work, The Outlook, The Missionary Review, The Literary Digest*, the *Annuals of the American Academy of Political and Social Science*, and *The Dial*. Du Bois's "The Talented Tenth" essay, on the other hand, was published the same year as *The Souls of Black Folk*, 1903, in a volume entitled, *The Negro Problem: A Series of Articles by Representative American Negroes of Today*, which Lewis (1993, p. 288) avers was compiled by "a now unidentifiable white editor," and which Gates (1996, p. 127) asserts is thought by many "to have been edited, or at least endorsed, by Du Bois's nemesis, Booker T. Washington." By plodding momentarily down the "pathological" path, which was in and of itself a risky and rare thing for a writer of African descent in the United States at the dawn of the twentieth century, Du Bois was attempting to lure his readers into his overall argument, which was that, like it or not, both Southern white supremacists and Northern liberal white racists were continuing to pillage black potential by applauding Washington's accommodationism and incessant emphasis on industrial education. From the Du Boisian dialectical perspective, Washington's accommodationism, fully financed by anti-black racists and wealthy whites, was robbing African Americans of their right to choose between in-

dustrial and liberal arts education. For further discussion of the Du Bois–Washington debate, please see the subsequent chapter in the present volume. On Du Bois's use of rhetorical strategies and devices, and on his development of a distinct "black" writing voice, the metaphor of the "veil," and the concept of "the color-line," see Adell (1994), E. Allen (1992), Baker (1972), Beavers (2000), Bell (1996), Blau and Brown (2001), Blight (1994), Brodwin (1972), Bruce (1992, 1995), Byerman (1978, 1981, 1994), Cain (1990a), Chaffee (1956), Darsey (1998), Echeruo (1992), V.P. Franklin (1995), Freedmen (1975), Gibson (1977), Gooding-Williams (1987, 1994), Jones (1998), Juguo (2001), Lemert (1994), Lloyd (1999), Mizruchi (1996), Moses (1975, 1990, 1993b), R.L. Moss (1975), Mtima (1999), Newsome (1971), Payne (1973), Posnock (1998), Quainoo (1993), Rampersad (1989, 1990, 1996a), Rawls (2000), Rutledge (2001), Schrager (1996), Stepto (1985), J.B. Stewart (1983), Stuckey (1987, 1994), Sundquist (1993, 1996), Taylor (1981), and Zamir (1994, 1995, 2008).

15. With regard to what I am referring to as Du Bois's "deep and abiding interests in coupling his philosophy of education and critical race theory with Marxist critiques of capitalism, critical class theory, and radical democratic socialism," please see my extended exploration in "Du Bois's Critique of Capitalism, Critical Marxism, and Discourse on Democratic Socialism" in Rabaka (2007a, p. 101–36), as well as the succeeding chapter of the present volume.

16. On Du Bois and his "race man" reputation, see Alridge (2003) and Carby (1998).

17. Some may find Guy-Sheftall's (re)construction of Du Bois as a male- "feminist" troubling. However, as Hazel Carby (1998) contends, it should be held in mind that Du Bois means "many things to many people" (p. 14). He is one of the many male and female "rediscovered ancestors" whose thought and texts are currently being engaged by contemporary theorists "in response to the needs of various agendas," academic and otherwise (p. 14). Where Guy-Sheftall (1990) and McKay (1990) read Du Bois as a male- "feminist," Joy James (1996b, 1997) proffered a "pro-feminist" Du Bois. More recently, Gary Lemons (2001) argued that Du Bois's pro-women's rights and women's suffrage work can actually be read as both "black feminist" *and* "womanist." It is not the intention of my remarks here to advance whether Du Bois was a "feminist" or a "womanist"—two terms, it should be pointed out, that were not *en vogue* in Africana intellectual arenas until well after his death in 1963. The primary purpose here is to discover what implications Du Bois's women's liberation work has for the development of an anti-racist, anti-sexist, anti-capitalist, and anti-colonial critical educational theory, what I am calling *Africana critical pedagogy*. Therefore, I draw from the women's liberation theory of a wide range of women *and* men of African descent who self-describe and self-define themselves as "black feminists," "African feminists," "feminists of color," and "womanists," among other nomenclature (see Byrd and Guy-Sheftall, 2001; Guy-Sheftall, 1995; hooks, 1984, 2000b; Hudson-Weems, 1998b, 1998c, 2001a). For a fuller treatment of Du Bois's contributions to the anti-sexist aspects of Africana critical theory, see my "W.E.B. Du Bois and the Damnation of Women: An Essay on Africana Anti-Sexist Critical Social Theory" and "The Souls of Black Female Folk: W.E.B. Du Bois and Africana Anti-Sexist Critical Social Theory" (Rabaka, 2003d, 2004).

The Du Bois–Washington Debate: Social Leadership, Intellectual Legacy, and the Lingering Problematics of African American Politics

It is ironic that Booker T. Washington, the most powerful black American of his time and perhaps of all time, should be the black leader whose claim to the title is most often dismissed by the lay public. Blacks often question his legitimacy because of the role that favor by whites played in Washington's assumption of power, and whites often remember him only as an educator or, confusing him with George Washington Carver, as "that great Negro scientist." This irony is something that Washington will have to live with in history, for he himself deliberately created the ambiguity about his role and purpose that has haunted his image. And yet, Washington was a genuine black leader, with a substantial black following and with virtually the same long-range goals for Afro-Americans as his rivals. . . . He was not called the Wizard for nothing.

—Harlan, "Booker T. Washington and
the Politics of Accommodation," p. 2, 4

Scholar and prophet; mystic and materialist; ardent agitator for political rights and propagandist for economic cooperation; one who espoused an economic interpretation of politics and yet emphasized the necessity of political rights for economic advancement; one who denounced segregation and called for integration into American society in accordance with the principles of human brotherhood and the ideals of democracy, and at the same time one who favored the maintenance of racial solidarity and integrity and a feeling of identity with Negroes elsewhere in the world; an equalitarian who apparently believed in innate racial differences; a Marxist who was fundamentally a middle-class intellectual, Du Bois becomes the epitome of the paradoxes in American Negro thought. In fact, despite his early tendencies toward an accommodating viewpoint, and despite his strong sense of race solidarity and integrity, Du Bois expressed more effectively than any of his contemporaries the protest tendency in Negro thought, and the desire for citizenship rights and integration into American society.

> —August Meier, *Negro Thought in America, 1880–1915: Racial Ideologies in the Age of Booker T. Washington*, p. 206

Given the persistent and intransigent nature of the American race system, which proved quite impervious to black attacks, Du Bois in his speeches and writings moved from one proposed solution to another, and the salience of various parts of his philosophy changed as his perceptions of the needs and strategies of black America shifted over time. Aloof and autonomous in his personality, Du Bois did not hesitate to depart markedly from whatever was the current mainstream of black thinking when he perceived that the conventional wisdom being enunciated by black spokesmen was proving inadequate to the task of advancing the race. His willingness to seek different solutions often placed him well in advance of his contemporaries, and this, combined with a strong-willed, even arrogant personality made his career as a black leader essentially a series of stormy conflicts. . . . For Du Bois, the blacks' only effective way to open the doors of opportunity was to adopt tactics of militant protest and agitation; by employing this style of propaganda, he made a key contribution to the evolution of black protest in the twentieth century—and to the civil rights movement.

> —Elliott M. Rudwick, "W.E.B. Du Bois: Protagonist of the Afro-American Protest," p. 64–65

INTRODUCTION: DU BOIS, WASHINGTON, AND THE RADICAL POLITICS OF AFRICAN AMERICAN POLITICS

Following the publication of both *The Souls of Black Folk* and his famous essay, "The Talented Tenth," in 1903, thirty-six-year-old W.E.B. Du Bois continued his devastating and intellectual history-making critique of Booker T. Washington's accommodationist thought in his often overlooked 1904 essay, "The Development of a People." In this obscure essay he asserted that African Americans have "two great needs: public schools and industrial schools" (Du Bois, 1982a, p. 214). In his posthumously published autobiography, *The Autobiography of W.E.B. Du Bois*, he asserted that his and Washington's social philosophies—"[t]hese two theories of Negro progress"—were "not absolutely contradictory" (Du Bois, 1968a, p. 236).[1]

Initially, Du Bois was open to Washington's accommodationism, but was soon frustrated by the Tuskegean's tyrannical rule over black America and the incessantly rising tide of racial violence that swept across the United States during Washington's years of political dominance (Logan, 1944, 1954, 1965;

Shapiro, 1988). Though he was not the first, nor the last, to criticize Washington, Du Bois's well-conceived anti-accommodationist arguments carried an unparalleled and almost hallowed weight amongst college-educated and professional African Americans: his beloved Talented Tenth, whom he sincerely believed would sacrifice and unselfishly serve in the cause of African American social and political advancement. In the critically acclaimed, widely read, and still-studied chapter, "Of Mr. Booker T. Washington and Others," from his classic, *The Souls of Black Folk*, Du Bois audaciously announced his opposition to Washington's accommodationism and put forward an alternative program for African American social development and cultural survival. He quickly became the leader of a small band of free-thinking blacks who began an outright agitation organization. They held their initial meeting in July 1905 on the Canadian side of Niagara Falls and dubbed themselves the Niagara Movement (Rudwick, 1957a).

Washington was deeply disturbed by the public appearance of opposition to his accommodationist policies. He used his considerable influence with wealthy whites and the black bourgeoisie to suppress progressive African American thought. Therefore, Du Bois and the Niagarites were portrayed in both the white and black presses as "radicals," "troublemakers" and, ironically, "traitors." The distinguished Washington scholar Louis Harlan (1982) sensitively wrote on this subject:

> Washington's outright critics and enemies were called "radicals" because they challenged Washington's conservatism and bossism, though their tactics of verbal protest would seem moderate indeed to a later generation of activists. They were the college-educated blacks, engaged in professional pursuits, and proud of their membership in an elite class—what one of them [i.e., Du Bois] called the Talented Tenth. The strong holds of the radicals were the northern cities and southern black colleges. They stood for full political and civil rights, liberal education, free expression, and aspiration. They dreamed of a better world and believed Booker T. Washington was a menace to its achievement. (p. 6)

Elliott Rudwick, a noted Du Bois scholar, has perceptively written of the power play between Washington's well-funded Tuskegee Machine and Du Bois's financially fledgling Niagara Movement. Rudwick's words help to paint a picture of the political landscape that Du Bois and Washington were operating in, and his words also help to highlight the fact that Washington wielded an enormous amount of power in both black and white America. Rudwick (1982b) revealingly wrote,

> In the large northern centers Washington had considerable contacts among white editors who easily concluded that the Niagara Movement was potentially damaging to harmonious race relations. Thus they followed the strong suggestions

of Washington and his agents to ignore the activities of Du Bois and his group. Since the Tuskegean was assumed to be blacks' only "real leader," white editors found nothing incongruous about giving the Niagara Movement the silent treatment. Indeed with the saintly image that Washington cultivated in the white media, the Niagara Movement's anti-Washington stance was beyond their comprehension. In 1906 the editor of the prominent white weekly, the *Outlook*, contrasted the prouncements of the Tuskegean's National Negro Business League with the recent Niagara manifesto, and Washington's "pacific" group was praised because it demanded more of blacks themselves, while Du Bois's "assertive" group unreasonably demanded more of whites on behalf of blacks — to the latter's moral detriment. The Business League was lauded for focusing on achieving an "inch of progress" rather than strangling itself in a "yard of fault-finding" as the Niagara Movement was doing. Washington's supporters in the black press made even more invidious contrasts. Thus the New York *Age* asserted that blacks needed "something cheerful," which the Tuskegean offered the masses, rather than the "lugubrious" and "bitter" commentary of Niagara's jealous "aggregation of soreheads." (p. 70)

Washington, drunk with the power whites bestowed upon him, dealt the Niagara Movement blow after bitter blow for five years until finally a defeated Du Bois reached out to anti-racist wealthy whites and founded the National Association for the Advancement of Colored People (NAACP) in 1909 (see Berg, 2005; L. Hughes, 1962; Jack, 1943; Jonas, 2005; Kellog, 1967; Meier, 1954; Meier and Bracey, 1993; Rudwick, 1960b). Partly due to the changing racial climate in the United States, and also consequent to his new association with the NAACP, Du Bois's thought increased in national influence. He edited the NAACP's national organ, *The Crisis*, for a quarter of a century, and from this platform he addressed and advised not simply black America, but white well-wishers and progressives as well (Arndt, 1970; Du Bois, 1972a, 1972b, 1983a, 1983b; Kimbrough, 1974; Rosenberg, 2000; Rudwick, 1958a, 1958b).

Although Du Bois had skirmishes with several prominent African American and Caribbean leaders — immediately Ida B. Wells, Marcus Garvey, Claude McKay, and A. Philip Randolph come to mind — his fifteen-year feud with Washington continues to serve as a touchstone for African American social and political thought. The Du Bois–Washington debate marked the maturation of African Americans, both socially and politically, and it also deepened and developed the dialectical external/internal style of criticism that has become a hallmark of African American social and political thought (see Brotz, 1992; Bush, 1999; Childs, 1989; Cruse, 1965, 1967, 1969, 2002; Gaines, 1996; Marable, 1985a, 1998; J.T McCarthy, 1991; Pohlman, 2003). With regard to the former contention, the Du Bois–Washington debate announced that many African Americans wanted nothing whatsoever to do with Washington's conservatism, bossism, and accommodationism. Du Bois and the Niagarites, and soon Du Bois, *The Crisis*, and the NAACP, offered African Americans a much-needed alternative to Washington's overarching political program and public policies, which were predicated on accommodating white supremacy and a blind acceptance of the myth of black inferiority. In terms of the latter assertion, the Du Bois–Washington debate provided Du Bois with one of his first opportunities to develop and critically apply his dialectical method that not only sought to critique white supremacist thought, but also weaknesses in black liberation thought.

The Du Bois–Washington debate reaches across the twentieth century and remains relevant at the dawn of the twenty-first century because it provides a well-known and virtually undisputed example of African American critical thought. Du Bois's inchoate dialectic did not simply critique white supremacy—if the critique of white supremacy has ever been simple—but, it also engaged black internalization of white-supremacist thought and practices, and it endeavored to offer solutions to the most pressing problems of black life. One of the major shortcomings of the scholarship on the Du Bois–Washington debate is that it often truncates and treacherously deals with the discursive dimensions of both Washington and Du Bois's social and political programs. In other words, the Du Bois–Washington debate previously has been almost exclusively examined from an historical perspective with little or no reference to its contribution to Africana critical thought traditions. In the subsequent sections I seek to remedy this oversight by providing Africana *transdisciplinary* analyses of the most important aspects of Washington and Du Bois's leadership and liberation thought. The concluding section critically compares their thought, demonstrates how Du Bois continued to develop his social, political, and educational philosophy after Washington's death, and the ongoing relevance of their debate for contemporary radical politics, critical social theory, and black leadership and liberation thought.

This chapter, then, does not endeavor an exhaustive treatment of the Du Bois–Washington debate, nor the historical and cultural conditions from which it emerged, but rather sets out to highlight the conceptual dimensions of their conflict and how it aided in enriching and expanding African American critical thought traditions.[2] Washington's work, though illusive, complicated, and complex, will not be as difficult to present as that of Du Bois because, by most accounts, Washington was religiously committed to his accommodationist stance, and his heyday only lasted two decades: from the time he delivered his Delphic Atlanta comprise address in 1895, to his untimely death in 1915, whereas Du Bois, similar to the critical social theories he produced, was multidimensional and constantly changing in light of new social scientific research and novel historical times. He had an almost unfathomable eighty-year publishing career, from 1883 to 1963, and spent more than half a century preoccupied with black leadership and black liberation. Therefore, one of the best ways to explore the Du Boisian dimension of the Du Bois–Washington debate is to identify the theory (or theories) that he created to combat and offer an alternative to Washington's accommodationism. That theory, of course, culminated in Du Bois's 1903 essay, "The Talented Tenth," which he continued to rethink and reconstruct long after Washington's death.

Below I revisit Du Bois's discourse on the Talented Tenth for its import to African American radical politics and Africana critical social theory. This radical re-reading stands in stark relief when compared with my brief interpretation of the same theory in the previous chapter: there I was concerned primarily with the ways in which Du Bois's theory of the Talented Tenth contributed to the discourse and development of Africana critical pedagogy, whereas here the focus will be on how his theory extends the realm of radical politics, social philosophy, and dialectical thought in African American intellectual and activist communities, and contributes to Africana critical theory of contemporary society. We begin with Washington since his was the dominant school of thought that Du Bois's Talented Tenth theory was created to critique.

PRELUDE TO WASHINGTON'S WIZARDRY: A NOTE ON ACCOMMODATIONISM

Accommodationism generally refers to a public policy in which African Americans are advised to accept white-supremacist, anti-black racist domination and discrimination in order to be gradually granted full citizenship and integration into U.S. society at some future time. As a major turn of the twentieth-century stream in African American social and political philosophy, accommodationism is usually associated with Booker T. Washington's thought and practices. Washington's philosophy of accommodationism is best characterized by its emphasis on African American vocational training and industrial education, pro-capitalist and anti-unionist stances, public acceptance of the dialectic of white supremacy and black inferiority, collaboration with influential and wealthy whites in order to paternally critique and correct "backward" and "childlike" blacks, and its euphemization of the importance of electoral politics and the African American struggle for civil rights and social justice. My examination of Washington's accommodationism will critically elaborate on each of the aforementioned aspects of his thought with an eye toward its contribution to the history of African American social and political philosophy and the discourse and development of contemporary black conservatism and black radicalism.[3]

BOOKER T. WASHINGTON'S
PHILOSOPHY OF ACCOMODATIONISM

Where many of the most noted nineteenth-century African American leaders were distinguished by their emancipatory efforts to free blacks from bondage and bring into being an authentic multicultural democratic America, Washington's words and deeds stand in stark relief (Cox, 1950a, 1950b; Franklin and Meier, 1982; Hawkins, 1974; Litwack and Meier, 1988). He has been hailed as *the* archetypal African American conservative because he urged blacks to acquiesce rather than radically oppose the racism of the established order.[4] Washington's economic strategy and educational philosophy are commonly contrasted with the social and political philosophy of other turn-of-the-twentieth-century African American leaders and intellectuals. Most often Washington's accommodationism and conservatism are compared with W.E.B. Du Bois's much mangled theory of the Talented Tenth, critical cultural nationalism, and radical democratic socialism. However, Du Bois was merely one of many critics who took issue with Washington's "Tuskegee machine." In fact, a short list of some of Washington's other—albeit often omitted—critics reads like an all-star roll call in twentieth-century African American social and political thought and radical journalism: Francis Grimke, William Monroe Trotter, George W. Forbes, T. Thomas Fortune, A. Philip Randolph, Oliver C. Cox, Kelly Miller, and J. Max Barber, among others. Each of these African American leaders took issue with Washington's social program for widely varied reasons, but at the heart of their individual critiques lay a common thread, a thread that generally involved Washington's emphasis on African American economic advancement and industrial education over the African American struggle for civil rights and racial justice (C.A. Bracey, 2008; Brundage, 2003; Carroll, 2003, 2006; Hawkins, 1974; M.R. West, 2005).

WASHINGTON'S POLITICAL PHILOSOPHY

What perplexed Washington's critics—many of whom were at one time Washington supporters—Du Bois, T. Thomas Fortune, and Francis Grimke notwithstanding—was his double dealing with regard to politics, economics, and education. On the issue of politics, Washington's conservative political philosophy counseled blacks not to seek immediate "social equality," but to be "patient, faithful, law-abiding, and unresentful" in the face of white-supremacist, anti-black racist domination and discrimination. In his famous 1895 address at the Cotton States Exposition in Atlanta (commonly referred to as the "Atlanta Compromise" address), Washington, in his customary fashion, catered to the whims and wishes of whites, stating, "The wisest among my race understand that the agitation of questions of social equality is the extremest folly." Washington wanted to assure whites that his ideology was one of conservative black economic and educational development, a brand of thought that did not demand redress for past or present white-supremacist wrongdoing and anti-black racism—that is, African holocaust, enslavement, colonization, and subsequent segregation in U.S. society.

Harlan has observed that though Washington constantly counseled blacks against getting involved in politics, he himself was a shrewd politician. Harlan's award-winning research painstakingly demonstrates that Washington actually was not against African Americans participating in U.S. politics, as much as he simply did not want blacks he did not approve of involved in the political arena. It is here that the ideological, and deeply political aspects of Washington's social thought and social programs come rushing to the fore. Harlan's words are worth quoting:

> It was in politics . . . that Washington built the most elaborate tentacle of the octopus-like Tuskegee Machine. In politics as in everything else, Washington cultivated ambiguity. He downgraded politics as a solution of black problems, did not recommend politics to the ambitious young black man, and never held office. But when Theodore Roosevelt became president in 1901 and asked for Washington's advice on black and southern appointments, Washington consented with alacrity. He became the chief black adviser of both Presidents Roosevelt and William Howard Taft. He failed in his efforts to liberalize the Republican policy on voting rights, lynching, and racial discrimination, however, and relations between the Republican party and black voters reached a low ebb. In patronage politics, however, Washington found his opportunity. For a man who minimized the importance of politics, Washington devoted an inordinate amount of his time and tremendous energy to securing federal jobs for his machine lieutenants. (1982, p. 5)

Similar to Harlan, August Meier's research reveals that "Washington's political involvement went even deeper." What, precisely, does Meier (1963) mean?

> Although he [Washington] always discreetly denied any interest in politics, he was engaged in patronage distribution under Roosevelt and Taft, in fighting the lily-white Republicans, and in getting out the Negro vote for the Republicans at

national elections. He might say that he disliked the atmosphere at Washington because it was impossible to build up a race whose leaders were spending most of their time and energy in trying to get into or stay in office, but under Roosevelt he became the arbiter of Negro appointments to federal office. Roosevelt started consulting Washington almost as soon as he took office, and later claimed that Washington had approved of his policy of appointing fewer but better-qualified Negroes. Numerous politicians old and new were soon writing to Tuskegee for favors, and in a few cases Roosevelt consulted Washington in regard to white candidates . . . Washington had at his disposal a number of collectorships of ports and internal revenue, receiverships of public monies in the land office, and several diplomatic posts, as well as the positions of auditor of the Navy, register of the Treasury and recorder of deeds. As Roosevelt wrote to a friend in 1903, his Negro appointees "were all recommended to me by Booker T. Washington." Furthermore, Roosevelt sought Washington's advice on presidential speeches and messages to Congress and consulted him on most matters concerning the Negro. Every four years also Washington took charge of the Negro end of the Republican presidential campaign. (p. 112)

Many of Washington's contemporary critics are quick to point to the fact that though he publicly advocated an apolitical or, as some have asserted, an *anti*-political philosophy for black development, he was nonetheless privately involved in the search for solutions to both black and white political problems. Despite his non-political public stance, the fact that Washington served as a sort of unofficial African American advisor to Presidents Cleveland, McKinley, Roosevelt, and Taft speaks volumes about his commitment to political involvement. Behind the white political scene, and in clandestine black political circles, Washington used his Tuskegee Machine and international influence to fight for civil rights and social justice. For example, in 1900 he covertly lobbied against anti-black racist election provisions in Louisiana's state constitution. Further, Washington's papers reveal that he personally "spent at least four thousand dollars in cash, out of my own pocket . . . in advancing the rights of the black man" in an effort to challenge Alabama's segregation laws in federal courts (quoted in Meier, 1963, p. 111; see also B.T. Washington, 1972–1989).

Washington's critics, however, both classical and contemporary, have maintained that no matter what he did privately, his stated public position and approach to anti-black racist policies gave whites the impression that blacks were not devoted to democracy as much as they were interested in earning a dollar (Brundage, 2003; Carroll, 2006; Cox, 1951). Washington went so far as to assert, "The opportunity to earn a dollar in a factory just now is worth infinitely more than the opportunity to spend a dollar in an opera-house." In other words, African Americans were asked to accept segregation provided they would have every opportunity to advance economically.

WASHINGTON'S ECONOMIC THEORY

With economic advancement Washington believed blacks would then be in a better position to gain and maintain power in U.S. society, which is to say that he did foresee blacks becoming a political force in the future. He asserted, "It is important and right that all privileges of the law be ours," and we will gain these "privileges" by "severe and constant struggle rather than artificial forcing." Politics and economics went hand in hand in Washington's ideology, but greater emphasis was placed on economics. In his assessment of blacks' situation at the turn of the twentieth century, Washington opined that a firm economic foundation would enable blacks to fight for their freedom faster than a purely political or agitative approach. He quickly befriended wealthy whites, such as Andrew Carnegie and John D. Rockefeller, and literally became the darling of turn-of-the-twentieth-century white philanthropy circles. It was in settings such as these that Washington mugged and masked most, telling "darky jokes" and deprecating and diminishing black dignity. Washington was so comfortable belittling black dignity before wealthy whites that Harlan notes his constant reiteration of his favorite "coon stories"—such as, "There seems to be a sort of sympathy between the Negro and the mule"—which helped to exacerbate and perpetuate racist myths and stereotypes about black inferiority (Harlan, 1972, 1983; see also Marable, 1998).

WASHINGTON'S PHILOSOPHY OF EDUCATION

What might be termed Washington's philosophy of education was essentially an extension of his political and economic thought. In fact, though much has been made of Washington's emphasis on vocational training and industrial education, historical records show that both Hampton and Tuskegee produced more black teachers at the turn of the twentieth century than manual or skilled laborers. One reason for this was the covert ideological character of Washington's educational program.

Washington's educational thought was based on that of his "tutor and idol," General Samuel Chapman Armstrong, who developed a pedagogy that was designed specifically to coerce blacks to accept and internalize post-Reconstruction white-supremacist, anti-black racist rule. Armstrong argued that blacks should be encouraged to take up industrial education as a way to subordinate and hold them as second-class citizens in the white-ruled, post-Reconstruction South. According to Armstrong, blacks were "not capable of self-government," and should be banned from the American political arena. He eagerly advertised himself as a "friend of the Negro," urging African

Americans to "let politics alone," claiming that black votes during Reconstruction enabled "some of the worst men" to become involved in politics, creating a situation that "no white race on this earth ought to endure or will endure" (quoted in J.D. Anderson, 1988, p. 37; see also Engs, 1999; Talbot, 1904).

Clearly Washington's aversion to public politics stemmed from Armstrong's influence on him. Throughout his public life Washington asserted that African Americans' first priority "was to get a foundation in education, industry and property." In order to build this foundation, Washington urged African Americans to forego open agitation against segregation and for political franchise. This public policy had severe and long-term consequences for African Americans: that is, educational and economic underdevelopment; continued and increased anti-black racist violence, especially lynchings; temporary throttling of black social and political theory and praxis; and censure and erasure of black intellectual independence (Brundage, 1993, 1997, 2005; Dray, 2002; Gilmore, 1996, 2008; Gilmore, Dailey and Simon, 2000; Hahn, 2003; Hale, 1998; Litwack, 1998; Logan, 1954, 1965; Tolnay, 1995). However, here it is important to note that no matter how powerful Washington was, there was an ever-increasing African American opposition to his accommodationist social programs. August Meier (1963) spoke directly to this issue when he wrote, "At no time were Washington's policies favored by all Negroes. Opposition to Washington existed from the time of the Atlanta Address, became more marked after 1900, and culminated in the founding of the National Association for the Advancement of Colored People" (p. 171).

In his classic essay, "The Evolution of Negro Leadership" (1901), which was a critical book review of Booker T. Washington's autobiography, *Up From Slavery*, W.E.B. Du Bois developed a sociology of African American politics that identified three basic trends: revolt and revenge; accommodation to the established order of the ruling race-class; and, dogged social development and cultural survival, "in spite of environing discouragements and prejudice" (Du Bois, 1977, p. 4). From the perspective of Du Bois's sociology of African American politics, Washington's leadership paradigm was simply one of three possible choices. For instance, Toussaint L'Ouverture, Richard Allen, Nat Turner, Blanche Bruce, Frederick Douglass, and John Mercer Langston—and Du Bois mentions several more "race leaders"—provided African Americans an "imprisoned group" or "a group within a group" with alternative leadership models (p. 4). Du Bois calmly declared,

> Mr. Washington came with a clear simple program, at the psychological moment; at a time when the nation was a little ashamed of having bestowed so much sentiment on Negroes and was concentrating its energies on Dollars. The

industrial training of Negro youth was not an idea originating with Mr. Washington, nor was the policy of conciliating the white South wholly his. But he first put life, unlimited energy, and perfect faith into this program; he changed it from an article of belief into a whole creed; he broadened it from a by-path into a veritable Way of Life. And the method by which he accomplished this is an interesting study of human life. (p. 4)

With his characteristic literary brevity and economy, Du Bois went on to lay out the nub of the opposition to Washington's accommodationism, which must have shocked and worried more than a few white readers unaware of the history and diversity of African American social and political philosophy. On behalf of the opposition, Du Bois stated, "We may not agree with the man at all points, but we admire him and cooperate with him so far as we conscientiously can" (p. 5). However, Washington's increasing silencing of "the voice of criticism" in the African American community was more than the admiring opposition could bear (Du Bois, 1986a, p. 398). Du Bois, who had long held his tongue and, since his youth, gravitated toward the radical political activism and social philosophy of Frederick Douglass, fired his opening salvo at the Tuskegee Machine. With passionate, but weighted words, Du Bois (1977) asserted the following:

> Among the Negroes, Mr. Washington is still far from a popular leader. Educated and thoughtful Negroes everywhere are glad to honor him and aid him, but all cannot agree with him. He represents in Negro thought the old attitude of adjustment to environment, emphasizing the economic phase; but the two other strong currents of feeling, descended from the past, still oppose him. One is the thought of a small but not unimportant group, unfortunate in their choice of spokesman, but nevertheless of much weight, who represent the old ideas of revolt and revenge, and see in migration alone an outlet for the Negro people. The second attitude is that of the large and important group represented by Dunbar, Tanner, Chesnutt, Miller, and the Grimkés, who, without any single definite program, and with complex aims, seek nevertheless that self-development and self-realization in all lines of human endeavor which they believe will eventually place the Negro beside the other races. While these men respect the Hampton-Tuskegee idea to a degree, they believe it falls far short of a complete program. They believe, therefore, also in the higher education of Fisk and Atlanta Universities; they believe in self-assertion and ambition; and they believe in the right of suffrage for blacks on the same terms with whites. (p. 5)

With these words an infamous episode in the history of African American social and political philosophy was born; the war between Washington and Du Bois, between the Tuskegee Machine and the Talented Tenth, would be waged not simply by these two social leaders, but by most of black America and, if the truth be told, many parts of white America as well. Du Bois daringly challenged Washington, and in doing so he developed one of his most significant contributions to early twentieth-century African American social and political philosophy. Perhaps subordinate only to his concept of double consciousness, Du Bois's theory of the Talented Tenth was simultaneously a theoretical blessing and a conceptual curse to black America, which is one of the reasons he revised it close to half a century after he initially proposed it, and over a quarter of a century after Washington's death and the demise of the Tuskegee Machine.

W.E.B. DU BOIS'S THEORY OF THE TALENTED TENTH

W.E.B. Du Bois's theory of the Talented Tenth registers right along with his concept of double consciousness as one of his most celebrated and controversial contributions to African American educational, social, and political thought traditions. However, unlike his concept of double consciousness, Du Bois returned to and revised his theory of the Talented Tenth, which Dan Green (1977) argued "was a lifelong theme" found throughout Du Bois's oeuvre, and "which encompasses his ideas of black leadership and a concomitant strategy to utilize the leadership as the most appropriate path toward black advancement" (p. 358). More recently, the noted African American radical feminist philosopher, Joy James (1997), has demonstrated that the Talented Tenth did not simply hold a pivotal place in Du Bois's early discourse, but that he constantly developed the concept throughout his corpus, ultimately overhauling it to include a critical rejection of white liberalism and black vanguardism, and a radical embrace and unfaltering faith in the black masses and black working classes' ability to provide, as he put it in *In Battle for Peace* (1952), "real, unselfish and clear-sighted leadership" (Du Bois, 1952, p. 77).[5]

Many scholars and critics have interpreted Du Bois's theory of the Talented Tenth as utterly elitist and thoroughly shot through with European ideals: from Eurocentric Enlightenment thought to European American aristocratic philosophy and political theory (Broderick, 1959; DeMarco, 1983; Wolters, 2001). However, other scholars and critics argue that Du Bois's much mangled theory of the Talented Tenth is actually not about the black bourgeoisie or an African American aristocracy leading the black masses and black working classes, but rather, as Du Bois (1996c) himself put it, about an assemblage of "men and women of character and almost fanatic devotion" to black liberation and, much later, radical democratic socialist transformation (p. 161; see also Battle and Wright, 2002; Dennis, 1977; Green, 1977; J.A. James, 1997).

Part of the confusion and contradictory interpretations of Du Bois's theory lies in his vagueness and, in his own words, his "youth and idealism" in his initial articulation of the Talented Tenth theory in 1903 (Du Bois, 1996c, p. 161). It also did not help matters much that it took nearly half a century to directly respond to criticisms and revise the theory, which he did in 1948. Taken together, Du Bois's 1903 and 1948 theories of the Talented Tenth represent and register as seminal and highly significant contributions to African American leadership and liberation thought, African American philosophy of education, and African American social and political philosophy. In what follows, let us look carefully and critically at the contributions this theory has made and continues to make to the discourse and debates surrounding African American radical politics and social theory.

THE TALENTED TENTH THESIS:
THE INITIAL ARTICULATION (1903)

Du Bois's initial articulation of the Talented Tenth was put forward in an essay appropriately titled, "The Talented Tenth," and was the second chapter of *The Negro Problem: A Series of Articles by Representative American Negroes of Today*, which included pieces by Booker T. Washington, Charles W. Chesnutt, Paul Laurence Dunbar, and T. Thomas Fortune, among others. "The Talented Tenth" is divided into three parts: Part one provides a philosophy of history that highlights and accents African American achievements against all the odds that holocaust and enslavement entail. Of particular note is the way in which Du Bois's philosophy of history places female freedom fighters right alongside their male counterparts, invoking the names of Phyllis Wheatley, David Walker, Sojourner Truth, Henry Highland Garnett, Harriet Tubman, Alexander Crummell and, "above all," Frederick Douglass (Du Bois, 1986a, pp. 842–46).

Though there has long been confusion amongst Du Bois's critics concerning the line that opens and closes the essay—"The Negro race, like all races, is going to be saved by its exceptional men"—he actually meant, as he made clear in his 1948 revision of the Talented Tenth thesis, that African American uplift rested squarely on the shoulders of both black "men and women of character," black men and women who, similar to the aforementioned freedom fighters, constantly seek "self-knowledge, self-realization, and self-control," and who possess a serious and sincere spirit of sacrifice, service, and struggle (Du Bois, 1986a, p. 842, 1996c, pp. 161, 165). However, Joy James (1997) has perceptively pointed out in *Transcending the Talented Tenth*, "Du Bois included women in the Talented Tenth," but his "referents were generally male;

Du Bois did not always use *men* as a generic reference to both sexes" (p. 19, original emphasis). Often when Du Bois used "men" the term signified something deeper; rather than merely persons of African descent who belonged to the male species, it represented a desire to have black males' masculinity, that gender-specific part of their identity and humanity, which need not be oppressive or negative toward women in any way whatsoever, recognized in a simultaneously white- *and* male-supremacist society. In other words, black men aspired to be respected, by white people as well as black women, as *gentlemen*, not as androgynous subhuman things or sex machines, or potential patriarchs or phallocentricists, but as humble human beings who have contributed to African American and world historic culture and civilization.

Unfortunately, too often the majority of black males have lacked the moral stamina to withstand the seductions of sexism, racial myths, and sexual stereotypes. Moreover, black men, especially in the post-enslavement period, have consistently lacked the wherewithal to view black women, not simply as sisters, but as comrades or fellow soldiers in the fight for freedom. Therefore, the desire to be respected as moral men who have significantly contributed to human culture and civilization has proven extremely illusive, and nowhere is this more obvious than in the myriad ways in which the Du Boisian dialectic ducks and dips into and out of sexist sentiments and patriarchal problematics.

For Du Bois, black manhood, as with black womanhood, engendered, literally, a life and death struggle with white supremacy and male supremacy, and he endeavored, again and again, to put forward black male and female models for this bitter battle for the souls of black folk without bowing to, or borrowing from, the long and horrible history of patriarchy. He was not always successful, to be perfectly honest but, Joy James observed, "by identifying women as members of the *public*, political race leadership, Du Bois's sexual politics were advanced for his era" (p. 19, original emphasis). This means, then, that for all of the continuous claims that Du Bois's classism and aristocratic attitude are on display throughout the Talented Tenth essay, his transgendered conception of the Talented Tenth—that is, of a cadre of African American male *and* female leaders "of character"—has often gone unrecognized.[6]

The first and last line of Du Bois's essay has been interpreted as an unmitigated endorsement of African American leadership and social development under the auspices of the black bourgeoisie or an African American aristocracy. According to Du Bois and many of his more sympathetic interpreters, though, he was not calling for leadership by the African American upper class, but leadership via the African American educated class, which, in his estimate of 1903, amounted to ten percent of the African American population; hence, the phrase "the Talented Tenth." The eminent historian, Evelyn Brooks-Higginbotham, has demonstrated that Du Bois did not coin this phrase, but borrowed it from the Northern white liberal, Henry Morehouse, who introduced it in an 1896 article in *The Independent* in which he stated that "not to make proper provision for the high education of the talented tenth man of the colored colleges is a prodigious mistake" (see E.B. Higginbotham, 1993).

Morehouse, who was a prominent member of the American Baptist Home Missionary Society (ABHMS), which established several Southern black colleges and universities, including one which bears his name, continued to wax with words that must have surely struck a chord with the young well-read, widely traveled and impeccably educated Du Bois when he, Morehouse, wrote, "Industrial education is good for the nine; the common English branches are good for the nine; [but] that tenth man ought to have the best opportunities for making the most of himself for humanity and God." The similarities between Morehouse and Du Bois's Talented Tenth, however, end here. Where Morehouse conceived of the Talented Tenth serving as guardians of the color-line, protectors of higher (read, white and bourgeois) culture, and essentially a black Southern social class, Du Bois's Talented Tenth were encouraged to break down racial barriers, immerse themselves in African American history and culture, and provide selfless leadership to the "nation within a nation," both in the North and in the South.[7]

As Du Bois continued to develop and deepen his consciousness, his conception of the Talented Tenth radically changed, until ultimately he called into question the entire idea of an educated elite leading the African American struggle for civil rights and racial justice (see Dennis, 1977; Tyner, 1997). But, at this early juncture in his illustrious career, Du Bois was blithely committed to a conception of black leadership that privileged college and university-educated black men and women. Non-academic African American intellectual-activists and black working-class leaders were never even considered in Du Bois's early theory of the Talented Tenth. In the first part of his essay on the Talented Tenth, then, Du Bois is at pains to predicate African American uplift on the African American intelligentsia using its knowledge of, and access to, crucial and critical resources in the best interest of the black masses, as opposed to merely its upper and/or middle class constituencies. Almost half a century later he would acknowledge the ambiguity inherent in, and, in effect, the long-term failure of, his early Talented Tenth theory, which is the main subject of the subsequent section.

The second part of the essay engages the issues surrounding African American education at the turn of the twentieth century, issues at the heart of the Du Bois–Washington debate. Where Washington was exclusively and firmly for industrial education and "trade training," Du Bois (1986a) declared that college education and "culture training" was a prerequisite for black leadership and black liberation (p. 855). However, and this is an important point that is often overlooked in discussions of the Du Bois–Washington debate, Du Bois did not deny that industrial education was extremely important to black life and social development. In his own words: "I am an earnest advocate of manual training and trade teaching for black boys, and for white boys, too. I believe that next to the founding of Negro colleges the most valuable addition to Negro education since the war has been industrial training for black boys" (p. 855).

Therefore, Du Bois (1968a) was not at all closed to the idea of industrial education for African Americans, which would also help to explain why he stated in his final autobiography, *The Autobiography of W.E.B. Du Bois*, that Washington and his "two theories of Negro progress were not absolutely contradictory" (p. 236). But, it must be calmly and clearly stated, Du Bois's thought went well beyond Washington's with its openness to *both* industrial and higher or liberal arts education. In fact, Du Bois's thought, being transdisciplinary and grounded in the academic or disciplinary developments of history, philosophy, sociology, political science, and economics (which he studied at Fisk, Harvard, and the University of Berlin), contained a broader and, perhaps, much more sophisticated conception of African American culture, social development, and future survival than Washington's hat-in-hand accommodationism. It is with this understanding that Louis Harlan (1982), one of Washington's foremost and most sympathetic interpreters, conceded in a discussion concerning Du Bois's opposition to Washington's accommodationist thought, "Du Bois took higher ground and perhaps a better vision of the future when he urged forthright protest against every white injustice, on the assumption that whites were rational beings and would respond dialectically to black protest. But few white racists of the early twentieth century cared anything for the facts" (p. 9).

In "The Talented Tenth," Du Bois made it clear that he had no deep desire to argue with Washington and the Tuskegeans over the fine points of African American education. The Atlanta educator and his Talented Tenth were more concerned with Washington occluding black youth's educational opportunities. From the Du Boisian perspective, Washington's accommodationism, fully financed by anti-black racists and wealthy whites, was robbing African Americans of their right to choose between industrial and liberal arts education. In an effort to hit at the heart of the Tuskegee Machine, Du Bois (1986e) boldly questioned the white world who placed Washington before blacks as the new risen "race leader" in the wake of Frederick Douglass' death:

> Do you Americans ever stop to reflect that there are in this land a million men
> of Negro blood, well-educated, owners of homes, against the honor of whose

womanhood no breath was ever raised, whose men occupy positions of trust and usefulness, and who, judged by any standard, have reached the full measure of the best type of modern European culture? Is it fair, is it decent, is it Christian to ignore these facts of the Negro problem, to belittle such aspiration, to nullify such leadership and seek to crush these people back into the mass out of which by toil and travail, they and their fathers have raised themselves? (p. 847)

Du Bois detected early on that the white world, as well as Washington himself, was benefiting from Washington's accommodationism and constant counsel to blacks that they should not agitate for their civil rights or get involved in politics. As August Meier (1963) has astutely observed, many African Americans believed that Washington's thought and "actions were motivated by his desire for money and praise" from wealthy whites (p. 171). John McCartney (1992) corroborates this claim by painstakingly pointing out that "in Washington's view the people who truly make the system work are the rich Americans" (p. 63). Why? Because from the Washingtonian point of view, first, wealthy whites believe in and practice charity. Second, wealthy whites understand themselves to be ordained by God to not only make large sums of money, but to use their capital, in Washington's words, as "an instrument which God has placed in their hands for doing good" (1996, p. 126). Third, Washington maintained that wealthy whites were the best guardians of American culture and civilization because they had long mastered politeness, patience, and self-control. And, finally, Washington believed that the religious or fanatical pursuit of wealth made one commit to, and deeply concerned about, America and its well-being, which, from the Washingtonian point of view, symbolized the kind of deep investment that a guardian of American civilization and culture must possess (see also B.T. Washington, 1899, 1900b, 1900c, 1902, 1904, 1906a). "In summary," McCartney (1992) writes, "self-control, patience, politeness, and the loss of self in a great cause, these are the necessary virtues for success in America, and Washington saw them best manifested in the rich and least manifested in black society of the time" (p. 63).

Du Bois and Washington's thought ironically dovetails here. However, unlike Washington, Du Bois had little or no faith in wealthy whites, or in the black bourgeoisie, for that matter. Indeed, similar to the Tuskegean, Du Bois was deeply interested in "self-control, patience, politeness, and the loss of self in a great cause," but Du Bois's conception of "a great cause" was markedly different from Washington's and, even in 1903, it was extremely critical of capitalism (and, especially, black capitalists).[8] The vanguard in Du Bois's leadership and liberation thought of 1903 was the educated among African Americans. However, his vanguard was not an "aristocracy" based on money or material possessions (à la Washington and the white-supremacist, patriar-

chal, capitalist, colonial world), but an "aristocracy of talent and character."
Du Bois (1986a) unapologetically asked black America this:

> Can the masses of the Negro people be in any possible way more quickly raised
> than by the effort and example of this aristocracy of talent and character? Was
> there ever a nation on God's fair earth civilized from the bottom upward? Never;
> it is, ever was and ever will be from the top downward that culture filters. The
> Talented Tenth rises and pulls all that are worth saving up to their vantage
> ground. This is the history of human progress; and two historic mistakes which
> have hindered progress were thinking first that no more could ever rise save the
> few already risen; or second, that it would better the unrisen to pull the risen
> down. (p. 847)

Where Washington's leadership model sought an external solution to the
problem of black social development and was predicated on wealthy whites'
philanthropy, by contrast Du Bois's leadership thought sought an internal solution to the problem of black social development and turned to the "talented"
and "gifted" among African Americans. Washington's social program would
leave African Americans at the mercy of rich and powerful whites, whereas
Du Bois's social program was predicated on "self-knowledge, self-realization, and self-control." In other words, as he put it in "Of Mr. Booker T. Washington and Others," Du Bois believed, in the tradition of Frederick Douglass,
that "manly self-respect is worth more than lands and houses, and that a people who voluntarily surrender such respect, or cease striving for it, are not
worth civilizing" (p. 399).

For Du Bois, then, the crucial question before black leaders and black
America was "How then shall the leaders of a struggling people be trained
and the hands of the risen few strengthened?" He went on and assuredly
shared with his eager readers that "[t]here can be but one answer." Then,
pulling no punches, Du Bois began his barrage:

> The best and most capable of their [black folks'] youth must be schooled in the
> colleges and universities of the land. We will not quarrel as to just what the uni-
> versity of the Negro should teach or how it should teach—I willingly admit that
> each soul and each race-soul needs its own peculiar curriculum. But this is true:
> A university is a human invention for the transmission of knowledge and culture
> from generation to generation, through the training of quick minds and pure
> hearts, and for this work no other human invention will suffice, not even trade
> and industrial schools. (p. 847)

Du Bois believed that blacks needed "broadly cultured men and women"
in leadership positions to guard against the manipulations and machinations
of the ruling race-class and the hundreds of "half-trained demagogues" and

opportunists (p. 855). Without "broadly cultured men and women," by which he meant men and women with an acute understanding of the historical and current life struggles of black people and an intense ethical obligation ("almost fanatic devotion") to black liberation, Du Bois surmised that blacks were, without a doubt, surely doomed to a slow and painful socio-cultural death at the hands of racism, capitalism, and colonialism (e.g., see Du Bois, 1982a, 1982e, 1985a).

The third part of the essay takes a headfirst and hard-nosed look at black leaders and intellectuals' relationship with and responsibility to the black liberation struggle. From Du Bois's optic, black leaders and intellectuals have an ethical obligation to use their training and knowledge, not to greedily grab all that they can and horde it for themselves and their families, but to improve the conditions of the black masses and working classes. Similar to Du Bois, one of Washington's major concerns with the African American intelligentsia was that they often pursued their own personal goals, as opposed to using their knowledge in the interest of the masses. However, the Tuskegean also accused black intellectuals of being "ignorant in regard to the actual needs of the masses of colored people" and, therefore, unprepared to contribute to black social development, which he believed needed trained and skilled laborers more than intellectuals who could quote lyrical lines of poetry and passages from classic texts (Washington, 1911, p. 127; see also Freedman, 1975; Greco, 1984). Du Bois (1986a), determined to dialectically demonstrate Washington's paradox, took great pleasure in pointing out that his, Washington's, own beloved Tuskegee had benefited enormously from blacks trained in the liberal arts and the sciences:

> Indeed the demand for college-bred men by a school like Tuskegee, ought to make Mr. Booker T. Washington the firmest friend of higher education. Here he has as helpers the son of a Negro senator, trained in Greek and the humanities, and graduated at Harvard; the son of a Negro congressman and lawyer, trained in Latin and mathematics, and graduated at Oberlin; he has as his wife, a woman who read Virgil and Homer in the same class room with me; he has as college chaplain, a classical graduate of Atlanta University; as teacher of science, a graduate of Fisk; as teacher of history, a graduate of Smith,—indeed some thirty of his chief teachers are college graduates, and instead of studying French grammars in the midst of weeds, or buying pianos for dirty cabins, they are at Mr. Washington's right hand helping him in a noble work. And yet one of the effects of Mr. Washington's propaganda has been to throw doubt upon the expediency of such training for Negroes, as these persons have had. (p. 860)

After exposing the inexcusable contradictions of Washington's program, Du Bois concluded the essay by offering white America a caveat, one that was drenched in pathos and centuries of planned pain, senseless suffering, and unmitigated sorrow. He closed "The Talented Tenth" addressing white America because it was white industrialists who placed Washington before black and white America, who financially supported, politically encouraged, and brazenly benefited from his accommodationism, and who manufactured and constantly tuned up his Tuskegee Machine. Du Bois began the essay re-calling the lives and achievements of dignified and distinguished African Americans, not simply to illustrate the antecedents of his Talented Tenth to blacks, but also to demonstrate to whites their immoral ignorance of African American history, culture, and struggle. As the essay opened, he sternly stated, "You misjudge us because you do not know us" (p. 842).

In so many words, Du Bois warned white America, just as he had warned black America, that they go the way of Washington at their own peril. Insofar as he was concerned, the problem and the solution had been clearly laid out in this essay, as well as in his other essays, such as "Of Mr. Booker T. Wash-ington and Others," "The Social Training of the Negro," "Possibilities of the Negro: The Advance Guard of the Race," and "The Training of Negroes for Social Power," among others: Either white America would aid black America on black America's own terms, or black America would, literally, turn white America's lily-white heaven on earth into a living hell. At the close of "The Talented Tenth, Du Bois thundered,

> Men of America, the problem is plain before you. Here is a race transplanted through the criminal foolishness of your fathers. Whether you like it or not the millions are here, and here they will remain. If you do not lift them up, they will pull you down. Education and work are the levers to uplift a people. Work alone will not do it unless inspired by the right ideals and guided by intelligence. Ed-ucation must not simply teach work—it must teach Life. The Talented Tenth of the Negro race must be made leaders of thought and missionaries of culture among their people. No others can do this work and Negro colleges must train men for it. The Negro race, like all other races, is going to be saved by its ex-ceptional men. (p. 861)

In 1903 Du Bois (1996c) naïvely "assumed," as he put it in 1948, that black leaders and black intellectuals would sacrifice and selflessly serve the black masses (p. 161). He quickly found out that the spirit of Jeffersonian individ-ualism and simple-minded selfishness was not something wholly plaguing whites, but that blacks were under its pernicious spell as well. It was with a sense of great disillusionment and deep depression that Du Bois returned to and revised his theory of the Talented Tenth into "the doctrine of the Guiding Hundredth" in 1948.

THE GUIDING HUNDREDTH THESIS:
REVISITING AND REVISING THE TALENTED TENTH (1948)

"The Talented Tenth Memorial Address" was delivered at the Nineteenth Grand Boulé Conclave of Sigma Pi Phi fraternity, in 1948. From the outset of the address Du Bois made it known that he had come to criticize, not simply others' black leadership and liberation thought but, in a rare self-reflective moment, his own black social development discourse. He was baffled and bemoaned the fact that so many black leaders and intellectuals aped the aristocratic attitudes of the white ruling race-class. He also chided himself for being naïve and not lucidly laying out the basic qualities and characteristics of the Talented Tenth in 1903—qualities and characteristics that ultimately revolved around the black intelligentsia's ethical obligations to the youth, the aged, and the infirmed, as well as the poor and poverty-stricken of black America.

However, it may be helpful to point out that Du Bois's critical discourse on the Talented Tenth was actually initiated eight years prior to "The Talented Tenth Memorial Address." In his classic memoir, *Dusk of Dawn*, he admitted that he indeed did conceive of the Talented Tenth as an aristocracy, but one based on "knowledge and character and not in its wealth." In his haste to dismantle the Tuskegee Machine, the young thirty-five-year-old Du Bois of 1903 did not theorize the possibility of intra-racial class struggle between the black intelligentsia and the black bourgeoisie. He innocently believed that the black bourgeoisie would bow to the learned leadership of the black intelligentsia and, what is more, he erroneously imagined that the black bourgeoisie and the black intelligentsia had few common class interests.[9]

When he published *Dusk of Dawn*, seventy-two-year-old W.E.B. Du Bois had been shunned by academe, censured and brow-beaten by Washington's black bourgeois and wealthy white conservative colleagues, mocked as a "mulatto" by Jamaican Pan-Africanist Marcus Garvey, ridiculed as an anti-revolutionary or, worse, a black bourgeois theorist by civil rights leader A. Philip Randolph, and, disparaged as a black separatist by black and white NAACP liberals (D.L. Lewis, 1993, 2000; Marable, 1986; Massiah, 1995). He was, in a word, *persona non grata* and utterly on his own, and his Talented Tenth had failed him just as they had failed black America. Finally, well-nigh four decades after he initially put forward his theory of the Talented Tenth, Du Bois seriously considered the contributions of the black masses and the black working classes to black leadership and liberation. Writing with a sense of revelation, in *Dusk of Dawn* he observed that

> our former panacea emphasized by Booker T. Washington was flight of class
> from mass in wealth with the idea of escaping the masses or ruling the masses

through power placed by white capitalists into the hands of those with larger income. My own panacea of earlier days was flight of class from mass through the development of a Talented Tenth; but the power of this aristocracy of talent was to lie in its knowledge and character and not in its wealth. The problem which I did not then attack was that of leadership and authority within the group, which by implication left controls to wealth—a contingency of which I never dreamed. But now the whole economic trend of the world has changed. That mass and class must unite for the world's salvation is clear. We who have had least class differentiation in wealth, can follow in the new trend and indeed lead it. (Du Bois, 1986d, pp. 712–13)

In Du Bois's original formulation of the Talented Tenth, an educated elite would lead in the best interest of black America, not simply the black middle class. When he revisited the concept in 1940 he took note, not only of his early intellectual elitism, but also of his naïveté where intra-racial class struggle was concerned. In *Dusk of Dawn*, Du Bois began to deconstruct the Talented Tenth, opening the theory to non-academic, working-class intellectual-activists and leaders. African American academics had not fulfilled the historical and cultural role that the architect of the modern Civil Rights movement had ascribed to them, and Marcus Garvey's parallel Pan-African movement, with its emphasis on the black masses and working classes, even though it ultimately failed, forced Du Bois to come to terms with his early ideas of an educated elite altruistically leading the black masses.

Garvey, self-educated and lovingly supported by the black masses and working classes, demonstrated to Du Bois the fallacy of his Talented Tenth leadership philosophy (see Ijere, 1974; McGuire, 1974; Mezu, Mezu and Bell, 1999; A.L. Reed, 1975, 1986; B.F. Rogers, 1955; Rudwick, 1959a; Wintz, 1996). But, as was conventionally the case with Du Bois (especially when it came to constructive criticism from non-academically trained leaders of black social movements), it took him several years—in this instance almost two decades—to redevelop this extremely important aspect of his social theory and social program for African American advancement. Therefore, in 1940, perhaps in quiet commemoration of Garvey's death earlier that year, Du Bois (1986a) began to search for new agents of African American liberation, irritatedly asserting, "None of us in the present pressure of race hate [can] afford to hold uncompromising and unchangeable views" (p. 733).

Washington had been dead for a quarter of a century and the Tuskegee Machine had been dismantled about the same amount of time, and still Du Bois, who constantly claimed that the feud between him and Washington was not personal but political, was not satisfied with black social development. The elite leadership model that he had borrowed from the Northern white liberals and learned so well in pursuit of his bachelor's, master's, and doctoral degrees at Harvard University had betrayed him and black America. The

Platonic leadership model of philosopher-kings/queens, which Du Bois had been doggedly attempting to African Americanize for four decades, was courting a *coup d'etat* in his discursive universe.

Despite his intellectual soul-searching and restless radical spirit, traces of elitism continued to contaminate Du Bois's leadership thought in *Dusk of Dawn*. Though he began to radically reform his conception of a black vanguard, he continued to embrace caste in his leadership thought. The intricacies of black intra-racial class interests and conflicts, as ever, eluded him, creating a conundrum in his thought for years to come. Du Bois, indeed, was moving in the right direction, but had not yet reached his *revolutionary* destination. Instead of calling for the complete abolition of any sort of elite leadership cadre, academic or non-academic, he opted for a democratic reform of academic-aristocratic black leadership, as opposed to a radical democratic leadership model, predicated on participatory democracy and collective leadership, a union of academic and non-academic intellectuals and leaders, cutting across caste and class lines and connecting with workers of widely varied occupations, and transgressing patriarchal conceptions of gender politics.

When he took the podium to deliver the "Talented Tenth Memorial Address," on August 12, 1948, Du Bois, then an octogenarian, critically returned to his early leadership thought, and physically returned to the site where he began his academic career, Wilberforce University. At Wilberforce, he would simultaneously eulogize the old, war-worn Talented Tenth thesis and conceptually christen the more democratic "doctrine of the Guiding Hundredth." Before an audience, who heretofore would have been ideal candidates for his erstwhile Talented Tenth cadre of race leaders, Du Bois criticized his elite leadership model, permanently disassociating himself and his discourse from the Talented Tenth.

In his address, Du Bois advocated the radical democratization and internationalization of black leadership and the black liberation struggle. Though he had intimated it previously, or so he thought, he now wanted to strongly stress that black leaders and the black liberation struggle must be preoccupied with more than merely the "race question" and achieving racial justice. With the work that many consider his magnum opus, *Black Reconstruction* (1935), Du Bois began an intense study of the political economy of race and racism, employing Marxist methodology and coupling it with the ever-evolving philosophy of race (and critical race theory) he had been developing for over half a century (see Bogues, 2003; C.J. Robinson, 2000). From the start of his Marxist studies, orthodox (or, rather, white) Marxists attacked his interpretation and application of Marxism to black America and later Pan-Africa, charging him with "revisionism" and dubbing Du Bois (as they did C.L.R. James),— as Anthony Bogues (2003) has so perceptively put it—a "black heretic." He was not dismayed, and after more than a decade of deeply dialoguing with Marxism and incorporating it into his political philosophy and social program(s), Du Bois, utilizing the Marxian dialectical method, deconstructed and reconstructed his leadership and liberation thought.

In the address before his black bourgeois audience, an audience who came to hear and be inspired by the architect of the African American aristocratic leadership model and movement, Du Bois demobilized the Talented Tenth, speaking at length about how Karl Marx and Marxism had entreated and inspirited him to look to "the masses of men" for "overwhelming floods of ability and genius." This, indeed, registered as a serious rupture with his previous leadership paradigm and liberation thought. Du Bois's "new idea for a Talented Tenth" aimed to transform, not only African American leadership models and contribute to the radical democratization of black social movements, but it also served as an undeniable sign that the aging octogenarian was making a solemn effort to critique and correct the latent elitism in his leadership and liberation thought (p. 168). In his own heartfelt words, Du Bois (1996c) candidly contended,

> Karl Marx stressed the fact that not merely the upper class but the mass of men were the real people of the world. He insisted that the masses were poor, ignorant, and sick, not by sin or by nature but by oppression. He preached that planned production of goods and just distribution of income would abolish poverty, ignorance and disease, and make the so-called upper-class, not the exception, but the rule among mankind. He declared that the world was not for the few, but for the many; that out of the masses of men could come overwhelming floods of ability and genius, if we freed men by plan and not by rare chance. Civilization not only could be shared by the vast majority of men, but such civilization founded on a wide human base would be better and more enduring than anything that the world has seen. The world would thus escape the enduring danger of being run by a selfish few for their own advantage. (pp. 162–63)

In discussing his shift of focus from an aristocratic leadership model to a radical democratic socialist leadership model in the interest of African Americans, Du Bois perceptively notes his efforts to African Americanize Marxism, to make it speak to the special needs of, as he put it elsewhere, "a nation within a nation," who were simultaneously struggling against capitalist exploitation and racial domination (see Du Bois, 1995a, pp. 563-570). Du Bois, similar to C.L.R. James, detected early in his Marxist studies that Marx and Marxism offered little with regard to anti-racist struggle—truth be told, like Hegel, Marx was a racist—but, Marxism did (and continues to) provide one of the most comprehensive critiques of capitalism and class struggle available to critical social theorists (Bannerji, 1995; Eze, 1997c; Flank, 2007; C.W. Mills, 2003; Serequeberhan, 1990).

In "My Evolving Program for Negro Freedom," written four years before he eulogized his Talented Tenth and gave birth to the Guiding Hundredth, Du Bois discussed in detail the protracted transformation of his social thought, which he claimed intensified with his 1926 sojourn to the Soviet Union. He openly admitted that he did not believe that Russian communism was the path for the United States, and certainly not for African Americans, but he did think that Russian communism offered many lessons concerning the development and differentiation of classes that could be extremely useful to African Americans in their liberation struggle. Traveling to the Soviet Union, and observing their sociopolitical experiment in communism firsthand, helped to concretize Du Bois's conception of Marxism and its significance for certain aspects of African American and Pan-African liberation movements; however, and this should be stressed, he remained critical of Marxism, among other critical social theories, that neglected to theorize the centrality of race and racism (as well as the ways in which it overlaps, interlocks, and intersects with capitalism and colonialism) in the modern world. His extremely important 1944 reflections on his 1926 journey to the Soviet Union and his present social program are worth quoting at length:

> I believe in the dictum of Karl Marx, that the economic foundation of a nation is widely decisive for its politics, its art and its culture. I saw clearly, when I left Russia, that our American Negro belief that the right to vote would give us work and decent wage; would abolish our illiteracy and decrease our sickness and crime, was justified only in part; that on the contrary, until we were able to earn a decent, independent living, we would never be allowed to cast a free ballot; that poverty caused our ignorance, sickness and crime; and that poverty was not our fault but our misfortune, the result and aim of our segregation and color caste; that the solution of letting a few of our capitalists share with whites in the exploitation of our masses, would never be a solution of our problem, but the forging of eternal chains. . . . Immediately, I modified my program again: I did not believe that the Communism of the Russians was the program for America; least of all for a minority group like the Negroes; I saw that the program of the American Communist party was suicidal. But I did believe that a people where the differentiation in classes because of wealth had only begun, could be so guided by intelligent leaders that they would develop into a consumer-conscious people, producing for use and not primarily for profit, and working into the surrounding industrial organization so as to reinforce the economic revolution bound to develop in the United States and all over Europe and Asia sooner or later. I believe that revolution in the production and distribution of wealth could be a slow, reasoned development and not necessarily a blood bath. I believed 13 millions of people, increasing, albeit slowly in intelligence, could so concentrate their thought and action on the abolition of their poverty, as to work in conjunction with the most intelligent body of American thought; and that in the fu-

ture as in the past, out of the mass of American Negroes would arise a far-seeing leadership in lines of economic reform. (Du Bois, 1995b, pp. 610–11)

In the eight years between *Dusk of Dawn* and "The Talented Tenth Memorial Address," Du Bois's leadership thought shows signs of intense transformation and critical rethinking. In fact, "My Evolving Program for Negro Freedom," could be seen as a prelude to the "The Talented Tenth Memorial Address," the former placing in plain public view Du Bois's protracted process of self-critique and self-transformation, and, the latter, symbolizing the complete reformulation, reconstruction, and radicalization of his leadership and liberation thought. "My Evolving Program for Negro Freedom" is additionally important in terms of examining Du Bois's leadership and liberation thought because it is one of the few pieces in his diverse and voluminous corpus where he economically periodizes his own unfolding philosophy of freedom.[10] Du Bois paints a political self-portrait, one that stands in stark relief to the intellectual elitism, youthful idealism, and political vanguardism of his original Talented Tenth theory. "My Evolving Program for Negro Freedom" did not simply note the shortcomings of his early leadership thought, as was the case in *Dusk of Dawn*, but it registered the kind of self-reflexive, dialectical, and critical attitude Du Bois would take toward the Talented Tenth, aristocratic, and conservative African American leadership and social movements for the remainder of his life. As he concluded his prelude to "The Talented Tenth Memorial Address," he wrote,

> The hope of civilization lies not in exclusion, but in inclusion of all human elements; we find the richness of humanity not in the Social Register, but in the City Directory; not in great aristocracies, chosen people and superior races, but in the throngs of disinherited and underfed men. Not the lifting of the lowly, but the unchaining of the unawakened mighty, will reveal the possibilities of genius, gift and miracle, in mountainous treasure-trove, which hitherto civilization has scarcely touched; and yet boasted blatantly and even glorified in its poverty. In world-wide equality of human development is the answer to every meticulous taste and each rare personality. (p. 617)

Du Bois continued to lay his leadership and liberation thought out, as if guiding his readers through the labyrinth of his logic, periodizing his political philosophy and social programs. He was, yet again, on the brink of breakthrough but, ironically, he would have to rupture his relationship with the very intellectual leadership cadre he created in order to move in a more radical direction. It seems as though Du Bois may have been holding out some kind of subtle and silent hope that his Talented Tenth would work with him to radically democratize, not only the United States, but also the wider world. Whether they would or would not, he was doggedly determined.

The periodization of his political philosophy and social programs that he provided in "My Evolving Program for Negro Freedom," then, can be seen as Du Bois's attempt to alert his Talented Tenth and the wider world to the radical transformation and internationalization of his social theory and political praxis—as if *Black Reconstruction, Black Folk, Then and Now, Dusk of Dawn* and, very soon, *Color and Democracy: Colonies and Peace* were not enough representative samples of his radically evolving critical social theory. His philosophy of freedom up to 1944, he observed, had taken the following "main paths":

1. 1885–1910
   "The Truth shall make ye free."
   This plan was directed toward the majority of white Americans, and rested on the assumption that once they realized the scientifically attested truth concerning Negroes and race relations, they would take action to correct all wrong.
2. 1900–1930
   United action on the part of thinking Americans, white and black, to force the truth concerning Negroes to the attention of the nation.
   This plan assumed that the majority of Americans would rush to the defense of democracy if they realized how race prejudice was threatening it, not only for Negroes but for whites, not only in America but in the world.
3. 1928–present
   Scientific investigation and organized action among Negroes, in close cooperation, to secure the survival of the Negro race, until the cultural development of America and the world is willing to recognize Negro freedom.
   This plan realizes that the majority of men do not usually act in accordance with reason, but follow social pressures, inherited customs, and long-established, often subconscious, patterns of action. Consequently, race prejudice in America will linger long and may even increase. It is the duty of the black race to maintain its cultural advance, not for itself alone, but for the emancipation of mankind, the realization of democracy, and the progress of civilization. (p. 618, all original emphasis)

In "The Talented Tenth Memorial Address" Du Bois, literally, picked up where he left off in "My Evolving Program for Negro Freedom." However, it should be said, with "The Talented Tenth Memorial Address," Du Bois moved beyond the mere narration and documentation of his political philosophy and put forward a concrete radical social program. In the period between the publication of *Dusk of Dawn* and his delivery of "The Talented

Tenth Memorial Address," Du Bois undertook an intense search for a revolutionary subject to bring about radical democratic socialist transformation in the interest of African Americans and other oppressed groups. He told his elite audience at Wilberforce that they, as with all of black America, must either take a pro or con position concerning American and global imperialism, calling for "special organization," which entailed "more than a tenth of our number" (Du Bois, 1996c, p. 168).

One of the many reasons Du Bois was consistently attacked by white Marxists during the latter years of his intellectual and political life was because his "revisionism" moved beyond Karl Marx and Marxists' most privileged agents of revolution: the *white* working class, or the "proletariat," in Marxian vernacular. Du Bois charged, not merely the white working class and labor unions with white supremacy, but he also asserted that most white Marxists' and their party politics suffered from white supremacy. As a result, he argued, white Marxists could not be counted as "comrades" (to borrow once again from Marxian vernacular) in African American and Pan-African liberation struggles.

In radically and anti-racistly calling into question traditional Marxian concepts of the proletariat as the privileged agent of revolution and the predestined revolutionary subject, Du Bois endeavored to demonstrate that the Marxian model simply could not be grafted onto a white supremacist capitalist society with transethnic, multi-racial, and multicultural workers. Race and racism, central social issues that Marxists have historically neglected, and of which Du Bois is considered to have pioneered the critical and systematic study, makes Marxism, as Cornel West (1993a) once put it, "indispensable" as a methodological orientation critical of capitalism and class struggle, but "ultimately inadequate" in grasping the distinctive features of anti-black racism and global white supremacy (p. 259). Du Bois, therefore, contributed critical race theory to Marxian discourse, laying a foundation for many of the first race-class concepts and opening Marxism to anti-racist categories of critical analysis; and, in so doing, he simultaneously broadened the base of both Marxism and his own burgeoning critical social theory.

Du Bois's "doctrine of the Guiding Hundredth" brought his theory of the Talented Tenth into dialogue with Marxism, as well as the "revolutionary thought" of other "prophets and reformers" (1996c, p. 162). Recalling his initial articulation of the Talented Tenth theory in 1903, Du Bois maintained that he had in mind "leadership of the Negro race in America by a trained few" (p. 159). Many interpreters of his theory understood him to be endorsing "the building of an aristocracy with neglect of the masses," which in most instances is precisely what his Talented Tenth did (p. 159). Du Bois asserted that this was not what he had in mind, and that his Marxist studies, along with the study of other "revolutionary thought," now provided him with a more intricate understanding of class conflict, the vicissitudes of capitalism, and the political economy of race and racism.

With "The Talented Tenth Memorial Address," then, Du Bois aimed to not only criticize and demobilize the Talented Tenth, but also to encourage his aristocratic audience to come to terms with the fact that the world had drastically changed since 1903. African Americans in mid-twentieth-century America, as with black folk at the beginning of "the American century," were wrestling with more than merely racial domination and discrimination. Capitalist exploitation was also a major contributor to African American oppression, but Du Bois did not sufficiently emphasize this crucial fact in his Talented Tenth thesis; racism was the overriding issue. In "The Talented Tenth Memorial Address," he told his audience that it was important to keep abreast of changes in thought, culture, and society; knowledge of these changes had prompted him to redevelop his leadership thought. Maintaining openness to change and the knowledge created to chart change, he contended, was a paramount necessity not only for intellectual-activists, but also for the organic intellectual-activists who lead the black masses and the black working classes. Therefore, Du Bois counseled his audience at Wilberforce on the relationship between emancipatory education and social transformation, stating, "It is necessary then for men of education continually to readjust their knowledge, and this is doubly necessary in this day of swift revolution in ideas, in ideals, in industrial techniques, in rapid travel, and in varieties and kinds of human contact" (p. 160).

The octogenarian's "new idea for a Talented Tenth" was ironically not an idea for a Talented Tenth at all, but a "concept of group leadership" under the auspices of "[o]ne one-hundredth, or thirty thousand persons," "men and women of character and almost fanatic devotion" to anti-racism, revolutionary democratic socialism, Pan-Africanism, and critical multiculturalism, among other efforts geared toward the "remaking of human culture" in the United States, and contributing to "the greater world of human culture" (pp. 161, 165–66, 168). The Guiding Hundredth, he eagerly announced in his Wilberforce address, is predicated on "group leadership, not simply educated and self-sacrificing, but with a clear vision of present world conditions and dangers, and conducting American Negroes to alliance with culture groups in Europe, America, Asia and Africa, and looking toward a new world culture" (p. 168). Du Bois's discourse on the Guiding Hundredth distinctly demonstrates many of the lessons he had learned from not only black America's betrayal at the hands of his Talented Tenth, but also the lessons he learned from half a century of participating in the Pan-African movement, toppling Booker T. Washington's Tuskegee Machine, bitterly battling Marcus Garvey and his

Back to Africa movement, witnessing two world wars, observing the rise of Russian communism, and, intensely studying Marxism for over a quarter of a century. The Guiding Hundredth, following in the footsteps of the widely or read, well-traveled, and world historical eighty-year-old W.E.B. Du Bois, was awesomely envisioned by its conceptual creator and discursive doyen, Du Bois himself, as simultaneously and multidimensionally internationalist, radical humanist, multiculturalist, pacifist, Pan-Africanist, democratic social-ist, anti-colonialist, anti-capitalist, anti-racist and, though he does not ade-quately emphasize it in this address, anti-sexist (Balfour, 2005; Gilkes, 1996; Gillman and Weinbaum, 2007; Hattery and Smith, 2005; Rabaka, 2003d, 2004; A.E. Weinbaum, 2001).

Even more than his theory of the Talented Tenth or his concept of double consciousness, it is clear that Du Bois intended his "doctrine of the Guiding Hundredth" to be both a concrete contribution to African American and Pan-African leadership and liberation thought, and, however subtly, a late-life conceptual creation by which his intellectual trajectory could be properly charted and critically characterized. In "The Talented Tenth Memorial Ad-dress," he placed some of the lessons he learned from his Marxist studies in plain view. Race and racism were, of course, ongoing issues confronting black leadership, but class and capitalism were also important issues. Du Bois now suggested that African American social leaders simultaneously be criti-cal race theorists and, à la Marxism, experts in "modern economics," which may also be interpreted as experts in the political economy of race and racism, as well as experts in the connections between colonialism and capi-talism. He autobiographically observed that

> very gradually as the philosophy of Karl Marx and many of his successors seeped into my understanding, I tried to apply this doctrine with regard to Ne-groes. My Talented Tenth must be more than talented, and work not simply as individuals. Its passport to leadership was not alone learning, but expert knowl-edge of modern economics as it affected American Negroes; and in addition to this and fundamental, would be its willingness to sacrifice and plan for such eco-nomic revolution in industry and just distribution of wealth, as would make the rise of our group possible. (Du Bois, 1996c, p. 163)

Along with its commitment to anti-racism, Du Bois advised his Talented Tenth audience to critically engage capitalism and embrace revolutionary democratic socialism. Where his Talented Tenth thesis was criticized for be-ing bourgeois, elitist and unconcerned with the black masses, his doctrine of the Guiding Hundredth was almost the complete opposite: revolutionary, col-lectively led by radical workers and insurgent intellectual-activists, and ut-terly concerned with the black masses. However, his emphasis on economics ultimately gave way to a discussion of character and service. It was no longer enough for the Talented Tenth to be talented, quipped Du Bois; they also had to be willing and able to struggle, sacrifice, and serve in the best interests of the black masses. Du Bois, then, charged the new Talented Tenth, his Guiding Hundredth, with the task of providing "self-sacrificing," "unselfish, farseeing" leadership through its "honesty of character and purity of motive" (p. 173). He criticized his 1903 articulation of the Talented Tenth thesis, observing that it "put in control and power, a group of selfish, self-indulgent, well-to-do men, whose basic interest in solving the Negro Problem was [purely] personal" (p. 162). Du Bois was upset with himself for not clarifying the central elements of the Talented Tenth thesis and, therefore, leaving his thought open to aristocratic interpretations and charges of intellectual elitism.

In his "youth and idealism," and perhaps in his desire to derail Washington's Tuskegee Machine as quickly as possible, Du Bois's Talented Tenth theory downplayed the black bourgeoisie's social strength, political power and, most of all, cultural confusion. As more members of the black middle class earned entry into mainstream America, their views and values were Americanized, undergoing a process of deracination and deradicalization, in which they (re)aligned themselves with the white middle class, as opposed to assisting, à la Du Bois's Talented Tenth theory, the black masses and working classes in their social development. "Immediately," Du Bois observed, "this posed a paradox." He continued:

> Those Negroes who had long trained themselves for personal success and individual freedom, were coming to regard the disappearance of segregation as an end and not a means. They wanted to be Americans, and they did not care so much what kind of folk Americans were, as for the right to be one of them. They not only, did not want to fight for a Negro culture, they even denied the possibility of any such animal, certainly its desirability even if it could be made to exist. The leaders, then, of my Talented Tenth over the mass of young colored men and women, college-trained and entering their careers, faced rejection and disappearance of the Negro, both as a race and as a culture. (p. 164)

With the disappearance and/or death of his Talented Tenth, Du Bois ventured once again to develop a leadership theory. This time he placed more emphasis on cultural grounding, the political economy of racism, the critique of capitalism, and the need for collective leadership, cutting across caste and class, and critical of bourgeois views and values. Du Bois was calling for "a new Talented Tenth," one that actually was not a Talented Tenth at all, but a "Guiding Hundredth." He had made a major mistake with his 1903 Talented Tenth theory and lived long enough to not simply see the error in his early thought, but to critique and offer correctives to it. With a solemn sense of self-reproach, he earnestly admitted:

> It is clear that in 1900, American Negroes were an inferior caste, were frequently lynched and mobbed, widely disfranchised, and usually segregated in the main areas of life. As student and worker at the time, I looked upon them and saw salvation through intelligent leadership, as I said, through a "Talented Tenth." And for this intelligence, I argued, we needed college-trained men. Therefore, I stressed college and higher training. For these men with their college training, there would be needed thorough understanding of the mass of Negroes and their problems; and, therefore, I emphasized scientific study. Willingness to work and make personal sacrifice for solving these problems was of course, the first prerequisite and *sine qua non*. I did not stress this, I assumed it. (pp. 160–61)

He continued:

> When I came out of college into the world of work, I realized that it was quite possible that my plan of training a Talented Tenth might put in control and power, a group of selfish, self-indulgent, well-to-do men, whose basic interest in solving the Negro Problem was personal; personal freedom and unhampered enjoyment and use of the world, without any real care, or certainly no arousing care, as to what became of the mass of American Negroes, or of the mass of any people. My Talented Tenth, I could see, might result in a sort of interracial free-for-all, with the devil taking the hindmost and the foremost taking anything they could lay hands on. (p. 162)

At this point in his life, Du Bois's "youth and idealism" were long gone and, therefore, no longer obscured his understanding of how egoistical, self-indulgent, and aristocratic academically trained African American leaders could be. To combat and correct the aristocratic impulse in African American leadership, he turned to the "revolutionary thought" of "great moral leaders," "prophets and reformers," who in "former ages" asked "charity for the poor and sympathy for the ignorant and sick" (p. 162). Of the "prophets and reformers," he found the philosophy of Karl Marx most useful for the reconstruction and radicalization of African American leadership and liberation movements, reminding his audience that it was Marx who pointed out that "the poor need not always be with us, and that all men could and should be free from poverty" (p. 162).

In his embrace of Marx and Marxism, Du Bois was led to broaden the base of his black leadership paradigm, highlighting class struggles, labor struggles, and political economy as they pertain to African Americans, and persons of African origin and descent worldwide. The old Talented Tenth philosopher-kings/

queens were replaced by anti-racist labor leaders, organic intellectual workers, and revolutionary theorist-activists, who, as Du Bois put it, understood
that "industry should be controlled by the state, and planned by science and
that all goods should be owned and distributed in such ways as result in the
greatest good to all. All persons should be educated according to ability and
should labor according to efficiency. Health and housing, social security, fa-
cilities for recreation and for human intercourse should be public responsibilities" (p. 167).

In the final analysis, it all came down to a question of character. In the Talented Tenth thesis, Du Bois emphasized education and economics, but neglected to connect them to personal character, social ethics, and a need to collectively embrace altruism and sacrifice. The Guiding Hundredth thesis,
however, was careful to couple black educational and economic needs with
an emphasis on social ethics, moral leadership, and the necessity of collective
sacrifice and struggle. In directly discussing the shift of focus in his leadership and liberation thought, Du Bois declared,

> In this reorientation of my ideas, my pointing out the new knowledge necessary
> for leadership and new ideas of race and culture, there still remains that funda-
> mental and basic requirement of character for any successful leadership toward
> great ideals. Even if the ideals are clearly perceived, honesty of character and
> purity of motive is needed without which no effort succeeds or deserves to suc-
> ceed. . . . We cannot have perfection. We have few saints. But we must have hon-
> est men or we die. We must have unselfish, far-seeing leadership or we fail. (p.
> 173)

The new black leaders, the Guiding Hundredth, had to be moral leaders as
well as social and political leaders. What is more, they were charged with the
task of sidestepping the conventional elitism and the vulgarities of vanguardism often associated with leadership cadres, Du Bois's bygone Talented
Tenth notwithstanding. With his "reexamined and restated theory of the 'Talented Tenth'," Du Bois conceived of the Guiding Hundredth as a dedicated
group of leaders from any and/or all classes of African Americans (and other
continental and diasporan Africans) devoted to revolutionary democratic socialist group leadership and anti-racist and revolutionary humanist social
change. This means, then, that his 1903 Talented Tenth thesis served more as
a stepping-stone theory than a full-blown and finished social program.

Du Bois developed the Talented Tenth thesis to speak to the specific social
and political problems confronting African Americans at the turn of the twentieth century. White supremacy and Booker T. Washington's acquiescence to
anti-black racism and industrial capitalism were the major targets of Du
Bois's original Talented Tenth thesis. With Washington dead by three decades

and his Tuskegee Machine dismantled, and with a host of new social and political problems confronting, not simply black America but the Pan-African world, Du Bois critically returned to his leadership and liberation thought. The Guiding Hundredth theory registers, therefore, as a mid-century critical update, expansion, and internationalization of the Talented Tenth thesis that, though often overlooked, symbolizes an important development in Du Bois's social and political philosophy, critical educational theory, and leadership and liberation thought. Over the sweep of half a century Du Bois theorized black leadership and liberation, his thought—to shamelessly borrow from Joy James (1997)—constantly "transcending the Talented Tenth."

Du Bois's dialectic, as we have witnessed throughout this chapter, knew no bounds and he was not afraid to turn his critical attention to not simply the anti-black racism of both white capitalists and white Marxists, but the theoretical inconsistencies and conservative ideologies of the black bourgeoisie and academically trained blacks. His critiques of black educational thought, black conservatism (à la Washingtonian accommodationism), and black leadership and liberation thought are complimented by his hard-hitting critique of black religious thought. Though rarely discussed, Du Bois put forward some of the most severe, albeit constructive, criticisms of black religion in the history of religious studies. Here, as with his critical thought on other topics, he passionately danced with the dialectic, bringing it to bear on Africana religious history and culture. What was Du Bois's philosophy of religion? What were his critical views on the black church and black preachers? How and what does his critical religious thought contribute to Africana Studies and the reconstruction of critical theory of contemporary society? It is to these questions that we now turn.

NOTES

1. The Du Bois–Washington debate was an important episode in African American intellectual history and, therefore, has been written about extensively. Such being the case, I have been selective in choosing the sources in which to develop my interpretation, an interpretation that engages this intellectual event for its import to Du Bois studies and the reconstruction of critical theory of contemporary society. Among the most noteworthy works I have relied on are the following: Alridge (2008), Aptheker (1949), Boxill (1997a), Bridges (1973), Frantz (1997), Freedman (1975), Greco (1984), T.E. Harris (1993), Hwang (1988), A. Johnson (1976), Kilson (2000b), McGuire (1974), Meier (1954), J.M. Moore (2003), W.J. Moses (2004), Mtima (1999), Payne (1973), Pugh (1974), Reedom (1977), Wintz (1996), and J.M. Wortham (1997).

2. For a critical discussion of the Du Bois–Washington debate from an historical perspective, see Jacqueline Moore's excellent *Booker T. Washington, W.E.B. Du Bois, and the Struggle for Racial Uplift* (2003). And, for a critical discussion of the debate from an educational perspective, see Derrick Alridge's ground-breaking *The Educational Thought of W.E.B. Du Bois: An Intellectual History* (2008).

3. My interpretation of Booker T. Washington has undoubtedly been influenced by the seminal work of Louis Harlan (1972, 1982, 1983, 1988), as well as Harlan and Smock (1972–1989). Harlan's eruditious and sensitive readings of his subject have endeared Washington to several generations of black intellectuals, who more than likely would have left Washington and his legacy in the historical waste bin.

4. Concerning the claim that Washington was the quintessential African American conservative, Harlan (1982) hits the issue head-on with words that are worthy of quotation:

> Washington was conservative by just about any measure. Though he flourished in the Progressive Era it was not he, but his opponents who were the men of good hope, full of reform proposals and faith in the common man. Washington's vision of the common man included the southern poor white full of rancor against blacks, the foreign-born anarchist ready to pull down the temple of American business, and the black sharecropper unqualified by education or economic freedom for the ballot. Though Washington opposed the grandfather clause and every southern device to exclude the black man from voting solely on account of his color, Washington did not favor universal suffrage. He believed in literacy and property tests, fairly enforced. He was no democrat. And he did not believe in woman suffrage, either. (p. 11)

Clearly, then, those who claim that Washington was a conservative are not simply complaining about his heavy-handed and narrow-minded emphasis on industrial education and plethora of accommodationist social programs, but pointing to something that transcends a mere ideological dispute, or a battle over which strategies and tactics are best suited for immediate and long-term black social development. Washington was a conservative through and through and, therefore, was criticized on account of his conservatism during an era which demanded radicalism.

5. On the origins of the concept of "the Talented Tenth" and Du Bois's essay by that name, see E.B. Higginbotham (1993) and D.L. Lewis (1993), and for critiques of Du Bois's use of the concept and his essay, see Broderick (1959), Bulmer (1995), Cain (1993), Carter (1998), DeMarco (1983), Dennis (1977, 1996a), W.A. Drake (1985), Drummer (1995), Gates and West (1996), Gatewood (1994), Green (1977), J.A. James (1997, 2000), Killian (1999), Kilson (2000b), Marable (1986), Meier (1959, 1963), A.L. Reed (1997), Rudwick (1956, 1960a, 1968, 1982a), E.C. Smith (1975), Travis (1996), Tyner (1997), and Zamir (1994, 1995).

6. For a more detailed discussion of Du Bois's complicated and often contradictory gender politics, anti-sexism, and, what Beverly Guy-Sheftall (1990, p. 13) has called, his "male-feminism," see my essays, "W.E.B. Du Bois and 'The Damnation of Women': An Essay on Africana Anti-Sexist Critical Social Theory" and "The Souls of Black Female Folk: W.E.B. Du Bois and Africana Anti-Sexist Critical Social Theory" (Rabaka, 2003d, 2004).

7. Du Bois's most elaborate explication of his "nation within a nation" thesis was put forward in his often overlooked 1935 conceptual gem, "A Negro Nation Within the Nation" (see Du Bois, 1995a, pp. 563–70; see also Rucker, 2002). In contrast to Henry Morehouse's Talented Tenth, Du Bois's Talented Tenth, as the aforementioned essay illustrates, and as Walter Rucker (2002) points out, were envisioned to be committed to black nationalism and revolutionary Pan-Africanism, among other race-specific political programs and social movements, at least until white Americans and the wider white world conscientiously committed themselves to critical multiculturalism, authentic anti-racism, and radical democratic socialism.

8. The acclaimed African American historian Wilson Jeremiah Moses (1978) argues that "Du Bois was anti-capitalist long before he was a socialist," and that it should be borne in mind that Du Bois "became a socialist by gradual stages" (p. 138). In "The Social Training of the Negro" (1901), Du Bois (1982a) prefigured his Talented Tenth thesis and later turn toward radical democratic socialism by emphasizing that "the strong talented characters of the race" should be "given careful thorough training in what the world agrees to be its best culture," and the "best" of the world's culture should be used by "the strong talented characters of the race" for black social development (p. 127). He continued,

> Negroes must do this work themselves, they must solve their own social problems as other nations have before. They may and must receive some outside aid, especially economic, but the main moral burden they must bear themselves. One thing however the Negro may demand as his right and that is the benefit of the experience of the nineteenth century, the benefit of the experience and thought of all those ages of research and culture which have made the world richer, healthier, wiser and better. And is not this information and the ability to use it the very essence of Higher Education? (p. 128)

The same year he published "The Talented Tenth," Du Bois penned and published two equally important essays, "Possibilities of the Negro: The Advance Guard of the Race," and "The Training of Negroes for Social Power," which illustrate his evolving leadership and liberation thought, and how that thought encouraged educated African Americans to selflessly use their training in the service of the "nation within a nation" (see Du Bois, 1982a). Clearly by 1903 Du Bois had not developed a sophisticated or systematic critique of capitalism (or the black bourgeoisie), but by strongly stressing that African American intellectuals and professionals should place their knowledge and expertise in the service of the wider black world, cutting across class and extending well beyond the United States' borders, he seemed to be promoting not only black self-determination and black self-reliance, but also putting forward an early paradigm for the very kind of cooperative economics and Pan-African socialism he would embrace a quarter of a century later (Contee, 1969a, 1969b, 1971, 1972; Pobi-Asamani, 1993; Rabaka, 2003e, 2005a; A.L. Reed, 1975; Romero, 1976).

9. It was the biting analysis of the acclaimed African American sociologist E. Franklin Frazier in his classic *The Black Bourgeoisie* (1962) that has enabled successive generations of blacks, as well as whites and other non-whites, to witness the wicked world of the black middle class. However, this work was not available to Du

Bois when he was developing his theory of the Talented Tenth or the Guiding Hundredth. Suffice to say that Frazier's research, and the wide range of work on the black middle class that has followed in its wake, points once again to the prescient intellectual-activist and radical political program that Du Bois was developing in his later years. For further discussion, see Frazier (1939, 1949, 1951, 1957, 1962, 1968, 1974, 1998), J.S. Holloway (2002), Platt (1991), and Teele (2002). And, for more on the developing discourse on the black middle class, see A.S. Barnes (1985), Bowser (2007), S.M. Collins (1997), M.E. Dyson (2005), Jewell (2007), K.R. Lacy (2007), Landry (1987), Pattillo-McCoy (2000), Summers (2004), and Tye (2004),

10. Du Bois penned several pieces that directly dealt with his personal political history and intellectual biography during his later years, among the more noteworthy efforts are: "From McKinley to Wallace: My Fifty Years as an Independent," "I Won't Vote," "A Vista of Ninety Fruitful Years," "A Negro Student at Harvard at the End of the Nineteenth Century," and "I Never Dreamed I Would See This Miracle." See Du Bois 1982d and 1986h. Of course, Du Bois's late life major autobiographical works are chock-full of references to his increasingly radical politics and commitment to revolutionary democratic socialism. See *Dusk of Dawn*, *In Battle for Peace*, and *The Autobiography of W.E.B. Du Bois* (Du Bois, 1952, 1968a, 1968b).

Chapter Four

The Prophet of Problems: Du Bois's Philosophy of Religion, Sociology of Religion, Critique of the Black (and White) Church, and Critical Theory of Liberation Theology[1]

May the Lord give us both the honesty and strength to look our own faults squarely in the face and not ever continue to excuse and minimize them, while they grow. Grant us that wide view of ourselves which our neighbors possess, or better the highest view of infinite justice and goodness and efficiency. In that great white light let us see the littleness and narrowness of our souls and the deeds of our days, and then forthwith begin their betterment. Only thus shall we broaden out of the vicious circle of our own admiration into great commendation of God. Amen.

—W.E.B. Du Bois, *Prayers for Dark People*, 19

Du Bois is remembered in terms of his embrace of atheistic communism and his crusade against segregation, but as has been said elsewhere, he was much committed to the use of religion as a means of social organization and as a source of a Pan-African spiritual cohesion. Thus, Du Bois, in important respects, bore a greater resemblance to de Maistre than to Marx, for he was committed to manipulation of religious symbols and institutions to give force and cohesion to the political aspirations of black Americans.

—Wilson Jeremiah Moses, "W.E.B. Du Bois and Antimodernism," 137

Here, then, is the problem of the color line and it is not only the most pressing social question of the modern world; it is an ethical question that confronts every religion and every conscience.

—W.E.B. Du Bois, *Du Bois on Religion*, 174

119

INTRODUCTION: TOWARD A CRITICAL THEORY OF
AFRICANA SPIRITUALITY AND RELIGION

While W.E.B. Du Bois's pioneering work as a historian, sociologist, political scientist, and race theorist has been heavily lauded and heatedly debated over the ensuing decades since his death, few theorists, and especially *critical* theorists, have sought to connect his wide-ranging anti-racism with his unrepentant criticisms of religion. Du Bois had a life-long, critical, and often contradictory relationship with religion, and particularly religion as it has historically been used or, rather, abused for Eurocentric-ideological-imperial purposes. His writings reveal a distinct Africana history, culture, philosophy, and struggle-informed perspective on religion that simultaneously accents the advances it has inspired, and highlights the hurt and harm it has caused throughout human history. Du Bois's approach to religion was rarely one that could be quickly or easily quarantined to traditional religious studies because of his *transdisciplinarity* and consistent emphasis on race, gender, class, and caste issues within the realm of religion. The emphasis on secular issues within the sacred world of religion led Du Bois to develop a distinct style of critical religious thought that paid more attention to the earthly deeds than the ethereal words of a religious tradition, institution, or adherent. This shift of focus, along with his disaffection for any specific religious denomination, gave Du Bois enormous insight into the ways in which religion has been and continues to be (ab)used in the interest of Eurocentric-ideological-imperial domination and discrimination.

Often Du Bois's writings on religion reveal as much about the political economy of race and racism as they do about the tenets of the religious tradition in question. He was apparently more preoccupied with, to use his words, "the problem of race and religion" than the problem of religion in any pure or narrow-minded sense (Du Bois, 2000b, p. 199). In fact, as many of his major studies in this area demonstrate, religion and racism have long been inextricable in the modern moment, and some of his work in this vein supports a similar claim with regard to religion and sexism.[2]

Recently religion has been conceived of as a site of and source for liberation, with religious studies scholars calling for a *theology of liberation* or *liberation theology* (see Berryman, 1987; Boff and Boff, 1987; Cone, 1970; Gutierrez, 1988; Segundo, 1976; C. Smith, 1991). Liberation theology is theology deeply rooted in lived experience and anti-imperial social and political praxis. It is primarily concerned with relating religion (usually some form of Christianity) to poor, poverty-stricken and oppressed peoples' social and political problems, those persons that liberation theologians call "the least of Christ's brothers and sisters" (Rowland, 1999, p. 3). Liberation theology is highly critical of the scholasticism of traditional Christian theology and seeks to make the words and deeds of Jesus Christ more accessible to the poor masses and working classes of the world, especially the so-called "Third World." It enables and encourages poor and marginalized masses to relate their suffering and social misery to Christ's suffering, crucifixion, and resurrection. According to liberation theologians, Christ always communed with the most needy and vulnerable (i.e., "the masses"), therefore, Christ's "presence is hidden in the poor," and it is the poor who have a special lesson to teach church leaders and not simply vice versa (p. 12).

Like liberation theology, Africana religious thought is primarily preoccupied with liberating the lives of the poor and dispossessed. But, unlike liberation theology, Africana religious thought has since its inception dialogued deeply with indigenous (dare I say "pre-colonial") African religious traditions and spirituality, and contained a critical anti-racist and anti-colonial component that has consistently problematized, if not downright dialecticized religion as a realm of potential good or bad (see L.E. Barrett, 1974; H.H. Mitchell, 1975; Muzorewa, 1985; G.E. Simpson, 1978). Religion has never and does not now guarantee Good or that God's will will be done. And, it is this conundrum, coupled with the contradictions of combining racism and religion for imperial intentions, that lies at the heart of Africana religious thought (see Cone, 1970; W.R. Jones, 1973; West and Glaude, 2003; Wilmore, 1983).

As early texts attest—texts such as Robert Alexander Young's *The Ethiopian Manifesto*, David Walker's *An Appeal in Four Articles*, Maria Stewart's *Meditations From the Pen of Mrs. Maria Stewart*, Frederick Douglass's *Narrative of the Life of Frederick Douglass*, Edward Blyden's *Christianity, Islam and the Negro Race*, and numerous others—Africana theorists have constantly criticized the (ab)use of religion for the purposes of domination and discrimination (Blyden, 1994; Douglass, 1994b; M.W. Stewart, 1987b; D. Walker, 1993; R.A. Young, 1996). This is to say that Africana theorists have long developed a habit of viewing religion dialectically—that is, simultaneously as *both* a site of spiritual liberation *and* a source of social domination. Though often overlooked Du Bois greatly contributed to this tradition, and his writings on religion may be regarded as an effort to deepen and develop a *critical theory of Africana spirituality and religion.*

This chapter, therefore, will explore Du Bois's dialectical discourse on spirituality and religion. It argues that his religious thought—being distinguished by its emphasis on Africana religiosity and spirituality, the relationship between and the political economy of religion and racism, and the ways oppressing and oppressed people use and/or abuse religion either as a form of social pacification or social protest—simultaneously deconstructs and reconstructs the conventional analytical categories of philosophy of religion, sociology of religion, and liberation theology. Du Bois's work in this area makes a profound contribution to contemporary critical theory insofar as it provides a paradigm that enables us to critique the ideological elements of religion while simultaneously accenting its more emancipatory aspects. His religious thought, like his critical social theory in general, is shown to be self-reflexive, constantly exhibiting the ability to revise and refine itself and, as a result, is remarkably relevant for contemporary religious criticism.

DU BOIS'S PHILOSOPHY OF RELIGION

In "W.E.B. Du Bois and Religion," Herbert Aptheker (1982) argues that "while Du Bois was an agnostic in his last years, he never was an atheist. Though the record shows a diminution as time passed in the confidence with which he held some religious concepts . . . he never quite rejected a belief in some creative and persistent force" (p. 5). Moreover, Manning Marable (1998) maintains, "Du Bois was simultaneously an agnostic and an Anglican, a staunch critic of religious dogma and a passionate convert to the black version of Christianity. His belief in his people was expressed in his own black faith for the world" (p. 60). As a child, Du Bois enjoyed church and, according to Aptheker (1982), "Outside of his school his major contact with the people of his town was through church" (p. 6). Du Bois (1968a) and he and his mother, Mary Silvina, "were the only colored communicants" of the Congregational church of his childhood, and he writes that his mother had "many acquaintances there" and that "the minister, Scudder, was especially friendly" (p. 88). In fact, in *The Autobiography of W.E.B. Du Bois*, he goes so far as to say, "I felt absolutely no discrimination, and I do not think there was any, or any thought" (p. 89). It was in the context of this thoroughly New England, though "especially friendly," congregation that Du Bois received most of his early religious training. However, as he pointed out a little later, "while I was in high school, the colored folk of the town, mostly newcomers . . . organized a small branch of the A.M.E. [African Methodist Episcopal] Zion church," which "we used to attend" from time to time (p. 90).

He fondly remembered the annual church festivals, its Sunday school, instruction in Hebrew and Greek, and the Sunday sermons. Arnold Rampersad (1990) has remarked that the foundation of Du Bois's "moral fervor was the iron of Puritan Ethics, initially instilled in him in the First Congregational Church of Great Barrington" (p. 5). The Congregationalism of Du Bois's boyhood was "deeply orthodox" and "[i]n its doctrine, if not its style, it reflected [a] severe Calvinism," with all its "seriousness and combativeness" (p. 5). It is important to observe with Rampersad that "[e]ven though Du Bois later scorned organized religion, these early Great Barrington years probably had a lasting impact on him and on the nebula of philosophic speculation surrounding his views of mankind" (p. 5). However, it should also be held in mind that even from an early age Du Bois exhibited a critical disposition toward religion and was an extremely independent ecumenical thinker.[3] Much later in his life he maintained,

> I have seen miracles in my life. As a boy we did not have the possibility of miracles emphasized in our schools. In the weekly Sunday School, we studied the bible with its tales of the impossible but I remember distinctly that I questioned the validity of some of them, like that story of Jonah. (Du Bois, 1968a, p. 413)

Throughout his long life Du Bois drew from his strict religious rearing, peppering his writings with religious themes, religious metaphors, and references to God (see Blum, 2007; Forney, 2002; Kahn, 2003; Marable, 1998). Though he was extremely critical of Christianity, he did not hesitate to use it to combat an unjust issue, provocatively explain a point, or ethically ground an argument. He had a peculiar predilection for religion, as the religiosity and profound spirituality of even his earliest writings reveal, and it was a constant source of both personal and professional inspiration and frustration.[4] Many of his religious writings harbor an autobiographical element, and are marked by a deep personal commitment to aligning the gentle words of Jesus with the deeds of those who claim to follow in his faithful footsteps. Moreover, Du Bois's religious writings are not immune to moral outrage and often display the critical questioning that ultimately became the cornerstone of his corpus. In "A Litany of Atlanta," for example, written in the aftermath of the 1906 Atlanta pogrom, he thundered,

> We are not better than our fellows. Lord, we are but weak and human men. When our devils do deviltry, curse Thou the doer and the deed—curse them as we curse them, do to them all and more than ever they have done to innocence and weakness, to womanhood and home.
> *Have mercy upon us, miserable sinners!*
> And yet, whose is the deeper guilt? Who made these devils? Who nursed them in crime and fed them on injustice? Who ravished and debauched their mothers and their grandmothers? Who bought and sold their crime and waxed fat and rich on public iniquity?
> *Thou knowest, good God!* (Du Bois, 2000b, p. 65, original emphasis)[5]

Du Bois (1997d) consistently affirmed his belief in "a vague Force which, in some uncomprehensible way, dominates all life and change" (p. 223). However, he was quick to correct anyone who might attempt to ascribe his beliefs—his liberation theology, if you will—to a specific organized religion or religious denomination (Blum, 2007; D.L. Lewis, 1993; Marable, 1986). Perhaps the epitome of a heretic in the eyes of "good," God-fearing, church-going folk, he began his "Credo" with the somber words "I believe in God," and then reposefully went on to announce,

> I believe in the Devil and his angels, who wantonly work to narrow the oppor-tunity of struggling human beings, especially if they be black; who spit in the faces of the fallen, strike them that cannot strike again, believe the worst and work to prove it, hating the image which their Master stamped on a brother's soul. (Du Bois, 1969a, p. 3)[6]

What bothered Du Bois (1968a) most was religious hypocrisy or, in his words, "religious lies" (p. 412). He quite simply had no tolerance for the abuse of religion, or for those who used religion as a tool to oppress or pacify. As Aptheker (1980), a personal friend of Du Bois and his literary executor, observed, "Du Bois's honesty was fierce" and "no one dared impugn his in-tegrity" (p. x). Therefore, when he found fault with a religious tradition (mostly Christianity, since it was the dominant religion of the United States during his lifetime), Du Bois was merely demanding an honesty and level of integrity from it, its leaders, and its adherents which he himself lived by. He consistently contended that religion was being used systematically to deceive, particularly the poor and children, thus socializing them to accept the lies and larceny of those in (Eurocentric-ideological-imperial) authority. His remarks are worth recollecting here at length:

> [T]he Soviet Union does not allow any church of any kind to interfere with ed-ucation, and religion is not taught in the public schools. It seems to me that this is the greatest gift of the Russian Revolution to the modern world. Most edu-cated modern men no longer believe in religious dogma. If questioned they will usually resort to double-talk before admitting the fact. But who today actually believes that this world is ruled and directed by a benevolent person of great power who, on humble appeal, will change the course of events at our request? Who believes in miracles? Many folk follow religious ceremonies and services; and allow their children to learn fairy tales and so-called religious truth, which in time the children come to recognize as conventional lies told by their parents and teachers for the children's good. One can hardly exaggerate the moral dis-aster of this custom. We have to thank the Soviet Union for the courage to stop it. (Du Bois, 1968a, p. 42)

And, continuing in the same vein, Du Bois stated,

> It is our great debt to the Soviet Union that it alone of nations dared stop that ly-ing to children which so long disgraced our schools. We filled little minds with

fairy tales of religious dogma which we ourselves never believed. We filled their thoughts with pictures of barbarous revenge called God which contradicted all their inner sense of decency. We repeated folk tales of children without fathers, of death which was life, of sacrifice which was shrewd investment and ridiculous pictures of an endless future. The Soviets have stopped this. They allow a child to grow up without religious lies and with mature mind make his own decision about the world without scaring him into Hell or rewarding him with a silly Heaven. (p. 412)

Du Bois's relationship with religion changed dramatically throughout his life, and where in his youth he was more or less quite content with the teachings of Jesus Christ, in adulthood he came to not only question its basic tenets, but many of the more mischievous people who claimed to be Christians. His was a complex and seemingly contradictory relationship with religion, one that went from earnestly affirming his faith in God, Jesus, and the redemption of "miserable sinners," to leveling some of the staunchest criticisms of Christianity, and religion in general, in modern memory—one need not mention his previously cited passionate praise of the Soviet Union's antireligion public policies. What is more, his many autobiographical writings are chock-full of discussions of his religious development and, therefore, attest to the importance of religion in his critical universe and corroborate the accuracy of the foregoing claims.

In his five major autobiographical works, *The Souls of Black Folk*, *Darkwater*, *Dusk of Dawn*, *In Battle for Peace*, and *The Autobiography of W.E.B. Du Bois*, Du Bois details his consecutive withdrawal and final cleavage from religion. Arriving for study at Fisk University, he reports that he almost immediately joined the campus Congregational church, eagerly "volunteering to teach Sunday school" (D.L. Lewis, 1993, p. 65). After settling into college life he penned a letter to his former congregation back in Great Barrington, in which he was proud to announce that "I am glad to tell you that I have united with the Church here and hope that the prayers of my Sunday School may help guide me in the path of Christian duty" (Du Bois 1968a, p. 110). However, his fellowship with the Congregational church at Fisk was fleeting, as he soon "became critical of religion and resentful of its practice" (Du Bois, 1968b, p. 33). What prompted the change in Du Bois's religious outlook? What could have possibly happened at Fisk, an African American *religious* university, to make him resent the very practice of religion? According to award-winning Du Bois biographer, David Levering Lewis (1993), the "course of events defies clear reconstruction" and, to make matters worse, Du Bois himself "never got the story quite straight," recollecting it differently in each of his autobiographical works (p. 65). What does seem certain, though, is that Du Bois's disdain for organized religion grew out of, believe it or not,

a controversy concerning dancing. In his last autobiography he candidly re-
called that

> "Pop" Miller did not allow my church membership to progress as placidly as I
> planned. He was an official of the church and a fundamentalist in religion. He
> soon had me and others accused before the church for dancing. I was astonished.
> I had danced all my life quite as naturally as I sang and ran. In Great Barrington
> there was little chance to dance on the part of anyone but in the small group of
> colored folk there was always some dancing along with playing games at
> homes. When I came South and was among my own young folk who not only
> danced but danced beautifully and with effortless joy, I joined and learned ea-
> gerly. I never attended public dance halls, but at the homes of colored friends in
> the city, we nearly always danced and a more innocent pastime I could not imag-
> ine. But Miller was outraged. What kind of dancing he was acquainted with I do
> not know, but at any rate in his mind dancing figured as a particularly heinous
> form of sin. I resented this and said so in very plain terms. The teachers inter-
> vened and tried to reconcile matters in a way which for years afterward made
> me resentful and led to my eventual refusal to join a religious organization. They
> admitted that my dancing might well be quite innocent, but said that my exam-
> ple might lead others astray. They quoted Paul: "If meat maketh my brothers to
> offend, I will eat no meat while the world standeth." I tried to accept this for
> years, and for years I wrestled with this problem. Then I resented this kind of
> sophistry. I began again to dance and I have never since had much respect for
> Paul. (Du Bois, 1968a, pp. 110–11)

Falsely accused of heresy, the young, popular black New Englander ("my
popularity rather went to my head") was surrounded by Southern sophists,
and where Fisk gave him his first exposure to "the South[,] the South of slavery, rebellion and black folk," and to "the scientific attitude," it also offered
him an acute awareness of the dormant dogma and ideological aspects of religion (Du Bois, 1968a, pp. 105–09, 1968b, p. 50). Du Bois had long held religion in high esteem, and now, in his first year at Fisk, in the motherless and
fatherless lad's newfound Southern home away from home, he was compelled to question his religious foundation. His religious questioning continued at Harvard and, as he noted in *Dusk of Dawn*, it did not wane when he
went to Germany to study at the University of Berlin, where he "turned still
further from religious dogma" (Du Bois, 1968b, p. 50). In his final autobiography Du Bois (1968a) paints a picture of himself as a constant critic of religion and narrates a rather nuanced ecumenical adventure:

> My religious development has been slow and uncertain. I grew up in a liberal
> Congregational Sunday School and listened once a week to a sermon on doing
> good as a reasonable duty. Theology played a minor part and our teachers had

to face some searching questions. At 17 I was in a missionary college where religious orthodoxy was stressed; but I was more developed to meet it with argument, which I did. My "morals" were sound, even a bit puritanic, but when a hidebound old deacon inveighed against dancing I rebelled. By the time of graduation I was still a "believer" in orthodox religion, but had strong questions which were encouraged at Harvard. In Germany I became a freethinker and when I came to teach at an orthodox Methodist Negro school I was soon regarded with suspicion, especially when I refused to lead the students in public prayer. When I became head of a department at Atlanta, the engagement was held up because again I balked at leading in prayer, but the liberal president let me substitute the Episcopal prayer book on most occasions. Later I improvised prayers [*Prayers for Dark People*] on my own. . . . From my 30th year on I have increasingly regarded the church as an institution which defended such evils as slavery, color caste, exploitation of labor and war. I think the greatest gift of the Soviet Union to modern civilization was the dethronement of the clergy and the refusal to let religion be taught in the public schools. (p. 285; see also Du Bois, 1980c)

For Du Bois, part of the problem of religion was the fact that it was being used as a tool for social pacification and to suppress forces for radical democratic socialist change. Throughout its long history religion has been contracted to uphold "such evils as slavery, color caste, exploitation of labor and war" and, we should add, the oppression of women and hatred of homosexuals. He was not against religion, but against the way many of its adherents interpreted or, rather, misinterpreted it for imperial purposes. In all of his religious questioning, including his increasingly radical criticisms of religion at the end of his life, Du Bois maintained an unfeigned and heartfelt belief in God (see Aptheker, 1980, 1982; Blum, 2007; Forney, 2002; Kahn, 2003; Marable, 1986, 1998).

It may be difficult for many of the more religious to digest, but the fact of the matter is, *God did not create religion.* God created human beings who in turn created religion but, I should reiterate, God did not create religion. Therefore, Du Bois felt no ethical obligation to follow the worldly whims and wishes of so-called religious leaders or institutions, especially when these leaders and institutions did not live by their own sacred texts and tenets. In one of the most significant summaries of Du Bois's (anti- and/or critical) religious development during his collegiate years, Du Bois biographer Arnold Rampersad (1990) has tellingly written,

The omniscient God of Du Bois's Congregational youth was slowly but surely displaced by the Unknowable of Herbert Spencer. Paradoxically, the search for truth was also the gospel of those who acknowledged this unknowable. For them, man scrutinized the universe unclouded by religious dogma: secular learning was religion enough. To those faithful to the old God, the new learning led almost inevitably to amorality and eventually to fatalism. As in his religion, so in his formal education, Du Bois would make a significant but unsteady transition between the old and new orders. (pp. 19–20)

Plowing his own spiritual path through the realm of religion, Du Bois brought his increasingly dialectical thought to bear on religious leaders, institutions, and practices.[7] He was particularly perplexed by the imperial aspects of modern religion, yet seemed to hold out a silent hope that it could be contracted not simply for personal salvation but for black liberation and radical democratic socialist transformation as well.[8] No matter what his personal views concerning religion, the dogged social scientist Du Bois never lost sight of the fact that the African American church, as he marveled in *The Philadelphia Negro*, "is by long odds the vastest and most remarkable product of American Negro civilization" (1996b, p. 21). In fact, for Du Bois, the African American church is distinguished not so much for the sacred communion it provided blacks, but for the educational initiatives, social services, and political power it bequeathed to successive struggling generations of black folk. Thus, the irreligious Du Bois undertook several systematic studies of religion. These studies focused more on the secular impact and role religion played in history, culture, politics, and society, and could be loosely characterized as Du Bois's sociology of religion.

DU BOIS'S SOCIOLOGY OF RELIGION

Religion is a recurring theme throughout Du Bois's wide and varied writings, and he has recently been recognized as "the first American sociologist of religion" for his pioneering 1903 volume, *The Negro Church* (see Zuckerman, Barnes and Cady, 2003; see also Blum, 2005a; C. Evans, 2007; Savage, 2000; R.A. Wortham, 2005a, 2005b; Zuckerman, 2002). Though I am generally critical of work that seeks to situate Du Bois within a specific disciplinary matrix, because his writings reveal him to be an unrepentant *transdisciplinary* theorist, I do think it important to engage interpretations of his thought and texts that subtly chronicle how he simultaneously contributed to the social sciences and humanities, broadly speaking. Looking at Du Bois through the lens of sociology of religion opens those scholars who maybe skeptical of my thesis that Du Bois was an important transdisciplinary theorist to the fact that he produced knowledge that not only combined the insights of sociology and religion but also, as we will soon see, generated a new kind of knowledge that cut across these disciplines, creating a new subdiscipline or field of academic inquiry.

The bulk of what Du Bois had to say concerning religion is buried in miscellaneous speeches, magazine articles, newspaper columns, novels, and book chapters. *The Negro Church* was his only book-length work on religion and, though he wrote much of it, it still stands in the end as an edited volume (see Du Bois, 2003). However, there are many additional major sources of Du Bois's sociology of religion, including 1) his autobiographical writings discussed above; 2) chapters from his well-known works, such as *The Philadelphia Negro* and *The Souls of Black Folk*, which specifically address religion; 3) his less popular and little-known texts, such as *The Negro in the South*, *John Brown*, and *The Gift of Black Folk*; 4) his creative writings, including five novels, numerous short stories, poems, and plays, which have been collected in *The Creative Writings of W.E.B. Du Bois*; and 5) his posthumously published volume of prayers, *Prayers for Dark People*, and three volumes of correspondence, *The Correspondence of W.E.B. Du Bois, 1877-1963* (see Du Bois 1962, 1970b, 1982a, 1982b, 1982c, 1982d, 1982e, 1983a, 1983b, 1996b, 1997a, 1997b, 1997c, 1997d; Du Bois and Washington, 1970).

As with Du Bois's philosophy of religion, a major preoccupation of his sociology of religion revolved around the problem(s) of race and racism. Africans were not "black," or assigned the racial designation of "blackness," in a color-blind and politically neutral social world. Far from it—and speaking with words bequeathed by the black existentialists—persons of African descent were "black" and only *became*, or were forced to *be*, "black" in response and in resistance to white-supremacist, anti-black, racist imperialism (Gordon, 1997a, 1997b, 2000a). Du Bois's sociology of religion, therefore, harbors a deep historical dimension, one that charts the changes and challenges of Africana religious thought and practices in traditional Africa, during the African holocaust and enslavement, and in so-called "freedom" (i.e., after the physical enslavement and material colonization of Africans and Africa—if we dare speak of anything after the horrors of holocaust, or as if it is possible to dream of a world in the wake of white-supremacist global imperialism).

Du Bois's sociological treatment of Africana religion fundamentally centers on syncretism—that is, on how enslaved Africans, as Albert Raboteau (1978) observed in *Slave Religion*, fused their traditional religious thought and practices with the Christian theology of their white oppressors (see also D.N. Hopkins, 2000; Hopkins and Cummings, 1991; Pitts 1993; Raboteau, 1995, 1999). It is in the explanation of this protracted sociocultural and historical process that Du Bois distinguishes himself not simply as a sociologist of religion, but also a historian of religion and political theologian. Without a doubt, argued Du Bois, there were white and black Christians, but they were bound together not by religion as much as by theology. In other words, I am hinting here at what Jacquelyn Grant (1989) eloquently argued in *White Women's Christ and Black Women's Jesus*—that is, that blacks and whites may be employing the same religious language and drawing from the same sacred text (the Bible), but their lived experiences, their histories, cultural contexts, and social situations inspire them to draw comparably different conclusions as to the nature and power of God.[9] What Du Bois's work demonstrates is that colonization and enslavement changed Africana people's theology, but it did not in every instance, and certainly it did not completely, destroy their religious thought and practices. This is an insight Du Bois culled from his lived or experiences, sociological observations, and data collection at Fisk, in Philadelphia's black community (under the auspices of the University of Pennsylvania), and at Atlanta University, among other sites, where black Christians practiced, literally, *lived* a wide variety of Africanized versions of Christianity and where, in their daily lives, conscious and unconscious African retentions reigned.[10]

As a historian of religion with strong sociological leanings, Du Bois chronicled, 1) the radical thought and rebellious lives of early African American religious leaders, 2) intra-African American class divisions and how secular distinctions such as these played themselves out in the realm of religion, 3) the dual sacred and secular nature of African American religion and the black church, 4) the conflicts within several white Christian denominations over the issue of whether enslaved Africans could or should be baptized; and, 5) why the white Baptists and Methodists were more successful in sowing the seeds of Christianity in the hearts and minds of the enslaved. Along with these issues, among others, Du Bois strongly stressed that African American religion, particularly as embodied in and flowing out of the black church, was not only "the first distinctively Negro American social institution" but, and most importantly, "the sole surviving social institution of the African fatherland." Religion, he wrote in *The Negro Church*, was the lone social sphere in which enslaved Africans had any agency, and even in this realm they were severely regulated. Du Bois (2000b), writing with a sense of unmitigated awe and critical discovery, declared,

At first sight it would seem that slavery completely destroyed every vestige of spontaneous social movement among Negroes; the home had deteriorated; political authority and economic initiative was in the hands of the masters; property, as a social institution, did not exist on the plantation; and, indeed, it is usually assumed by historians and sociologists that every vestige of internal development disappeared, leaving the slaves no means of expression for their common life, thought, and striving. This is not strictly true; the vast power of the priest in the African state has already been noted; his realm alone—the province of religion and medicine—remained largely unaffected by the plantation system in many important particulars. The Negro priest, therefore, early became an important figure on the plantation and found his function as the interpreter of the supernatural, the comforter of the sorrowing, and as the one who expressed, rudely, but picturesquely, the longing and disappointment and resentment of a stolen people. From such beginnings arose and spread with marvelous rapidity the Negro Church, the first distinctively Negro American social institution. It was not at first by any means a Christian Church, but a mere adaptation of those heathen rites which we roughly designate by the term Obe Worship, or "Voodoism." Association and missionary effort soon gave these rites a veneer of Christianity, and gradually, after two centuries, the Church became Christian, with a simple Calvinistic creed, but with many of the old customs still clinging to the services. It is this historic fact that the Negro Church of today bases itself upon the sole surviving social institution of the African fatherland, that accounts for its extraordinary growth and vitality. . . . This institution, therefore, naturally assumed many functions which the other harshly suppressed social organs had to surrender; the Church become the center of amusements, of what little spontaneous economic activity remained, of education, and of all social intercourse. (p. 113)

African American religion was forged in the fires of abolitionist struggle, and the quest for freedom was not quenched with the bellowing, but weak-willed words of the Emancipation Proclamation. Therefore, Du Bois studied the impact of African American religion, basically the black church, on African American social development and cultural survival post-enslavement. African American religious thought and practices, Du Bois had a hunch, changed during the decades after enslavement because, though they had de jure freedom, blacks were still in a white-supremacist, hyper-racially-ruled social world and did not have de facto freedom. American apartheid thus lingered on, leaving its stench and stain on everyone and everything it came into contact with, even religion (see Du Bois, 1995c; Frederickson, 1981; Massey and Denton, 1993; Shapiro, 1988).

In *The Philadelphia Negro* of 1899, he analyzed a wide-range of African American religious practices that illustrated the dramatic (sacred *and* secular) changes in black church life in the three and a half decades since the issuing of the Emancipation Proclamation. Beginning with the history of the black church, Du Bois then turned his attention to its organizational structures and social functions, and was undoubtedly the first to systematically study and document its political positions, educational initiatives, amusement/entertainment activities, missionary efforts, charitable organizations, insurance societies, and homes for the aged and infirm. He examined congregational economic life, from debts and membership contributions to the value of church properties and the salaries of pastors. Further, Du Bois critically observed how black class divisions within the churches and various denominations played themselves out, causing continuous stratification and discontinuous congregational affiliation. He painstakingly detailed an intricate interrelation of church and/or religion-related social and political programs, and the lingering leitmotif of African retentions, which I have come to think is one of the hallmarks of his work, is ubiquitous. In words that read more like a sorrow-filled sinner testifying in a black church at Sunday morning service, Du Bois (1996b) wrote,

> We often forget that the rise of a church organization among Negroes was a curious phenomenon. The church really represented all that was left of African tribal life, and was the sole expression of the organized efforts of the slaves. It was natural that any movement among freedmen should center about their religious life, the sole remaining element of their former tribal system. . . . The Negro is, to be sure, a religious creature—most primitive folk are—but his rapid and even extraordinary founding of churches is not due to this fact alone, but is rather a measure of his development, an indication of the increasing intricacy of his social life and the consequent multiplication of the organ which is the function of his group life—the church. . . . The Negro church is the peculiar and characteristic product of the transplanted African, and deserves especial study. As a social group the Negro church may be said to have antedated the Negro family on American soil; as such it has preserved, on the one hand, many functions of tribal organization, and on the other hand, many of the family functions. Its tribal functions are shown in its religious activity, its social authority and general guiding and coordinating work; its family functions are shown by the fact that the church is a center of social life and intercourse; acts as newspaper and intelligence bureau, is the center of amusements—indeed, is the world in which the Negro moves and acts. So far-reaching are these functions of the church that its organization is almost political. (pp. 197, 201)

His inexcusable politically incorrect language aside ("The Negro is, to be sure, a religious creature—most primitive folk are")—which demonstrates that even the architect of Africana studies was not immune to internalized racism and the diabolical dialectic of white superiority and black inferiority!—Du Bois accentuated both the social and political functions of the black church.[11] In his estimate, it is "the most remarkable product of American Negro civilization" because "[i]t is a democratic church; a church where the governing power is largely in the hands of the mass of membership" (Du Bois, 1985a, p. 84). The democratic nature of the black church is a recurring theme in Du Bois's writings on religion, especially when he compared it with the white church, because in spite of what he was wont to term its "primitivisms" and "nativisms," yet and still, he stated, "The Negro church is at least democratic. It welcomes everybody. It draws no color line" (Du Bois, 2000b, p. 141). He asserted that the black church is further distinguished because it serves as a multipurpose site for moral instruction, political education, social development, and racial/cultural awareness.

African American women's special role in creating and sustaining the black church was not lost on Du Bois, and they received unprecedented praise from his pen. Radical religious convictions were not simply the cornerstone of individual black women's struggles against various forms of oppression, but they were also at the heart of women's collective efforts to organize African Americans in the interest of social development. In *Darkwater*, Du Bois put forward the oft-noted names of Harriet Tubman and Sojourner Truth, fervently recalling, not merely their profound religiosity, but how their religious beliefs inspired and, perhaps even, invoked their legendary "feminist-abolitionism" (Du Bois, 1969a, pp. 175–77; see also Guy-Sheftall, 1990; Yee, 1992). The organizations that ultimately came to be called "the black women's club movement" all emerged from the religious cultural context of the black church and, it should be duly noted, the National Association of Colored Women (NACW)—that is, the national association of black women's clubs—was "the first truly black national organization that functioned with strength and unity" (Hine and Thompson, 1998, p. 180; see also Collier-Thomas, 1980, 1993; E.L. Davis, 1996; Giddings, 1984; E.B. Higginbotham, 1993; Salem, 1990, 1993; Wesley, 1984; D.G. White, 1999). So powerful and pervasive was the influence of the black women's club movement on Du Bois, when he turned to social organization and radical political activism, he used the black women's club movement as a model, going so far as to name the social organization he helped to found (along with two of the major leaders of the black women's club movement, Ida B. Wells and Mary Church Terrell), the National Association for the Advancement of Colored People (NAACP) (see D.L. Lewis, 1993; Rabaka, 2003d, 2004). In *The Gift of Black Folk* of 1924, he candidly conceded that

we have noted then the Negro woman in America as a worker tending to emancipate all women workers; as a mother nursing the white race and uniting the black and white races; as a conspirator urging forward emancipation in various sorts of ways; and we have finally only to remember that today the women of America who are doing humble but on the whole the most effective work in the social uplift of the lowly, not so much by money as by personal contact, are the colored women. Little is said or known about it but in thousands of churches and social clubs, in missionary societies and fraternal organizations, in unions like the National Association of Colored Women, these workers are founding and sustaining orphanages and old folk homes; distributing personal charity and relief; visiting prisoners; helping hospitals; teaching children; and ministering to all sorts of needs. Their work, as it comes now and then in special cases to the attention of individuals of the white world, forms a splendid bond of encouragement and sympathy, and helps more than most realize in minimizing racial difficulties and encouraging human sympathy. (Du Bois, 1970b, p. 149)

Without a doubt, Du Bois (1969a) declared in *Darkwater*, "[i]t was . . . strong women that laid the foundations of the great Negro church of today, with its five million members and ninety millions of dollars in property" (p. 174; see also Du Bois, 2003; E.B. Higginbotham, 1993; Zuckerman, Barnes and Cady, 2003). He acknowledged the role of "early church mothers," such as Mary Still, in the establishment of the African Methodist Episcopal Church (p. 174). And, he suggested that "such [was the] spiritual ancestry" that spurred Harriet Tubman's legendary efforts to liberate the enslaved, sympathize with John Brown's revolutionary abolitionism, and enlist in the Union Army (p. 174).

In an audacious turn of phrase, Du Bois further accentuated black women's special "spiritual ancestry" by placing the religious and resistance activities of black women on a par with those of black men, going so far as to recall Sojourner Truth's classic query to Frederick Douglass, "Frederick, *is God dead?*," when the male-feminist abolitionist, in a moment of desperation, declared that African Americans would have to fight for their freedom by force of arms. Douglass is reported to have stated, "It must come to blood; they [enslaved Africans] must fight for themselves, and redeem themselves, or it would never be done." Truth was apparently troubled, according to Harriet Beecher Stowe and a host of white writers, by Douglass's radical tenor and questioned his faith in God, who—as Stowe's recounting of the story goes—would guide African Americans to an imminent victory over slavery and white supremacy (Douglass, 1994a, p. 719; Painter, 1996, pp. 160–63). Du Bois (1969a) also acknowledged the work of Kate Ferguson, a nineteen-year-old African American widow, who "took the children of the streets of New York, white and black, into her empty arms, taught them, found them homes" and, most pertinent to the present discussion, "established the first modern Sunday School in Manhattan" (pp. 177–78).

In his writings on religion Du Bois also spoke highly of African American clergy, and often exhibited a great deal of sympathy for their peculiar simultaneous positions as "spiritual guides" and social leaders of their people. For instance, in his chapter on Alexander Crummell and in "Of the Faith of the Fathers," both in *The Souls of Black Folk*, he heartily advanced the following: "The Preacher is the most unique personality developed by the Negro on American soil. A leader, a politician, an orator, a 'boss,' an idealist—all these he is, and ever, too, the center of a group of men" (Du Bois, 1986a, p. 494; see also Du Bois, 1996b, pp. 205–07, 2000b, pp. 21–22, 1982a, pp. 328–29). Black ministers were often misunderstood, he argued, and very few were qualified to criticize them, as there were no serious studies (antedating Du

Bois's) of their dual social and religious roles. In perhaps his earliest essay on religion, "The Problem of Amusement" (originally published in 1897), Du Bois (1978) contended,

> The minister who directs this peculiar and anomalous institution must not be criticized with full knowledge of his difficult role. He is in reality the mayor, the chief magistrate of a community, ruling to be sure, but ruling according to the dictates of a not over-intelligent town council, according to time honored custom and law; and above all, hampered by the necessities of his budget; he may be a spiritual guide, he must be a social organizer, a leader of actual men; he may desire to enrich and reform the spiritual life of his flock, but above all he must have church members; he may desire to revolutionize church methods, to elevate the ideals of the people, to tell the hard, honest truth to a people who need a little more truth and a little less flattery—but how can he do this when the people of this social organism demand that he shall take from the purely spiritual activities of his flock, time to minister to their amusements, diversion, and physical comfort; when he sees the picnic masquerading as a camp-meeting, the revival becoming the social event of the season, the day of worship turned into a day of general reception and dining out, the rival church organizations plunging into debt to furnish their houses of worship with an elegance that far outruns the financial ability of a poverty-stricken people; when the church door becomes the trysting place for all the lovers and Lotharios of the community; when a ceaseless round of entertainments, socials, and necktie parties chase the week through—what minister can be more that most ministers are coming to be, the business managers of a picnic ground? (p. 229)

Finally, with regard to Du Bois's reverence for African American religion, it must be said that he held black church music in especial high esteem. He frequently wrote beamingly and bemusingly of African American religious music, calling it "the most original and beautiful expression of human life and longing yet born on American soil" (1986a, p. 494). And, few scholars of African American religious music, or black music in general, can resist commenting on that hauntingly famous passage from *The Souls of Black Folk* where Du Bois wrote,

> Little of beauty has America given the world save the rude grandeur God himself stamped on her bosom; the human spirit in this new world has expressed itself in vigor and ingenuity rather than in beauty. And so by fateful chance the Negro folk-song—the rhythmic cry of the slave—stands today not simply as the sole American music, but as the most beautiful expression of human experience born this side the seas. It has been neglected, it has been, and is, half despised, and above all it has been persistently mistaken and misunderstood; but notwithstanding, it still remains as the singular spiritual heritage of the nation and the greatest gift of the Negro people. (p. 537)

From the Du Boisian perspective, the black church was the cornerstone of African American culture, and in his studies he traced its connections to the spiritual and broader cultural traditions of Africa, while simultaneously demonstrating the process by which various groups of enslaved Africans became a single people, *African Americans*. In *Slave Culture*, Sterling Stuckey (1987) pointed out that even before enslaved Africans reached the shores of North America, they began to create a new culture, one where traditional "tribalisms" were nothing more than "a lingering memory in the minds of American slaves" (p. 3). People from as far north as Senegal were piled onto people from Namibia and Angola in the south, people from Kenya in the east were sandwiched between Ghanaians and Nigerians from the west, and in their long and horror-filled voyage to the Americas they initiated the protracted and arduous process of creating a new culture. This new culture was primarily one of resistance, but it must be borne in mind that the bulk of this defiance was grounded in and grew out of the enslaved Africans' hark back to the religions and social justice traditions of their ancestors, which, for all of the reasons observed above, are historically embodied in the black church (see Battle, 2006; Billingsley, 1999; Fulop and Raboteau, 1996; Lincoln, 1974; Lincoln and Mamiya, 1990; H.H. Mitchell, 2004; Pinn and Pinn, 2002; Sernett, 1999; T. Walker, 1991; Wilmore, 1989).

For Du Bois, then, the African American church was based as much on African religious thought and practices as it was on European and European American Christian theology, and its contributions to African American culture, both sacred and secular, were not only worthy of religious and social study, but, he believed, provided a paradigm and should be recounted for present and future generations of African Americans and others struggling against oppression. He, therefore, often acknowledged and emphasized what he understood to be the overarching achievements of African American religion, and the black church in specific. In weighted words from one of his classic passages from the pages of *The Crisis*, he sternly stated,

> Before such an organization [the black church] one must bow with respect. It has accomplished much. It has instilled and conserved morals, it has helped family life, it has taught and developed ability and given the colored man his best business training. It has planted in every city and town of the Union, with few exemptions, meeting places for colored folk which vary from shelters to luxurious and beautiful edifices. (Du Bois, 1972b, p. 332)

However, here the Du Boisian dialectic rears its head. One of the many things that distinguish Du Bois's writings on religion is that they expose both the positives and negatives of religion. In other words, his religious thought is deeply dialectical, as with the best of his work. As we have seen above, Du Bois undoubtedly saw a certain value and had a deep and sincere respect for religion. But, by the same token, he was also one of its harshest critics, especially when religion was (ab)used to uphold racism, sexism, or classism. Aptheker's work offers great insight on this issue:

> Neither in his youth nor in later life did Du Bois attend any church with any regularity, but he was well aware of the enormous influence of the church upon the history and lives of black people and upon his own life. . . . The fact is that Du Bois disliked denominational religion and detested that "Christianity" which became an excuse for the status quo—whether slavery or racism or war: the religion, as he once put it, of J.P. Morgan rather than of Jesus Christ. A reason for this sharp feeling was Du Bois's admiration for what he took to be the revolutionary, or at least radical and challenging, character of the actual teachings of Jesus . . . [H]e viewed the black church as, at its best, the "basic rock" of his people, their shield and sword, their solace and goad; an indispensable source of their persistence and historical confidence despite all oppression. (Aptheker, 1980, pp. vii–viii)

The fact of the matter is Du Bois problematicized more than he praised religion. To be sure, he acknowledged its positive social and historical significance, but his comments were often more critical and condemning than they were congratulatory and commending. Few scholars of religion have recognized the potential *and* actual (or historical) pitfalls of religion as long and as loudly as Du Bois did, and few have exhibited the kind of care he did in discussing taboo and tough topics in a critical language laced with love and fiery words filled with a radical humanism that would make both Mohandas Gandhi and Martin Luther King, Jr., blush. Du Bois, demonically dancing with the dialectic, criticized black and white religious leaders and institutions alike. He argued that religious hypocrisy, as with other vices and vulgarities emerging from the bowels of human existence, is not the exclusive domain of a single racial group, gender, or social class, but remains open to any and all who would enter into its evil.

His contempt for the black church and its bourgeois practices was notorious, as was his disdain for its leadership. From the Du Boisian dialectical perspective, the black church seemed to be involved in and promoting everything but its "chief duty," that of "character building" (Du Bois, 1973, p. 114). Part of the problem, to be sure, was with its leadership. The "average Negro preacher," Du Bois (1996b) put it plainly, "is a shrewd manager, a respectable man, a good talker, a pleasant companion, but neither learned nor spiritual, nor a reformer" (p. 206). In "The Minister," an address delivered at the 1906 Hampton Annual Conference, Du Bois (1982a) boldly criticized African

American ministers, saying, as only he could, the too-often "Unsaid Thing" on the tip of everyone's tongues:

> On the whole the Negroes of the United States are not satisfied with their ministers. . . . [O]n the whole there is deep and wide-spread dissatisfaction with the average Negro minister. . . . There have been among Negro ministers in the past so many men of immoral life and men so lacking in dignity and high purpose that continually the educated classes of the race, the young aspiring graduates of our schools, the fathers of rising families have been dissatisfied with this class of men and have withdrawn themselves from them. (p. 328)

However, here it is important to highlight the fact that Du Bois did not lay the blame completely on the black clergy; black congregations were also at fault. They were, to be sure, a difficult and contradictory group to lead and, as Du Bois observed, increasingly the traditional leaders of the church were being led, if not by the entire congregation, then by the rich and politically powerful of the church (i.e., the black bourgeoisie). This is an intricate issue, one that points to the pitfalls of African American religion in general, the relationship between black clergy and black congregations more specifically, and, most importantly from a Du Boisian dialectical perspective, the moral mission of Africana people. In words that brilliantly capture this conundrum, Du Bois (1996b) wrote,

> In direct moral teaching and in setting moral standards for the people . . . the church is timid, and naturally so, for its constitution is democracy tempered by custom. Negro preachers are often condemned for poor leadership and empty sermons, and it is said that men with so much power and influence could make striking moral reforms. This is but partially true. The congregation does not follow the moral precepts of the preacher, but rather the preacher follows the standard of his flock, and only exceptional men dare seek to change this. And here it must be remembered that the Negro preacher is primarily an executive officer, rather than a spiritual guide. (pp. 205–06)

On the one hand, Du Bois praised the social function of the black church, acknowledging it as the cornerstone of African American culture and commending it for its contributions to African American social development and cultural survival. On the other hand, he criticized the black church for failing to develop the special moral mission of African Americans. He was highly disappointed with the pomp and circumstance of black church life, and said so in clear and critical terms. The "reform of the pulpit" was only part of the work that Du Bois (1982a) saw at hand (p. 329). If the black church was to truly embrace both its sacred and secular obligations and live out its creed, then it must not only demand that its clergy be persons (men *and* women) of "integrity, learning, and deep spiritual earnestness" (Du Bois, 1996b, p. 206). It must also call upon its congregations to be persons of "integrity, learning, and deep spiritual earnestness."[12] In the 1938 classic commencement address, "The Revelation of Saint Orgne the Damned," which he was invited to deliver in commemoration of the fiftieth anniversary of his graduation from Fisk, Du Bois (1973) put forward perhaps his most trenchant criticisms of the black church:

> [B]ehold . . . the Black Churches of America. . . . Their five millions of members in 40,000 groups, holding $2,000,000,000 in their hands, are the most strongly organized body among us; the first source of our group culture, the beginning of our education—what is this church doing today towards its primary task of teaching men right and wrong, and the duty of doing right? The flat answer is nothing if not less than nothing. Like other churches and other religions of other peoples and ages, our church has veered off on every conceivable side path, which interferes with and nullifies its chief duty of character building. It has built up a body of dogma and fairy tales, fantastic fables of sin and salvation, impossible creeds and impossible demands for ignorant unquestioning belief and obedience. Ask any thorough churchman today and he will tell you, not that the object of the church is to get men to do right and make the majority of mankind happy, but rather that the whole duty of man is to "believe in the Lord Jesus Christ and be saved;" or to believe in the "one Holy Catholic church," infallible and omniscient. (pp.113–14)

In response to the issues he raised Du Bois boldly restated the fundamental role of the black church, and it is interesting to note that his position was remarkably consistent with that of his first writings on black religion in "The Problem of Amusement" and *The Philadelphia Negro*, pieces which he penned four decades prior to "The Revelation of Saint Orgne the Damned"! He audaciously asserted that "the function of the Negro Church, instead of being that of building edifices, paying old debts, holding revivals and staging entertainments, has got to be brought back, or shall we say forward, to the simple duty of teaching ethics. For this purpose the Hebrew scriptures and the New Testament canon will not suffice" (p. 114).

Why would a strictly scriptural or religious response to African American problems not be a viable solution? Because clergy and laity alike had for hundreds of years been interpreting and misinterpreting, using and abusing both Christian theology and religion in general, not for the spreading of a spirit of selflessness and lovingkindness, but to teach selfishness, competitiveness, and the diabolical "good" of guile (see also K. Marx, 1974, 2002; Marx and Engels, 1964, 2008). Moreover, even more than the black church, the white church was not only guilty of the foregoing but, according to Du Bois, served in many respects as a model for much of the religious mayhem of the black church. In his 1907 "Religion in the South" he railed against white religion and whites' tendency to blame blacks for their own social degradation:

> Not only is there . . . falseness when the [white] South excuses its ethical para-
> dox by pointing to the low condition of the Negro masses, but there is also a
> strange blindness in failing to see that every pound of evidence to prove the
> present degradation of black men but adds to the crushing weight of indictment
> against their past treatment of this race. A race is not made in a single genera-
> tion. If they accuse Negro women of lewdness and Negro men of monstrous
> crime, what are they doing but advertising to the world the shameless lewdness
> of those Southern men who brought millions of mulattoes into the world, and
> whose deeds throughout the South and particularly in Virginia, the mother of
> slavery, have left but few prominent families whose blood does not today course
> in black veins? Suppose today Negroes do steal; who was it that for centuries
> made stealing a virtue by stealing their labor? Have not laziness and listnessness
> always been the followers of slavery? If these ten millions are ignorant by
> whose past law and mandate and present practice is this true? (Du Bois, 1982e,
> pp. 92–93)

To be sure, black religion had/has its problems, and Du Bois did not mince any words bringing his concerns to the attention of the black church. How-ever, he emphasized, the black church and the white church had different kinds of problems, perhaps not at every instance, but enough to level compa-rably different critiques. His major criticism of the white church revolved around its claim of Christian love. How is it possible that white clergy and laity could avow the cardinal creed of Christian love, and then schizophreni-cally and systematically sanction and exercise the oppression of their black fellow Christians?

Christianity, it could be said, has been the subterfuge by which whites have religiously disarmed blacks, among others. In fact, Christianity spread the spirit of Europe and its imperial push for global dominance more than it has ever imparted Christian ethics. No matter what the "true" tenets of Christian-ity may be, its historical manifestations violently register again and again in the all too familiar hegemonic language(s) of racism, sexism, colonialism, and, of course, capitalism. The corroboration of this claim is written all over colored and colonized (and formerly colonized) people's faces (*and* their bod-ies as well). Thus, the theodicean question returns: How could a religion that has unleashed such evil in the world be good? The time for timid talk was long gone, if there ever was a time to talk to oppressors in such a way. Du Bois offered his studied answer to this question more times than many white Christians would care to recall. On what he called, the "utter failure of white religion," Du Bois (1970c) stated, "A nation's religion is its life and as such white Christianity is a miserable failure" (p. 309). In connection to this, he asserted elsewhere that

> it is painfully true that White Christianity has in the twentieth century been curiously discredited. . . . Here in the twentieth century of the Prince of Peace the leading nations representing His religion have been murdering, maiming and hurting each other on a scale unprecedented in the history of Mankind . . . into the White Church of Christ race prejudice has crept to such an extent it is openly recognized and in the United States at least it is considered the natural and normal thing that white and colored people should belong mostly to different organizations and almost entirely to different congregations. . . . These facts do not impugn Christianity but they do make terrible comment upon the failure of its white followers. (Du Bois, 1985a, p. 84)

Du Bois was careful not to condemn Christianity, but had great contempt for *white* Christianity, which could more properly be called *white-supremacist, patriarchal, capitalist, colonial* Christianity. It was what seemed to be the inherent racist nature of white religion that bothered him. He perplexingly mused, white Christianity "theoretically opens the door to all men and yet closes it forcibly and insultingly in the face of black men" (Du Bois, 1982e, p. 92). He noted a recurring theme of religious hypocrisy in the way whites (mis)interpreted and practiced Christianity. In "The Church and the Color Line" of 1929, he thundered,

> [W]hen the church meets the Negro problem, it writes itself down as a deliberate and systematic liar. It does not say "Come unto me all ye that labor"; it does not "love its neighbor as itself"; it does not welcome "Jew and Gentile, barbarian, Scythian, bond and free;" and yet it openly and blatantly professes all this. . . . The church has opposed every great modern social reform; it opposed the spread of democracy, universal education, trade unionism, the abolition of poverty, the emancipation of women, the spread of science, the freedom of art and literature, and the emancipation of the Negro slave. When the reform was gained, the church righted itself, led usually by some schismatic and heretical part of itself, came over on the Lord's side and usually did not hesitate both to claim a preponderant share of the glory of victory and again to emphasize its supernatural claims. (Du Bois, 1970c, p. 217)

Du Bois's critique of the hypocrisy of white Christianity did not end here; there was more. Indeed, there was much more that he took issue with. Many of his criticisms centered on how the white church sanctioned African holocaust, colonization, and enslavement, a historical fact that many black Christians had (and continue to have) a hard time coming to terms with. For example, in "Will the Church Remove the Color Line?" of 1931, there stands a little-known passage that says more about white Christian hypocrisy in one paragraph than many are likely to be exposed to attending the most progressive black churches of the present age faithfully for a number of years. Du Bois (2000b) wrote,

> [P]erhaps many of us would rather forget it [African holocaust and enslavement]; yet we cannot forget that under the aegis and protection of the religion of the Prince of Peace—of a religion which was meant for the lowly and unfortunate—there arose in America one of the most stupendous institutions of human slavery that the world has seen. The Christian Church sponsored and defended this institution, despite occasional protest and effort at amelioration here and there. The Catholic church approved of and defended slavery; the Episcopal church defended and protected slavery; the Puritans and Congregationalists recognized and upheld slavery; the Methodists and Baptists stood staunchly behind it; the Quakers gave their consent to it. Indeed, there was not a single branch of the Christian Church that did not in the end become part of an impregnable bulwark defending the trade in human beings and the holding of them as chattel. (pp. 174–75)

Du Bois also had harsh, but morally justified words to say with regard to the white church's position on segregation. Not only did the white church want to conveniently omit its role in the holocaust and enslavement of African people, but it wanted to do so while slyly supporting twentieth-century segregation, and, therefore, blacks' ongoing dehumanization and social degradation. In "The Church and the Negro" in 1913, Du Bois (2000b) declared,

> The church aided and abetted the Negro slave trade; the church was the bulwark of American slavery; and the church is the strongest seat of racial and color prejudice. If one hundred of the best and purest colored folk of the United States should seek to apply for membership in any white church in this land tomorrow, 999 out of every 1,000 ministers would lie to keep them out. They would not only do this, but would openly and brazenly defend their action as worthy of followers of Jesus Christ. (p. 99)

In "The Color Line and the Church" in 1929, Du Bois continued this line of thinking, demonstrating in it and the writings cited above his undeniable contributions to the sociology of religion—principally, that religion is inextricably from the history and culture of society, and always intersecting with and informing the general thought and practices of society. He put it plainly: "The American Church of Christ is Jim Crowed from top to bottom. No other institution in America is built so thoroughly or more absolutely on the color line. Everybody knows this" (Du Bois, 2000b, p. 169).

A major assertion of the sociology of religion is that religion is not simply about the sacred or transcendent, the intangible or other-worldly (i.e., God, heaven, the soul, faith, belief, miracles, and prayer), but that religion is also concerned with everyday reality and social phenomena (see Beckford, 1989, 2003; Beckford and Demerath, 2007; Christiano, 2008; Davie, 2007; Dillon, 2003; Frazier, 1974; Weber, 1963; Zuckerman, 2003). Moreover, the sociology of religion grapples with (or *should* wrestle with) the ways in which religion hints at the fact that it is a human product, perhaps divinely inspired, but a human product nonetheless, and one that plays itself out, not in heaven, but here on earth within the web of the wider social world. From this optic, religion may be conceived of as being meticulously marked by particular sociohistorical events, social thought, social practices, social organizations, and social institutions, and it is precisely the way in which Du Bois critically engaged religion and religious institutions, focusing on their *sociality*, that distinguish his writings on religion and places the bulk of his work in this area under the rubric of the sociology of religion (see A.E. Aldridge, 2000; Bainbridge, 1997; Fenn, 2001; M.B. Hamilton, 1998, 2001; Johnstone, 1997; B.S. Turner, 1997).

In Du Bois's dialectical treatment of religion he was able to touch on and turn his readers' attention to its potential for good *or* bad. Religion was never neutral, but always and ever an alternative site where knowledge and power are contested and acquired. Du Bois composed some of the most beautiful passages one could possibly read concerning African American religion and the black church. However, he also leveled some of the harshest criticisms of African American religion and the black church ever recorded. What is it about Du Bois's dialectic that makes him seem so schizophrenic, praising the black church on one page and condemning it on the next? And, what of his work on white Christianity and the white church? He certainly does not seem schizophrenic in that regard. He is straightforward and to the point: He thinks white Christians and white Christianity reek of religious hypocrisy, to put it plainly.

Because religion, as with any area of culture, is a shared human project and a social construction, it almost inherently points to human potentials and moral pitfalls (Pinn, 1995, 2002b, 2003). Du Bois's writings on religion seek to simultaneously salvage its good and, literally, excommunicate its bad. Many scholars of religion and social scientists have misunderstood his work in this area, among several other areas, because, as he put it, "so far as the American world of science and letters was concerned, we [Africana intellectual-activists] never 'belonged'; we remained unrecognized in learned societies and academic groups" (Du Bois, 1968a, p. 228). His work, as I am certain many must wryly contend concerning the work of contemporary Africana Studies scholars, is merely the work of "Negroes studying Negroes, and after all, what [have] Negroes to do with America or science [or, human culture and civilization, some might even sardonically add]?" (p. 228).

In short, from his research on African American religion during enslavement to his portraits of radical black religious leaders, from his pioneering studies of black congregational life to his critiques of both black and white Christianity, from his discussions of the role of African American women in the black church to his passionate praise of African American religious music, there can be little doubt that Du Bois significantly contributed to the sociology of religion (and by extension, religious studies and sociology, in the conventional sense). He was not simply the first black sociologist of religion, or the first sociologist of black religion, but the first sociologist to analyze the role of religion in American society, which, I should reiterate, is the precise point of the sociology of religion.

DU BOIS AND CRITICAL
THEORY OF LIBERATION THEOLOGY

Du Bois's sociology of religion and philosophy of religion lend themselves to the development of a *critical theory of liberation theology* insofar as, first, critical social theory seeks to employ every available resource to critique all forms of domination and provide a bedrock for the radical democratic socialist transformation of contemporary society. Secondly, a critical theory of liberation theology is premised on a theology of liberation, which, of course, begins with thought on God, but it is also rooted in the social and political realities of poor and marginalized people, those struggling against the contemporary beasts of burden: capitalism, colonialism, racism, and sexism, among other imperial issues. A critical theory of liberation theology, then, draws from the discourses of both critical theory and liberation theology in the interest of critiquing the ideological and oppressive aspects of religion and their role in and relationship to contemporary society. Moreover, a critical theory of liberation theology contains the characteristic dialectical and self-reflexive quality of the best of critical social theory and, therefore, seeks to reconstruct both critical theory and liberation theology through theoretical synthesis and critical dialogue on domination and human liberation.[13]

An Africana critical theory of liberation theology places liberation theology in dialogue with classical and contemporary critical social theory, and particularly the Africana critical thought tradition. It challenges traditional liberation theologians to open themselves epistemically to the contributions of Africana radical political theory and revolutionary social thought. From the optic of Africana critical theory, this dialogue will be philosophically fruitful insofar as Africana radical political theory and revolutionary social thought are often omitted from the social theories and political thought that most mainstream liberation theologians employ in their efforts to bridge the growing gap between church and society. Further, many of the social problems that liberation theologians currently seek to address have been, and are being, brilliantly engaged in the discourse(s) of Africana philosophy and Africana social and political thought (Dawson, 2001; Eze, 1997a, 1997b; R.M. Franklin, 1990; Gordon and Gordon, 2006a, 2006b; L. Harris, 1983; Lott and Pittman, 2003; Pohlman, 2003; Serequeberhan, 1991; Wiredu, 2004).

Traditionally, liberation theology prides itself on the fact that it is not quarantined to luxurious church sanctuaries and university lecture halls, but rather emerges in the midst of anti-imperial struggle and social conflict (C. Boff, 1987; McGovern, 1989; Milbank, 1990). Christopher Rowland (1999) contends, "The key thing is that one first of all *does* liberation theology rather than learns about it. Or, put another way, one can only learn about it by embarking on it" (p. 4, original emphasis). Embarking on liberation theology means, first of all, coming to terms with the fact that it is a very varied intellectual and political tradition that seeks to situate theology and religion in contemporary social contexts and cultural conditions. It means acknowledging the wide range of theoretical and political practices that have come to be identified as liberation theology, practices which, it should be emphasized, have consistently dialogued with the discourses of the academy (though not necessarily the discursive practices of Africana intellectuals in the academy or the social and political theories of organic Africana intellectual-activists working outside the orbit of the academy). Hence, among the more popular versions of liberation theology there are Marxist, feminist, postmodernist, and postcolonialist schools of thought, as well as cultural and ethnic-studies, based liberation theologies, which accent issues of ethnicity, history, and geography often along with the class and gender analysis of Marxist and feminist liberation theologies (Berryman, 1987; Boff and Boff, 1987; Hennelly, 1995; Rowland, 1999; Segundo, 1976; C. Smith, 1991).

By focusing on the progressive and regressive aspects of religion, Du Bois's sociology of religion demonstrates its *dialecticality* and, like the liberation theologians, places *liberation* at the heart of his discourse on theology and religion. Where liberation theologians conventionally stress poor and vulnerable peoples' struggles against secular oppression, Du Bois (1972b) criticized, not simply imperial society, but the church for acquiescing to the whims and wishes of rich and ruling-class congregants and betraying the "working man" (p. 330). In *The Philadelphia Negro*, he also criticized the church for taking too great a portion of poor families' income, money he maintained that could be better spent on bare necessities and much-needed family possessions, such as homes:

> Much of the money that should have gone into homes has gone into costly church edifices, dues to societies, dress and entertainment. If the Negroes had bought little homes as persistently as they have worked to develop a church and secret society system, and had invested more of their earnings in savings-banks and less in clothes they would be in far better condition to demand industrial opportunity than they are today. (Du Bois, 1996b, p. 185)

A critical theory of liberation theology does not simply use sacred texts to point to secular wrongs, as it seems is the case with much of modern critical theology. It does not see religion or the church as politically neutral, nor does it understand the Bible or any other sacred text to be a source free from the trappings of a particular race, gender, or class's all too human heavenly and/or earthly desires. It is, to put it plainly, a critical theory of liberation theology primarily preoccupied with the radical reconstruction of theology and religion in the interest of human liberation and radical democratic socialist transformation.

Du Bois's philosophy of religion and sociology of religion are relevant to the development of a critical theory of liberation theology insofar as his writings on religion exhibit an openness to the role that not only Christianity but traditional African religions and Islam have played in continental and diasporan African history and culture—antedating Ali Mazrui's "triple heritage" thesis by well over half a century (Mazrui, 1986). In *The Negro Church*, Du Bois (2000b) discussed "primitive Negro religion," by which he meant the religion of "the African tribes," and made dazzling claims concerning retentions of ancient African religious beliefs and practices (p. 110). He stated with clear confidence, "There can be no reasonable doubt, however, but that the scattered remains of religious systems in Africa today among the Negro tribes are survivals of the religious ideas upon which the Egyptian religion was based" (p. 110).

In *Black Folk Then and Now*, Du Bois (1939) continued to chronicle the character of traditional African religions, stating again, "The basis of Egyptian religion was 'of a purely Nigritian character,' and, in its developed form, Sudanese tribal gods were invoked and venerated by the priest" (p. 108). He went on to discuss the religions of the Bori, Yoruba, Hausa, and Ewe, among others, asserting that

> the religion of Africa is the universal animism or fetishism of primitive peoples, rising to polytheism and approaching monotheism chiefly, but not wholly, as a

result of Christianity and Islamic missions. Of fetishism there is much misapprehension. It is not mere senseless degradation. It is a philosophy of life. Among primitive Negroes there can be . . . no such divorce of religion from practical life as is common in civilized lands. Religion is life, and fetish an expression of the practical recognition of the dominant natural forces which surround the Negro. (p. 106)

With regard to Islam, Du Bois claims, it "came by conquest, trade, and proselytism. As a conqueror it reached Egypt in the seventh century and had by the end of the fourteenth century firm footing in the Egyptian Sudan" (p. 108). In addition, he acknowledged Islam (which he refers to throughout his early works as "Mohammedism") as a religion which "[t]oday . . . dominates Africa north of ten degrees north latitude and is strong between five and ten degrees north latitude. In the east it reaches below the Victoria Nyanza" (p. 108). In *The World and Africa*, Du Bois (1965) writes at length about Islam's imperial legacy in Africa, what he called "the process of arabization in North Africa" and the "arabization of the Nile valley" (p. 185). He even went so far to discuss the extremely taboo topic of the prophet Muhammad personally enslaving Africans, but then, he quickly claimed, "He [the prophet Muhammad] liberated all his slaves, and they were all well-known figures in the early history of Islam" (p. 183). Though he despised the imperial legacy of Islam in Africa, Du Bois often posed it as a counter to the Christianity of Africa's European colonizers. In *The Negro Church*, he wrote, "Mohammedism entered Africa in the seventh and eighth centuries and had since that time conquered nearly all North Africa, the Sudan, and made inroads into the populations of the west coast . . . and especially is it preserving the natives against the desolations of Christian rum" (Du Bois, 2000b, p. 111).

Du Bois's openness to non-Christian theologies and religions, particularly African traditional theologies and religions, is also evident in his own personal beliefs and worship practices, which, as mentioned above, cannot comfortably be characterized as Christian. Noted African American theologian, Gayraud Wilmore (1983), perhaps put it best when he stated that Du Bois "was a religious man in the broadest sense, but one who did not regard himself as a churchman" (p. 136). Wilmore continues,

His religion obtrudes through his secular writings under a nimbus of African spirituality and transcendental mystique. He was once Knight Commander of the Liberian Order of African Redemption, which had strong religious overtones. On his 25th birthday he vowed to become the Moses of black people and improvised a ritual of regeneration, using wine, candles, oil, and oranges. In the throes of the rite he prayed, sang, and made "a sacrifice to the *Zeitgeist* of Work, God and Mercy." (pp. 258–59, emphasis in original; see also Du Bois, 1985a, pp. 26–29)

Du Bois, therefore, aids in the development of a critical theory of liberation theology insofar as his writings on religion compare and contrast the wide range of theologies and religions throughout the African world. His philosophy of religion and sociology of religion constantly dovetailed with his increasingly critical dialectic, and this enabled him to highlight both the positive and negative impact of theology or religion on Africana people, their history and culture. Indeed, Christianity garnered the bulk of his religious criticism because it was, and remains, the dominant religion of the United States and the religion to which most people of African descent adhere in the Western hemisphere. His critique of Christianity, then, must be viewed as nothing less than a continuation of his critique of Western European and white American imperial thought and culture, and, equally important, accommodationist and assimilationist tendencies in Africana religious thought and practices.

Liberation theology, in the traditional sense, is often content to leave its central theological components as they are, which is to say, conventional liberation theology's Christological core is rarely questioned, and in this sense it seems utterly unaware of non-Christian theologies and religious realities (Hennelly, 1990; McGovern, 1989). The critical theory of liberation theology that I am developing here, then, challenges conventional liberation theology to dialogue with the wide range of theologies and religions in the world, especially the African world. It, therefore, neither begins nor ends with Jesus Christ and Christianity, but is open to the prophets (or prophetesses), priests (or priestesses), and theologies of other spiritual traditions and religions. In this sense, critical theory of liberation theology, as I envision it, is not Christian but, I should add, it is also not anti-Christian. It is, in a word, more of a methodological and metatheoretical move toward our current (I could say *continental* and *diasporan African*, but it is certainly applicable to oppressed others') religious reality, a reality that has been and continues to be marked and molded by diasporan diversity (L.E. Barrett, 1974; Blakely, van Beek and Thomson, 1994; Mazrui, Opkewho, and Davies, 1999; B. Ray, 2000).

Critical theory of liberation theology hinges on hermeneutics and *emancipatory epistemology*—that is, *a theory of knowledge deeply concerned with critical interpretation and struggles for liberation*. A major goal of emancipatory epistemology is to contest flat-footed, reductionistic, and absolutist conceptions of meaning, what we call in Africana philosophy—borrowing the buzzwords of the black existentialists and postmodernists—"essentializing" and "totalizing" meanings. In essence, and more methodologically speaking, this means warding off narrow-minded and totalizing thought that resists or rejects difference and diversity, whether religious, cultural, racial, sexual, or what have you. Emancipatory epistemology sidesteps claims of closure and stubbornly struggles to keep the realm of knowledge open.

Theology, religion, and the church have long been immune, in the minds of many, to criticism, but Du Bois dialectically points us in a different direction. His critique of Christianity, again the dominant religion of the society in which he lived and worked, contributes to the development of a critical theory of liberation theology in that it prefigures and provides a paradigm for the reconceptualization and reconstruction of liberation theology, the role of religion in society, and the ways in which Africana religious thought broadens the epistemic base of both critical social theory and liberation theology. Long before the liberation theologians began their discourse on those who are "poor and Christian," "the weakest and the insignificant", before liberation theologians began to use the Bible to buttress their claim that it is important to "understand the grace and salvation of Jesus in the context of the present and from the situation of the poor", before the liberation theologians pointed out that poverty-stricken people's "faith affects in many different ways their experience of poverty and oppression, and this experience of poverty and oppression makes its mark on their experience of the gospel," W.E.B. Du Bois developed a critical discourse on theology and religion that accentuated the often overlooked situation of persons who are poor, black, and Christian (Gutierrez, 1999, pp. 19, 25–26). He chastised the Christian Church for not living by its creed, for allowing racism and segregation to creep into its congregations, and for bastardizing the life and legacy of Jesus Christ. How could they call themselves Christians, Du Bois furiously wondered, if they do not adhere to the cardinal principles of Christianity: Christ's word and the Golden Rule? In his 1913 *Crisis* essay, "The Church and the Negro," he wrote,

> The relation of the church to the Negro is, or should be, a very simple proposition. Leaving aside the supernatural significance of the church, we have here groups of people working for human uplift and professing the highest and most unselfish morality as exemplified by the life and teaching of Jesus of Nazareth and the Golden Rule. By this standard all church members should treat Negroes as they themselves would wish to be treated if they were colored. They should do this and teach this, if need be, die for this creed. (Du Bois, 2000b, p. 99)

Like liberation theologians, Du Bois conceived of Christ as someone who would side with the poor and the most marginalized in society (Araya, 1987; L. Boff, 1988; Gutierrez, 1983, 1994). In his writings on religion Du Bois illustrated time and time again how the teachings of Jesus could be used to combat the increasing invisibility of poverty and the oppression of the poor. In this sense, his work connects with contemporary liberation theology, especially the thought of leading Latin American liberation theologian, Gustavo Gutierrez (1999), where he writes,

> These times . . . bear the imprint of a new presence of the poor, the marginalized and the oppressed. Those who were for so long "absent" in our society and in the Church have made themselves—and are continuing to make themselves—present. It is not a matter of physical absence: we are talking of those who have had scant or no significance, and who therefore have not felt (and in many cases still do not feel) in a position to make plain their suffering, their aspirations and their hopes. (p. 20; see also Gutierrez, 1996)

Not simply in society, but within the hallowed walls of the Christian church, African Americans have been (and in some senses remain) invisible and "have not felt (and in many cases still do not feel) in a position to make plain their suffering, their aspirations and their hopes." The situation sometimes seems worse when we turn to the discourse of liberation theology where, once again, race and racism have reared their ugly heads, which is to say that liberation theology is often locked along the racial divide, with each theologian tending to his or her own racial flock, often forgetting that religion at its best does not promote racial (or gender or class or sexual orientation) oppression and distinctions but critically combats any and all forms of imperial thought and practices.

In contrast with most mainstream liberation theologians who have a longstanding tendency of focusing almost exclusively on Latin America and the Caribbean (Erskine, 1981; Pinn and Valentin, 2001), Du Bois's liberation theology centers on the poor and, perhaps, the most vulnerable members of North American society, African Americans. With words that will surely shock many contemporary liberation theologians and white Christians alike, Du Bois (2000b) provocatively declared,

> Jesus Christ was a laborer and black men are laborers; He was poor and we are poor; He was despised of his fellow men and we are despised; He was persecuted and crucified, and we are mobbed and lynched. If Jesus Christ came to America He would associate with Negroes . . . and working people; He would eat and pray with them, and He would seldom see the interior of the Cathedral of Saint John the Divine. (pp. 99–100)

Prefiguring the discourse of black theology by nearly half a century, Du Bois's words capture one of its core concerns: that is, the contradictions of coupling racism and religion, particularly Christianity (Cone and Wilmore, 1993; Hopkins, 1999a; 1999b; Kunnie, 1994; Pinn, 2003). Black theology, as defined by one of its founding figures, James Cone (1969), begins with "the Black condition" (p. 18). "It is a theology which confronts white society as racist Antichrist, communicating to the oppressor that nothing will be spared in the fight for freedom" (p. 135). A central issue in the discourse of black theology is the racialization of God; therefore, God's racial identity is of prime importance to black theologians (Cone and Wilmore, 1993). Cone (1970) contends, "The Blackness of God and everything implied by it in a racist society is the heart of Black Theology's doctrine of God," in that "there is no place for a colorless God in a society where people suffer precisely because of their color" (p. 120).

In order to understand black theology's concept of blackness, one must first explore the history of race and racism, and the social significance of skin color in Western culture and social consciousness (Jordan, 1968; Pieterse, 1992; Goldberg, 1993). Another founding figure in black theology, Deotis Roberts (2003), pointed out long ago that in a white-supremacist society, such as the United States, whiteness is the opposite of blackness, even in the realm of religion. Where whiteness represents all that is good, beautiful, and divine, blackness signifies all that is bad, ugly, and evil. And more, in white-supremacist society blackness symbolizes subhumanity and intellectual inferiority, the exact opposite of what whiteness means: the highest mark of humanity and super superiority, not simply intellectually but in every possible way.

Black theology begins with the black condition because it is a condition not of Africana people's creation or social construction, but a condition of continued coercion, violence, and oppression. Blackness, then, for the black theologians is not necessarily a biological concept, but an existential paradigm and point of departure (Gordon, 1995a, 1997a). It is, in a word, a concept that captures the historical and cultural legacy of black people's resistance to white supremacy and anti-black racism, among other imperialisms unleashed by Europe's push for global dominance. Therefore, when the black theologians argue for Jesus's blackness they are not putting forward a biological or crude racial claim as much as they are contending, as Cone (1970) did in his classic *A Black Theology of Liberation,* that the ministry and moral life and legacy of Jesus is more meaningful if it is acknowledged that, according to the New Testament of the Bible, the image of Jesus which has precedence over all others is that of Christ as "the Oppressed One," and that his entire life and legacy rest squarely on his identification with the poor, downtrodden, and dispossessed (pp. 202–10).

The God of black liberation theology, then, is "the God of and for the oppressed of the land who makes himself known through their liberation" (p. 116; see also Cone, 1975). Cone's conception of black liberation theology, as a consequence, means nothing less than "doing God's work in history by righting the wrongs done against his people." (Cone, 1969, p. 47). Hence, based on this interpretation, blacks—undoubtedly some of the most oppressed people in the world—are one of God's covenant communities. This is a theme that runs throughout Du Bois's writings on religion, and its similarity with Conian theology is striking.[14] Aptheker (1980) observed, "If Du Bois is not the first who writes of a Black God, he is certainly among the earliest to express this view and he repeatedly draws a parallel between lynching as practiced by Americans and crucifixion as practiced by the Romans" (p. viii; see also Blum, 2007).

For Du Bois, as for Cone and contemporary black liberation theologians, religion should foster not simply a love of God, but a love for oneself and humanity. Too often Christianity has been used to crush the human spirit encased in black (and especially female) bodies and, though black theologians have yet to acknowledge it, Du Bois was one of the first to systematically criticize both white and black Christianity's supposed color-blindness and religious racial neutrality.[15] He called on the black church to remember its rebellious roots and abolitionist activities, which is one of the reasons he continuously chronicled the contributions of black religious leaders to Africana radical thought and revolutionary struggles.[16] Coincidently, Cone (1969) makes a similar claim, pleading with black clergy and laity to recall that "the Black church was born in protest," has a "heritage of radical involvement in the world" and, therefore, possesses a past that "is a symbol of what is actively needed in the present" (pp. 112-113).

CONCLUSION: DU BOIS, BLACK LIBERATION THEOLOGY, AND CRITICAL THEORY OF CONTEMPORARY SOCIETY

It would be very difficult to say with any precision "what is actively needed in the present"; however, I believe that Du Bois, Cone, and many of the liberation theologians point us in some promising directions. The "this-world" or earthly focus of liberation theologians' brand of Christianity is certainly a move in the right direction, but their blindness to other forms of faith, religions, spiritual traditions, and non-Christian prophets (or prophetesses) and priests (or priestesses) speaks volumes about the ways in which Christianity is continually being (ab)used for global imperial and cultural hegemonic purposes. Where I am perplexed by the insularity of some the liberation theologians' discourse, I am also deeply moved by their awe-inspiring efforts to encourage Christians and contemporary Christianity to not simply speak truth *to* global imperial power, but to speak truth *about* global imperial power. Speaking truth to power in more ways than one places the powerful at the discursive center. It presumes that the powerful possess a moral consciousness and an ethical authority which history has hinted again and again they simply do not. Du Bois and the liberation theologians, then, are not as interested in speaking truth to the powerful as much as they are concerned with speaking truth about the powerful to the powerless. This practice promotes the empowerment of the powerless in a way that speaking truth to the powerful often only flatters them and warns them of what they need to alter in their efforts to maintain the established imperial order (see Marable, 1992, 1996).

Du Bois's philosophy of religion and sociology of religion, though primarily preoccupied with the critique of Christianity and its impact on U.S. society, could be extremely useful in reconstructing liberation theology, broadening its base to encompass critical race theory, radical politics, social analysis, cultural criticism, anti-colonialism, and feminist theory. His writings on religion could also aid in epistemically opening liberation theology to the spiritual knowledge(s) of non-Christian, albeit God-loving laities. What is more, Du Bois's emphasis on social ethics in his writings on religion certainly stands as a testament and offers a prodigious moral model of what religion should really be about: *not* about saving souls and using guile to get into heaven, *not* about religious chauvinism or racial exclusionism in the realm of religion, *not* about building big churches or worship centers, and certainly *not* about promoting patriarchal and bourgeois values. On the contrary, as we have witnessed, and as he himself testified with his own words above, religion at its best should really be about enhancing the quality of life on earth, about promoting and practicing loving-kindness and compassion, about being selfless as opposed to selfish, and about respecting and valuing the wide range of human diversity and human difference that God has omnisciently placed on earth.

In 1910, while professor of history and economics at Atlanta University, Du Bois the agnostic composed a prayer that beautifully captures his belief, not in any specific religion or spiritual tradition, but in the God of and for the oppressed and struggling people of the world. Here, then, I conclude with his heartfelt prayer:

> Give us grace, O god, to dare to do the deed which we well know cries to be done. Let us not hesitate because of ease, or the words of men's mouths, or our own lives. Mighty causes are calling us — the freeing of women, the training of children, the putting down of hate and murder and poverty — all these and more. But they call with voices that mean work and sacrifice and death. Mercifully grant us, O God, the spirit of Esther, that we say: I will go unto the King and if I perish, I perish — Amen. (Du Bois, 1980c, p. 21)

Du Bois's critical religious thought was part of his diverse and ongoing efforts to bring dialectical thought to bear on not only the ideologies of imperialism but the institutions of imperialism. Inextricable from his critiques of black education, black leadership, black liberation thought, and black religion, and along with each of the institutions that these discourses spawned, are Du Bois's critiques of the U.S. government's sanction of the enslavement and ensuing segregation of persons of African descent. The government may not be held accountable for the anti-black racial violence of white terrorist groups, such as the Klu Klux Klan, the White Knights and neo-Nazi skinheads, or the racist acts of its individual white racist citizens, but, Du Bois firmly believed, the government is responsible for endorsing and enforcing federal laws, establishing federal institutions, and promoting social and cultural practices and values which uphold and perpetuate white supremacy and anti-black racism. Du Bois's critiques of the U.S. government's racial rule, its horrible history of racial exclusion and racial violence, along with its public profession and public projection of racelessness or racial neutrality, and his continuous calls for racial redress, distinctly contributes to modern reparations discourse and contemporary critical race theory. An exploration of these contributions will, consequently, constitute the primary preoccupation of the next chapter.

NOTES

1. This chapter is lovingly dedicated to my mother, Reverend Marilyn Giles, who has been an ordained Baptist minister for more than a quarter of a century, and who continues to struggle with the constant intentional erasure or, at the very least, the intense invisibility of black women, especially womanist theologians and ministers, in the Southern Baptist black church. Her indelible influence on my philosophy of religion, sociology of religion, and conceptions of both black liberation and womanist theology cannot be overstated. Iwori Meji 3:2; Owonrin Meji 6:1; Iwori Odi 75:1; Oturupon Bara 176:1; Oturupon Ogunda 206:1; Exodus 20:12; Deuteronomy 5:16; Matthew 15:4; Matthew 19:19; Mark 7:10; Mark 10:19; Luke 18:20; Ephesians 6:2.

2. With regard to Du Bois's work that connects not simply racism, but also sexism to religion, see, for example, "The Burden of Black Women" (1914), "The Gospel According to Mary Brown" (1919), "The Damnation of Women" (1920), and "The Freedom of Womanhood" (1924) in Du Bois (1969a, 1970b, 1982a, 1982b).

3. For a discussion of black ecumenism, see Sawyer (1994).

4. With regard to religion being both an "inspiration and frustration" for Du Bois, I observe below his acute and pioneering awareness of the black church as the center of African American life and culture, and also I note how perplexed he was, as early as his teenage years at Fisk, with dogmatic religion, religious hypocrisy, religion that prohibits or restricts progressive social and political theory and praxis, and religion being (ab)used to dehumanize or dispossess. The pertinent passages from his texts are presented and commented on below.

5. For further discussion of what has come to be called the "Atlanta Race Riot," see Bauerlin (2001), Burns (2006), Godshalk (2005), and Mixon (2005).

6. Du Bois's "Credo" has a pivotal place in his oeuvre for several reasons. First, it was one of the only published pieces in his long literary career in which he openly espoused a belief in God. Second, it was one of the first to blazon out at the dawn of the twentieth century a growing spirit of black nationalism and critical opposition to Booker T. Washington's accommodationism. Du Bois (1969a) declared that he believed in God and in "all men, black and brown and white," who, from his perceptive point of view, "are brothers, varying through time and opportunity, in form and gift and feature, but different in no essential particular, and alike in soul and the possibility of infinite development" (p. 3). And then, his radical humanism took a back seat to what he saw as the necessity of black nationalism (and, I would include, Pan-Africanism) in the face of European imperialism, and specifically anti-black racist white supremacy. He unapologetically announced,

> Especially do I believe in the Negro Race: in the beauty of its genius, the sweetness of its soul, and its strength in that meekness which shall yet inherit this turbulent earth.
> I believe in Pride of race and lineage and self: in pride of self so deep as to scorn injustice to other selves; in pride of lineage so great as to despise no man's father; in pride of race so chivalrous as neither to offer bastardy to the weak nor beg wedlock of the strong, knowing that men may be brothers in Christ, even though they may not be brothers-in-law. (p. 3)

A final reason Du Bois's "Credo" is distinguished amongst his other writings is because of its unprecedented popularity. Du Bois biographer David Levering Lewis noted that the piece was literally celebrated by blacks of all political persuasions and white conservatives and liberals alike. So popular was Du Bois's "Credo" that, Lewis (1993) claims, it was "reprinted widely in the African American press and made available on cardboard rectangles slightly larger than playing-card size by a Memphis printing establishment" (p. 313). An extremely important piece with regard to Du Bois's writings on religion, the Lewis work offers a succinct synopsis of the historical context in which it was produced, its personal and political purposes, and its impact on blacks as wells as whites during those turbulent times. His words are worth quoting at length:

> Like so much else that he wrote, the "Credo" was meant to serve a dual purpose: manifesto to a few thousand influential whites outlining the social and civil rights ideals Du Bois and his few supporters embodied; and catechism for great numbers of ordinary men and women of his race whose beleaguered pride was faltering. . . . Du Bois sprinkled it with pieties about peace and beauty and goodness—patience, even—and appeared to profess a belief in God and spoke of green pastures beside still waters, for he especially needed to persuade a white public schooled in the black world by *Up From Slavery* [Booker T. Washington's 1901 accommodationist autobiography] that he was not a rash and godless intellectual, but a committed exponent of Judeo-Christian harmony and justice. "Credo" was a majestic incantation whose surface and subliminal meanings were easily misread. White readers of a sanctimonious or myopic bent were profoundly gratified by the expression of religious sentiments, as were the overwhelming majority of his own

people. Perceptive readers, on the other hand, heard, in a staccato modeled on Zola's *J'accuse*, distinct sounds of white supremacy crumbling. A good many black people heard the thunder of avenging racial parity. They would hang the "Credo" on their living room walls after Du Bois included it in *Darkwater* sixteen years later, just as their grandchildren would mount "I Have a Dream" on theirs. (p. 312)

7. A note on the dialectical nature of Du Bois's thought is necessary in order to quell longstanding confusion. Francis Broderick (1955, 1958c, 1959), August Meier (1959, 1963) and Elliott Rudwick (1956, 1958b, 1959b, 1968), among others, have each made mention of the contradictory character of Du Bois thought. However, in their criticisms they fail to adequately acknowledge and assess the social forces and social phenomena, public policies and political programs—which Du Bois apparently was consistently conscious of—that continental and diasporan Africans were struggling against. Africana history has shown that blacks exist in a totalitarian reality that is simultaneously and thoroughly white supremacist, sexist, capitalist, and colonialist—A reality extremely arduous to explain to whites primarily because one of the fundamental features of being white in a white-supremacist world is an exaggerated and over-inflated sense of self and (consciously or unconsciously) participating in the public practice of racistly rendering blacks non-existent or, as Ralph Ellison might put it, invisible (see Bogues, 2003; C.W. Mills, 1997, 1998, 2003). It is this invisibility that most members of the ruling race (and we could add *gender* and *class*) literally do not detect which makes many of Du Bois's positions seem contradictory and intellectually incoherent. The duality that Du Bois's critics describe is actually quite common in Africana social and political thought, and it neither began nor ended with Du Bois, but is symptomatic of blacks' efforts to live (not simply survive) and work in a world ravaged by racism and imperialism, in societies where white supremacy and capitalist patriarchy are institutionally sanctioned and socially accepted (see Boxill, 1997c; Cain, 1993; Childs, 1989; Wintz, 1996). The dialectical nature of Du Bois's thought, to be sure, is one of his greatest contributions to the Africana tradition of critical theory, and his search for solutions to the most pressing social problems, along with his ability to consistently put forward radical political programs and ethical alternatives, remains unparalleled.

8. Du Bois believed that religion, and Christianity in specific, could be employed as an instrument in both the quest to achieve black liberation and radical democratic socialist transformation. In *W.E.B. Du Bois: American Prophet*, the noted religious historian Edward Blum (2007) importantly observed, "At first glance, Du Bois's assertion that religious leaders and ideas helped rationalize and legitimate capitalistic exploitation seems to show that he was using a fairly simple Marxian approach. But looking at a variety of Du Bois's other texts suggests that he broke with the Marxian base-superstructure analysis by claiming that an ideological value, 'true Christianity,' could make social change; if a renewal of true Christianity struck society and masses of people subscribed to the radical teachings of Christ, a new economic base could result, one of economic justice and brotherhood. By focusing on racism and religion as powerful social forces, Du Bois offered a sophisticated revision of Marxian theory. In Du Bois's scholarly writing, a religious renewal could have the power to change eco-

nomic structures, a position that would have been anathema to any strict Marxist" (p. 111; see also Blum, 2005b).

9. For further discussion of womanist theology, and the ways in which it is distinctly different from white feminist theology, but deeply connected to the discourses of liberation theology, especially black liberation theology, please see Cannon (1988, 1995), M.A. Coleman (2008), Crawford (2002), Floyd-Thomas (2006a, 2006b), Gilkes (2001), Mitchem (2002), Riggs (1994), and Townes (1993, 1995, 2006).

10. For further discussion of African retentions in African American religious thought and practices, please see Baer and Singer (2002), S.T. Barnes (1997), Bascom (1980), L.E. Barrett (1974), Bastide (1971, 1978), Cornelius (1999), Gomez (2005), J.E. Holloway (1991), R.E. Hood (1990), P.E. Johnson (1994), J.M. Murphy (1994), Ohadike (2007), Sernett, (1999), G.E. Simpson (1978), Sobel (1979), C.S. Wilder (2001), and J.R. Young (2007).

11. Wilson Jeremiah Moses (1978, 1996, 1998) and Adolph Reed (1997) have each expertly addressed and thoroughly criticized Du Bois's digestion of Eurocentric-ideological-imperial concepts of progress and civilization.

12. In *Afrotopia*, Moses (1998), who argues that Du Bois was "[p]reeminently a dialectician" that "frequently championed opposing positions, sometimes within the scope of a single paragraph," gives us a bird's-eye view of Du Bois's dialectical approach to African American religion. He states that because Du Bois's thought was primarily dialectical,

> It is therefore not surprising that from time to time Du Bois wrote optimistically of the church's past and present role in organizing the political and economic consciousness of black communities. In his assessment of African American religion, Du Bois represented contradictory tendencies toward modernism and traditionalism. Toward the end of his chapter entitled "The Faith of the Fathers" in *The Souls of Black Folk*, he spoke as the prophet of a new "awakening . . . when the pent-up vigor of ten million souls shall sweep irresistibly toward the Goal." At other locations in that same essay, he wrote almost nostalgically of the waning of a mythical Afro-Christian virtue, which was supposedly giving way to the tawdry values of modern capitalism. He was ambivalent with respect to the role that religion played in African American acculturation, suggesting at times that it symbolized the retention of African traditions, at others viewing it as evidence of African American acceptance of American values. He posed the question of whether religion had functioned historically as a force for social reform or as a form of escapism. (pp. 136–37)

13. My conception of a critical theory of liberation theology is derived from several sources, the most noteworthy among them Alcoff and Mendieta (2000), C. Boff (1987), M.M. Campbell (1999), Cone (1970, 1999), Cone and Wilmore (1993), Dussel (1976, 1978, 1985, 1988, 2003), Forrester (1988), W.R. Jones (1973), Kee (1990), Kunnie (1994), Lakeland (1990), Mendieta (2005), J.W. Perkins (2004), Pinn (2001), Reddie (2003, 2006a, 2006b, 2008), Reddie and Jagessar (2007), Seibert (1985, 1989), C. Smith (1991), and West (1982, 1988a).

14. Several critical treatments of Cone's theology have been helpful here. Among the more noteworthy, see Burrow (1994), Hopkins (1999b), and Singleton (2002).

15. On Christianity being used in both a white supremacist and patriarchal manner to crush black women's spirit, see Cannon (1988, 1995), Gilkes (2001), Grant (1989), Townes (1993, 1995, 2006), and D.S. Williams (1993).

16. There are several recent works which continue the tradition of documenting and critically engaging the ideas and actions of church leaders and religious radicals. For example, see F.O. Best (1998), J.B. Childs (1980), F.C. Harris (1999), E.B. Higginbotham (1993), Pinn (2002a), Simms (2000), Wilmore (1983), H.J. Young (1977), and J.U. Young (1992).

Chapter Five

Critical Reparations Theory: Du Bois's Revolutionary Pan-Africanism and Revolutionary Humanism

From the very beginning of this nation, in the late eighteenth century, and even before, in the colonies, decade by decade and indeed year by year, the Negroes of the United States have appealed for redress of grievances, and have given facts and figures to support their own contention.

—W.E.B. Du Bois, *The Negro*, 241–42

It is important for philosophers to analyze the concept of reparations if we are to become clear about the morality of such an issue.

—Howard McGary, *Race and Social Justice*, 93

Du Bois had probably been the first black American to develop explicitly the concept of Pan-Africanism; certainly of all the black American intellectuals, he was the one most deeply identified with Africa itself—at a time when most Afro-Americans were embarrassed by the "primitiveness" of the ancestral societies.

—Elliott M. Rudwick, "W.E.B. Du Bois: Protagonist of the Afro-American Protest," 78

RACISM, REPARATIONS, AND DU BOIS'S PLACE IN THE DISCOURSE

The discourse and debates surrounding reparations for people of African origin and descent has historically and continues currently to offer Africana social and political philosophers, among many others, a treasure trove of theoretical and practical insights. These insights, if studied carefully and critically,

could, and I argue *should*, aid Africana critical theorists in their endeavors to
(1) seek redress for past and present anti-African racist wrongdoing, (2) transform their respective societies through the radical redistribution of social
wealth and political power, and (3) put forward preventive measures to ensure
that holocaust, enslavement, colonization, and segregation never happen to
any people, anywhere again. The modern African American reparations
movement by most accounts has two leading tendencies. The first tendency
grew out of the radical thought and political practices of the Black Power
Movement (1965–1975).[1] For some scholars, such as Howard McGary
(1977–1978), it was Student Non-Violent Coordinating Committee (SNCC)
official James Forman's "Black Manifesto," which argued that churches, synagogues, and other (state, public, and private) institutions who historically
and currently put forward and practice anti-black racism—what we are wont
to refer to, following the Caribbean political philosopher, Charles Mills
(2001, 2003), as "white supremacy"—owed African Americans $500 million
in reparations that began this tendency. However, as McGary is quick to point
out, it was Forman's abrupt interruption of the scheduled Sunday service at
the prestigious Riverside Church and the rhetorical excesses of his reading of
the 2,500-word manifesto, rather than the actual words of the manifesto,
which received media attention (Forman, 1997; Lecky and Wright, 1969;
McGary, 1977–1978). Other scholars, such as Robin D.G. Kelley (2002), lo-
cate the genesis of the first tendency in an outgrowth of the Black Power
movement's Republic of New Africa (RNA), whose central theorist, Imari
Obadele, among others, founded the National Coalition of Blacks for Reparations in America (N'COBRA) in 1987. Perhaps more than any other organization, N'COBRA has consistently contributed to modern reparations discourse and debate.[2] The first tendency, then, is clearly characterized by its
black nationalist and grassroots radicalism.

   The second leading tendency of the modern African American reparations
movement was inspired by Randall Robinson's *The Debt: What America
Owes to Blacks* (2000), which warned that racial problems in the U.S. would
continue and more than likely will increase if the historical and current injustices against African Americans were not quickly and adequately addressed.
The leading figures of this tendency include an all-star cohort of African
American lawyers led by Johnnie Cochran and Harvard University law professor, Charles Ogletree. Their basic approach to reparations is decidedly le-
galistic and involves elaborate legal theory and strategy that, in many senses,
parallels the politics of the National Association for the Advancement of Colored People (NAACP), especially during Thurgood Marshall's tenure with
the Association. Along with Cochran and Ogletree, other prominent African
American attorneys with unquestionable credentials in winning litigation

around victim compensation claims are involved, including Richard Scruggs, who won a $368.5 billion settlement from the tobacco industry, and Alexander Pires, who won more than $1 billion from the U.S. Department of Agriculture for decades of racially discriminatory policies against African American farmers. There are also African American Senators, Congresspersons and other prominent politicians involved in this stream of the reparations struggle that either influenced, or were influenced by Robinson's *The Debt*. For example, Massachusetts State Senator Bill Owens introduced Senate Bill 1621 in the late 1980s, calling on the state to provide reparations to African Americans for enslavement and subsequent segregation and human rights violations. And, more recently, Michigan Congressman John Conyers reintroduced (as he has consistently done for over two decades) HR 40 to Congress, which simultaneously signaled to many that the black reparations struggle, just as Robinson predicted, is currently and will remain a permanent part of the African American search for social justice.

With so many promising developments in the reparations movement it seems almost silly not to expect opposition from white conservatives, white liberals, and their black conservative counterparts (see A.L. Reed 2000). David Horowitz (2001), for instance, one of many white liberals who turned conservative, claims that the very idea of reparations is racist. Noted African American historian, John Hope Franklin (2001) quickly, albeit eloquently, took Horowitz and those of his ilk to task, observing that even whites who did not enslave Africans benefited and continue to benefit both materially and psychologically from the racist sociohistoric hierarchy and institutions that African holocaust, enslavement, colonization, and segregation made possible. When the whites saw that many blacks in the modern reparations movement felt that whites had no moral authority to judge the legitimacy and validity of their reparations claims, and especially after centuries of extreme human rights violations and outright racist reasoning regarding blacks and other people of color, they quickly called on their black conservative counterparts to parrot their anti-black ideological positions. Thomas Sowell, Shelby Steele, Condoleeza Rice, and Walter Williams, among others, attacked reparations as promoting "black dependency," playing on "white guilt," "demonizing all white people," utterly unrealistic, financially farfetched, monetarily misguided, and so on. But, none of the white or black conservatives' arguments against reparations seriously took into consideration the fact that financial or monetary compensation is merely one item on the modern reparations movement's multipoint program. In fact, many reparations theorists argue that compensation can and should take various forms, examples of which include, but are not limited to government provided housing, health care, education (from grade school to college), and economic/entrepreneurial development funds.

In light of all of these developments in the discourse and debates in the modern African American reparations movement—that is, considering the two major tendencies and their criticisms of each others' tactics and the white and black conservatives' criticisms of the two tendencies and their tactics—it may be beneficial at this point to turn to the history of African American political philosophy and social movements. More than mere intellectual exercise, taking a turn toward the history of African American political philosophy and social movements promises to offer us a unique opportunity to learn lessons from the life-work of theorists and political activists whose thought and practices often prefigure and provide us with sociohistoric situation-specific points of departure and paradigms of possibility that can be used in our ongoing struggles. Though there are many classical African American social and political theorists whose ideas and activism have great import for the modern reparations movement, it is to the radical political thought and multimovement leadership practices of W.E.B. Du Bois that I now intend to turn.

With regard to the modern reparations movement, Du Bois's pioneering work with the Pan-African movement and his efforts to argue for redress for anti-African racist wrongdoing and human rights abuses, by bringing the U.S. and other European imperial powers before the League of Nations and the United Nations, register as clear-cut examples of some of the ways in which his radical thought contributes to modern reparations discourse. The contention here, however, is not that Du Bois put forward a systematic or sophisticated reparations argument, but that there is a sense in which his thinking at specific intervals in his oeuvre lays a philosophical foundation and provides paradigms for modern Africana reparations arguments and movements. One of the central tasks of this chapter, then, will be to outline and develop Du Bois's position on reparations by taking a piecemeal approach to several of his seminal works on Africana social, political, and economic justice.

DU BOIS, REVOLUTIONARY PAN-AFRICANISM, AND BLACK RADICAL POLITICS

Africana intellectuals and political leaders generally regard Du Bois as "the Father of Pan-Africanism." Martin Luther King, Jr., the "Moses" of the Civil Rights movement, observed at the centennial celebration of Du Bois's birth that early in his career Du Bois "became aware that the expansion of imperialism was a threat to the emergence of Africa. He recognized the importance of the bonds between American Negroes and the land of their ancestors and he extended his activities to African affairs. After World War I he called Pan-African congresses in 1919, 1921, and 1923, alarming imperialists in all countries and disconcerting Negro moderates in America who were afraid of this restless, militant, black genius" (M.L. King, 1970, p. 22).

The Trinidadian historian and Pan-African Marxist, C.L.R. James (1977), wrote that "more than any other citizen of Western civilization (or of Africa itself) [Du Bois] struggled over many years and succeeded in making the world aware that Africa and Africans had to be freed from the thralldom which Western civilization had imposed on them" (p. 202). Du Bois, James continued, was "from start to finish . . . the moving spirit and active organizer" of five Pan-African congresses (p. 208). Additionally, Kwame Nkrumah, leader of the Ghanaian independence movement and first prime minister of Ghana, called Du Bois a "treasured part of Africa's history" and chronicled his special contributions to the discourse and development of Pan-Africanism in several works (Nkrumah, 1973a, pp. 42–43, 1970a, pp. 122–35).

Du Bois scholars harboring diverse intellectual agendas and political persuasions have also hailed Du Bois as "the Father of Pan-Africanism." Two-time Pulitzer Prize–winning Du Bois biographer David Levering Lewis (1993) noted that Nkrumah and other continental African leaders, such as Nnamdi Azikiwe and Jomo Kenyatta, saw Du Bois as a "Pan-African Moses" whose long labor in anti-imperialist efforts paved the way for their own Pan-African theories and practices (p. 8). The Nigerian philosopher Segun Gbadegesin (1996) observed, "It cannot be doubted that W.E.B. Du Bois remains the most famous intellectual defender of the Pan-African idea and movement" (p. 221). Moreover, Manning Marable and Arnold Rampersad relate that Du Bois's *The Negro*, not only provided "the Bible of Pan-Africanism," but also "established a tradition of black socialist historiography that would be enriched in subsequent decades by other Pan-African scholars such as C.L.R. James and Walter Rodney" (Rampersad, 1990, p. 234; Marable, 1986, p. 93; see also Du Bois, 1970b).

What then is Pan-Africanism according to "the Father of Pan-Africanism"? And, how has it helped to shape and frame Africana reparations arguments and movements? In answer to the first question, Du Bois (1971a) declared that "Pan-Africa[nism] means intellectual understanding and cooperation among all groups of Negro descent in order to bring about at the earliest possible time the industrial and spiritual emancipation of Negro peoples" (p. 208). Pan-Africanism is a movement with a threefold philosophical foundation. First, there are the moral claims of the Pan-African movement, which are deeply rooted in African history, culture, religion, and values. From the African point of view, holocaust, enslavement, colonization, and segregation are morally repugnant and reprehensible, and anyone or any group that perpetrates such horrors and affronts against humanity brings the hatchet down on their own heads. Each person in African cosmology and theology has an inherent worth, dignity, and divinity, and all human beings are equal before God. Therefore, atrocious acts such holocaust, enslavement, colonization, and segregation represent and register as crimes not only against African people, but crimes against the Creator and all creation as well.[3]

Second, as Africans on the continent and in the diaspora became conscious of their common experience of domination and discrimination at the hands of European imperial powers, they formed a united front to fight for their freedom (Esedebe, 1994; Langley, 1973, 1979; V.B. Thompson, 1969). This gave the Pan-African movement a definite political dimension that built on the moral base discussed above. Third, combining the moral claims and political programs of the movement, continental and diasporan Africans quickly became conscious of the concept of race and the reality of racism. Instead of "incessant [racial] self-questioning and the hesitation that arises from it," the Pan-Africanists argued that Africans should invert racism and use it as fuel to fire "race action," "race responsibility," and "race enterprises" (Du Bois, 1986a, p. 821). According to Du Bois's critical theory of race, it is not race and race consciousness that cause racism and other racial injustices, but racial exclusivity and racial domination and discrimination. As Lucuis Outlaw (1990)—echoing Du Bois—observed in "Toward a Critical Theory of Race," race and race consciousness can be utilized in efforts aimed at radically altering the white-supremacist social world in which race was/is conceived and constructed in constraining and conflictual terms (see also Outlaw, 1995, 1996a, 1996b, 2000). Hence, *race*, albeit a radically reconstructed revolutionary humanist concept of race, may be the very vehicle that the racialized (need to) use to struggle for and initiate their long overdue, but all too human, liberation. As Du Bois (1986d) declared in *Dusk of Dawn*,

> So long as we [are] fighting a color line, we must strive by color organization. We have no choice. If in time, the fight for Negro equality degenerates into organized murder for the suppression of whites, then our last case is no better than our first; but this need not be, if we are level-headed and clear-sighted, and work for the emancipation of all men from caste through the organization and determination of the present victims of caste. (p. 781)

From the foregoing, we can clearly see that for Du Bois and his anti-colonial colleagues Pan-Africanism was much more than mere "racial romanticism" (see Broderick, 1958, 1959; Gilroy, 1993a; Wolters, 2001). It was a multidimensional movement based on the premise that persons of African descent (as all human beings) deserve and must demand mutual respect and moral recognition. Further, Pan-Africanism was not so much about "race" as it was rallying continental and diasporan Africans to fight *against* racism (Aptheker, 1983; Du Bois, 1985a). This means, then, that Du Bois's entire approach to race was more instrumental than anything else. Time and time again he told his readers that although race is not real or has no scientific basis, we must not fall into the trap of thinking that racism, racial violence, and/or racial oppression are not real. From his Pan-African perspective, the history of the modern world told tale after tale of the reality of racism, racial violence, and racial oppression (see Du Bois, 1945, 1948, 1958, 1960, 1968b, 1969, 1985a, 1986a).

DU BOIS'S PAN-AFRICAN PETITIONS TO THE LEAGUE OF NATIONS AND PROPOSAL FOR AN "INTERNATIONAL INSTITUTE FOR THE STUDY OF THE NEGRO PROBLEM"

This brings us to the answer to the second question: How has Du Boisian Pan-Africanism helped to shape and (re)frame reparations arguments and movements? Immediately our attention is drawn to the various declarations, resolutions and manifestos Du Bois penned under the auspices of the Pan-African congresses. As Du Bois himself details in his own histories of Pan-Africanism, such as "A Second Journey to Pan-Africa," "The Pan-African Congresses: The Story of a Growing Movement," "The Pan-African Movement," and "Pan-Africanism: A Mission in My Life," the political program and moral mission of Pan-Africanism gave it a dual theoretical and practical thrust (Du Bois, 1958, 1970a, 1971b, 1995a). First, Pan-Africanism speaks to Africans' right to *self-determination*, *self-definition*, and *self-defense*. The overarching aims are geared toward protest against European imperial aggression, affirming Africans' humanity in the face of this dehumanizing onslaught, and reminding Africans and others that "the Negro people, as a race, have a contribution to make to civilization and humanity, which no other race can make" (Du Bois, 1986a, p. 825). In "The Conservation of Races," right before admonishing African Americans to "take their just place in the van of Pan-Negroism," Du Bois (1986c) stated, "For the development of Negro genius, of Negro literature and art, of Negro spirit, only Negroes bound and welded together, Negroes inspired by one vast ideal, can work out in its fullness the great message we have for humanity" (p. 820).

In some senses, "The Conservation of Races" registers as Du Bois's earnest attempt to struggle through the difficulties of employing biological criteria for group classification of differences in the human species, something that was en vogue in the social scientific community of his time. A lot of what he set down in the essay is antiquated and reads from our current optic as just outright wrongheaded racial reasoning.[4] But, we will get more out of his essay if we sidestep some of these *raciological* issues—issues that have to do with the scientific and systematic analysis of race—great and grave though these issues may be, and focus on his identification of the need for a policy to protect specific groups from the genocidal and white-supremacist practices of European and U.S. imperialism. It must be borne in mind, when we read "The Conservation of Races" today, that the Native American populations of the U.S. were reduced to 5 percent of their original population in a little more than a century (see Drinnon, 1980; H. Jackson, 1993; F. Jennings, 1976; A. Smith, 2005; Stannard, 1992). With the rhetoric and realities of Manifest Destiny, Du Bois had every reason to believe that Africans in the diaspora and on the continent had a similar fate in store (Fehrenbacher, 1970; Horsman, 1981; R.J. Miller, 2006; M.A. Morrison, 1997; Stephanson, 1996). His essay was and remains a solemn salvo to Africana intellectuals and activists to take action against such disaster. Therefore, those Africana intellectuals and activists who are very critical of Du Bois's political philosophy and public policy should think long and hard about what our present may have been like had he not led movements and built institutions to combat the anti-black racist practices and policies of the U.S. and European imperial governments. In an effort to prevent racial genocide, Du Bois had no other recourse, we could aver, than to advocate and articulate anti-racist racial identification for continental and diasporan African liberation.

In innumerable and unimaginable ways, holocaust, enslavement, colonization, and segregation greatly hindered Africana people from developing and delivering their "great message" to the world, as Du Bois wrote in "The Conservation of Races." Where some would sit and whine and wince at the very thought of Africana agitation, Du Bois consistently advocated "concerted thought and action," contending "we must do something. We cannot stand still; we cannot permit ourselves simply to be the victims of exploitation and social exclusion" (pp. 755, 695). One of the things Du Bois did was draft Pan-African petitions to the League of Nations, the forerunner to the United Nations, which was "conceived to promote [international] Peace and Justice" after World War I (Bendiner, 1975; Callahan, 2004; Egerton, 1978; Ostrower, 1979; Riches, 1933). In 1919 and again in 1921, Du Bois brought the conditions of continental and diasporan Africans to the attention of the League of Nations. He knew the League had "little, if any, direct power," but he wanted them to use their "vast moral power" to shape international public opinion and initiate an international discourse and dialogue on African holocaust, enslavement, colonization, and segregation. The 1921 Pan-African petition to the League of Nations read in part, "We ask and urge that the League of Nations take a firm stand on the absolute equality of races, and that it suggest to the colonial powers connected with the League of Nations to form an International Institute for the Study of the Negro Problem, and for the evolution and protection of the Negro race" (Du Bois, 1970a, pp. 192).

If, indeed, part of our modern plea for reparations revolves around public admission of and public apology for the holocaust committed against Africana people, then, Du Bois's Pan-African petitions to the League of Nations prefigure contemporary efforts to challenge and change racist reasoning regarding the African holocaust. Du Bois wanted to persuade the League of Nations, as a world or international court, to move beyond the rabid racist reasoning of European colonialism and U.S. imperialism and to acknowledge that the holocaust committed against Africana people was a centuries-spanning collective criminal act perpetrated by various European imperial governments. The "International Institute for the Study of the Negro Problem" that Du Bois envisioned would examine the past racist practices of holocaust, enslavement, and colonization, and the current continuing effects that these human rights violations have on hyper-segregated, contemporary, continental and diasporan Africans. In connecting past anti-African practices with present anti-African practices, the research programs, panels, and publications flowing from Du Bois's proposed "International Institute for the Study of the Negro Problem" would provide persons of African descent with firmer historical and moral footing on which to make claims for reparations. It would also educate non-Africans about the African holocaust and its lingering legacy on contemporary Africana life conditions, and encourage governments and their citizens to rethink the reparations issue in light of new research, new interpretations, and a rekindled international interest in reparations for people of African descent. And finally, Du Bois's "International Institute" would also help to highlight the simple sociohistoric fact that although the African holocaust has ended and old forms of enslavement and colonization are no longer practiced, there are many new forms of "semi-" or "quasi-" colonialism and enslavement (see Du Bois, 1945, 1985; Nkrumah, 1965, 1973a; Rabaka, 2003c, 2005a). The contemporary sociohistoric situations of apartheid in South Africa, Jim Crow laws in the United States, and the conditions of Afro-Brazilians quickly come to mind (see Fredrickson, 1981; J.E. Harris, 1993; Massey and Denton, 1993; Mazrui, Okpewho and Davies, 1999; Whitten and Torres, 1998; Vann Woodard, 1974). Reparations, then, is not so much about righting "old wrongs," or past injustices, as much as it is about combating their contemporary impact and effects on all of our life-worlds and lived experiences and the life-worlds and lived experiences of future generations, those "beautiful ones," as Ayi Kwei Armah (1969) so eloquently put it, who "are not yet born."

The second central objective of Pan-Africanism is concerned with connecting and creating a critical consciousness of continental and diasporan Africa and Africans amongst persons of African descent themselves. One of the great challenges of the modern Africana reparations movement has to do with persuading persons of African descent to see themselves and their ancestors as human beings who have an inherent worth and who deserve mutual respect and moral recognition. If continental and diasporan Africans do not see each other and their ancestors as human persons with rights to be respected and protected, and if continental and diasporan Africans, in fact, approach each other with disdain and in dignity-denying terms, then the reparations movement is left without a rallying point, and persons of African descent have no compelling reasons to make moral claims for the insults and injustices committed against them and their ancestors. Du Bois's Pan-African thought provides a model for modern reparations theorists in that it was extremely critical of Eurocentric dignity-denying interpretations of Africa and Africans. In "Pan-Africa and New Racial Philosophy," for example, Du Bois (1971a) thundered,

> American Negroes, West Indians, West Africans and South Africans must proceed immediately to wipe from their minds the preconcepts of each other which they have gained through white newspapers. They must cease to think of Liberia and Haiti as failures in government; of American Negroes as being engaged principally in frequenting Harlem cabarets and Southern lynching parties; of West Indians as ineffective talkers; and of West Africans as parading around in breech-clouts. These are the pictures of each other which white people have painted for us and which with engaging naiveté we accept, and then proceed to laugh at each other and criticize each other before we make any attempt to learn the truth. (p. 208)

Du Bois knew that as long as continental and diasporan Africans viewed themselves and their history and culture through the eyes of their racial rulers, they would not only not understand why reparations are important, but also they would not understand their own (inherent) human worth and human wealth. Reparations, then, in some senses begins with black folk repairing the damage done to their self-conceptions and axiological universe(s). Du Bois's work with the Pan-African movement contributes to the modern movement for reparations in the fact that it forces the finance-focused naysayers to admit that reparations is about acknowledging past human rights violations; ending present human rights violations; and educating continental and diasporan Africans, as well as non-African others, about the history of African holocaust, enslavement, colonization, and segregation and the historic and current political, economic, and ethical implications of these atrocious acts. About a quarter of a century after he petitioned the League of Nations on behalf of black folk, Du Bois appealed to the newly formed United Nations Commission on Human Rights on behalf of a specific group of people of African descent–African Americans. It is to this discourse that we now turn.

DU BOIS'S *APPEAL TO THE WORLD* AND THE UNITED NATIONS FOR AFRICAN AMERICAN REPARATIONS

In 1946, Du Bois prepared *An Appeal to the World: A Statement on the Denial of Human Rights to Minorities in the Case of Citizens of Negro Descent in the United States of America and An Appeal to the United Nations for Redress* in which he made several significant contributions to reparations theory and the modern movement for reparations. The ninety-four-page petition added up to an eloquent and irrefutable indictment of the U.S. with regard to its past and present violations of African American human rights. Du Bois (1970a) began his discourse by noting that African Americans "form largely a segregated caste, with restricted legal rights, and many illegal disabilities. They are descendants of the Africans brought to America during the sixteenth, seventeenth, eighteenth and nineteenth centuries and reduced to slave labor" (p. 227). In thinking about this document in critical terms, we need to note that from the outset Du Bois introduces the fact that African Americans' ancestors were taken from Africa and enslaved. This is important because we see from the beginning that his theory of reparations is historically grounded and culturally rooted in the realities of the African American experience. Additionally, this point of departure is also important because it gives Du Bois grounds on which to make claims for redress based on descendancy.

Most reparations theorists maintain that holocaust, enslavement, and/or colonization are extreme human rights abuses and, taking into consideration human rights law and policy, each living victim of these crimes is entitled individually to seek and receive reparations from those who committed or permitted these wrongs (see Bittker, 2003; Boxill, 1972; Brooks, 1999, 2004; Martin and Yaquinto, 2007; McGary, 1974; Munford, 1996; Winbush, 2003). But what happens when there are no living victims to pursue claims of reparations? In such a situation the descendants of a victim of a human rights violation are then entitled to reparations. In other words, the right of reparations is not extinguished with the death of the victim, but can be pursued by his or her heirs (see Bittker, 2003; Boxill, 2003; Matsuda, 1995; McGary, 1977–1978, 1984; Munford, 1996). Here, however, we step onto tough terrain. We know well that the older the injury, or the more time elapsed between the crimes committed and the claims of reparations, the harder it is for people to recognize and feel responsible for the wrong done. For instance, European Americans generally reject African American claims for reparations for enslavement and various other historic human rights abuses. In fact, as with the example of Horowitz and his colleagues, many European Americans maintain that the whole idea of reparations for African Americans is not only unfair, but "reverse-racism." They confuse and collapse reparations, a series of anti-racist policies and, perhaps, payment programs (monetary and non-monetary) sanctioned by the state as restoration and compensation for human rights abuses, with racism—that is, systemic domination and discrimination based on biological/"racial" categorization (see Banks, 2001; Feagin, 2000; A. L. Reed, 2000). In light of the fact that many white (and black) conservatives purposely confuse and misconstrue the central claims of the modern reparations movement, reparations theorists are charged with a special task to work on conceptual clarity when building their theories of reparations. The new theories of reparations will have to have both the political brawn and polemical bite of traditional reparations theory and a new polyvocal tone that is accessible to persons across the wide spectrum of our contemporary multi-issue-oriented political world and ethical universe (Baraka, 2003; Berry, 2005; Brophy, 2002a, 2002b, 2006; Cartlidge, 2007; De Greiff, 2006; Hakim, 2005; Harvey, 2007; C.P. Henry, 2007; Martin and Yaquinto, 2007; McPhail, 2002; Miller and Kumar, 2007; Salzberger and Turck, 2004; Schedler, 1998; Torpey, 2006).

One of the first things a theory of reparations must do is properly identify and determine who committed the human rights abuse. Since both the perpetrators and the victims are deceased in the case of European Americans and African Americans it is very difficult to point to and punish actual individuals who committed the crimes. But, when we bear in mind that these individuals were citizens of a country that not only condoned but continues to benefit from these crimes, then we are given liberty to charge the U.S. government with responsibility. Why? Because governments (or "nation-states") have an intergenerational and/or transgenerational life (see Barkan, 2000; Dunleavy, 1993; Goldberg, 2001; Nozick, 1975; Skinner, 1997). This Du Boisian approach to reparations focuses on both historic anti-African human rights abuses and their contemporary effects. The U.S. government may not feel compelled to compensate enslaved African ancestors, but it can compensate contemporary African Americans by rectifying the current colonial/capitalist/sexist/racist reality—that is, the U.S. government could begin the reparation process by ending the ongoing white-supremacist, patriarchal, capitalist, colonial exploitation and oppression of African Americans. Du Bois (1970a) spoke to this issue in *An Appeal to the World* when he wrote,

> The so-called American Negro, therefore, while it is in no sense absolutely set off physically from its fellow American, has nevertheless a strong, hereditary cultural unity, born in slavery, of common suffering, prolonged proscription and curtailment of political and civil rights; and especially because of economic and social disabilities. Largely from this fact, have arisen their cultural gifts to America—their rhythm, music and folk song; their religious faith and

customs; their contribution to American art and literature; their defense of their country in every war, on land, sea and in the air; and especially the hard, continuous toil upon which the prosperity and wealth of this continent has largely been built. (p. 227)

Du Bois highlights and accents the initial violation of African American human rights by the U.S. government and its citizens: collective kidnapping and enslavement. Then, he observes the continued abuse of African American human rights because of the state-sanctioned Jim Crow character of U.S. society after enslavement. Next, he moves away from traditional reparations claims and on to new terrain by focusing on the violation of African American civil, social, political, and economic rights in the post-enslavement state-sanctioned segregated U.S. society (Chafe, Gavins and Korstad, 2001; Gilmore, Dailey and Simon, 2000; Martin and Yaquinto, 2007; Packard, 2003; Vann Woodard, 1974; Wormser, 2003). Du Bois's approach to reparations seems to suggest that the link between past and present inhuman and anti-African racist practices is extremely important to establish, because it enables Africana reparations theorists to make concrete connections and claims about the historic denial of African American human rights and their current social, political, and economic conditions.

Above Du Bois observes that African Americans have bequeathed several seminal "cultural gifts" to America and, he stresses, "especially the hard, continuous toil upon which the prosperity and wealth of this continent has largely been built." Here, as in his classic *Black Reconstruction*, he minces no words and makes it known that it was several centuries of coerced African labor under enslavement that rests at the heart of this country's successful industrialization and economic growth and prosperity. Because the United States and its citizens have received economic and social benefits and privileges as a result of the enslavement of Africans, and because even after their enslavement African Americans' human, civil, social, political, and economic rights continue to be violated, Du Bois indicted the U.S. government.

Even after enslavement, the U.S. government created and enforced American apartheid (or "Jim Crow") and other racially discriminatory laws that contributed to African Americans' current social, political, and economic deprivation and destitution. Du Bois's theory of reparations, then, is dialectical in the sense that it not only calls for redress for past wrongs but, equally, for present wrongs as well. His focus on the denial of African American civil rights and their economic disenfranchisement under contemporary U.S. law gives greater urgency to the issue than traditional reparations claims, because he is asking the current government to rectify current injustices rather than historic ones. Du Bois's theory of reparations assumes that U.S. citizens, and specifically the white ruling race/class, will be more receptive to ending present racist practices connected to past racist practices than to providing compensation for historic injustices standing alone.

THE QUESTION OF COMPENSATION
AND CRITICAL RACE THEORY

One of the major weaknesses of Du Bois's reparations theory revolves around the question of compensation. Earlier I stated that one of the first things a viable theory of reparations must do is properly identify and determine the nature of the injustice and who committed the offense. Once we identify who did what, then we have to be clear on what it is that we are demanding as compensation. Du Bois's theory of reparations in many instances does not spell out in any accessible or clearly defined terms what appropriate or adequate compensation should entail and, therefore, leaves the door open for the white ruling race/class to wiggle their way out of reparations.

Certainly Du Bois (1971b) advocated "socialized medicine, dentistry and nursing," "the re-distribution of wealth," and "revolutionary change", by which he meant much more than reforming the racial sociopolitical hierarchy and putting blacks in the place of whites, and airbrushing capitalism, reforming and reframing it, (re)making it black user-friendly (pp. 157–58, 169). Even a cursory reading of Du Bois reveals that he grew increasingly critical of capitalism as he deepened and developed his critical theoretical perspective on racism. Capitalism could neither be sanitized nor modernized to fulfill the vital needs of African Americans, or any cultural group for that matter (and the same could and should be said of sexism, racism, and colonialism). That being the case, Du Bois militantly embraced an alternative conception of humanity and society that he understood to offer the most comprehensive critique of and challenge to capitalism: revolutionary democratic socialism (Horne, 1986; D.L. Lewis, 1993, 2000; Marable, 1986; Rabaka, 2007a; C.J. Robinson, 2000).

Du Bois's revolutionary democratic socialism was decidedly anti-racist, anti-colonialist, *and*, of course, anti-capitalist, always and ever pointing to the historical and current connections between the contradictions and crimes of capitalism and bourgeois banditry, colonial exploitation and cultural deracination, and racial violence and ethnic oppression. Further, his version and unique vision of revolutionary democratic socialism was also deeply self-reflexive and self-critical, practicing an unprecedented internal ideological critique which was predicated on raising white socialists' (and communists') awareness of the political economy of racism and the pitfalls of whiteness within their own ranks and political parties. His anti-colonialist and anti-racist revolutionary democratic socialism, in a word, simultaneously ruptured and destabilized the established order's ideological imperatives of maintaining and reproducing a white-supremacist, capitalist society, and it demystified and decolonized white (and many black) Marxists' theories and praxes, accentuating the fact that white workers' (and white socialists') *whiteness* provides them with the privileges of racial kinship with white capitalists in a white supremacist society and world. For Du Bois, then, reparations was never simply about repairing the unfathomable moral and cultural damage mercilessly inflicted upon African Americans and other persons of African descent, which is to say that reparations was never simply about people of African descent coming to terms with their brutal and broken pasts, but it was also about revolutionizing race relations—not simply black and white race relations, but blacks with the world—and, equally important, "the re-distribution of wealth" and political power by cutting capitalism and colonialism off at their knees.

A critical reading of Du Bois's reparations theory demonstrates that he did not argue for "revolutionary change[s]" in the interest of African Americans alone, but was deeply and increasingly committed to revolutionary humanism, revolutionary democratic socialism, insurgent internationalism, and critical multiculturalism in the interest of suffering and suppressed humanity as a whole. Du Bois's dialectic of nationalism and internationalism created an untamable tension in his theory of reparations, one that provides his work in this area with theoretic strengths as well as political weaknesses. What is more, because his theory of reparations cast such a wide theoretical and political net, many modern reparations theorists either overlook or unwittingly misinterpret Du Bois's major contributions to contemporary reparations discourse.

As demonstrated above, Du Bois was without a doubt the doyen of Africana reparations discourse in the first half of the twentieth century. But, even when we take all of the aforementioned into consideration there is still a sense in which his reparations theory seriously suffers because he did not thoroughly think through and outline, in an accessible manner, the major questions of compensation. It can be said, then, that Du Bois succeeded on identifying who committed the injustice and determining the nature of the injustice, but failed to follow through on articulating what African Americans, the victims of these human rights violations, want and deserve as a result of and repair for these injustices. Keeping in mind what we have learned from Du Bois's contributions to reparations discourse, we will conclude by building on his reparations theory and developing its weakest point, the question of compensation.[5] In order to comprehend the question of compensation a brief discussion of critical race theory is required, because unless we understand what race is and isn't, and unless we radically engage race and racism from the critical theoretical perspective of those who have been and continue to be hyper-raced in a white-supremacist society, such as the United States, then reparations arguments for racially motivated human rights violations will appear abstract, unimportant, and perhaps even absurd.

No longer considered the exclusive domain of legal studies scholars and radical civil rights lawyers and law professors, critical race theory has blossomed and currently encompasses and includes a wide range of theory and theorists from diverse academic disciplines (Essed and Goldberg, 2001; Outlaw, 1990; Valdes, Culp and Harris, 2002). Its most prominent practitioners, initially law professors and "left scholars, most of them scholars of color," borrowed from many of the political and theoretical breakthroughs of black nationalism, radical feminism, New Left Marxism, poststructuralism, and postmodernism (Crenshaw, Gotanda, Peller and Thomas, 1995, p. xiii). They also employed and experimented with new cutting-edge literary techniques and social science methodologies that shaped and shaded their work and burgeoning sociolegal discourse, ultimately giving it a fierceness and flair unheard of in the history of legal studies. Early critical race theorists' work acutely accented "the vexed bond between law and racial power" (p. xiii). The emphasis on race and power quickly led them to the critique of "white supremacy and the subordination of people of color," not simply in the legal system, but in society as a whole (p. xiii).

Most notably, critical race theory essentially entails a claim that race and racism are central to European modernity; an insistence that European modernity spawned a homogenizing social, political, legal and medical system that glosses over the heterogeneity of non-Europeans (non-whites); a declaration that racism interlocks with sexism and classism to form an overarching system of oppression that thrice threatens modern movements for radical multicultural democracy; a critique of the established orders' claims of colorblindness and racially neutral rule; a critique of whiteness and white supremacy; a call for racial justice; and a controversial claim that the raced (i.e., non-whites or "people of color") may have to employ race and their experiences of white-supremacist racism as a rallying point to mobilize a movement *against* white-supremacist, patriarchal, capitalist, colonialism (see Crenshaw, et al., 1995; Delgado, 1995; Delgado, Stefancic and Harris, 2001; Essed and Goldberg, 2001; Goldberg, Musheno and Bower, 2001; Goldberg and Solomos, 2002; Wing 1997, 2000).

Du Bois's philosophy of race and theory of reparations, as we have witnessed throughout this chapter, in many senses foreshadows contemporary critical race theory and, therefore, contributes several paradigms and theoretic points of departure. However, as with so many other aspects of his thought, Du Bois's writings on race and racism have been relegated to the realm, at best, of sociology (and, more specifically, sociology of race), which downplays and diminishes their transdisciplinarity and seminal significance for Africana Studies and the reconstruction of contemporary critical social theory and radical politics. Therefore, his writings on race have been virtually overlooked and/or rendered intellectually invisible by critical race theorists.[6]

In *Critical Race Theory*, Richard Delgado (1995) states that though it began organizing as a "self-conscious entity" in 1989, critical race theory's "intellectual origins go back much further" (p. xiv). He states, "The movement has predecessors—Critical Legal Studies, to which it owes a great debt, feminism, and Continental social and political philosophy. It [also] derives its inspiration from the American civil rights tradition, including Martin Luther King, W.E.B. Du Bois, Rosa Parks, and Cesar Chavez, and from nationalist movements, including Malcolm X and the Panthers" (p. xiv). What I wish to highlight here is, first, though it generously draws from European and white American thought traditions, African American political thought and social movements have been at the heart of and enormously influential on critical race theory's discourse and debates. This is an important point to make since there has been a relative silence regarding critical race theory in African American Studies in specific, and Africana Studies more generally. If, in fact, African American radical intellectuals, social critics, and political activists have been at the heart of this discourse, central to its formation, and many of its major advocates and practitioners, then African American Studies scholars and students would be remiss to continue to allow critical race theory to go unengaged.[7]

A second issue I wish to emphasize here involves Du Bois's place in critical race scholarship. Many, if not all, of the key concerns of critical race theory are prefigured in Du Bois's discourse on race and racism in ways that makes one wonder whether critical race theory is simply a continuation, or a contemporary version of Du Boisian race theory by another name. For instance, Du Bois's critique of European modernity, albeit often masked and muted, found it, Euro-modernity, morally weak and wanting because each of its inventions and innovations was accompanied by unprecedented human domination and environmental destruction. Put another way, Du Bois's contributions to critical race theory accent the fact that when and where whites broke new ground, in whatever technical capacity and in whichever area of existence, they did so on the graves of people of color, imperially embalming the earth and making the life-worlds, countries, and continents of people of color a massive mortuary. From Du Bois's view, no amount of racial naïveté could (or can) save non-whites. They, therefore, had/have no other recourse but to argue for and embrace, as Du Bois did time and time again throughout his long career, *race-consciousness*. This is one of the central themes of contemporary critical race theory, and Kimberlé Crenshaw and company claim, "With its explicit embrace of race-consciousness, Critical Race Theory aims to reexamine the terms by which race and racism have been negotiated in American consciousness, and to recover and revitalize the radical tradition of race-consciousness among African Americans and other peoples of color— a tradition that was discarded when integration, assimilation and the ideal of color-blindness became the official norms of racial enlightenment" (Crenshaw et al., 1995, p. xiv).

It is virtually impossible to argue that Du Bois did not contribute to "the radical tradition of race-consciousness among African Americans and other peoples of color." In fact, Du Bois's faultfinders and fans alike would agree that his pioneering work as a Pan-Africanist and soldier for African American civil rights and social justice, and specifically his groundbreaking quarter of a century contributions to the National Association for the Advancement of Colored People (NAACP), irrefutably demonstrate his commitment to a *critical race-consciousness.*

At certain intervals in Du Bois's discourse this impulse to embrace critical race-consciousness registered as racial separatism, at others times black nationalism and Pan-Africanism, and yet at other moments the radical humanism and revolutionary internationalism I observed above. However, no matter which position Du Bois embraced and argued for, an *anti-racist social ethics* was ever at work and at the heart of his agenda and ultimate objectives.[8] Moreover, the emphasis on ethics made many of his positions— including and extending beyond his anti-racism—temporal tactics that were extremely time and space sensitive.

One of the most intriguing issues that Du Bois's discourse on race and racism brings to the fore is the often-overlooked fact that it is possible to reject biology-based concepts of race, and any and all forms of racism, without denying the sociohistoric and politico-economic reality of race and racism. The so-called "anti-race" theorists who argue that concepts of race and race-consciousness on the part of the racially oppressed are the cause of and perpetuate racism and racial oppression are, quite simply, thinking wrong about race and have not done their homework on the origins and evolution(s), and the historic sociopolitical uses and abuses, of race and racism. Racism, as critical race theorists never weary of reminding us, is "systematic" and, at this point, deeply "ingrained" in social, political, intellectual, and cultural consciousness (Crenshaw, et al., 1995, p. xiv). It is an invisible invader and an often-illusive intruder that has impacted and affected, perhaps, almost every life experience human beings have had in the modern (and postmodern) moment. Even if utter abandonment of race concepts and race-consciousness were possible, the material and morphological, religious and rancorous, public and private consequences of the last five hundred years of racialized human existence—that is, rote racialization and racial injustice, and the sociocultural memories associated with these phenomena—would remain.

The African American reparations struggle is intrinsically related to critical race theory in that it is not simply a struggle *for* reparations, but also a struggle *against* racism, and specifically white supremacy. It is not merely a movement for redress, but also a consciousness-raising movement deeply concerned with what W. James Booth (2001) has recently referred to as "memory-justice," and what Du Bois (1995c) dubbed the "buried truths" that must be resurrected in the quest not only for reparations but also the antiracist and anti-capitalist reconstruction of democracy in the United States. By coupling Du Bois's reparations theory with critical race theory I intend to provide inchoate answers to the critical question of compensation: What do African Americans desire and deserve as compensation for holocaust, enslavement, colonization, segregation, Black Codes, Jim Crow laws, the continued reality of anti-black racism, and their sociohistoric and politico-economic deprivation and destitution?

First, the government needs to officially and publicly acknowledge its complicity in these crimes against humanity. This is an important first step because African Americans are perpetually surrounded by people who disingenuously say that they know about "slavery," and that African Americans, the naysayers nonchalantly say, should "just get over it." However, from the African American perspective a distinction must be made between "knowledge" and "acknowledgement." All U.S. citizens may "know" about the governments' violations of African Americans' human and civil rights, but the government's formal "acknowledgement" of these injustices is a simultaneously crucial and critical part of the repair process.

Second, after the government acknowledges its historic violation of African American human rights, it should quickly take concrete steps to end current anti-African (and other racist) practices. At this point the government might make pledges of money in an effort to remedy its racist practices, but a more moral and meaningful remedy would be federal laws and legal actions that involve the radical reorganization of the basic (racist/sexist/capitalist) structure of U.S. society, making it a true multicultural, participatory democracy in all U.S. citizens' image and interests.[9] From this stance, the government should not be given the easy out of paying African Americans off for "slavery"—which, in point of fact, anything that they could possibly offer would be an insult and insufficient since there is no price that can be put on a single human life, let alone millions and millions of human lives. Part of the repair process involves the government telling the truth about its complicity in this crime against humanity, and making a political commitment to right these wrongs. In the long run, the truth-telling and the political commitment will more than likely generate the type of deep and sustained ethical investment necessary to remedy the contemporary effects of holocaust, enslavement, colonization, and segregation than quick-scheme, rush-up-hush-up, one-shot, out-of-the-context pledges and plans of compensation. Further, the government's acknowledgement of the extent to which past racist practices inform present racist practices would set a standard and enable its current and future leaders and citizens to assess its progress toward remedying the contemporary effects of anti-African (and other racist) practices.

Third, after the government acknowledges its abuse of African American human rights and initiates the repair process by sanctioning new laws geared toward radically reorganizing the U.S. social structure, then we can address the issue of financial and non-financial compensation. Since one of the major objectives of the theory of reparations that I am developing here is to rectify the contemporary effects of past racist practices, I am proposing that any reparations made be used for African Americans *collectively* rather than individually (see C.P. Henry, 2007; Marable, 2002; McGary, 1977–1978; Nickel, 1973). Financial compensation could be invested in and used for African American education, housing, health care, job training, and/or land acquisition. However, we should be clear here, financial compensation is only one part of the repair process, and should never take precedence over the non-financial aspects of the African American reparations agenda. Again, we will probably get more moral mileage out of the truth-telling and the political commitment part of the repair process than any quick-scheme, let's-hurry-up-and-pay-them-off plans of compensation. Moreover, because part of the whole point of this approach to reparations is to remedy ongoing human rights abuses, and white-supremacist, anti-black racism in specific, then the non-financial moral concerns are an incredibly critical component of African American reparations claims.

Non-financial compensation could involve the establishment of national African holocaust monuments and museums, institutes and centers for the study of African American history and culture (à la Du Bois's 1921 proposal to the League of Nations), and other federally funded educational programs that take the museum exhibitions and institutes' findings and shares them with the general U.S. public and wider world. This would not only build a public morality for and give proper respect and recognition to African Americans in U.S. history and culture, but it would also enable African Americans and others to learn the great and grave lessons that African holocaust and enslavement in the United States have to teach. However, here it must be observed that any discussion of holocaust memorials, monuments, or museums should be directed, first and foremost, to Native Americans, who suffered the first holocaust in the Western hemisphere and who, along with their contemporary Latino and Chicano kith and kin, have been and continue to be erased from and rendered invisible in U.S. history, culture, and social consciousness.

DU BOIS AND CRITICAL REPARATIONS THEORY

In closing, it should be said that the foregoing thoughts are meant merely as hints as to what Du Bois's social and political philosophy contributes to modern reparations discourse. Certainly there are several other ways that we could analyze his thought for its import to modern reparations theory. However, as stated earlier, one of central objectives of this study is not so much to suggest that Du Bois put forward any type of systematic or sophisticated theory of reparations, but simply to call our attention to an overlooked archive for modern reparations arguments. Clearly Du Bois's work in this area has many deficiencies. However, instead of simply throwing the baby out with the bath water, as is so often the case with Africana (and especially Du Bois's) thought, the suggestion here is that we keep in mind that his work is couched in a specific historical, cultural, and intellectual milieu, and that we look at it more as a model and map for our liberation theory and praxis than an unalterable blueprint. As illustrated above, limitations in Du Bois's logic can often easily be overcome by turning to contemporary critical theoretical developments and frameworks. In this instance, where Du Bois's theory of reparations was found wanting on the question of compensation, I quickly turned to the discourse of critical race theory and, using Du Bois's theory as a point of departure, developed a theory of reparations that speaks to the specific needs of our age.

African Americans' current cries for reparations are part and parcel of an older and wider, world-historic discourse on the denial of continental and diasporan Africans' humanity and distinct human personality. By using Du Bois's theory of reparations as a paradigm and point of departure, and coupling it with contemporary reparations theory and critical race theory, the emphasis here has been on exposing some of the connections between historic violations of continental and diasporan Africans' human rights and their current conditions. Du Bois's dialectical approach to reparations provides modern reparations theorists with a foundation on which to develop a more nuanced multiperspectival reparations theory that seriously and simultaneously considers the conundrums of the contemporary world. The resistance to reparations in recent years is very different from that which Du Bois confronted; however, his work continues to provide answers to the mind-numbing and spirit-crushing riddle(s) of racism. His reparations theory can and, as I have argued throughout this chapter, should be used to inspire contemporary reparations theorists and activists to renew their commitments to, not simply reparations, but to the myriad anti-imperial struggles throughout the (post)modern world. Du Bois's reparations theory, with its emphasis on the connections between racism and the rise of capitalism, and its stress on the kinship between capitalism and colonialism, also accentuates the fact that an Africana critical theory of contemporary society is needed now, perhaps, more than ever before.

NOTES

1. Several of my colleagues and comrades are at the forefront of what is currently being called "Black Power Studies," and it is their work, among the work of others, which most informs my conception of the radical politics of the Black Power Movement. Please see Brisbane (1974), S. Brown (2003), Carson (1981), Cleaver and Katsiaficas (2001), Collier-Thomas and Franklin (2001), Conyers (2006), Glaude (2002), Jeffries (2002), C.E. Jones (1998), Joseph (2006a, 2006b), W.E. Martin (2005), McCartney (1992), Muse (1968), Ogbar (2004), Peeks (1971), Pinkney (1976), Pohlman (2003), Ransby (2003), D.E. Robinson (2001), Springer (1999, 2005), Van Deburg (1992, 1997a), and K. Woodard (1999).

2. For a more detailed discussion of Obadele, the Republic of New Africa (RNA), and N'COBRA's reparations plan(s), see Aiyetoro (2003), Eustace and Obadele (2000), Joseph (2006a), Lumumba, Obadele and Tafia (1993), Obadele (1975, 1997), Ogbar (2004), R.C. Smith (2003), and Van Deburg (1997b).

3. This interpretation of African ethics, cosmology, and theology has been greatly influenced by Blakely, van Beek, and Thomson (1994); Fulop and Raboteau (1996); Gyekye (1995, 1996); Idowu (1975); Karenga (1999, 2004); Mbiti (1975, 1989); B.C. Ray (2000); Wilmore (1989); and Zahan (1979).

4. Anthony Appiah (1985, 1992) has made several solid criticisms of Du Bois's philosophy of race, and specifically as articulated in "The Conservation of Races." However, his interpretation often unfairly lifts Du Bois's thought out of its historical and cultural context and criticizes it from an imagined raceless and/or post-racism point of view. Needless to say, several Africana philosophers have criticized Appiah's (mis)interpretation and (mis)treatment of Du Bois's philosophy of race. For further discussion, see Gooding-Williams (1996), Lott (1997, 2000, 2001), Outlaw (1995, 1996b), and Rabaka (2003b, 2005a).

5. My conception of compensation(s) has been deeply influenced by distributive justice discourse, contemporary human rights theory, and critical race theory. For critical discussions, see Boxill (1992, 2003), Dworkin (1977), Essed and Goldberg (2001), Goldberg (1993, 1997, 2001, 2003), Goodin and Pettit (1993, 1997), Habermas (1994), Kolm (1993), Kymlicka (1997), McGary (1999), C.W. Mills (1997, 1998, 1999, 2000), Nozick (1975, 1997), Outlaw (1990, 1996a, 2005), J. Rawls (1971, 1997), West (1982, 1988, 1993), Wing (1997, 2000), and Zegeye, Harris and Maxted (1991).

6. For a few examples of works that offer interdisciplinary interpretations of Du Bois, and which treat his critical social and radical political thought, see Cain (1993), Coates, Browning and Beenah (1996), Dennis (1997), W.A. Drake (1985), Horne (1986), Marable (1986), Nonini (1992), Owen (1973), Rabaka (2003c, 2003d, 2003e, 2007a), Richards (1970), C.J. Robinson (2000), Vivian (1997), W.D. Wright (1985), and Yuan (1998). Also, as may be extremely evident at this point, the present chapter in its entirety can be read as an intense *transdisciplinary* (re)interpretation of Du Bois's reparations discourse that brings it, however briefly, into dialogue with contemporary discursive formations and practices: from critical race and radical feminist theory to postmodern and postcolonial theory, among others.

7. There have, of course, been exceptions, more or less intellectual flirtations between critical race and Africana theorists: for instance, works such as L.E. Collins (2003), Gordon (1999), and Outlaw (1990). However, these works are more in the realm of intellectual history, sort of documenting the often-omitted Africana dimension of critical race theory. What I propose to do here is to use Du Bois as a theoretic point of departure to highlight and accent the major themes of critical race theory as it is currently practiced. In addition, my work here also endeavors to place new issues on critical race theory's agenda, issues that will continue to be downplayed and diminished until Du Bois's anti-racist discoveries (among other Africana theorists') are critically engaged for their contribution to contemporary race and racism discourse. For further discussion of Du Bois's contributions to critical race theory, and the need to further develop a critical dialogue between Africana Studies and critical race theory, please see my essays: "W.E.B. Du Bois's 'The Comet' and Contributions to Critical Race Theory: An Essay on Black Radical Politics and Anti-Racist Social Ethics" and "The Souls of White Folk: W.E.B. Du Bois's Critique of White Supremacy and Contributions to Critical White Studies" (Rabaka, 2006c, 2006d).

8. My interpretation of Du Bois's social ethics, as well as my general argument throughout the preceding paragraphs, has been deeply influenced by Ramona Edelin's doctoral dissertation, "The Philosophical Foundations and Implications of William Edward Burghardt Du Bois's Social Ethic" (1981), which carefully and critically elaborates Du Bois's life-long preoccupation with and predilection for social ethics.

9. Perhaps the most promising development in this vein has been the discourse and debates revolving around critical race theory. If any part of our reparation plan involves litigation and new (anti-racist) legislation, we will be remiss not to draw from the efforts of critical race theorists. For further discussion, see Crenshaw, Gotanda, Peller and Thomas (1995), Delgado (1995), Delgado and Stefancic (1997), Delgado, Stefancic and Harris (2001), Essed and Goldberg (2001), Goldberg, Musheno and Bower (2001), Goldberg and Solomos (2002), Outlaw (1990, 2005), C.W. Mills (1997, 1998, 2003), Valdes, Culp and Harris (2002), and Wing (1997, 2000).

Chapter Six

Conclusion: The Souls of Black Radical Folk: Du Bois, Africana Studies, and the Crises of Contemporary Critical Social Theory

In the folds of this European civilization I was born and shall die, imprisoned, conditioned, depressed, exalted and inspired. Integrally a part of it and yet, much more significant, one of its rejected parts; one who expressed in life and action and made vocal to many, a single whirlpool of social entanglement and inner psychological paradox, which always seem to me more significant for the meaning of the world today than other similar and related problems.

Little indeed did I do, or could I conceivably have done, to make this problem or to loose it. Crucified on the vast wheel of time, I flew round and round with the Zeitgeist, waving my pen and lifting faint voices to explain, expound and exhort; to see, foresee and prophesy, to the few who could or would listen. Thus very evidently to me and to others I did little to create my day or greatly change it; but I did exemplify it and thus for all time my life is significant for all lives of men.

—W.E.B.Du Bois, *Du Bois: Writings*, 555

Du Bois continued to write and lecture until the end of his life, but the output of his last three decades had slight impact among his black American contemporaries. Then, ironically, shortly after his departure from the United States, Du Bois's reputation soared, and he was transformed into a prophet. In the early 1960s the militant integrationist phase of the black direct-action protest movement was building toward its climax, and his enormous contributions became widely recognized and revered among young activists. . . . Then a few years afterwards, with the decline of militant integrationism and the ascendancy of the Black Power Era with its separatist thrust, the relevance of his nationalist writings became widely appreciated. W.E.B. Du Bois, the propagandist, had now become symbol and prophet, and events both in the United States and abroad vindicated the celebrated

183

words he had used in *The Souls of Black Folk* in 1903: "The problem of the Twentieth Century is the problem of the color-line."

> —Elliott M. Rudwick, "W.E.B. Du Bois:
> Protagonist of the Afro-American Protest," 82–83

[U]nderneath the conservative popular base is the substratum of the outcasts and outsiders, the exploited and persecuted of other races and other colors, the unemployed and the unemployable. They exist outside the democratic process; their life is the most immediate and the most real need for ending intolerable conditions and institutions. Thus their opposition is revolutionary even if their consciousness is not. Their opposition hits the system from without and is therefore not deflected by the system; it is an elementary force which violates the rules of the game and, in doing so, reveals it as a rigged game. When they get together and go out into the streets, without arms, without protection, in order to ask for the most primitive civil rights, they know that they face dogs, stones, and bombs, jail, concentration camps, even death. Their force is behind every political demonstration for the victims of law and order. The fact that they start refusing to play the game may be the fact which marks the beginning of the end of a period.

> —Herbert Marcuse, *One-Dimensional Man: Studies in
> the Ideology of Advanced Industrial Society*, 256–57

The challenge to critical theorists to rethink their presuppositions according to the realities of non-European cultures and technologies remains the most underthematized aspect of critical theories new and old. . . .

> —William S. Wilkerson and Jeffrey Paris,
> *New Critical Theory: Essays on Liberation*, 8

DU BOIS'S DISTINCTION: CRITICALLY ENGAGING THE ARCHITECT OF AFRICANA STUDIES

One of the major themes of Du Bois's discourse revolves around race and racism or, more specifically, the critical, systematic, and social scientific study of race and the political economy of racism. However, race and racism were only part of the problem that faced a dying humanity from Du Bois's point of view. There were other important life-threatening and liberty-denying issues, some of them involving sexism, capitalism and colonialism, among infinite others. Nevertheless, no matter what issue Du Bois critically engaged, it should be emphasized that his major preoccupation was ever the dialectic of oppression and liberation—which is to say, the central dialectic (and defining characteristic) of critical theory (Marcuse, 1997a, 2001, 2004, 2007a, 2007b; Mendieta, 2007; Outlaw, 2005; Rasmussen, 1999; Rasmussen and Swindal, 2004; Wilkerson and Paris, 2001).

"For Du Bois," Cheryl Townsend Gilkes (1996) asserted, "oppression always was the central issue" (p. 117). She continued: "Early in the history of sociology, W.E.B. Du Bois emphasized . . . gender, race, and class. . . . Sociology for Du Bois was a means to seek solutions to social problems" (pp. 112–13; see also Bracey, Meier and Rudwick, 1971; Dennis, 1972, 1975, 1996a; Du Bois, 1978; D.S. Green, 1973; Green and Driver, 1976; A.J. Jones, 1976; Lemert, 2000b; Rudwick, 1960a, 1969, 1974; R.A. Wortham, 2005a, 2005b; Zuckerman, 2004). Sociology, it should be duly noted, was simply one of many disciplines that Du Bois contributed to, and methodologically drew from in his infatigable efforts to "seek solutions to social problems." His work was wide-ranging and anticipated several contemporary theoretical revolutions and radical political positions, and particularly Africana Studies' emphasis on linking academic excellence and intellectual innovation with political activism and social organizing, as well as its transdisciplinarity and utilization of multiple methodologies (see Aldridge and Young, 2000; Aldridge and James, 2007; Asante and Karenga, 2005; Bobo and Michel, 2000; Bobo, Hudley and Michel, 2004; Conyers, 2005; Gordon and Gordon, 2006a, 2006b; Hudson-Weems, 2007; Marable, 2000, 2005). One of the deans of black biography, and a noted Du Bois scholar, Arnold Rampersad (1996b), recently declared,

> I would like to suggest that Du Bois bears a special relationship to some of the more perplexing trends and currents in contemporary American intellectual life, and especially where the university is concerned. I refer here not to all of the intellectual ferment of this generation but to certain of its salient aspects. The most obvious, perhaps, is the rise of "Black Studies" in the last twenty years or so. Also germane is the rise of scholarly work emphasizing the diasporic aspect of African culture; with his publication of *The Negro* in 1915, Du Bois virtually inaugurated that aspect of African Studies. His career relates, in addition, to the general assertion of the importance of the troika of Race, Class, and Gender as the major tool in critical discourse across a wide range of disciplines in American universities. (p. 290)[1]

Here Rampersad identifies three key intellectual currents to which Du Bois, either directly or indirectly, contributes. Du Bois, first and foremost, contributes to the simultaneously intellectual and sociopolitical transdisciplinary discipline of Africana Studies. The second intellectual tradition he contributes to (or, actually, establishes) is a branch of or subdiscipline internal to Africana Studies commonly referred to as Diaspora Studies. Further, the third thought tradition Du Bois's work helps to highlight foreshadows the modern mantra of and politico-philosophical focus on race gender, and class that has offered countless contemporary academics a transdisciplinary *lingua franca*. Du Bois's contributions to each of the aforementioned intellectual currents enable contemporary Africana Studies scholars and critical theorists to engage his discourse from their respective interdisciplinary angles, and provide useful paradigmatic tools and discursive devices that could be employed in the reconceptualization and reconstruction of both Africana Studies and critical social theory.

Du Bois's contributions to the history and development of Africana Studies have yet to be adequately treated. Although many Africana Studies scholars consider him the architect of Africana Studies, they have not produced the kinds of critical studies, systemic analyses, and discipline-specific detailed discussions of his corpus and its relationship to Africana Studies which would corroborate their claims. Along with my previous book, *Du Bois and the Problems of the Twenty-First Century*, this study has endeavored to open this long-closed and deeply buried intellectual history, as well as explore the relationship(s) between Africana Studies, radical politics, and critical social theory. However, it should be pointed out that Africana Studies scholars are not alone in their neglect of Du Bois and his discourse.

TOWARD A CRITICAL DISCUSSION OF THE DEPRESSING STATE OF DU BOIS STUDIES

Since Du Bois is highly regarded as one of the preeminent scholars of not simply African American but American intellectual history, it is amazing that there is such a shameful paucity of scholarship and critical discourse (especially *critical theoretical* discourse) on him. Returning to Rampersad (1996b), he characterized the depressing state of Du Bois studies best when he wrote,

> Until now, the record of such scholarship has been uneven at best and poor by almost any standard when one considers the importance of Du Bois. I refer not to the quality of the books published on Du Bois by skilled scholars such as Francis Broderick and Elliott Rudwick, but to the quantity of such work, which has never matched or even approached the conspicuous importance of Du Bois as an American writer on the subjects of race and African American history, sociology, and culture. The notable exception in scholarship has been, of course, Professor Herbert Aptheker. Nevertheless, scarcely half a dozen scholarly books have been published on Du Bois's life and work. (p. 289)[2]

One of the reasons that there are so few studies on Du Bois involves the racial exclusionary practices and/or the institutionalized racism of many traditional academic disciplines.[3] Du Bois has never received his due recognition in disciplines he helped to establish or significantly contributed to, disciplines such as sociology, history, political science, and education, among others (see Alridge, 2008; Anderson and Zuberi, 2000; Bell, Grosholz and Stewart, 1996; Blackwell and Janowitz, 1974; Katz and Sugrue, 1998; Logan, 1971; Meier and Rudwick, 1986; Rudwick, 1969, 1974; Zamir, 2008). He and his discourse, consistently defying and redefining conventional academic culture, radical politics, and social thought, serve as heresy for many monodisciplinary scholars. Deeply connected to the Western academy, state-sanctioned politics often point to academic anxieties over not simply radical social change but also theoretical revolution(s). Furthermore, similar to academics (as opposed to intellectual-activists) in a repressed society, the politics of the established order repudiates transformations of consciousness that incite treasonous thoughts and/or seditious acts against the state. The highest treason, then, is that which lays hold of the hearts and minds of the masses and problematizes and destabilizes the "divine" authority and "democracy" of the government and its academic arm.

Du Bois's discourse urges unorthodox and heretical states of consciousness that advance theoretical revolutions and radical politics that threaten the established order and its educational institutions and ideological hegemony. Therefore, as his *In Battle for Peace* eloquently illustrates, the government attempted to suppress and harass Du Bois and disrupt the educational institutions, political associations, and social movements he allied with (Du Bois, 1995d; Nikopoulos, 2003). The government and its academic arm and intellectual infantry has a long history of co-opting critical thought and radical movements, modifying and elevating them into the mainstream so as to weaken their radical or revolutionary potential.[4] However, unofficial narratives consistently and critically shadow official documents. Censored and heavily edited heretical texts continue to challenge conventional views and values. Hidden histories and unofficial stories do not usually make it into the mainstream, but the fact remains that they often subtly and silently reach and raise consciousness amongst radicals, providing them with alternative narratives and critical paradigms of self and social transformation. As the revered radical historian Robin D.G. Kelley (2002) recently wrote, "Without new visions we don't know what to build, only what to knock down. We not only end up confused, rudderless, and cynical, but we forget that making a revolution is not a series of clever maneuvers and tactics but a process that can and must transform us" (p. xii).

The influence of unorthodox and unofficial politics and academics is often widespread and incalculable, and subject to emerge at any moment, rupturing the rules of the repressed society. Accompanying official texts and history, alternative narratives and critical paradigms foster dialectical thought on official

orthodoxy and unofficial heterodoxy that complicate, contradict, and sometimes even complement each other. Kelley (2002) continues:

> [T]he desires, hopes, and intentions of the people who fought for change cannot
> be easily categorized, contained, or explained. Unfortunately, too often our stan-
> dards for evaluating social movements pivot around whether or not they "suc-
> ceeded" in realizing their visions rather than on the merits or power of the vi-
> sions themselves. By such a measure, virtually every radical movement failed
> because the basic power relations they sought to change remain pretty much in-
> tact. And yet it is precisely these alternative visions and dreams that inspire new
> generations to continue to struggle for change. (p. vii)

Nowhere, perhaps, is this more evident than in Du Bois's discourse and the
intellectual and political debates surrounding and (re)framing the radical
and/or revolutionary potential of Africana Studies and critical theory.

James Stewart (1984) argues that another reason scholars have a hard time
with or simply do not engage Du Bois's oeuvre is because "Du Bois rejected
the fragmentation of experience into disciplinary compartments, the attempt
by the social sciences to use the natural sciences as a developmental model,
because he believed that it was, in fact, man who causes 'movement and
change'" (p. 305). Thus, it is Du Bois's transdisciplinarity in the interest of
radically transforming the conditions of Africa and Africans, along with other
oppressed and struggling people, that challenges and, perhaps even more,
dumbfounds traditional monodisciplinary theorists and at the same time accents the fact that he was, indeed, an undeniable architect of the transdisciplinary discipline of Africana Studies, as well as an authentic critical social
theorist. But, again, Africana Studies scholars and critical theorists must do
more than merely claim Du Bois as a transdisciplinary intellectual-activist ancestor; they must comprehensively and accessibly engage his corpus for its
contribution to their respective insurgent intellectual arenas and radical political agendas.

A third reason Du Bois has been and continues to be overlooked in the
academy is because of his unorthodox appropriation and eclectic utilization
of multiple methodologies, what Stewart (1984) dubbed "Du Bois's increasing belief in the complementarity of methodologies" (p. 302). This issue is directly and deeply connected to Du Bois's transdisciplinarity and, again, helps
to highlight his status as a doyen of Africana Studies discourse and a major
contributor to critical theoretical discourse. His multi-methodological approach manifested itself most in groundbreaking scholarly studies such as
The Philadelphia Negro, *The Souls of Black Folk*, *The Negro*, *Darkwater*, *The
Gift of Black Folk*, *Black Reconstruction*, *Black Folk, Then and Now*, *Color
and Democracy*, and *The World and Africa*, among others; innumerable ef-

forts at autobiography—for instance, *Darkwater*, *Dusk of Dawn*, *In Battle for Peace*, and *The Autobiography of W.E.B. Du Bois*; edited volumes, specifically the Atlanta University studies; editorship of and publications in periodicals, such as *The Moon*, *The Horizon*, *The Crisis*, and *Phylon*; literally hundreds of critical essays and scholarly articles on a staggeringly wide range of topics; public intellectualism, political activism, and participation in national and international social movements, such as Pan-Africanism, the Niagara Movement, the NAACP, the New Negro Movement, the Harlem Renaissance, the Civil Rights Movement, the Women's Liberation Movement, and the Peace Movement, among others; and countless creative writings, which encompass novels, short stories, poetry, and plays. Stewart also stated that "Du Bois's early rejection of his socialization as a classically trained traditional Western scholar and the subsequent self-definition of an alternative program bear strong similarities to Black Studies" (p. 303). From this angle, then, Du Bois is not simply an architect of Africana Studies, but a paradigmatic figure who could (and, I think, indeed *does*) provide many Africana Studies scholars (and critical theorists) lost in the labyrinth of the academy with intellectual guidance and political direction.

Du Bois's multi-methodological approach prefigures contemporary Africana Studies' methodologies in that it was deeply dialectical, critical of traditional disciplines' omission of important race, gender, class, and cultural issues, and interested in drawing from and contributing to continental and diasporan African political-theoretical and social-activist traditions. His conception of the "complementarity of methodologies," along with his consistent focus on Pan-African social and political issues, simultaneously places him in the transdisciplinary intellectual arena now known as Africana Studies, and challenges those theorists in traditional disciplines who would, in a monodisciplinary manner, claim Du Bois for their specific disciplines or disciplinary agendas. Commenting on Du Bois's conception of the "complementarity of methodologies," Stewart asserted that Du Bois's multi-methodological approach to the Africana experience was not simply theoretical eclecticism on his part, but a conscious effort to critically comprehend continental and diasporan African history, culture, and struggle in its totality and complexity. Stewart (1984) stated that

> Du Bois perceived that certain methodologies of analysis and styles of presentation were more appropriate than others for capturing the complexity of the Black experience and for communicating that complexity in a manner that generated new insights for non-Blacks and self-reflection among Blacks leading to social action. There is no doubt that Du Bois's methodological predilections violated traditional standards of historical research. . . . To understand Du Bois's methodology it is necessary to examine the connotation of the word "fact" as it

relates to social science. What constitutes fact in social science is that which can be verified with respect to a particular paradigm. Throughout his career, Du Bois operated from a mind-set that posited the existence of systematic biases in the determination of what constituted "fact" with respect to the Black experience. Consequently, to seek substantial correspondence between his interpretation and the conventional wisdom was necessarily self-defeating. A more salient strategy was to construct alternative explanations and subject them to testing procedures that were indigenous to the alternative paradigm. This is what Du Bois did. At the same time, Du Bois was always concerned with preserving his reputation as a bona fide scholar among traditionalists. . . . Du Bois's increasing disenchantment with the methodology of the traditional social sciences took a variety of forms. (pp. 303-305)

Du Bois's emphasis on "alternative explanations," the development of an "alternative paradigm," and, as Stewart put it elsewhere, "a non-traditional program of instruction" does not simply resonate with Africana Studies; it is the transdisciplinary discipline's very conceptual core (p. 307; see also Aldridge and James, 2007; Aldridge and Young, 2000; Anderson and Stewart, 2007; Asante and Karenga, 2006; Gordon and Gordon, 2006a, 2006b; Hudson-Weems, 2007; J.B. Stewart, 2004). Therefore, Du Bois's multi-methodological approach is inextricable from his transgressive transdisciplinarity, both of which place him well beyond the boundaries of traditional disciplines and their monodisciplinary maneuvers. As I have argued in chapter 3 of the present volume and elsewhere (Rabaka, 2003b), Du Bois's philosophy of education points to Africana Studies' "non-traditional program of instruction," and it reveals Africana philosophy of education to be a critical educational theory that is geared toward translating theory into progressive social praxis. However, the range and reach of Du Bois's discourse amazingly does not stop here.

Constantly cutting across disciplines and breaking through artificial academic boundaries, Du Bois's discourse is dialectical, meaning it does not simply challenge traditional disciplines, but it also offers an internal challenge to, and critique of non-traditional disciplines, such as—and I am thinking here especially of—Africana Studies. Du Bois challenges Africana Studies scholars, and particularly the self-conscious discipline definers and developers, to beware of the pitfalls of disciplinary development and the poison of intellectual esoterica. If, indeed, Africana Studies is a progressive social praxis-promoting transdisciplinary discipline, then Africana Studies scholars (and their authentic intellectual-activist allies) must constantly be concerned with critical consciousness raising, radical politics, theoretical revolutions, and—I should strongly stress—world historical, national and international, real-life social and political revolutions and movements geared toward not only black liberation but also multi-racial and transethnic human liberation, women's liberation and gender justice, revolutionary decolonization, and revolutionary democratic socialist (among other egalitarian) alternatives.

Once again Rampersad (1996b) enters the intellectual fray and offers insights. He argues that there are aspects of Du Bois's work that are actually *anti-disciplinary*, by which he means that Du Bois's corpus contains several texts that not only problematize but go against the whole notion of an academic discipline. As he pointed out, particularly in his autobiographical writings, soon after he published his 1899 classic, *The Philadelphia Negro*, Du Bois lost faith in a purely social scientific or academic solution to African American and Pan-African social and political problems (see Du Bois, 1952, 1968a, 1968b, 1969a; see also D.L. Lewis, 1993, chapter 9). Along with his loss of intellectual faith came an intense critique of the academy and, more specifically, academic disciplines. His intellectual soul-searching led him to develop scholastic and political positions that, Rampersad contends, parallel many of the thought traditions en vogue in "the volatile dynamic of American intellectual life today." Rampersad (1996b) punctiliously revealed that

> if it would be difficult to relate Du Bois directly . . . to those intricacies of deconstruction and poststructuralism that have seized the attention of large sections of the American academy in the past dozen years or so, his life and career are connected nevertheless both to certain direct aspects of these intellectual forces and to certain germane trends and tensions. I refer both to the rise of relatively new and discrete disciplines and departments and to our vastly increased sense of the benefits of the interdisciplinary approach. I am thinking also about the growing tension between traditional humanistic discourse and the new antihumanist and posthumanist emphasis that has surfaced so strongly among the latest generation of scholars, and definitely among many of the brightest and most politically engaged among them. In Du Bois, I would suggest, one sees elements of this antihumanism and posthumanism peering out in spite of the deep commitment to humanism that Du Bois long cherished. I have referred to disciplinarity and interdisciplinarity; but I am also thinking of the increasing tendency of the cultural studies movement toward an anti-disciplinarity that is distinct from interdisciplinarity. In other words, I refer to important elements in the volatile dynamic of American intellectual life today, which is itself but a token of the volatile and sometimes ominous quality of contemporary American culture in general; and I see Du Bois, born almost 125 years ago and dead now almost 30 years, as having been intimately involved, in one way or another, in many of these questions I have mentioned. (pp. 290–91)

Du Bois's discourse can be said to prefigure not only posthumanist, poststructuralist, postmodernist, and postcolonial thought, but also several traditions of thought internal to and emanating from contemporary Africana Studies. For instance, Rampersad (1996b) observed above that Du Bois was instrumental in establishing the diasporan dimension of Africana Studies with his seminal 1915 text, *The Negro*. Furthermore, in his magisterial *Black Marxism*, Cedric Robinson (2000) argued that Du Bois was one of the first persons of African descent to systematically and critically study Marxism, developing many of the first race-class theories and, consequently, he aided in inaugurating black Marxism. Noted Du Bois scholar Elliott Rudwick (1982b) contentiously corroborated Robinson's claims when he observed, "Du Bois was both a pioneering advocate of black capitalism, and later was one of the country's most prominent black Marxists," although, Rudwick went on to assert, "his quasi-socialistic brand of economic nationalism was never widely accepted" (pp. 64, 78).

Also, as Cheryl Gilkes (1996) asserted above, Du Bois was one of the first classical sociologists to challenge "the subordination of the problems of gender and race in the development of sociological theory" (p. 117). She went further to argue that for Du Bois, social problems were highly "complex, and first of all demanded respect for the ideas of people of all nationalities, all races, and of both women and men" (p. 119). Thus, Du Bois, the mastermind behind black Marxism, has also been hailed as an extremely early critic of the overlapping, interlocking, and intersecting nature of race, gender, and class in human life-worlds and lived experiences in the modern moment.

In fact, the preeminent Du Bois biographer, David Levering Lewis (2000), definitively declared that Du Bois was undoubtedly "the first sociologist of race" (p. 550). Contributing the first social scientific studies of race, racism, and the ways in which white supremacy impacts and influences race relations, ideology, individuals, and institutions, Du Bois launched critical race theory and critical white studies, and foreshadowed and laid the foundation for subsequent studies, sociological or otherwise, of race and racism (Baber, 1992; L.D. Bobo, 2000; Chaffee, 1956; Coates, Browning and Beenah, 1996; Dennis, 1977; B.S. Edwards, 2001, 2006; Gordon, 2000b, 2000c; Green and Smith, 1983; T.L. Lott, 1997, 2000, 2001; Miles, 2003; Moses, 1993a; Mostern, 1996; Outlaw, 1995, 1996b, 2000; Rabaka, 2006c, 2007a, 2007b; A.W. Rawls, 2000; Schrager, 1996; Shuford, 2001; Sullivan, 2003; C.M. Taylor, 1981; P.C. Taylor, 2000; K.H. Wilson, 1999). Recently the sociologist Phil Zuckerman (2004) perceptively pointed out that "what class was for Karl Marx and what gender was for Charlotte Perkins Gilman, race was for Du Bois: the most socially significant construct of modernity, the grand fissure of human relations. For Du Bois, 'the color-line' was the problem of the 20th century, and his entire scholarly output was related in some way to explaining, exploring, and deconstructing that color-line" (p. 5).

Du Bois's critical social theory is distinguished when compared and contrasted with the theories of other classical social theorists, say, for instance, Marx and Gilman, because his work increasingly deepened and developed political and sociological analyses of race, gender, and class. Neither the work of Marx nor Gilman demonstrates a conjunctive critical engagement with and ideological critique of racism, sexism, *and* capitalism. In fact, in many instances, Marx's work has been shown to be, however subtly, racist and sexist. Marx scholar Edward Reiss (1997) has written that "in many ways and by modern, liberal standards, Marx was quite chauvinist. . . . Generally, he had a romantic, Victorian view of women" (p. 114). The same sexist sentiment, or, rather, masculinism to be more precise, has been detected in most of the discourse and theories emanating from male Marxists and their various Marxian traditions (see Bannerji, 1995; M. Barrett, 1980; Boxer and Quartaert, 1978; Braun, 1987; M.J. Buhle, 1981; Cliff, 1984; Di Stephano, 1991, 2008; Eisenstein, 1979; A. Ferguson, 1986, 1998; K.E. Ferguson, 1980; Guettel, 1974; Hansen and Philipson, 1990; Hennessey and Ingraham, 1997; Holmstrom, 2002; Jaggar, 1983; G. Martin, 1986; Meulenbelt, 1984; Randall, 1992; Roberts and Mizuta, 1993; Rowbotham, 1973, 1979; Sargent, 1981; Sayers and Osborne, 1990; Slaughter and Kern, 1981; D.E. Smith, 1977; Vogel, 1983, 1995; B. Weinbaum, 1978). With regard to Marx on the pressing sociopolitical problem of racism, Reiss (1997) further revealed that

> Marx himself did *not* fully explore racism. Clearly it has something to do with suspicion and fear (of other beliefs, other values, other cultures) and something to do with ignorance—not understanding others. Marx occasionally descended to racist slurs, particularly against rival Lassalle, whom he abused as a "Jewish Nigger." Several anti-Semitic comments suggest that he was insecure about his own Jewish background. And he was deeply prejudiced against the Slavs. (p. 124, emphasis in original; see also Bannerji, 1995; Flank, 2007; C.W. Mills, 2003; C.J. Robinson, 2001; Serequeberhan, 1990)

Du Bois work demonstrates his preoccupation with not simply the social and political problems confronting continental and diasporan Africans but a profound and prophetic revolutionary humanism that extended to other non-whites as well as whites, including Jews. Du Bois religious biographer Edward Blum (2007) asserted that "Du Bois attacked whitewashed histories of Judaism, Islam, and Christianity" (p. 125). Further, following closely on the heels of the Jewish holocaust, Du Bois revised the Jubilee Edition of *The Souls of Black Folk*, removing any statements that might be interpreted (or misinterpreted) as anti-Semitic. Du Bois did not want his work associated with any form of oppression, or used to dominate or discriminate, especially against Jews, some of whom have roots in Africa that have been traced back more than 3,000 years (Chouraqui, 1973; Gustav, 1955; Herrman, 1935; Hirschberg, 1974; Mendelssohn, 1920). Blum's work is extremely important here in helping to drive this point home:

> During the 1940s and 1950s, moreover, Du Bois showed greater interest in and sensitivity toward Jews in the United States and the world. He lobbied for the creation of Israel, lectured on several occasions before the American Jewish Congress, and, in the Jubilee Edition of *The Souls of Black Folk*, removed eight negative statements toward Jews. The [Jewish] Holocaust had a marked effect on how Du Bois viewed the relationship between blacks and Jews. Du Bois now believed that their experiences were similar and drew attention to "the way in which African and Jewish history have been entwined for 3,000 years." Du Bois used the image of Nazism to warn against race supremacists in the United States. In 1950, for instance, speaking before the Jewish People's Fraternal Order, he declared, "It has been said more than once that if and when fascism comes to America . . . it will be the Negro people followed by the Jewish people who will feel the fury of barbaric sadism." For this reason, "the Negro people have an obligation to support the fight for a free Israel as the Jewish people have an obligation to support the fight for a free Africa" (p. 193; see also Horne, 1986, pp. 283-284; Sevitch, 2002)[5]

We witness here that where Marx is generally regarded as a liberal racist and sexist, though he, too, was not always able to side-step the pitfalls of patriarchy, male supremacy, and masculinism, part of Du Bois's distinction as a critical social theorist revolves around his innovative and insightful discussions of the ways in which racism, sexism, and capitalism represent overlapping, interlocking, and intersecting systems of exploitation and oppression (Gilkes, 1996; Gilman and Weinbaum, 2007; J.A. James, 1997; Rabaka, 2003d, 2004). Therefore, even as Du Bois argued that Marx and Marxism provide one of the most comprehensive critiques of capitalism available to critical social theorists, he simultaneously exploded its obsessive economism and emphasized the importance of the critique of racism and sexism as well. Furthermore, when compared with the important work of Charlotte Perkins Gilman, Du Bois's social theory, once again, demonstrates its distinctiveness. Where Marx was found wanting with regard to critical engagements and ideological critiques of racism and sexism, even though she contributed much to the discourse and development of the sociology of gender, Gilman (1908) unapologetically embraced white-supremacist, anti-black racism (see also Lengermann and Niebrugge-Brantley, 2007). Writing on Gilman's anti-black racism, Zuckerman (2004) bemoaningly mused, "For Gilman, the central fissure was between men and women, whereas for Du Bois it was between blacks and whites. Unfortunately, while Du Bois wrote sympathetically of the plight of women and was a vocal advocate of female suffrage, Gilman wasn't as sympathetic to the plight of blacks in America; in an article published in the *American Journal of Sociology* in 1908, Gilman argued that it was the innate inferiority of black people that best accounted for their poor social conditions. Her racism only got worse as she aged" (pp. 8-9). Horne (1986), D.L. Lewis (1993, 2000), and Marable (1986) each argue that Du Bois grew increasingly more radical (if not, ultimately, *revolutionary*) as he got older, and inextricable from his critiques of capitalism, racism, and sexism was his pioneering Pan-Africanism and critique of colonialism. His critical social theory, in several ways, therefore, can be said to go above and beyond the limitations of conventional Eurocentric and patriarchal radical politics and critical social theory.

Elsewhere I have contended that Du Bois's discourse both contributes to and critically destabilizes postcolonialism because it points to a period or stage/state in between colonialism and postcolonialism, what Du Bois conceptually characterized as "quasi-colonialism" or "semi-colonialism" (Rabaka, 2003c, 2005a). My work in this area, in addition, lucidly demonstrates that Du Bois was developing a critical discourse on decolonization long before many of the major anti-colonial theorists who have been appropriated (and, often misappropriated) by contemporary postcolonial theorists were born—theorists such as Frantz Fanon, Albert Memmi, and Edward Said. This means, then, that when all the smoke clears and all the dust settles, Du Bois's discourse transgresses, transcends, and transverses traditional Eurocentric and patriarchal critical social theory. Indeed, and in partial agreement with Rampersad, Du Bois's work contentiously demonstrates striking similarities with contemporary Western European and European American schools of thought as well as contemporary Africana thought traditions, displaying its epistemic openness and anti-disciplinarity, breaking through both intellectual and social barriers, crossing cultural and political borders, and demonstrating a distinct philosophical and filial connection to both black and white theories, along with a wide range of theory put forward by other non-white insurgent intellectual-activist traditions. However, as the foregoing analysis lucidly illustrates, Du Bois's insurgent intellectual and radical political legacy also acutely demonstrates the myriad ways in which the Africana tradition of critical theory is distinctly different from European, European-American, white Marxist, and white feminist traditions of critical theory.

Du Bois's thought resists restriction to a single academic discipline and does, indeed, harbor aspects of what could be called an anti-disciplinary approach to knowledge and phenomena. However, Du Bois's anti-disciplinarity dovetails with Africana Studies' emphasis on interdisciplinarity, multidisciplinarity, transdisciplinarity, and supradisciplinarity.[6] In this sense, Du Bois was intellectually and politically prophetic, not necessarily in his ability to foresee the future, but in his ability to anticipate future political developments and discursive dilemmas. Du Bois's anti-disciplinarity offers contemporary Africana Studies scholars a caveat: We must be wary of those among us who would attempt to make Africana Studies a black version of traditional white disciplines, severing the connection between blacks on the campus and the black community, creating an intellectual oasis in the academy that caters to the wishes and whims of whites and only speaks of and to the black community in condescending and acrimonious tones.

DU BOIS, THEORETICAL REVOLUTIONS, AND THE CRISES OF CRITICAL SOCIAL THEORY

Du Bois's work has previously been engaged and presented in one-dimensional ways that obscure its resilience and relevance for contemporary cultural critique, radical politics, and revolutionary social movements. One-sided biographical and intellectual-historical studies of Du Bois that read and render his thought and texts in arbitrary and artificial terms not only obfuscate Du Bois's intellectual past—and, therefore, much of modern black intellectual history—but these studies also adumbrate (classical and contemporary) Africana Studies' contributions to the quickly emerging interdisciplinary intellectual present. As I have endeavored to illustrate in the foregoing sections of this chapter, Du Bois was an early transdisciplinarian whose history- and culture-centered theorizings consistently identified key sociopolitical problems and utilized a wide range of work from various disciplines in an effort to produce viable solutions to those problems. The "problems" that Du Bois's thought sought to grasp and grapple with went well beyond the realm of race and racism, and often encompassed other enigmatic issues, such as sexism, civil rights, capitalism, (neo)colonialism, and education, which all remain on the radical political agenda.

Though his work is most frequently read for its contributions to the critique of racism, and white supremacy in specific, Du Bois actually understood racism to be one of many interlocking oppressive systems that threaten not only the souls of black folk, but also the heart and soul of humanity. As Du Bois developed his discourse, various themes and theories were either embraced or rejected contingent upon particular historical and cultural conditions, which, reiteratively, help to highlight the fact that his social and political theory was deeply grounded in history and culture. The deep historical and cultural dimension in Du Bois's thought suggests that he took seriously the role of a critical social theorist as someone who is concerned with crises in human life and who is committed to constantly (re)conceptualizing what is essential to human liberation and creating a new social world. As a critical social theorist, Du Bois's distinction is undoubtedly apparent when we note his ability to synthesize historical studies, cultural criticism, radical political theory, and economic analysis with social philosophy and public policy in an effort to (1) discover the fundamental features of contemporary society, (2) identify its most promising potentialities and paths to a liberated future, and (3) accessibly advance ways that the current society could be transformed to realize these newly identified egalitarian goals.[7]

As far back as his 1898 essay, "The Study of Negro Problems," Du Bois (1978) declared, "Whenever any nation allows impulse, whim or hasty conjecture to usurp the place of conscious, normative, intelligent action, it is in grave danger. The sole aim of any society is to settle its problems in accordance with its highest ideals, and the only rational method of accomplishing this is to study those problems in the light of the best scientific research" (p. 75). Sidestepping the scientism and quest for rationalism in the quote, Du Bois seems to suggest two things. First, just as society changes, so too must the social theory that seeks not simply to chart those changes but to have an emancipatory influence on them. And, second, social theory must be much more *critical*, meaning it is imperative for it to constantly carry out ideological critique, as there are many imperial and neo-imperial "impulse[s], whim[s]" and "hasty conjecture[s]" that are blocking human beings from realizing their "highest ideals."[8]

Conventionally Du Bois's corpus has been categorized as falling into three distinct stages: First, there is his early elitist, social scientist, and quasi-cultural nationalist stage, from 1896 to 1903; second, his Pan-African socialist or "black Marxist" middle stage, from 1904 to 1935; and, third, his revolutionary, radical humanist, internationalist, and peace activist final stage, from 1936 to the end of his life in 1963 (see Broderick, 1959; DeMarco, 1983; J.B. Moore, 1981; Rudwick, 1968; Wolters, 2001). Many problems, however, arise when Du Bois is periodized and interpreted in this way. At first issue is the simple fact that this scheme shrouds the complexity and transdisciplinarity of the first and second stages and, therefore, does not adequately prepare or equip social theorists of the present age with the intellectual history and conceptual tools necessary to critically interpret and understand Du Bois's later life ("third stage") ruptures with his early elitism and mid-period political radicalism. Earlier in this chapter, I have demonstrated that Du Bois's thought does not fit into the nice and neat conceptual categories of traditional disciplines, but may best be interpreted by examining it as transdisciplinary theory with emancipatory intent. What appears to many Du Bois scholars and critics as three distinct stages in his oeuvre is actually a single, protracted, critical, and conjunctive thought process that—on careful and close reading—reveals recurring themes of epistemic openness and radical political receptiveness.

Throughout each of the "three stages," Du Bois's writings return again and again to the critique of domination and discrimination, human liberation, democratic political action, and radical social transformation. Though he began with bourgeois (and sometimes even Eurocentric imperial) notions of social uplift, by the so-called "second stage" Du Bois was clearly collapsing conventional social scientific categories and exploring new social identities and programs of radical political action.[9] He incorporated a wide-range of academic theory and grassroots political praxis into his burgeoning critical social theoretical framework; thus his thought displays an unusual openness to and critical engagement of black nationalism, black separatism, Pan-Africanism, African communalism, Ethiopianism, Marxism, Leninism, Maoism, German romanticism, German nationalism, British socialism, American pragmatism, Third Worldism, multiculturalism, feminism, and womanism, among other thought traditions.

It would seem that the leitmotifs in Du Bois's thought would make his ideas more accessible and easier to interpret. However, it must be emphasized that though there are many recurring themes in his writings, he consistently revised his social theory and political analysis throughout each of the "three stages." Consequently, there are specific issues—usually race, gender, and class issues—that transgress the traditional "three stages" conceptualization of Du Bois's corpus, and which are persistently and perhaps perplexingly present at each stage. I argue, once more, that it is the *transdisciplinary* nature of his work that makes it so difficult to interpret in a one-dimensional or monodisciplinary (as opposed to multidisciplinary) manner. Also, Du Bois's transdisciplinarity, which is to say the way his work constantly transcends and transgresses the arbitrary and artificial boundaries of traditional disciplines, coupled with his accent on political economy and social theory, and his consistent emphasis on race, gender, and class issues, make his work an ideal model for reconceiving and recreating critical theory of contemporary society as well as Africana Studies.

Interpretations of Du Bois based on the tripartite paradigm, then, are extremely problematic and often theoretically myopic, frequently displaying the disciplinary desires of the critic to fashion a Du Bois for their specific (postmodern) purposes.[10] However, Du Bois will not be anyone's theoretical straw man (or, "race man" either), if you will. His thought, like that of other provocative thinkers, must be approached from an angle that is sensitive to intellectual, historical, and cultural context in order to be adequately, and one could say *correctly*, interpreted. For instance, as I argued in chapter 3 of the present study, Du Bois carried out one of the most devastating critiques of black leadership and black liberation thought in the first half of the twentieth century. But, one will hardly be able to fully appreciate the originality of his arguments, the radicalism of his political actions, and their relevance to critical theory of contemporary society unless his anti-accommodationism is linked to his later *simultaneously* anti-racist, anti-capitalist, anti-colonial, and anti-sexist social theorizing (Rabaka, 2007a).

By taking a conceptual (as opposed to the conventional chronological) approach to Du Bois's research and writings, I have been able to accent some of the significant developments of his thought that speak to ongoing and important issues revolving around race, gender, class, and the reconstruction of critical theory. Instead of viewing changes in his thought as signs of confusion, vacillation or intellectual inertia, I have emphasized the subtle logic of the modifications Du Bois made in his thinking by placing it in the context of continental and diasporan African intellectual history, culture, and struggle, as well as the wider world of intellectual history, culture, and struggle. Additionally, engaging Du Bois's corpus conceptually has also enabled me to stress its strengths and weaknesses as a paradigm and point of departure for developing a more multicultural, transethnic, anti-racist, anti-sexist, and sexual orientation-sensitive critical theory of contemporary society. Similar to several other critical social theorists, Du Bois oriented his political theory toward what he perceived as the most progressive political struggles (or, lack thereof) of a particular moment and, thus, articulated possibilities and potentialities specific to *his* contemporary society and social reality, rather than putting forward a blueprint for future social change or an architecture for emancipation in an epoch to come. To put it plainly, this is the central task of contemporary critical theorists, Africana or otherwise.[11]

This means, then, that "we are on our own"—as the post-Marxists and post-feminists regularly remind us (Aronson, 1995; Gamble, 2002). However, it does not mean that we should abandon those aspects of Du Bois's social thought that may aid us in our endeavors to develop a new, more multicultural, transethnic, transgender, transgenerational, transnational, sexual orientation-sensitive, and environmental justice-committed critical theory of contemporary society. Critical theory seeks to comprehend, critique, and offer alternatives to the contradictions of current culture and society. Therefore, it is always in need of revision and, literally, demands development because its basic concepts and categories are time- and situation-sensitive. In other words, the basic concepts and categories of critical theory are historical, and history, to put it plainly, has never bowed to the wishes and whims of any human being or human group. Hence, history is always unfolding and playing itself out in new and unimagined ways. Critical theory, then, being a form of historical and cultural critique, must remain receptive to the various ways in which the world is changing if it is to truly transform contemporary culture and society (see Foucault, 1997, 1998, 2000; Gramsci, 1975, 1985, 1995;

Habermas, 1984, 1987a, 1989a, 1989b, 1996; Marcuse, 1997a, 2001, 2004, 2007a, 2007b; Rasmussen, 1999; Rasmussen and Swindal, 2004; L. Ray, 1993).

DU BOIS, THE SOULS OF BLACK RADICAL FOLK, AND THE RACE(IST) POLITICS OF CRITICAL SOCIAL THEORY

In this study I have endeavored to elucidate ways in which Du Bois contributes to critical theory in general, and a new, broader-based critical theory that seriously engages and takes as its point of departure the social and political thought of Africana radicals and revolutionaries. Throughout his life, Du Bois's critique of racism was relentless and, however flawed, remains one of his greatest contributions to both classical and contemporary social theory. However, as this study illustrates, Du Bois's much-heralded concepts of race and critiques of racism are virtually incomprehensible and seemingly incoherent without taking into consideration his bravura and often simultaneous critiques of Eurocentric and bourgeois education, sexism (and, particularly patriarchy), black civil rights and social justice struggles, (neo)colonialism, and capitalism, among other issues. Where most critical theorists, at least in the Frankfurt School and other Western Marxist traditions of critical theory, identified capitalism as the primary problem and essential source of human suffering and social misery, Du Bois's critical theory, though it began with a race base, ultimately developed a conjunctive model that did not privilege one social or political problem over another.

This study has also analyzed and explained the many tensions and ambiguities in Du Bois's corpus by demonstrating how his thought and texts are deeply connected to, and, as is usually the case, in critical dialogue with specific historical happenings, cultural conditions, and political practices. This dual emphasis approach enables us to see, first, how Frankfurt School and Western Marxist critical theory has long overlooked racism, sexism, and colonialism, thus making it the very "one-dimensional" thought that Marcuse (1964) warned against, and, second, it allows us to observe how Du Bois and Africana Studies relate to the reconstruction of critical theory. Over the last quarter of a century there have been consistent calls within critical theoretical discourse for a "return to Marx" in order to reconstruct critical theory and make it more viable in light of the vicissitudes of contemporary capitalism. However, what many of these otherwise sophisticated critical social theorists fail to perceive is that it was and remains their overdependency on Marx and Marxism that has made so much of their work theoretically myopic and intellectually insular.

Like a dog chasing its own tail, many white Marxists and critical theorists have locked their discourses into a vicious cycle, going round and round, covering a lot of the same theoretical terrain and identifying similar economic issues as the infinite cause of contemporary social suffering without opening their conceptual universes to the world of ideas and the radical thought traditions of those of "other races and other colors," as Marcuse (1964) aptly put it in *One-Dimensional Man* (p. 256). Many of these same Marxists and critical theorists bemoan the sorry state of contemporary critical social theory, but are either too intellectually timid, intellectually elitist or, dare I say, racially exclusivist to move beyond merely mentioning the fact that critical theory should be *equally* anti-racist, anti-sexist, and anti-colonial. Mentioning racism, sexism, and/or colonialism in passing, at the end of an article, or at the back of a book, and always in subordination to "the evils of capitalism," does not do a favor for the billions of human beings who suffer at the hands of these overlapping, interlocking, and intersecting systems of exploitation and oppression. In fact, if the truth be told, it is the exact kind of cosmetic multiculturalism and tired tokenism that profoundly perturbs non-white radical and revolutionary intellectual-activists and makes them constantly question the sincerity of white "critical" social theorists.

If, indeed, critical theory is theory critical of domination and discrimination, and a social theory that simultaneously offers accessible and ethical alternatives to the key social and political problems of the present age, then any theory claiming to be a "critical theory of contemporary society" must thoroughly theorize not only capitalism, but also racism, sexism, and colonialism, and how each of the aforementioned interconnects and intersects to deform and destroy life and the ongoing prospects of liberation. Du Bois, thus, emerges from this study as a transdisciplinary, multi-faceted, and philosophically fascinating paradigmatic figure whose work indisputably contributes to contemporary efforts to reconceptualize and reconstruct critical theory. Critical theory cannot and will not be able to revise itself unless and until it seriously considers the contributions of non-white/non-European social theorists and intellectual-activists. This generation of critical theorists, then, has a unique and time-sensitive task before it and, simply said, it is as follows: We must put into principled practice *immediately* what critical theory has so long advanced theoretically. In terms of the Africana tradition of critical theory that critical theoretical admonition, perhaps, has been captured best by Frantz Fanon (1967), in *Black Skin, White Mask*, when he wrote,

I, the man of color, want only this:
That the tool never possess the man. That enslavement of man by man cease forever. That is, of one by another. That it be possible for me to discover and to love man, wherever he may be . . .

It is through the effort to recapture the self and to scrutinize the self, it is through the
    lasting tension of their freedom that men will be able to create the ideal conditions
    of existence for a human world.
Superiority? Inferiority?
Why not the quite simple attempt to touch the other, to feel the other, to explain the
    other to myself?
Was my freedom not given to me then in order to build the world of the *You*? (pp.
    231–32; original emphasis)

TOWARD AN AFRICANA CRITICAL THEORY OF CONTEMPORARY SOCIETY: DU BOIS, EPISTEMIC OPENNESS, AND TRANSDISCIPLINARITY— TRANSGRESSING, TRANSCENDING, AND TRANSVERSING EUROCENTRIC CRITICAL THEORY, CONCEPTUAL INCARCERATION, AND INTELLECTUAL INSULARITY

In summary, it must be openly admitted that the theoretic tensions noted in
the previous paragraphs point to and produce an extremely uneasy combination of criticisms and interpretations that defy simple synopsis or conventional conceptual rules. Consequently, most of Du Bois's critics have heretofore downplayed and diminished the real brilliance and brawn of his work by
failing to grasp its antinomies and they have, therefore, put forward a divided
and distorted Du Bois, who is either, for example, a Pan-Africanist *or* Eu-
rophile, a black nationalist *or* radical humanist, a social scientist *or* propagandist, a race man *or* radical women's rights man, a bourgeois elitist *or* dogmatic Marxist. Each of the aforementioned superficial ascriptions falls short
of capturing the complex and chameleonic character of Du Bois's discourse
and the difficulties involved in interpreting it employing the one-sided, single-subject theoretical, and monodisciplinary devices that his research, writings, and radicalism consistently transgressed, transcended, and transversed—hence, my characterization of Du Bois as a *transdisciplinarian*.

Many dismiss Du Bois and charge his work with being dense because it
employs a wide range of theory from several different disciplines, while others, such as myself, are attracted to his work because it is theoretically thick,
rich in both radicality and originality, and boldly crosses so many academic
and political boundaries. No matter what one's ultimate attitude toward Du
Bois, I believe the fact that his thought and texts continue to cause contemporary controversies, and that it has been discussed and debated *across the
disciplines* for more than a century, in some degree points to the multidimensionality and transdisciplinarity of his ideas, which offer enigmatic insights
for everyone either to embrace enthusiastically or demur definitively. Hence,

the dialectic of attraction and repulsion in Du Bois studies can partly be attributed to the ambiguities inherent in his thought and the monodisciplinary anxieties of many of the interpreters of his work. Suffice to say this is the case, then several previous studies of his thought are seriously flawed because they have sought to grasp and grapple with Du Bois's oeuvre using a monodisciplinary instead of a multidisciplinary model.

Whatever the deficiencies of his thought and the problems with his approach to critical issues confronting Africana and other oppressed people, Du Bois forces his readers to think deeply, to criticize thoroughly, and to move beyond the imperial impulses of the established order. Many critics have made solid criticisms of some aspect of Du Bois's thought but, when analyzed objectively, his life-work and intellectual legacy is impressive and inspiring, as is his loyalty to the most radical and revolutionary thought and practice traditions in Africana and world history. His impact and influence has been widespread, not only cutting across academic disciplines, but setting aglow several revolutionary social movements and radical political programs.

Where some theorists dogmatically hold views simply because they are fashionable or politically popular, Du Bois's work draws from a diverse array of often eclectic and enigmatic sources and, therefore, offers no closed system or absolute truths. His thought was constantly open and routinely responsive to changing historical, and cultural conditions, both nationally and internationally. There are several, sometimes stunning transformations in his theory that are in most instances attempts to answer conundrums created by changing sociopolitical, historical and cultural conditions. In conclusion, then, I want to suggest that it is the openness and consistently non-dogmatic radicalism of Du Bois's project, the richness and wide range and reach of his ideas, and the absence of any finished system or closed body of clearly defined truths that can be accepted or rejected at ease, which constitute both the contemporary philosophical fascination with and continuing critical importance of W.E.B. Du Bois and his discourse.

NOTES

1. I rely heavily on Rampersad's recent reflections on Du Bois and Du Bois Studies throughout this section, and would suggest those interested in his more detailed discussion of Du Bois consult his classic treatment in *The Art and Imagination of W.E.B. Du Bois* (1990).

2. For Aptheker, Broderick, and Rudwick's major contributions to Du Bois Studies, please see Aptheker (1948, 1949, 1961, 1963, 1964, 1965, 1966, 1971, 1973, 1980, 1981, 1982, 1983, 1985, 1989, 1990, 1997), Broderick (1955, 1958a, 1958b, 1958c, 1959, 1974) and Rudwick (1956, 1957a, 1957b, 1957c, 1958a, 1958b, 1959a,

1959b, 1960a, 1960b, 1968, 1969, 1974, 1982a, 1982b). While I utterly agree with Rampersad's assertion that these scholars significantly contributed to the discourse and development of Du Bois Studies, I also think that it is important to point out that none of the aforementioned transgressed the boundaries of their traditional disciplines and *consciously* sought to simultaneously contribute to both Du Bois *and* Africana (or African American) Studies. At this point, that is, at the dawn of the twenty-first century, it is extremely important for Du Bois scholars to draw from the wide range of methodological and theoretical work that Africana Studies has to offer, because many of the new Africana Studies theories and research methods emerge from discursive communities that Du Bois either directly or indirectly established or influenced. In terms of Africana Studies scholars interested in Du Bois, Du Bois's discursive contributions (especially with regard to *The Philadelphia Negro* and *The Souls of Black Folk*) are often overlooked or taken for granted because of his popularity both within and without Africana Studies, causing many to claim (often before they seriously engage his work) that Du Bois belongs to this or that traditional discipline. However, prejudgment and petty intellectual turf wars will not suffice. There simply is no substitute for Africana Studies scholars doing the long and hard work that needs to be done (especially on his work after *The Souls of Black Folk*) in order to assess Du Bois's intellectual and political legacy for its contribution to the discourse and development of Africana Studies.

3. For critical discussions of the racial exclusionary practices and/or the institutionalized racism of traditional academic disciplines, see Eze (1997c), Goldberg (1993, 2002), Gordon (2006a, 2006b), Gordon and Gordon (2006a, 2006b) and Kelley (1997a).

4. Here, and throughout this section, I am generously drawing from Antonio Gramsci's conceptual contributions: "ideological hegemony," "organic intellectual," "historical bloc," "war of position," "war of maneuver," and "ensemble of ideas and social relations," etc. His work has deeply influenced my conception of critical theory as a form of ideological and cultural critique, as well as a radical political praxis-promoting social theory. In particular, Gramsci asserts that class domination is exercised as much through popular and unconscious consensus (or the internalization of imperialism) as through physical coercion (or the threat of it) by the state apparatus, especially in advanced capitalist societies where education, religion, law, health care, media, and popular culture, among other areas, are controlled by the ruling class, and his work innovatively emphasizes the ideological and "counter-hegemonic" dimension that radical politics and critical social theory today must deepen and further develop. However, in terms of Africana critical theory of contemporary society and the life-worlds of people of African origin and descent, and people of color in general, class domination and capitalism represent one of many overlapping, interlocking, and intersecting systems of domination and discrimination that must be ideologically and physically combated and discontinued. Therefore, Gramsci's work provides several insights, but must be synthesized with other theory, especially critical race theory, anti-racist feminist theory, womanist theory, postcolonial theory, and liberation theology, among others, if it is to aid in the (re)construction of a new, more multicultural, radical anti-racist, anti-colonial, and gender justice-seeking critical theory of contem-

porary society. For further discussion, see Gramsci (1971, 1973, 1975, 1977, 1978, 1985, 1994, 1995, 2000).

5. With regard to some of the major primary sources on Du Bois's critique of anti-Semitism and the connections he made between the African and Jewish liberation struggles, please see his essays "The Shape of Fear" (1925), "Anti-Semitism" (1940), "Book Review of *Essays on Anti-Semitism* and *Jews in a Gentile World: The Problems of Anti-Semitism*" (1942), "America's Responsibility to Israel" (1948), "Speech Before the Jewish Peoples Fraternal Order" (1950), "Negro-Jewish Unity" (1950), and "The Negro and the Warsaw Ghetto" (1952) (Du Bois, 1977, 1980e, 1986g, 1986h).

6. For classic and contemporary discussions of Africana Studies' interdisciplinarity, multidisciplinarity, transdisciplinarity, and/or supradisciplinarity, see Aldridge and Young (2000), Aldridge and James (2007), T. Anderson (1990), Anderson and Stewart (2007), Asante (1990, 1993, 1998, 2003a, 2007a, 2007b), Asante and Karenga (2006), Azevedo (2005), Ba Nikongo (1997), Bobo and Michel (2000), Bobo, Hudley and Michel (2004), Conyers (2003, 2005), Fossett and Tucker (1997), Gordon and Gordon (2006a, 2006b), P.A. Hall (1999), Hudson-Weems (2007), Karenga (1988, 2001, 2002), Marable (2000, 2005), Norment (2001), Rabaka (2006a, 2006b, 2007a), J.B. Stewart (1992, 2004), and J. Turner (1984).

7. With regard to the last three points, which provide a basic outline for my conception of critical theory, I have generously drawn from the work of Joy James (1996a, 1997, 1999), whose texts have consistently raised the issue of connecting theory to praxis; the realities of the "ugliness" of anti-racist, anti-sexist, and anti-imperial struggle (both inside and outside "radical" thought traditions and movements); and, the need for progressive intellectual-activists to move "beyond literary insurgency or rhetorical resistance to bring the element of the fight into our daily lives with the specificity of political struggles around economic, sexual, and racial violence" (James, 1996a, p. 23). Here I am also borrowing, however loosely, from the theoretical orientations and methodological work of Marcuse (1969, 1972a, 1997a, 2001, 2004, 2007a, 2007b), Habermas (1984, 1986a, 1986c, 1987a), and Foucault (1977a, 1977b, 1984, 1988, 1997, 1998, 2000). Foucault's conception of and contributions to critical theory, in particular, helped me to hone a critical methodological perspective that transgresses not only the boundaries of traditional academic disciplines, but also the Frankfurt School critical theorists' obsession with Marx and Marxism as the major theoretical thread that connects one version of critical theory to another. Where Foucault turned to Nietzsche and other counter- or post-Marxian thinkers to develop his critical theoretical discourse, I, of course, have labored with Du Bois, and have plans to call on several other Africana social and political theorists (see Rabaka, 2009).

8. For a series of critical discussions on the centennial of Du Bois's essay, "The Study of Negro Problems," and its relevance for contemporary Africana and global radical politics, social thought, progressive movements, philosophy, economic analysis, cultural criticism, feminism, and radical humanism, see Anderson and Zuberi (2000). The influence of this essay on my conception of critical theory, Africana critical theory, cannot be overemphasized.

9. Wilson Moses (1978, 1996, 1998) and Paul Gilroy (1993a) have demonstrated that the "Eurocentric imperial" aspects of Du Bois's early social uplift theory were derived, in part, from his affinity to German nationalism, which he admired, arguably, since his undergraduate days at Fisk. For further discussion, see also Barkin (1998, 2000), Beck (1996), R.A. Berman (1997), Broderick (1958b), D.L. Lewis (1993), A.L. Reed (1997), Schafer (2001), and Zamir (1995).

10. I have in mind here, particularly, the work of Appiah (1992), Gilroy (1993a), Posnock (1995, 1997, 1998) and West (1989).

11. In terms of the time-sensitivity and theoretical specificity of critical theory, Herbert Marcuse (1970a) made an excellent statement regarding the critical theorist's primary task of wrestling with the most pressing issues of their epoch, as opposed to pointing to or pointing out the future "forces of transformation." In his own words,

> If Marx saw in the proletariat the revolutionary class, he did so also, and maybe even primarily, because the proletariat was free from the repressive needs of capitalist society, because the new needs for freedom could develop in the proletariat and were not suffocated by the old, dominant ones. Today [in 1967] in large parts of the most highly developed capitalist countries that is no longer the case. The working class no longer represents the negation of existing needs. That is one of the most serious facts with which we have to deal. As far as the forces of transformation themselves are concerned, I grant you without further discussion that today nobody is in a position to give a prescription for them in the sense of being able to point and say, "Here you have your revolutionary forces, this is their strength, this and this must be done." The only thing I can do is point out what forces potentially make for a radical transformation of the system. (Marcuse, 1970a, p. 70; see also Marcuse, 1964, 1965a, 1965b, 1965c, 1967, 1968, 1969, 1970b, 1972, 1972b, 1973).

This means, then, that critical theorists need not feel compelled to accept the call of the prophet, though, it should be duly noted, Du Bois has regularly been interpreted from this angle (see Blum, 2007; Bogues, 2003; Duberman, 1968; Gooding-Williams, 1991; L.J. Henderson, 1970; T. Nelson, 1958, 1970; West, 1989, 1996; Zamir, 1994). Critical theory is, or, rather, at its best *should be*, deeply rooted in empirical and historical research, and its theoretical positions *should be* linked to concrete social and political struggles. Therefore, though a part of its focus is on the future, critical theory is ultimately a theory of the present whose philosophical foundation rests on and revolves around classical and contemporary radical/revolutionary thought and practices.

Bibliography

Adell, Sandra. (1994). *Double Consciousness/Double Bind: Theoretical Issues in Twentieth-Century Black Literature*. Urbana: University of Illinois Press.

Adorno, Theodor W. (1991). *The Culture Industry: Selected Essays on Mass Culture* (Jay M. Bernstein, Ed.). New York: Routledge.

———. (2000). *The Adorno Reader* (Brain O'Connor, Ed.). Malden, MA: Blackwell.

Adu-Poku, S. (2001). "Envisioning (Black) Male Feminism: A Cross-Cultural Perspective." *Journal of Gender Studies* 10, 157–67.

Agger, Ben. (1992a). *The Discourse of Domination: From the Frankfurt School to Postmodernism*. Evanston, IL: Northwestern University Press.

———. (1992b). *Cultural Studies as Critical Theory*. Washington, D.C.: Falmer Press.

———. (1993). *Gender, Culture, and Power: Toward a Feminist Postmodern Critical Theory*. Westport, CT: Praeger.

———. (1998). *Critical Social Theory*. Boulder, CO: Westview.

———. (2006). *Critical Social Theories: An Introduction*. Boulder: Paradigm Publishers.

Aiyetoro, Adjoa. (2003). "The National Coalition of Blacks for Reparations in America (N'COBRA): Its Creation and Contribution to the Reparations Movement." In Raymond A. Winbush (Ed.), *Should America Pay?: Slavery and the Debate on Reparations* (pp. 209–25). New York: HarperCollins.

Alcoff, Linda Martin. (1998). "Racism." In Alison M. Jaggar and Iris Marion Young (Eds.), *A Companion to Feminist Philosophy* (pp. 475–84). Malden, MA: Blackwell.

———. (2006). *Visible Identities: Race, Gender, and the Self*. New York: Oxford University Press.

Alcoff, Linda Martín, and Mendieta, Eduardo. (Eds.). (2000). *Thinking from the Underside of History: Enrique Dussel's Philosophy of Liberation*. Lanham, MD: Rowman and Littlefield.

Aldridge, Alan E. (2000). *Religion in the Contemporary World: A Sociological Introduction*. Malden, MA: Polity Press.

Aldridge, Delores. (1988). *New Perspectives on Black Studies*. Special Issue, *Phylon* 49, (1).

Aldridge, Delores P., and James, E. Lincoln. (Eds.). (2007). *Africana Studies: Philosophical Perspectives and Theoretical Paradigms*. Pullman, WA: Washington State University Press.

Aldridge, Delores, and Young, Carlene. (Eds.). (2000). *Out of the Revolution: An Africana Studies Anthology*. Lanham, MD: Lexington.

Alexander, Elizabeth. (1995). "'We Must Be About Our Father's Business: Anna Julia Cooper and the In-Corporation of the Nineteenth Century African American Woman Intellectual." *Signs* 20 (2), 336–56.

Alexander, Jeffrey C. (Ed.). (2001). *Mainstream and Critical Social Theory: Classical, Modern, and Contemporary*. Thousand Oaks, CA: Sage.

Alexander, M. Jacqui, and Mohanty, Chandra Talpade. (Eds.). (1997). *Feminist Genealogies, Colonial Legacies, Democratic Futures*. New York: Routledge.

Alexandre, Pierre. (1972). *Languages and Language in Black Africa*. Evanston, IL: Northwestern University Press.

Alkalimat, Abdul. (1986). *Introduction to Afro-American Studies: A People's College Primer*. Chicago: Twenty-First Century Books and Publications.

——. (Ed.). (1990). *Paradigms in Black Studies: Intellectual History, Cultural Meaning, and Political Ideology*. Chicago: Twenty-First Century Books and Publications.

Alkebulan, Paul. (2007). *Survival Pending Revolution: The History of the Black Panther Party*. Tuscaloosa, AL: University of Alabama.

Allen, Ernest, Jr. (1992). "Ever Feeling One's Twoness: 'Double Ideas' and 'Double Consciousness' in *The Souls of Black Folk*." *Critique of Anthropology* 12 (3), 261–75.

Allen, Ernest, and Chrisman, Robert. (2001). "Ten Reasons to Respond to David Horowitz." *The Black Scholar* 31 (2), 49–55.

Allen, Robert. (1974). "The Politics of the Attack on Black Studies." *Black Scholar* 6 (1), 1–7.

——. (1998). "Past Due: The African American Quest for Reparations." *The Black Scholar* 28 (2), 2–17.

Allen, Theodore W. (1994). *The Invention of the White Race* (Volume 1). New York: Verso.

——. (1997). *The Invention of the White Race* (Volume 2). New York: Verso.

Alridge, Derrick P. (1997). "The Social, Economic, and Political Thought of W.E.B. Du Bois during the 1930s: Implications for Contemporary African American Education." Ph.D. dissertation, Pennsylvania State University.

——. (1999a). "Conceptualizing a Du Boisian Philosophy of Education: Toward a Model for African American Education." *Educational Theory* 49 (3), 359–79.

——. (1999b). "Guiding Philosophical Principles for a Du Boisian-Based African American Educational Model." *Journal of Negro Education* 68 (2), 182–99.

——. (2003). "W.E.B. Du Bois: Race Man, Teacher, and Scholar." In Sherry Field and Michael Bergson (Eds.), *They Led by Teaching: Influential Educators* (pp. 102–14). Indianapolis, IN: Phi Delta Pi Publications.

———. (2008). *The Educational Thought of W.E.B. Du Bois: An Intellectual History.* New York: Teachers College Press.

Alva, J.J.K. de. (1995). "The Postcolonization of the (Latin) American Experience, A Reconsideration of 'Colonialism,' 'Postcolonialism' and 'Mestizaje'." In Gyan Prakash (Ed.), *After Colonialism: Imperial Histories and Postcolonial Displacements* (pp. 241–75). Princeton, NJ: Princeton University Press.

Alway, Joan. (1995). *Critical Theory and Political Possibilities: Conceptions of Emancipatory Politics in the Works of Horkheimer, Adorno, Marcuse, and Habermas.* Westport, CT: Greenwood Press.

America, Richard F. (Ed.). (1990). *The Wealth of the Races: The Present Value of Benefits From Past Injustices*: New York: Greenwood Press.

———. (1993). *Paying the Social Debt: What White America Owes Black America.* Westport, CT: Praeger.

———. (1995). "Racial Inequality, Economic Dysfunction, and Reparations." *Challenge* 38 (6), 40–45.

———. (1996). "Reparations and the Competitive Advantage of Inner Cities." *Review of Black Political Economy* 24 (2/3), 193–206.

———. (2000). "Reparations and Higher Education." *Black Issues in Higher Education* 16 (23), 104.

———. (1999). "Reparation and Public Policy." *Review of Black Political Economy* 26 (3), 77–83.

Anderson, Elijah, and Zuberi, Tukufu. (Eds.). (2000). *The Study of African American Problems: W.E.B. Du Bois's Agenda, Then and Now.* Thousand Oaks, CA: Sage.

Anderson, John D. (1988). *The Education of Blacks in the South, 1860–1935.* Chapel Hill: University of North Carolina Press.

Anderson, Perry. (1976). *Considerations on Western Marxism.* London: New Left Books.

Anderson, Talmadge. (Ed.). (1990). *Black Studies: Theory, Method and Cultural Perspective.* Pullman, WA: Washington State University Press.

Anderson, Talmadge, and Stewart, James B. (2007). *Introduction to African American Studies: Transdisciplinary Approaches and Implications.* Balitmore, MD: Black Classic Press.

Andrews, Malachi. (1973). *Black Language.* Los Angeles: Seymour-Smith Publishing.

Andrews, William L. (Ed.). (1985). *Critical Essays on W.E.B. Du Bois.* Boston: G.K. Hall.

Andrews, William L., Foster, Frances Smith, and Harris, Trudier. (Eds.). (1997). *The Oxford Companion to African American Literature.* New York: Oxford University Press.

Anthias, Floya, and Lloyd, Cathie. (Eds.). *Rethinking Anti-Racism: From Theory to Practice.* New York: Routledge.

Anthias, Floya, and Yuval-Davis, Nira. (1992). *Racialized Boundaries: Race, Nation, Gender, Color and Class in the Anti-Racist Struggle.* New York: Routledge.

Antonio, Robert J., and Kellner, Douglas. (1994). "Postmodern Social Theory: Contributions and Limitations." In David Dickens and Andrea Fontana (Eds.), *Postmodernism and Social Inquiry* (pp. 127–52). New York: Guilford.

Appiah, Kwame Anthony. (1985). "The Uncompleted Argument: Du Bois and the Illusion of Race." *Critical Inquiry* 12 (1), 21–37.

———. (1990). "Racisms." In David Theo Goldberg (Ed.), *Anatomy of Racism* (pp. 3–17). Minneapolis, MN: University of Minnesota Press.

———. (1992). *In My Father's House: Africa in the Philosophy of Culture.* New York: Oxford University Press.

———. (1995). "The Uncompleted Argument: Du Bois and the Illusion of Race." In Albert G. Mosley (Ed.), *African Philosophy: Selected Readings* (pp. 199–215). Englewood Cliffs, NJ: Prentice Hall.

———. (1994). "Identity, Authenticity, Survival: Multicultural Societies and Social Reproduction." In Amy Gutmann (Ed.), *Multiculturalism* (pp. 149–65). Princeton: Princeton University Press.

———. (1996). "Race, Culture, Identity." In Kwame Appiah and Amy Gutman, *Color Conscious: The Political Morality of Race* (pp. 3–75). Princeton: Princeton University Press.

———. (1997). "'But Would That Still Be Me?': Notes on Gender, 'Race,' Ethnicity as a Source of Identity." In Naomi Zack (Ed.), *Race/Sex: Their Sameness, Difference, and Interplay* (pp. 75–82). New York: Routledge.

Appiah, Kwame Anthony, and Gates, Henry Louis, Jr. (1999). *Africana: The Encyclopedia of the African and African American Experience.* New York: Basic/Civitas Books.

Appleby, Joyce, Covington, Elizabeth, Hoyt, David, Latham, Michael, and Snieder, Allison. (Eds.). (1996). *Knowledge and Postmodernism in Historical Perspective.* New York: Routledge.

Aptheker, Bettina. (1975). "W.E.B. Du Bois and the Struggle for Women's Rights: 1910–1920." *San Jose Studies* 1 (2), 7–16.

Aptheker, Herbert. (1948). "W.E.B. Du Bois: The First Eighty Years." *Phylon* 9, 58–69.

———. (1949). "The Washington-Du Bois Conference of 1904." *Science and Society* 13, 344–51.

———. (1961). "Dr. Du Bois and Communism." *Political Affairs* 40 (December), 13–20.

———. (1963). "To Dr. Du Bois—With Love." *Political Affairs* 42 (February), 35–42.

———. (1964). "Du Bois on Douglass: 1895." *Journal of Negro History* 49 (October), 264–68.

———. (1965). "Some Unpublished Writings of W.E.B. Du Bois." *Freedom* 5 (Winter), 103–28.

———. (1966). "W.E.B. Du Bois: The Final Years." *Journal of Human Relations* 14, 149–55.

———. (1971). "*The Souls of Black Folk*: A Comparison of the 1903 and 1952 Editions." *Negro History Bulletin* 34 (January).

———. (Ed.). (1973). *An Annotated Bibliography of the Published Writings of W.E.B. Du Bois.* Millwood, New York: Kraus-Thompson.

———. (1980). "Introduction to *Prayers for Dark People*." In W.E.B. Du Bois, *Prayers for Dark People* (pp. iv-xi). Amherst, MA: University of Massachusetts.

———. (1981). "W.E.B. Du Bois and Africa." *Political Affairs* 60 (March).

———. (1982). "W.E.B. Du Bois and Religion: A Brief Reassessment." *Journal of Religious Thought* 59 (Spring-Summer), 5–11.

———. (1983). *W.E.B. Du Bois and the Struggle Against Racism*. New York: United Nations Center Against Apartheid.

———. (1985). "Introduction to Du Bois's Creative Writings." In Herbert Aptheker (Ed.), *Creative Writings by W.E.B. Du Bois: A Pageant, Poems, Short Stories, and Playlets* (pp. ix-xii). White Plains, NY: Kraus International.

———. (1989). *The Literary Legacy of W.E.B. Du Bois*. White Plains, NY: Kraus International.

———. (1990). "W.E.B. Du Bois: Struggle Not Despair." *Clinical Sociology Review* 8, 58–68.

———. (1997). "Personal Recollections: Woodson, Wesley, Robeson, and Du Bois." *Black Scholar* 27 (2), 42.

Arato, Andrew, and Gebhardt, Eike, (Eds.). (1997). *The Essential Frankfurt School Reader.* New York: Continuum.

Araya, Victorio. (1987). *God of the Poor: The Mystery of God in Latin American Liberation Theology*. Maryknoll, NY: Orbis.

Arisaka, Yoko. (2001). "Women Carrying Water: At the Crossroads of Technology and Critical Theory." In William S. Wilkerson and Jeffrey Paris (Eds.), *New Critical Theory: Essays on Liberation* (pp. 155–74). Lanham, MD: Rowman and Littlefield Publishers.

Armah, Ayi Kwei. (1969). *The Beautiful Ones Are Not Yet Born*. London: Heinemann.

Arndt, Murray Dennis. (1970). "The *Crisis* Years of W.E.B. Du Bois, 1910–1934." Ph.D. dissertation, Duke University.

Arnold, N. Scott. (1990). *Marx's Radical Critique of Capitalist Society*. New York: Oxford University Press.

Aronowitz, Stanley. (1990). *The Crisis Historical Materialism*. Minneapolis: University of Minnesota Press.

———. (1996). *The Death and Rebirth of American Radicalism*. New York: Routledge.

Aronson, Ronald. (1995). *After Marxism*. New York: Guilford.

Arrington, Robert L. (Ed.). (1999). *A Companion to the Philosophers*. Malden: Blackwell.

Asante, Molefi Kete. (1969). *The Rhetoric of Black Revolution*. Boston: Allyn and Bacon.

———. (1972). *Language, Communication, and Rhetoric in Black America*. New York: Harper and Row.

———. (1973). *Transracial Communication*. Englewood Cliffs, NJ: Prentice-Hall.

———. (1987). *The Afrocentric Idea*. Philadelphia: Temple University Press.

———. (1988). *Afrocentricity*. Trenton: Africa World Press.

———. (1990). *Kemet, Afrocentricity, and Knowledge*. Trenton: Africa World Press.

———. (1993). *Malcolm X as Cultural Hero and Other Afrocentric Essays*. Trenton: Africa World Press.

———. (1998). *The Afrocentric Idea*. Philadelphia: Temple University Press.

——. (1999). *The Painful Demise of Eurocentricism.* Trenton: Africa World Press.

——. (2000). *The Egyptian Philosophers: Ancient African Voices from Imhotep to Akhenaten.* Chicago: African American Images.

——. (2001). *African American History: A Journey of Liberation.* Saddle Brook, NJ: Peoples Publishing Group.

——. (2002). *Culture and Customs of Egypt.* Westport, CT: Greenwood Press.

——. (2003a). *Afrocentricity: Theory of Social Change.* Chicago: African American Images.

——. (2003b). *Erasing Racism: The Survival of the American Nation.* Amherst, NY: Promethues Books.

——. (2005a). *Race, Rhetoric, and Identity: The Architecton of Soul.* Amherst, NY: Humanity Books.

——. (2005b). *Ebonics: An Introduction to African American Language.* Chicago: African American Images.

——. (2005c). *Cheikh Anta Diop: An Intellectual Portrait.* Chicago: Third World Press.

——. (2007a). *An Afrocentric Manifesto.* Oxford: Polity Press.

——. (2007b). *The History of Africa: The Quest for Eternal Harmony.* New York: Routledge.

Asante, Molefi K., and Asante, Kariamu Welsh. (Eds.). (1985). *African Culture: The Rhythms of Unity.* Westport, CT: Greenwood.

Asante, Molefi K., and Abarry, Abu S. (Eds.). (1996). *The African Intellectual Heritage.* Philadelphia: Temple University.

Asante, Molefi K., and Gudykunst, William. (Eds.). (1989). *Handbook of Intercultural and International Communication.* Thousand Oaks, CA: Sage.

Asante, Molefi K., and Karenga, Maulana. (Eds.). (2006). *The Handbook of Black-Studies.* Thousand Oaks, CA: Sage.

Asante, Molefi K., and Rich, Andrea. (Eds.). (1970). *The Rhetoric of Revolution.* Durham, NC: Moore Publishing.

Asante, Molefi K., and Robb, Steve. (Eds.). (1971). *The Voice of Black Rhetoric.* Boston: Allyn and Bacon.

Asante, Molefi K., and Vandi, Abdulai S. (Eds.). (1980). *Contemporary Black Thought: Alternative Analyses in Social and Behavioral Science.* Beverly Hills, CA: Sage.

Asare, William Kweku. (2002). *Slavery Reparations in Perspective:* Victoria, B.C.: Trafford.

Ashcroft, Bill, Griffiths, Gareth, and Tiffin, Helen. (1989). *The Empire Writes Back: Theory and Practice in Postcolonial Literatures.* New York: Routledge.

——. (Eds.). (1995). *The Post-Colonial Studies Reader.* New York: Routledge.

——. (Eds.). (1998). *Key Concepts in Postcolonial Studies.* New York: Routledge.

Awkward, Michael. (2000). "A Black Man's Place in Black Feminist Criticism." In Joy A. James and T. Denean Sharpley-Whiting, (Eds.), *The Black Feminist Reader* (pp. 88–108). Malden, MA: Blackwell.

Axelsen, Diana E. (1984). "Philosophical Justifications for Contemporary African Social and Political Values and Strategies." In Richard A. Wright (Ed.), *African Phi-*

losophy: An Introduction (3rd Edition, pp. 227–44). Lanham, MD: University of America Press.

Azevedo, Mario. (Ed.). (2005). *Africana Studies: A Survey of Africa and the African Diaspora.* Durham: Carolina Academic Press.

Baber, Willie L. (1992). "Capitalism and Racism: Discontinuities in the Life and Work of W.E.B. Du Bois." *Critique of Anthropology* 12 (3), 339–64.

Babbitt, Susan E., and Campbell, Sue. (Eds.). (1999). *Racism and Philosophy.* Ithaca: Cornell University Press.

Baer, Hans A., and Singer, Merrill. (2002). *African American Religion: Varieties of Protest and Accommodation.* Knoxville: University of Tennessee Press.

Bailey, Ronald. (1970). "Why Black Studies?" *The Education Digest* 35 (9), 46–48.

Bainbridge, William S. (1997). *The Sociology of Religious Movements.* New York: Routledge.

Baker, Houston A., Jr. (1972). "The Black Man of Culture: W.E.B. Du Bois and *The Souls of Black Folk*." In Houston Baker, *Long Black Song* (pp. 96–108). Charlottesville: University of Virginia Press.

Baker, Houston A., Jr., Diawara, Manthia, and Lindeborg, Ruth H. (Eds.). (1996). *Black British Cultural Studies: A Reader.* Chicago: University of Chicago Press.

Balbus, Isaac D. (1982). *Marxism and Domination.* Princeton: Princeton University Press.

Baldwin, James. (1955). *Notes of a Native Son.* Boston: Beacon.

Balfour, Lawrie. (2003). "Unreconstructed Democracy: W.E.B. Du Bois and the Case for Reparation." *American Political Science Review* 97 (1), 33–44.

———. (2005). "Representative Women: Slavery, Citizenship, and Feminist Theory in Du Bois's 'The Damnation of Women.'" *Hypatia* 20 (3), 127–48.

Bambara, Toni Cade. (Ed.). (1970). *The Black Woman: An Anthology.* New York: Signet.

Ba Nikongo, Nikongo. (Ed.). (1997). *Leading Issues in African American Studies.* Durham, NC: Carolina Academic Press.

Banks, Williams L. (2001). *The Case Against Black Reparation.* New York: Infinity.

Bannerji, Himani. (1995). *Thinking Through: Essays on Feminism, Marxism, and Anti-Racism.* Toronto: Women's Educational Press.

Baraka, Amiri. (1966). *Home: Social Essays.* New York: Morrow.

———. (1970). *It's Nation Time!* Chicago: Third World Press.

———. (1971). *Raise, Race, Rays, Raze: Essays Since 1965.* New York: Random House.

———. (Ed.). (1972). *African Congress: A Documentary of the First Modern Pan-African Congress.* New York: Morrow.

———. (1984). *Daggers and Javelins: Essays, 1974–1979.* New York: Morrow.

———. (1994). *Conversations with Amiri Baraka* (Charles Reilly, Ed.). Jackson: University Press of Mississippi.

———. (1995). *Wise, Why's, Y's: Social and Political Essays.* Chicago: Third World Press.

———. (1997). *The Autobiography of LeRoi Jones/Amiri Baraka.* Chicago: Lawrence Hill.

———. (2000). *LeRoi Jone/Amiri Baraka Reader* (William J. Harris, Ed.). New York: Thunder's Mouth Press.

———. (2003). *The Essence of Reparations: Afro-American Self-Determination and Revolutionary Democratic Struggle in the United States.* St. Martin, Caribbean: House Nehesi Publishing.

Baraka, Amiri, and Neal, Larry. (Eds.). (1968). *Black Fire: An Anthology of Afro-American Writing.* New York: Morrow.

Baraka, Amiri, and Fundi. (1970). *In Our Terribleness: Some Elements and Meaning in Black Style.* Indianapolis: Bobbs-Merrill.

Baraka, Amiri, and Baraka, Amina. (Eds.). (1983). *Confirmation: An Anthology of African American Women.* New York: Quill.

Barkan, Elazar. (2000). *The Guilt of Nations: Restitution and Negotiating Historical Injustices.* New York: Norton.

Barkin, Kenneth. (1998). "W.E.B. Du Bois and the Kaiserreich Articles: An Introduction to Du Bois's Manuscripts on Germany." *Central European History* 31 (3), 155–71.

———. (2000). "'Berlin Days,' 1892-1894: W.E.B. Du Bois and German Political Economy." *Boundary 2* 27 (3), 79–101.

Barnes, Annie S. (1985). *The Black Middle Class Family: A Study of Black Subsociety, Neighborhood, and Home Interaction.* Bristol, IN: Wyndham Hall Press.

Barnes, Sandra T. (Ed.). (1997). *Africa's Ogun: Old World and New.* Bloomington, IN: Indiana University Press.

Barnett, Bernice McNair, and Mooney, Jessica. (2001). "W.E.B. Du Bois and Joe Feagin: Liberation Sociologists and Activist Intellectuals Affirming Diversity Along Race, Gender, and Class Lines." *Society for the Study of Social Problems.*

Barrett, Leonard E. (1974). *Soul-Force: African Heritage in Afro-American Religion.* Garden City, NY: Anchor.

Barrett, Margaret Dwight, and Carey, Phillip. (Eds.). (2003). *The Diaspora: Introduction to Africana Studies.* Kendall/Hunt Publishing.

Barrett, Michele. (1980). *Women's Oppression Today: Problems in Marxist Feminist Analysis.* London: Verso.

Bartolovich, Crystal (2000). "Global Capital and Transnationalism." In Henry Schwarz and Sangeeta Ray (Eds.), *A Companion to Postcolonial Studies* (pp. 126–61). Malden: Blackwell.

Bascom, William R. (1980). *Sixteen Cowries: Yoruba Divination from Africa to the New World.* Bloomington, IN: Indiana University Press.

Bastide, Roger. (1971). *African Civilization in the New World.* New York: Harper and Row.

———. (1978). *The African Religions of Brazil: Twoard a Sociology of the Interpretation of Civilization.* Baltimore: Johns Hopkins University Press.

Bates, Robert H., Mudimbe, V.Y., and O'Barr, Jean. (Eds.). (1993). *Africa and the Disciplines: The Contributions of Research in Africa to the Social Sciences and Humanities.* Chicago: University of Chicago Press.

Batstone, David, Mendieta, Eduardo, Lorentzen, Lois Ann, and Hopkins, Dwight N. (Eds.). (1997). *Liberation Theologies, Postmodernity, and the Americas.* New York: Routledge.

Battle, Juan, and Wright, Earl, II. (2002). "W.E.B. Du Bois's Talented Tenth: A Quantitative Assessment." *Journal of Black Studies* 32 (6), 654–72.

Battle, Michael. (2006). *The Black Church in America: African American Christian Spirituality.* Malden: Blackwell.

Bauerlin, Mark. (2001). *Negrophobia: A Race Riot in Atlanta, 1906.* San Francisco: Encounter Books.

Baulding, Lisa. (Producer). (1992). *W. E. B. Du Bois of Great Barrington.* [Documentary]. WGBY-TV Springfield, MA: PBS Video.

Bay, Mia. (1998). "'The World Was Thinking Wrong About Race': *The Philadelphia Negro* and Nineteenth-Century Science." In Michael B. Katz and Thomas J. Sugrue (Eds.), *W.E.B. Du Bois, Race, and the City: The Philadelphia Negro and Its Legacy* (pp. 41–60). Philadelphia: University of Pennsylvania Press.

Beale, Frances. (1995). "Double Jeopardy: To Be Black and Female." In Beverly Guy-Sheftall (Ed.), *Words of Fire: An Anthology of African American Feminist Thought* (pp. 146–56). New York: Free Press.

Beavers, Herman. (2000). "Romancing the Body Politic: Du Bois's Propaganda of the Dark World." *Annals of the American Academy of Political and Social Science* 568 (March), 250–64.

Beck, Hamilton. (1996). "W.E.B. Du Bois as a Study Abroad Student in Germany, 1892–1894." *Frontiers: The Interdisciplinary Journal of Study Abroad* 2 (1), 45–63.

Beckford, James A. (1989). *Religion and Advanced Industrial Society.* Boston: Unwin Hyman.

——. (2003). *Social Theory and Relgion.* Cambridge: Cambridge University Press.

Beckford, James A., and Demerath, N. Jay. (Eds.). (2007). *The Sage Handbook of the Sociology of Religion.* Thousand Oaks, CA: Sage.

Bell, Bernard W. (1985). "W.E.B. Du Bois's Struggle to Reconcile Folk and High Art." In William L. Andrews (Ed.), *Critical Essays on W.E.B. Du Bois* (pp. 106–22). Boston: G.K. Hall.

——. (1996). "Genealogical Shifts in Du Bois's Discourse on Double-Consciousness as the Sign of African American Difference." In Bernard W. Bell, Emily R. Grosholz, and James B. Stewart (Eds.), *W.E.B. Du Bois: On Race and Culture* (pp. 87–110). New York: Routledge.

Bell, Bernard W., Grosholz, Emily R., and Stewart, James B. (Eds.). (1996). *W.E.B. Du Bois: On Race and Culture.* New York: Routledge.

Bell, Derrick. (1995). "Racial Realism—After We're Gone: Prudent Speculations on America in a Post-Racial Epoch." In Richard Delgado (Ed.), *Critical Race Theory: The Cutting Edge* (pp. 2–8). Philadelphia: Temple University Press.

Bell, Linda A., and Blumenfeld, David. (Eds.). (1995). *Overcoming Racism and Sexism.* Lanham, MD: Rowman and Littlefield.

Bell, Richard H. (2002). *Understanding African Philosophy: A Cross-Cultural Approach to Classical and Contemporary Issues in Africa.* New York: Routledge.

Bendiner, Elmer. (1975). *A Time for Angels: The Tragicomic History of the League of Nations.* New York: Knopf.

Benhabib, Seyla. (1986). *Critique, Norm, and Utopia.* New York: Columbia University Press.

————. (1992). *Situating the Self: Gender, Community, and Postmodernism in Con-temporary Ethics*. New York: Routledge.

Benhabib, Seyla, and Cornell, Drucilla. (1987). *Feminism as Critique: Essays on the Politics of Gender in Late-Capitalist Societies*. London: Polity Press.

Berg, Manfred. (2005). *The Ticket to Freedom: The NAACP and the Struggle for Black Political Integration*. Gainesville, FL: University Press of Florida.

Berman, Nathan. (2000). "Shadows: Du Bois and the Colonial Prospect, 1925." *Villanova Law Review* 45 (5), 959–70.

Berman, Russell A. (1989). *Modern Culture and Critical Theory: Art, Politics, and the Legacy of the Frankfurt School*. Madison, WI: University of Wisconsin Press.

————. (1997). "Du Bois and Wagner: Race, Nation, and Culture Between the United States and Germany." *German Quarterly* 70 (2), 123–35.

Bernasconi, Robert. (Ed.). (2001). *Race*. Malden, MA: Blackwell.

Bernasconi, Robert, and Lott, Tommy L. (Eds.). (2000). *The Idea of Race*. Indianapolis: Hackett.

Bernstein, Jay M. (Ed.). (1995). *The Frankfurt School: Critical Assessments*. London: Routledge.

Berry, Mary Frances. (1972). "Reparations for Freedmen, 1890–1916: Fraudulent Practices or Justice Deferred?" *Journal of Negro History* 57 (3), 219–30.

————. (1994). *Black Resistance, White Law: A History of Constitutional Racism in America*. New York: Allen Lane.

————. (2000). "Du Bois as Social Activist: Why We Are Not Saved." *Annals of the American Academy of Political and Social Science* 568 (March), 100–10.

————. (2005). *My Face Is Black, Is True: Callie House and the Struggle for Ex-Slave Reparations*. New York: Knopf.

Berryman, Phillip. (1987). *Liberation Theology: Essential Facts about the Revolutionary Movement in Latin America and Beyond*. Philadelphia: Temple University Press.

Best, Felton O. (Ed.). (1998). *Black Religious Leadership from the Slave Community to the Million Man March: Flames of Fire*. Lewiston, NY: Edwin Mellen Press.

Best, Steven. (1995). *The Politics of Historical Vision: Marx, Foucault, Habermas*. New York: Guilford.

Best, Steven and Kellner, Douglas. (1991). *Postmodern Theory: Critical Interrogations*. New York: Guilford.

————. (1997). *The Postmodern Turn*. New York: Guilford.

————. (2001). *The Postmodern Adventure*. New York: Guilford.

Bhavnani, Kum-Kum. (Ed.). (2001). *Feminism and Race*. New York: Oxford University Press.

Bienen, Henry. (1977). "State and Revolution: The Work of Amilcar Cabral." *Journal of Modern African Studies* 15 (4), 555–95.

Billingsley, Andrew. (1999). *Mighty Like a River: The Black Church and Social Reform*. New York: Oxford University Press.

Birt, Robert E. (Ed.). (2002). *The Quest for Community and Identity: Critical Essays in Africana Social Philosophy*. Lanham, MD: Rowman and Littlefield.

Bittker, Boris I. (2003). *The Case for Black Reparations*. Boston: Beacon.

Blackburn, Robin. (1972). *Ideology in Social Science: Readings in Critical Social Theory.* New York: Pantheon.

Blackey, Robert. (1974). "Fanon and Cabral: A Contrast in Theories of Revolution for Africa." *Journal of Modern African Studies* 12 (2), 191–209.

Blackwell, James E., and Janowitz, Morris. (Eds.). (1974). *Black Sociologists: Historical and Contemporary Perspectives.* Chicago: University of Chicago Press.

Blakely, Thomas D., van Beek, Walter E.A., and Thomson, Dennis L. (Eds.). (1994). *Religion in Africa.*

Blakeney, Ronnie F., and Snarey, John R. (2001). "The Ripples in Placid Lakes: W.E.B. Du Bois Revisted." *Theory and Research in Social Education* 29 (4), 742–48.

Blassingame, John. (Ed). (1973). *New Perspectives on Black Studies.* Chicago: University of Illinois Press.

Blau, Judith R., and Brown, Eric S. (2001). "Du Bois and Diasporic Identity: The Veil and Unveiling Project." *Sociological Theory* 19 (2), 219–33.

Blaut, James M. (1993). *The Colonizer's Model of the World: Geographical Diffusionism and Eurocentric History.* New York: Guilford.

Blee, Kathleen M. (1991). *Women of the Klan: Racism and Gender in the 1920's.* Berkeley: University of California Press.

———. (2002). *Inside Organized Racism: Women in the Hate Movement.* Berkeley: University of California Press.

Blight, David W. (1994). "W.E.B. Du Bois and the Struggle for American Historical Memory." In Genevieve Fabre and Robert O'Meally (Eds.), *History and Memory in African American Culture* (pp. 45–71). New York: Oxford University Press.

———. (2001). "The Enduring Du Bois." *American Prospect* 12 (5), 57–59.

Bloom, Harold. (2001). *W.E.B. Du Bois.* Broomall: Chelsea House Publishers.

Blum, Edward J. (2004). "The Soul of W.E.B. Du Bois." *Philosophia Africana* 7 (2), 1–16.

———. (2005a). "Religion and the Sociological Imagination of W.E.B. Du Bois." *Sociation Today* 3 (1). Online at: www.ncsociology.org/sociationtoday/v31/blum .htm (Accessed 23 February 2005).

———. (2005b). "'There Won't be Any Rich People in Heaven': The Black Christ, White Hypocrisy, and the Gospel According to W.E.B. Du Bois." *Journal of African American History* 90 (4), 368–86.

———. (2007). *W.E.B. Du Bois: American Prophet.* Philadelphia, PA: University of Pennsylvannia Press.

Blyden, Edward W. (1994). *Christianity, Islam, and the Negro Race.* Baltimore: Black Classic Press.

———. (1995). *African Life and Customs.* Baltimore, MD: Black Classic Press.

Bobo, Jacqueline. (1995). *Black Women as Cultural Readers.* New York: Columbia University.

———. (Ed.). (2001). *Black Feminist Cultural Criticism.* Malden, MA: Blackwell.

Bobo, Jacqueline, and Michel, Claudine. (Eds.). (2000). *Black Studies: Current Issues, Enduring Questions.* Dubuque, IA: Kendall/Hunt.

Bobo, Jacqueline, Hudley, Cynthia, and Michel, Claudine. (Eds.). (2004). *The Black Studies Reader.* New York: Routledge.

Bobo, Lawrence D. (2000). "Reclaiming a Du Boisian Perspective on Racial Attitudes." *Annals of the American Academy of Political and Social Science* 568 (March), 186–202.

Boff, Clodovis. (1987). *Theology and Praxis: Epistemological Foundations*. Maryknoll, NY: Orbis.

Boff, Leonardo. (1988). *When Theology Listens to the Poor*. San Francisco, CA: Harper & Row.

Boff, Leonardo, and Boff, Clodovis. (1987). *Introducing Liberation Theology*. Maryknoll, NY: Orbis.

Bogues, Anthony. (Ed.). (1983). *Marxism and Black Liberation*. Cleveland: Hera Press.

——. (2003). *Black Heretics, Black Prophets: Radical Political Intellectuals*. New York: Routledge.

Bolner, James. (1968). "Toward a Theory of Racial Reparations." *Phylon* 29 (1), 41–47.

Bonilla-Silva, Eduardo. (2001). *White Supremacy and Racism in the Post-Civil Rights Era*. Boulder, CO: Lynne Rienner.

——. (2003). *Racism Without Racists: Color-Blind Racism and the Persistence of Racial Inequality in the United States*. Lanham, MD: Rowman and Littlefield.

Bonilla-Silva, Eduardo, and Doane, Ashley. (Eds.). (2003). *White Out: The Continuing Significance of Racism*. New York: Routledge.

Booth, W. James. (2001). "The Unforgotten: Memories of Justice." *American Political Science Review* 95, 777–91.

Bottomore, Tom. (1985). *The Frankfurt School*. New York: Tavistock.

Bourne, Jenny. (1983). "Towards an Anti-Racist Feminism." *Race & Class* 25, 1–22.

Bowser, Benjamin P. (2007). *The Black Middle Class: Social Mobility and Vulnerability*. Boulder, CO: Lynne Rienner.

Bowser, Benjamin, and Whittle, Deborah. (1996). "Personal Reflections on W.E.B. Du Bois: The Person, Scholar and Activist." *Research in Race and Ethnic Relations* 9, 27–65.

Boyd, Melba Joyce. (1994). *Discarded Legacy: Politics and Poetics Frances E. W. Harper*. Detroit: Wayne State University.

Boxer, Marilyn J., and Quataert, Jean H. (Eds.). (1978). *Socialist Women: European Socialist Feminism in the Nineteenth and Early-Twentieth Centuries*. New York: Elsevier North-Hollad.

Boxill, Bernard. (1972). "Morality of Reparations." *Social Theory and Practice* 2, 113–22.

——. (1977-78). "Du Bois and Fanon on Culture." *Philosophical Forum* 9 (2–3), 326–38.

——. (1992). *Blacks and Social Justice*. Lanham, MD: Rowman and Littlefield.

——. (1996). "Du Bois on Cultural Pluralism." In Bernard W. Bell, Emily R. Grosholz, and James B. Stewart (Eds.), *W.E.B. Du Bois: On Race and Culture* (pp. 57–86). New York: Routledge.

——. (1997a). "Washington, Du Bois and Plessy vs. Ferguson." *Law & Philosophy* 16 (3), 299–330.

———. (1997b). "Two Traditions in African American Political Philosophy." In John P. Pittman (Ed.), *African American Perspectives and Philosophical Traditions* (pp. 119–35). New York: Routledge.

———. (1997c). "Populism and Elitism in African American Political Thought." *Journal of Ethics* 1 (3), 209–38.

———. (2003). "The Morality of Reparations II." In Tommy L. Lott and John P. Pittman (Eds.), *A Companion to African American Philosophy* (pp. 134–50). Malden: Blackwell.

Bracey, Christopher A. (2008). *Saviors or Sell-Outs: The Promise and Peril of Black Conservatism, from Booker T. Washington to Condoleezza Rice*. Boston: Beacon.

Bracey, John, Meier, August, and Rudwick, Elliott. (Eds.). (1971). *The Black Sociologists: The First Half Century*. Belmont, CA: Wadsworth.

Brady, Jeanne. (1994). "Critical Literacy, Feminism, and a Politics of Representation." In Peter McLaren and Colin Lankshear (Eds.), *Politics of Liberation: Paths from Freire* (pp. 142–53). New York: Routledge.

Braley, Mark Steven. (1994). "The Circle Unbroken: W.E.B. Du Bois and the Encyclopedic Narrative." Ph.D. dissertation, Princeton University.

Braun, Lily. (1987). *Selected Writings on Feminism and Socialism*. Bloomington, IN: Indiana University Press.

Breines, Winifred. (2006). *The Trouble Between Us: An Uneasy History of White and Black Women in the Feminist Movement*. New York: Oxford University Press.

Brewer, Anthony. (1980). *Marxist Theories of Imperialism*. London: Routledge & Kegan Paul.

Brewer, Rose. (1993). "Theorizing Race, Class and Gender: The New Scholarship of Black Feminist Intellectuals and Black Women's Labor." In Stanlie James and Abena Busia (Eds.), *Theorizing Black Feminism: The Visionary Pragmatism of Black Women* (pp. 13–30). New York: Routledge.

Bridges, Charles Wesley, II. (1973). "The Curriculum Theory Context of Activity Analysis and the Educational Philosophies of Washington and Du Bois." Ph.D. dissertation, Ohio State University, Columbus, OH.

Brisbane, Robert H. (1974). *Black Activism: Racial Revolution in the United States, 1954–1970*. Valley Forge, PA: Judson Press.

Broderick, Francis L. (1955). "W.E.B. Du Bois: The Trail of His Ideas." Ph.D. dissertation, Harvard University.

———. (1958a). "The Academic Training of W.E.B. Du Bois." *Journal of Negro Education* 27 (Winter), 10–16.

———. (1958b). "German Influence on the Scholarship of W.E.B. Du Bois." *Phylon* 19 (December), 367–71.

———. (1958c). "The Tragedy of W.E.B. Du Bois." *Progressive* 22 (February), 29–32.

———. (1959). *W.E.B. Du Bois: Negro Leader in a Time of Crisis*. Palo Alto, CA:

———. (1974). "W.E.B. Du Bois: History of an Intellectual." In James E. Blackwell and Morris Janowitz (Eds.), *Black Sociologists: Historical and Contemporary Perspectives* (pp. 3–24). Chicago: University of Chicago Press.

Brodwin, Stanley. (1972). "The Veil Transcended: Form and Meaning in W.E.B. Du Du Bois's *The Souls of Black Folk*." *Journal of Black Studies* 2 (3), 303–21.

Brooks, Roy L. (Ed). (1999). *When Sorry Isn't Enough: The Controversy over Apologies and Reparations for Human Injustice.* New York: New York University.

———. (2004). *Atonement and Forgiveness: A New Model for Black Reparations.* Berkeley, CA: University of California Press.

Brophy, Alfred L. (2002a). *Reconstructing the Dreamland: The Tulsa Riot of 1921: Race, Reparations, and Reconciliation.* New York: Oxford University Press.

———. (2002b). "Losing the [Understanding of the Importance of] Race, Evaluating the Significance of Race and the Utility of Reparations." *Texas Law Review* 80 (4), 911–32.

———. (2006). *Reparations: Pro & Con.* New York: Oxford University Press.

Brotz, Howard. (Ed.). (1992). *African American Social and Political Thought, 1850–1920.* New Brunswick, NJ: Transaction.

Brown, Lee M. (Ed.). (2004). *African Philosophy: New and Traditional Perspectives.* New York: Oxford University Press.

Brown, Scot. (2003). *Fighting for Us: Maulana Karenga, the Us Organization, and Black Cultural Nationalism.* New York: New York University Press.

Bruce, Dickson D., Jr. (1992). "W.E.B. Du Bois and the Idea of Double Consciousness." *American Literature* 64 (June), 299–309.

———. (1995). "W.E.B. Du Bois and the Dilemma of Race." *American Literary History* 7 (2), 334–43.

Brundage, William F. (1993). *Lynching in the New South: Georgia and Virginia, 1880–1930.* Urbana: University of Illinois Press.

———. (Ed.). (1997). *Under Sentence of Death: Lynching in the South.* Chapel Hill, NC: University of North Carolina.

———. (Ed.). (2003). *Booker T. Washington and Black Progress: Up From Slavery 100 Years Later.* Gainesville, FL: University Press of Florida.

———. (2005). *The Southern Past: A Clash of Race and Memory.* Cambridge, MA: Belknap/Harvard University Press.

Bubner, Rudiger. (1988). *Essays in Hermeneutics and Critical Theory.* New York: Columbia University Press.

Buhle, Mari Jo. (1981). *Women and American Socialism, 1870–1920.* Urbana: University of Illinois Press.

Buhle, Paul. (1991). *Marxism in the United States.* London: Verso.

Bulmer, Martin. (1991). "W.E.B. Du Bois as a Social Investigator: The PhiladelphiaNegro, 1899." In Martin Bulmer and Kevin Bales (Eds.), *The Social Survey in Historical Perspective, 1880–1940.* Cambridge: Cambridge University Press.

———. (1995). "The Challenge of African American Leadership in an Ambiguous World: W.E.B. Du Bois, Cater G. Woodson, Ralph Bunche and Thurgood Marshall in Historical Perspective." *Ethnic & Racial Studies* 18 (3), 629–47.

Burbridge, Lynn C. (1999). "W.E.B. Du Bois as Economic Analyst: Reflections on the 100th Anniversary of *The Philadelphia Negro*." *Review of Black Political Economy* 26 (3), 13–31.

Burks, Ben. (1997). "Unity and Diversity through Education: A Comparison of the Thought of W.E.B. Du Bois and John Dewey." *Journal of Thought* 32 (1), 99–110.

Burns, Rebecca. (2006). *Rage in the Gate City: The Story of the 1906 Atlanta Race Riot.* Cinncinati, OH: Emmis.

Burrow, Rufus. (1994). *James H. Cone and Black Liberation Theology*. Jefferson, NC: McFarland & Co.

Busby, Margaret. (Ed.). (1992). *Daughters of Africa: An International Anthology of Words and Writings by Women of African Descent from Ancient Egyptian to the Present*. New York: Pantheon.

Bush, Roderick D. (1999). *We Are Not What We Seem: Black Nationalism and the Class Struggle in the American Century*. New York: New York University Press.

Butler, Johnnella E. (1981). *Black Studies—Pedagogy and Revolution: A Study of Afro-American Studies and the Liberal Arts Tradtion Through the Discipline of Afro-American Literature*. Lanham, MD: University Press of America.

———. (2000). "African American Studies and the "Warring Ideals": The Color Line Meets the Borderlands." In Manning Marable (Ed.), *Dispatches from the Ebony Tower: Intellectuals Confront the African American Experience* (pp. 141–52). New York: Columbia University Press.

———. (Ed.). (2001). *Color-Line to Borderlands: The Matrix of American Ethnic Studies*. Seattle, WA: University of Washington Press.

Butler, Johnnella E., and Walter, John C. (Eds.). (1991). *Transforming the Curriculum: Ethnic Studies and Women's Studies*. Albany, NY: State University of New York Press.

Byerman, Keith E. (1978). "Two Warring Ideals: The Dialectical Thought of W.E.B. Du Bois." Ph.D. dissertation, Purdue University.

———. (1981). "Hearts of Darkness: Narrative Voices in *The Souls of Black Folk*." *American Literary Realism* 14, 43–51.

———. (1994). *Seizing the Word: History, Art, and Self in the Work of W.E.B. Du Bois*. Athens: University of Georgia Press.

Byrd, Rudolph P., and Guy-Sheftall, Beverly. (Eds.). (2001). *Traps: African American Men on Gender and Sexuality*. Indianapolis: Indiana University Press.

Cabral, Amilcar. (1972). *Revolution in Guinea: Selected Texts*. New York: Monthly Review Press.

———. (1973). *Return to the Source: Selected Speeches of Amilcar Cabral*. New York: Monthly Review Press.

———. (1979). *Unity and Struggle: Speeches and Writings of Amilcar Cabral*. New York: Monthly Review Press.

Cahill, Susan. (Ed.). (1982). *Motherhood*. New York: Avon.

Cain, William E. (1990a). "W.E.B. Du Bois's *Autobiography* and the Politics of Literature." *Black American Literature Forum* 24, 299–313.

———. (1990b). "Violence, Revolution, and the Cost of Freedom: John Brown and W.E.B. Du Bois." *Boundary* 2 (17), 305–30.

———. (1993). "From Liberalism to Communism: The Political Thought of W.E.B. Du Bois." In Amy Kaplan and Donald E. Pease (Eds.), *Culture of United States Imperialism* (pp. 456–73). Durham: Duke University Press.

Calhoun, Craig. (1995). *Critical Social Theory: Culture, History, and the Challenge of Difference*. Malden, MA: Blackwell.

Calhoun-Brown, Alison. (1999). "The Image of God: Black Theology and Racial Empowerment." *Review of Religious Research* 40, 197–212.

———. (1998). "While Marching to Zion: Otherworldliness and Racial Empowerment in the Black Community." *Journal for the Scientific Study of Religion* 37, 426–39.

Callahan, Michael D. (2004). *A Sacred Trust: The League of Nations and Africa, 1929–1946*. Portland, OR: Sussex Academic Press.

Callari, Antonio, Cullenberg, Stephen, and Biewener, Carole. (Eds.). (1995). *Marxism in the Postmodern Age: Confronting the New World Order*. New York: Guilford.

Campbell, Margaret M. (1999). *Critical Theory and Liberation Theology: A Comparision of the Initial Work of Jurgen Habermas and Gustavo Gutierrez*. New York: Peter Lang.

Cannon, Katie G. (1988). *Black Womanist Ethics*. Atlanta: Scholars Press.

———. (1995). *Katie's Canon: Womanism and the Soul of the Black Community*. New York: Continuum.

Capeci, Dominic J., Jr., and Knight, Jack C. (1996). "Reckoning with Violence: W.E.B. Du Bois and the 1906 Atlanta Race Riot." *Journal of Southern History* 62 (4), 727–67.

Caraway, Nancie. (1991). *Segregated Sisterhood: Racism and the Politics of American Feminism*. Knoxville: University of Tennessee.

Carbado, Devon W. (Ed.). (1999). *Black Men on Race, Gender, and Sexuality: A Critical Reader*. New York: New York University Press.

Carby, Hazel V. (1987). *Reconstructing Womanhood: The Emergence of the Afro-American Woman Novelist*. New York: Oxford University Press.

———. (1998). *Race Men: The W.E.B. Du Bois Lectures*. Cambridge: Harvard University Press.

Carey, Stephen Anderson. (1992). "Black Men's Du Boisian Relationships to Southern Social Institutions in the Novels of John Oliver Killens." Ph.D. dissertation, University of Texas, Dallas.

Carroll, Rebecca. (Eds.). (2003). *Saving the Race: Conversations on Du Bois from a Collective Memoir of The Souls of Black Folk*. New York: Harlem Moon.

———. (Ed.). (2006). *Uncle Tom or New Negro?: African Americans Reflect on Booker T. Washington and Up from Slavery One Hundred Years Later*. New York: Broadway Books/Harlem Moon.

Carson, Clayborne. (1981). *In Struggle: SNCC and the Black Awakening of the 1960s*. Cambridge: Harvard University Press.

Carter, Cynthia Lorraine Jacobs. (1998). "Higher Education and the Talented Tenth at the New Millennium: A Study of Five Black Women of the African Diaspora." Ph.D. dissertation, George Washington University.

Cartlidge, Cherese. (2007). *Reparations for Slavery*. New York: Lucent.

Carver, Terrell. (Ed.). (1991). *The Cambridge Companion to Marx*. New York: Cambridge University Press.

Castle, George. (Ed.). (2001). *Postcolonial Discourse: An Anthology*. Malden, MA: Blackwell.

Castoriadis, Cornelius. (1991). *Philosophy, Politics, Autonomy* (David Ames, Ed.). New York: Oxford University Press.

———. (1997). *The Castoriadis Reader* (David Ames, Ed.). Malden, MA: Blackwell.

Castronovo, Russ. (2000). "Within the Veil of Interdisciplinary Knowledge?: Jefferson, Du Bois, and the Negation of Politics." *New History* 31 (4), 781–804.

Cell, John W. (1982). *The Highest Stage of White Supremacy: The Origins of Segregation in South Africa and the American South.* Cambridge: Cambridge University Press.

Césaire, Aimé. (1972). *Discourse on Colonialism.* New York: Monthly Review Press.

Chabal, Patrick. (1981a). "The Social and Political Thought of Amilcar Cabral: A Reassessment." *Journal of Modern African Studies* 19 (1), 31–56.

———. (1981b). "National Liberation in Portuguese Guinea, 1956–1974." *African Affairs* 80 (318), 75–99.

———. (1983). *Amilcar Cabral: Revolutionary Leadership and People's War.* Cambridge: Cambridge University Press.

Chafe, William H., Gavins, Raymond, and Korstad, Robert. (Eds.). (2001). *Remembering Jim Crow: African Americans Tell About Life in the Segregated South.* New York: New Press.

Chaffee, Mary Law. (1956). "William E. B. Du Bois's Concept of the Racial Problem in the United States." *Journal of Negro History* 41, 241–58.

Chambers, Iain, and Curti, Lidia. (Eds.). (1996). *The Post-Colonial Question: Common Skies, Divided Horizons.* New York: Routledge.

Chandler, Nahum Dimitri. (1997). "The Problem of Purity: A Study in the Early Work of W.E.B. Du Bois." Ph.D. dissertation, University of Chicago.

Chatterjee, Partha. (1993). *The Nations and Its Fragments: Colonial and Postcolonial Histories.* Princeton: Princeton University Press.

Chilcote, Ronald H. (1968). "The Political Thought of Amilcar Cabral." *Journal of Modern African Studies* 6 (3), 373–88.

———. (1991). *Amilcar Cabral's Revolutionary Theory and Practice.* Boulder, CO: Lynne Rienner.

Childs, John Brown. (1980). *The Politics of the Black Minister.* Boston: G.K. Hall.

———. (1989). *Leadership, Conflict and Cooperation in Afro-American Social Thought.* Philadelphia: Temple University Press.

Childs, Peter, and Williams, R.J. Patrick. (1997). *An Introduction to Postcolonial Theory.* New York: Prentice-Hall.

Chouraqui, Andre. (1973). *Between East and West: A History of the Jews of North Africa.* New York: Atheneum.

Chrisman, Robert. (2005). "Black Studies, the Talented Tenth, and the Organic Intellectual." *Black Scholar* 35 (2), 5–10.

Christian, Barbara. (1985). *Black Feminist Criticism, Perspectives on Black Women Writers.* New York: Pergamon.

———. (1989). "But Who Do You Really Belong To—Black Studies or Women's Studies?" *Women's Studies* 17 (1-2), 17–23.

———. (1994). "Diminishing Returns: Can Black Feminism(s) Survive the Academy?" In David Theo Goldberg (Ed.), *Multicultarism: A Critical Reader* (pp. 168–79). Cambridge: Blackwell.

Christian, Mark (2002). "An African Centered Perspective on White Supremacy." *Journal of Black Studies* 33 (2), 179–98.

———. (2006). "Philosophy and Practice for Black Studies: The Case of Researching White Supremacy." In Molefi K. Asante and Maulana Karenga (Eds.), *The Handbook of Black Studies* (pp. 76–88). Thousand Oaks, CA: Sage.

Christiano, Kevin. (2008). *Sociology of Religion: Contemporary Developments.* Landam, MD: Rowman and Littlefield.

Chukwu, Cletus N. (2002). *Introduction to Philosophy in an African Perspective.* Eldoret, Kenya: Zapf Chancery.

Clack, Beverly. (Ed.). (1999). *Misogyny in the Western Philosophical Tradition: A Reader.* New York: Routledge.

Clarke, John Henrik, Jackson, Esther, Kaiser, Ernest, and O'Dell, J.H. (Eds.). (1970). *Black Titan: W.E.B. Du Bois.* Boston: Beacon.

Cleaver, Kathleen, and Katsiaficas, George. (Eds.). (2001). *Liberation, Imagination, and the Black Panther Party: A New Look at the Panthers and Their Legacy.* New York: Routledge.

Cliff, Tony. (1984). *Class Struggle and Women's Liberation: 1640 to Today.* London: BookMarks.

Coates, Rodney D., Browning, Sandra Lee, and Beenah, Moshay. (1996). "Race, Class, and Power: The Impact of Du Bois's Scholarship and Revolutionary Agenda." *Research in Race & Ethnic Relations* 9, 211–239.

Coetzee, Pieter H., and Roux, Abraham P.J. (Ed.). (1998). *The African Philosophy Reader.* New York: Routledge.

Cole, Eve Browning. (1993). *Philosophy and Feminist Criticism.* New York: Paragon House.

Cole, George D.H. (1950-65). *History of Socialist Thought*, vols. 1–4. New York: MacMillan.

Coleman, Monica A. (2008). *Making a Way Out of No Way: A Womanist Theology.* Minneapolis, MN: Fortress Press.

Collier-Thomas, Bettye. (1980). *NCNW: National Council of Negro Women.* Washington, D.C.: National Council of Negro Women.

——. (1993). "National Council of Negro Women." In Darlene Clark Hine, Elsa Barkley Brown, and Rosalyn Teborg-Penn (Eds.), *Black Women in America: An Historical Encyclopedia* (Volume 2, pp. 853-864). Brooklyn: Carlson.

Collier-Thomas, Betty, and V.P. Franklin (Eds.). (2001). *Sisters in the Struggle: African American Women in the Civil Rights-Black Power Movement.* New York: New York University Press.

Collins, Lee E. (2002). "Critical Race Theory: Themes, Perspectives, and Directions." In James L. Conyers, Jr. (Ed.), *Black Cultures and Race Relations* (pp. 154–68). Chicago: Burnham.

Collins, Patricia Hill. (1990). *Black Feminist Thought: Knowledge, Consciousness, and the Politics of Empowerment.* New York: Routledge.

——. (1993). "Feminism in the Twentieth Century." In Darlene Clark Hine, Elsa Barkley Brown, and Rosalyn Teborg-Penn (Eds.), *Black Women in America: An Historical Encyclopedia* (Volume 1, pp. 418–25). Brooklyn: Carlson.

——. (1996). "The Social Construction of Black Feminist Thought." In Ann Garry and Marilyn Pearsall (Eds.), *Women, Knowledge, and Reality: Explorations in Feminist Philosophy* (pp. 222–48). New York: Routledge.

——. (1998). *Fighting Words: Black Women and the Search for Social Justice.* Minneapolis: Minnesota.

——. (2000). *Black Feminist Thought: Knowledge, Consciousness, and the Politics of Empowerment* (2nd Edition). New York: Routledge.

——. (2005). *Black Sexual Politics: African Americans, Gender, and the New Racism.* New York: Routledge.

——. (2006). *From Black Power to Hip Hop: Racism, Nationalism, and Feminism.* Philadelphia: Temple University Press.

Collins, Randall. (2000). *The Sociology of Philosophies: A Global Theory of Intellectual Change.* Cambridge: Harvard University Press.

Collins, Sharon M. (1997). *Black Corporate Executives: The Making and Breaking of a Black Middle Class.* Philadelphia, PA: Temple University Press.

Cone, James H. (1969). *Black Theology and Black Power.* New York: Seabury Press.

——. (1970). *A Black Theology of Liberation* Philadelphia: Lippincott.

——. (1972). *The Spirituals and the Blues: An Interpretation.* New York: Seabury Press.

——. (1984). *For My People: Black Theology and the Black Church.* Maryknoll, NY: Orbis.

——. (1975). *God of the Oppressed.* New York: Seabury Press.

——. (1986). *Speaking the Truth: Ecumenism, Liberation, and Black Theology.* Grand Rapids, MI: W.B. Eerdmans.

——. (1999). *Risks of Faith: The Emergence of a Black Theology of Liberation, 1968-1998.* Boston: Beacon Press.

Cone, James H., and Wilmore, Gayraud S. (Eds.). (1993). *Black Theology: A Documentary History* (2 Volumes). Maryknoll, NY: Orbis.

Contee, Clarence G. (1969a). "W.E.B. Du Bois and African Nationalism, 1914–1945." Ph.D. dissertation, American University, Washington, D.C.

——. (1969b). "The Emergence of Du Bois as an African Nationalist." *Journal of Negro History* 54 (January), 48–63.

——. (1970). "W.E.B. Du Bois and *Encyclopedia Africana.*" *Crisis* 77, 375–79.

——. (1971). "A Crucial Friendship Begins: Du Bois and Nkrumah, 1935–1945." *Crisis* 78, 181–85.

——. (1972). "Du Bois, the NAACP, and the Pan-African Congress of 1919." *Journal of Negro History* 57, 13–28.

Conyers, James L. (Ed.). (2003). *Afrocentricity and the Academy: Essays on Theory and Practice.* Jefferson, NC: McFarland & Co.

——. (2005). *Africana Studies: A Disciplinary Quest for Both Theory and Method.* Jefferson: McFarland & Co.

——. (2006). *Engines of the Black Power Movement: Essays on the Influence of Civil Rights Actions, Arts, and Islam.* Jefferson, NC: McFarland & Co.

Conyers, James L., and Smallwood, Andrew P. (Eds.). (2008). *Malcolm X: A Historical Reader.* Durham, NC: Carolina Academic Press.

Cook, Mercer, and Henderson, Stephen E. (Eds.) (1969). *The Militant Black Writer in Africa and the United States.* Madison: University of Wisconsin Press.

Cooper, Anna Julia. (1998). *The Voice of Anna Julia Cooper: Including* A Voice From the South *and Other Important Essays, Papers, and Letters* (Charles Lemert and Esme Bhan, Eds.). Lanham, MD: Rowman and Littlefield.

Cooper-Lewter, Nicholas, and Mitchell, Henry. (1986). *Soul Theology: The Heart of American Black Culture.* New York: Harper & Row.

Corlett, J. Angelo. (2003). *Race, Racism, & Reparations*: Ithaca: Cornell University Press.

Cornelius, Janet D. (1999). *Slave Missions and the Black Church in the Antebellum South.* Columbia, SC: University of South Carolina Press.

Cortada, Rafael. (1974). *Black Studies in Urban and Comparative Curriculum.* Lexington, MA: Xerox College Publishing.

Cox, Oliver C. (1948). *Caste, Class, and Race: A Study in Social Dynamics.* New York: Monthly Review Press.

——. (1950a). "The New Crisis in Leadership Among Negroes." *Journal of Negro Education* 19, 459–65.

——. (1950b). "Leadership Among Negroes in the United States." In Alvin W. Gouldner (Ed.), *Studies in Leadership* (pp. 79–96). New York: Harper.

——. (1951). "The Leadership of Booker T. Washington." *Social Forces* 30, 91–97.

——. (1959). *The Foundations of Capitalism.* New York: Philosophical Library.

——. (1962). *Capitalism and American Leadership.* New York: Philosophical Library.

——. (1964). *Capitalism as a System.* New York: Monthly Review Press.

——. (1976). *Race Relations: Elements of Social Dynamics.* Detroit: Wayne State University Press.

——. (1987). *Race, Class, and the World System* (Herbert M. Hunter and Sameer Y. Abraham, Eds.). New York: Monthly Review Press.

——. (2000). *Race: A Study in Social Dynamics.* New York: Monthly Review Press.

Crawford, A. Elaine Brown. (2002). *Hope in the Holler: A Womanist Theology.* Louisville, KY: Westminster John Know Press.

Crenshaw, Kimberle, Gotanda, Neil, Peller, Gary, and Thomas, Kendall. (Eds.). (1995). *Critical Race Theory: The Key Writings That Formed the Movement.* New York: New Press.

Cross, Theodore. (1996). "Du Bois's *The Philadelphia Negro*: 100 Years Later." *Journal of Blacks in Higher Education* 11 (Spring), 78–84.

Crossley, Nick. (Ed.). (2005). *Key Concepts in Critical Social Theory.* Thousand Oaks, CA: Sage.

Croutchett, Larry. (1971). "Early Black Studies Movements." *Journal of Black Studies* 2 189–200.

Cruse, Harold. (1965). *Marxism and the Negro Struggle.* New York: Pioneer Publishers.

——. (1967). *The Crisis of the Negro Intellectual: A Historical Analysis of the Failure of Black Leadership.* New York: Quill.

——. (1969). *Rebellion or Revolution?* New York: Morrow.

——. (2002). *The Essential Harold Cruse: A Reader* (William J. Cobb, Ed.). New York: Palgrave.

Daniel, Walter C. (1990). "W.E.B. Du Bois's First Efforts as a Playwright." *CLA Journal* 33 (4), 415–27.

Daniels, Phillip T.K. (1980). "Black Studies: Discipline or Field of Study?" *Western Journal of Black Studies* 4 (3), 195–99.

——. (1981). "Theory Building in Black Studies." *Black Scholar* 12 (3), 29–36.

Dant, Tim. (2003). *Critical Social Theory: Culture, Society, and Critique.* Thousand Oaks, CA: Sage.

Darsey, Jay. (1998). "'The Voice of Exile': W.E.B. Du Bois and the Quest for Culture." *Communication Abstracts* 21 (6).

Davie, Grace. (2007). *The Sociology of Relgion.* Thousand Oaks, CA: Sage.

Davies, Carole Boyce, Gadsby, Meredith, Peterson, Charles, and Williams, Henrietta, (Eds.). (2003). *Decolonizing the Academy: African Diaspora Studies.* Trenton, NJ: Africa World Press.

Davis, Adrenne D. (2000). "The Case for Reparations to African Americans." *Human Rights Brief: Center for Human Rights and Humanitarian Law, A Legal Resource for the International Human Rights Community* 7 (8), 3–12.

Davis, Angela Y. (1981). *Women, Race and Class.* New York: Vintage.

———. (1989). *Women, Culture, and Politics.* New York: Vintage.

———. (1995). "Reflections on the Black Woman's Role in the Community of Slaves." In Beverly Guy-Sheftall (Ed.), *Words of Fire: An Anthology of African American Feminist Thought* (pp. 200–18). New York: Free Press.

———. (1998a). *The Angela Y. Davis Reader* (Joy A. James, Ed.). Malden, MA: Blackwell.

———. (1998b). "Angela Y. Davis: An Interview." In George Yancy (Ed.), *African American Philosophers: 17 Conversations* (pp. 13–31). New York: Routledge.

Davis, Elizabeth L. (1996). *Lifting As They Climb: The National Association of Colored Women.* New York: G.K. Hall.

Davis, William Allison. (1974). *Du Bois and the Problem of the Black Masses.* Atlanta: Atlanta University Press.

Dawson, Michael C. (2001). *Black Visions: The Roots of Contemporary African American Political Ideologies.* Chicago: University of Chicago Press.

Deegan, Mary Jo. (1988). "W.E.B. Du Bois and the Women of Hull House, 1895–1899." *American Sociologist* 19 (4), 301–11.

———. (2001). "American Pragmatism and Liberation Sociology: The Theory and Praxis of Jane Addams, W.E.B. Du Bois, G.H. Mead, and Joe Feagin." Paper presented at the annual meeting of the *Society for the Study of Social Problems.*

De Greiff, Pablo. (Ed.). (2006). *The Handbook of Reparations.* New York: Oxford University Press.

Delgado, Richard. (Ed.). (1995). *Critical Race Theory: The Cutting Edge.* Philadelphia: Temple University Press.

———. (2007). *The Law Unbound!: A Richard Delgado Reader.* Boulder, CO: Paradigm Publishers.

Delgado, Richard, and Stefancic, Jean. (Eds.). (1997). *Critical White Studies: Looking Behind the Mirror.* Philadelphia: Temple University Press.

Delgado, Richard, and Stefancic, Jean. (2001). *Critical Race Theory: An Introduction.* New York: New York University Press.

DeMarco, Joseph P. (1974). "The Rationale and Foundation of Du Bois's Theory of Economic Cooperation." *Phylon* 35 (March), 5–15.

———. (1983). *The Social Thought of W.E.B. Du Bois.* Lanham, MD: University Press of America.

Dennis, Rutledge M. (1972). "W.E.B. Du Bois as Sociologist." *Journal of African American Studies* 2, 62–79.

———. (1975). "The Sociology of W.E.B. Du Bois." Ph.D. dissertation, Washington State University.

———. (1977). "Du Bois and the Role of the Educated Elite." *Journal of Negro Education* 46 (4), 388–402.

———. (1996a). "Continuities and Discontinuities in the Social and Political Thought of W.E.B. Du Bois." *Research in Race & Ethnic Relations* 9, 3–23.

———. (1996b). "Du Bois's Concept of Double Consciousness: Myth and Reality." *Research in Race & Ethnic Relations* 9, 69–90.

———. (1997). "Introduction: W.E.B. Du Bois and the Tradition of Radical Intellectual Thought." *Research in Race & Ethnic Relations* 10, xi-xxiv.

Dews, Peter. (1987). *Logics of Disintegration: Post-Structuralist Thought and the Claims of Critical Theory.* New York: Verso.

Dickens, David R., and Fontana, Andrea. (1994). (Eds.). *Postmodernism and Social Theory.* New York: Guilford.

Digby, Tom. (Ed.). (1998). *Men Doing Feminism.* New York: Routledge.

Diggs, Irene. (1974). "Du Bois and Women: A Short Story of Black Women, 1910–1934." *Current Bibliography on African Affairs* 7 (Summer), 260–307.

———. (1976). "Du Bois and Children." *Phylon* 37 (December), 370–99.

Dill, Bonnie Thornton. (1979). "The Dialectics of Black Womanhood: Towards a New Model of American Femininity." *Signs: A Journal of Women and Culture in Society* 4 (3), 543–55.

———. (1983). "Race, Class, and Gender: Prospects for an All-Inclusive Sisterhood." *Feminist Studies* 9 (1), 131–50.

Dillard, Joey L. (Ed.). (1975). *Perspectives on Black English.* The Hague: Mouton.

Dillon, Michele. (Ed.). (2003). *Handbook of the Sociology of Religion.* New York: Cambridge University Press.

Diop, Cheikh Anta. (1974). *The African Origin of Civilization: Myth or Reality.* Chicago: Lawrence Hill Books.

———. (1978a). *The Cultural Unity of Black Africa.* Chicago: Third World Press.

———. (1978b). *Black Africa: The Economic and Cultural Basis for a Federated State.* Chicago: Lawrence Hill Books.

———. (1987). *Precolonial Black Africa.* Chicago: Lawrence Hill Books.

———. (1991). *Civilization or Barbarism: An Authentic Anthropology.* Chicago: Lawrence Hill Books.

———. (1996). *Towards the African Renaissance: Essays in Culture and Development.* London: Karnak House.

Dirilik, Arif. (1994). "The Postcolonial Aura: Third World Criticism in the Age of Global Capitalism." *Critical Inquiry* 20 (2), 328–56.

———. (1997). *The Postcolonial Aura: Third World Criticism in the Age of Global Capitalism.* Boulder: Westview.

Di Stephano, Christine. (1991). "Masculine Marx." In Mary Lyndon Shanley and Carole Pateman (Eds.), *Feminist Interpretations and Political Theory* (pp. 146–64). University Park, PA: Penn State University Press.

————. (Ed.). (2008). *Feminist Interpretations of Karl Marx.* University Park, PA: Pennsylvania State University Press.

Dixson, Adrienne D., and Rousseau, Celia K. (Eds.). (2006). *Critical Race Theory in Education: All God's Children Got a Song.* New York: Routledge.

Dobratz, Betty A., and Shanks-Melie, Stephanie L. (1997). *"White Power, White Pride!": The White Separatist Movement in the United States.* New York: Twayne.

Douglass, Frederick. (1950–1975). *The Life and Writings of Fredrick Douglass* (Volumes 1–5, Philip S. Foner, Ed.). New York: International.

————. (1992). *Frederick Douglass on Women's Rights* (Philip S. Foner, Ed.). New York: Da Capo Press.

————. (1994a). *Autobiographies: Narrative of the Life, My Bondage and My Freedom, Life and Times.* New York: Library of America.

————. (1994b). *Narrative of the Life of Frederick Douglass. In Autobiographies: Narrative of the Life, My Bondage and My Freedom, Life and Times.* New York: Library of America.

————. (1999). *Frederick Douglass: Speeches and Selected Writings* (Philip S. Foner, Ed., abridged and adapted by Yuval Taylor). New York: Library of America.

Dove, Nah. (1998a). *Afrikan Mothers: Bearers of Culture, Makers of Social Change.* Albany: State University of New York Press.

————. (1998b). "Africana Womanism: An Afrocentric Theory." *Journal of Black Studies* 28 (5), 515–39.

Dowdy, Lewis Carnegie, Jr. (1989). "The Impact of the Philosophies of the Presbyterian Church, U.S.A., Booker T. Washington, and W.E.B. Du Bois on the Educational Program of Johnson C. Smith University." Ph.D. dissertation, Rutgers State University of New Jersey, New Brunswick.

Drachler, John. (1975). *Black Homeland/Black Diaspora: Cross Currents of the African Relationship.* Port Washington, NY: Kennikat Press.

Drake, St. Clair. (1986-87). "Dr. W.E.B. Du Bois: A Life Lived Experimentally and Self-Documented." *Contributions in Black Studies* 8, 111–34.

Drake, William Avon. (1985). "From Reform to Communism: The Intellectual Development of W.E.B. Du Bois." Ph.D. dissertation, Cornell University, Ithaca, NY.

Dray, Phillip. (2002). *At the Hands of Persons Unknown: The Lynching of Black America.* New York: Random House.

Dred Scott vs. Sanford 1857: 60 US (19 How.).

Drinnon, Richard. (1980). *Facing West: The Metaphysics of Indian Hating and Empire Building.* New York: Meridian.

Drummer, Raydora Susan. (1995). "Transformational Leadership in the Life of W.E.B. Du Bois: 1900–1930." Ph.D. dissertation, Michigan State University.

Duberman, Martin. (1968). "Du Bois as Prophet." *New Republic* (March 23rd), 36–39.

Dubiel, Helmut. (1985). *Theory and Politics: Studies in the Development of Critical Theory.* Cambridge: MIT Press.

Du Bois, David Graham. (1978). "The Du Bois Legacy Under Attack." *Black Scholar* 9 (January-February), 2–12.

————. (1982). "W.E.B. Du Bois: The Last Years." *Race & Class* 24 (Autumn), 178–83.

———. (1998). "David Du Bois Reflects Upon His Father, W.E.B. Du Bois's Commitment to the Struggle of African People." *Crisis* 105 (3), 18.

Du Bois, W.E.B. (1898). "The Study of Negro Problems." *Annals of the American Academy of Political and the Social Science* 11 (January), 1–23.

———. (1906). *The Health and Physique of the Negro American*. Atlanta: Atlanta University Press.

———. (1911a). *The Quest of the Silver Fleece: A Novel*. Chicago: McClurg.

———. (1911b). "Writers." *Crisis* 1 (6), 20–21.

———. (1928). *Dark Princess: A Romance*. New York: Harcourt, Brace & Co.

———. (1930a). *Africa, Its Geography People and Products*. Girard, Kansas: Haldeman-Julius.

———. (1930b). *Africa, Its Place in Modern History*. Girard, Kansas: Haldemen-Julius.

———. (1938). *A Pageant in Seven Decades, 1868–1938*. Atlanta: Atlanta University Press.

———. (1939). *Black Folk Then and Now: An Essay in the History and Sociology of the Negro Race*. New York: Henry Holt.

———. (1945). *Color and Democracy: Colonies and Peace*. New York: Hartcourt Brace.

———. (1947). *An Appeal to the World: A Statement on the Denial of Human Rights to Minorities in the Case of Citizens of Negro Descent in the United States of America and An Appeal to the United Nations for Redress*. New York: National Association for the Advancement of Colored People Publications.

———. (1948). "A Program of Emancipation for Colonial Peoples." In Merze Tate (Ed.), *Trust and Non-Self Governing Territories: Papers and Proceedings of the Tenth Annual Conference of the Division of the Graduate School Howard University*, April 8–9, 1947. *Howard University Studies in the Social Sciences* 6 (1), 96–104.

———. (1952). *In Battle for Peace: The Story of My 83rd Birthday*. New York: Masses & Mainstream.

———. (1957). *The Ordeal of Mansart*. New York: Mainstream.

———. (1958). *Pan-Africa, 1919–1958*. Accra, Ghana: Bureau of African Affairs.

———. (1959). *Mansart Builds a School*. New York: Mainstream.

———. (1960a). *W.E.B. Du Bois: A Recorded Autobiography* [Compact Disc]. Washington, D.C.: Folkways.

———. (1960b). *W.E.B. Du Bois: Socialism and the American Negro* [Compact Disc]. Washington, D.C.: Folkways.

———. (1960c). *Africa in Battle Against Colonialism, Racism, and Imperialism*. Chicago: Afro-American Heritage Association.

———. (1961a). *Africa: An Essay Toward a History of the Continent of Africa and Its Inhabitants*. Moscow: Soviet Institute of African Studies.

———. (1961b). *Worlds of Color*. New York: Mainstream.

———. (1962). *John Brown*. New York: International Publishers.

———. (1965). *The World and Africa: An inquiry into the part which Africa has played in world history*. New York: International Publishers.

———. (1968a). *The Autobiography of W.E.B. Du Bois: A Soliloquy on Viewing My Life from the Last Decade of Its First Century*. New York: International Publishers.

———. (1968b). *Dusk of Dawn: An Essay Toward an Autobiography of a Race Concept*. New York: Schocken.

——. (1969a). *Darkwater: Voices from Within the Veil.* New York: Schocken.

——. (1969b). *The Souls of Black Folk.* New York: New American Library.

——. (1969c). *An ABC of Color: Selections from over a Half Century of the Writings of W.E.B. Du Bois.* New York: International Publishers.

——. (Ed.). (1969d). *Atlanta University Publications, 1896–1916* (Numbers 1–20, 2 Volumes). New York: Arno Press.

——. (1970a). *The Negro.* New York: Oxford University Press.

——. (1970b). *The Gift of Black Folk: The Negro in the Making of America.* New York: Simon & Schuster.

——. (1970c). *W.E.B. Du Bois: A Reader* (Meyer Weinberg, Ed.). New York: Harper and Row.

——. (1970d). *W.E.B. Du Bois Speaks: Speeches and Addresses, 1899–1963* (2 Volumes, Philip S. Foner, Ed.). New York: Pathfinder Press.

——. (1970e). *The Selected Writings of W.E.B. Du Bois* (Walter Wilson, Ed.). New York: Mentor Books.

——. (1971a). *The Seventh Son: The Thought and Writings of W.E.B. Du Bois* (Volume 1, Julius Lester, Ed.). New York: Vintage Books.

——. (1971b). *The Seventh Son: The Thought and Writings of W.E.B. Du Bois* (Volume 2, Julius Lester, Ed.). New York: Vintage Books.

——. (1971c). *W.E.B. Du Bois: A Reader* (Andrew Paschal, Ed.). New York: Collier Books.

——. (1972a). *The Emerging Thought of W.E.B. Du Bois* (Henry Lee Moon, Ed.). New York: Simon & Schuster.

——. (1972b). *W.E.B. Du Bois: The Crisis Writings* (Daniel Walden, Ed.). Greenwich, CT: Fawcett.

——. (1973). *The Education of Black People: Ten Critiques, 1906–1960* (Herbert Aptheker, Ed.). New York: Monthly Review Press.

——. (1977). *Book Reviews by W.E.B. Du Bois* (Herbert Aptheker, Ed.). Millwood, NY: Kraus-Thomson.

——. (1978). *W.E.B. Du Bois on Sociology and the Black Community* (Dan S. Green and Edwin D. Driver, Eds.). Chicago: University of Chicago Press.

——. (1980a). *Contributions of W.E.B. Du Bois in Government Publications and Proceedings* (Herbert Aptheker, Ed.). Millwood, NY: Kraus-Thomson.

——. (1980b). *Selection from Phylon* (Herbert Aptheker, Ed.). Millwood, NY: Kraus-Thomson.

——. (1980c). *Prayers for Dark People* (Herbert Aptheker, Ed.). Amherst: University of Massachusetts Press.

——. (1980d). *Selections from the Brownies Book* (Herbert Aptheker, Ed.). Millwood, NY: Kraus-Thomson.

——. (1980e). *The Papers of W.E.B. Du Bois* (89 reels of microfilm; Herbert Aptheker, Ed.). Sanford, NC: Microfiliming Corporation of America.

——. (1982a). *Writings in Periodicals Edited by Others*, vol. 1 (Herbert Aptheker, Ed.). Millwood, NY: Kraus-Thomson.

——. (1982b). *Writings in Periodicals Edited by Others*, vol. 2 (Herbert Aptheker, Ed.). Millwood, NY: Kraus-Thomson.

——. (1982c). *Writings in Periodicals Edited by Others*, vol. 3 (Herbert Aptheker, Ed.). Millwood, NY: Kraus-Thomson.

——. (1982d). *Writings in Periodicals Edited by Others*, vol. 4 (Herbert Aptheker, Ed.). Millwood, NY: Kraus-Thomson.

——. (1982e). *Writings in Non-Periodical Literature Edited by Others* (Herbert Aptheker, Ed.). Millwood, NY: Kraus-Thomson.

——. (1983a). *Selections from The Crisis,* vol. 1 (Herbert Aptheker, Ed.). Millwood, NY: Kraus-Thomson.

——. (1983b). *Selections from The Crisis,* vol. 2. (Herbert Aptheker, Ed.). Millwood, NY: Kraus-Thomson.

——. (1985a). *Against Racism: Unpublished Essays, Papers, Addresses, 1887–1961* (Herbert Aptheker, Ed.). Amherst, MA: University of Massachusetts Press.

——. (1985b). *Creative Writings by W.E.B. Du Bois: A Pageant, Poems, Short Stories and Playlets* (Herbert Aptheker, Ed.). Millwood, NY: Kraus-Thomson.

——. (1985c). *Selections from Horizon* (Herbert Aptheker, Ed.). White Plains, NY: Kraus-Thomson.

——. (1986a). *Du Bois: Writings* (Nathan Irvin Huggins, Ed.). New York: Library of America Press.

——. (1986b). "Careers Open to College-Bred Negroes." In *Du Bois: Writings* (Nathan Irvin Huggins, Ed.). New York: Library Press of America.

——. (1986c). "The Conservation of Races." In *Du Bois: Writings* (Nathan Irvin Huggins, Ed.). New York: Library Press of America.

——. (1986d). *Dusk of Dawn.* In *Du Bois: Writings* (Nathan Irvin Huggins, Ed.). New York: Library Press of America.

——. (1986e). "The Talented Tenth." In *Du Bois: Writings* (Nathan Irvin Huggins, Ed.). New York: Library Press of America.

——. (1986f). *Pamphlets and Leaflets* (Herbert Aptheker, Ed.). New York: Kraus-Thomson.

——. (1986g). *Newspaper Columns by W.E.B. Du Bois*, vol. 1 (Herbert Aptheker, Ed.). White Plains, NY: Kraus-Thomson.

——. (1986h). *Newspaper Columns by W.E.B. Du Bois*, vol. 2 (Herbert Aptheker, Ed.). White Plains, NY: Kraus-Thomson.

——. (1989). *The Souls of Black Folk.* New York: Bantam-Doubleday.

——. (1992). *The World of W.E.B. Du Bois* (Meyer Weinberg, Ed.). Westport, CT: Greenwood.

——. (1995a). *W.E.B. Du Bois Reader* (David Levering Lewis, Ed.). New York: Henry Holt.

——. (1995b). "My Evolving Program for Negro Freedom." In *W.E.B. Du Bois Reader* (David Levering Lewis, Ed.). New York: Henry Holt.

——. (1995c). *Black Reconstruction in America, 1860–1880.* New York: Touchstone.

——. (1995d). *The FBI File on W.E.B. Du Bois, 1942–1963.* Wilmington, DE: Scholarly Resources.

——. (1996a). *The Oxford W.E.B. Du Bois Reader* (Eric Sundquist, Ed.). New York: Oxford University Press.

——. (1996b). *The Philadelphia Negro: A Social Study.* Philadelphia: University of Pennsylvania Press.

———. (1996c). "The Talented Tenth Memorial Address." In Henry Louis Gates, Jr. and Cornel West, *The Future of the Race* (pp. 159–79). New York: Alfred A. Knopf.

———. (1997a). *The Souls of Black Folk* (Robert Gooding-Williams and David W. Blight, Eds.). Boston: Bedford Books.

———. (1997b). *The Correspondence of W.E.B. Du Bois: Volume I—Selections, 1877–1934* (Herbert Aptheker, Ed.). Amherst, MA: University of Massachusetts Press.

———. (1997c). *The Correspondence of W.E.B. Du Bois: Volume II—Selections, 1934–1944* (Herbert Aptheker, Ed.). Amherst, MA: University of Massachusetts Press.

———. (1997d). *The Correspondence of W.E.B. Du Bois: Volume III—Selections, 1944–1963.* (Herbert Aptheker, Ed.). Amherst, MA: University of Massachusetts Press.

———. (1998a). "The Socialism of the German Socialists." *Central European History* 31 (3), 189–225 [Special Issue on "W.E.B. Du Bois and the Kaiserreich Articles"].

———. (1998b). "The Present Condition of German Politics—1893." *Central European History* 31 (3), 171–89 [Special Issue on "W.E.B. Du Bois and the Kaiserreich Articles"].

———. (1999a). *Darkwater: Voices from within the Veil.* Mineola, NY: Dover.

———. (1999b). *The Souls of Black Folk: Authoritative Text, Contexts, and Criticism* (Henry Louis Gates, Jr., and Terri Hume Oliver, Eds.). New York: Norton.

———. (2000a). "The Salvation of the American Negro Lies in Socialism." In Manning Marable and Leith Mullings (Eds.), *Let Nobody Turn Us Around: Voices of Resistance, Reform, and Renewal, An African American Anthology* (pp. 409–19). Lanham, MD: Rowman & Littlefield.

———. (2000b). *Du Bois on Religion* (Phil Zuckerman, Ed.). Walnut Creek: Altamira.

———. (2000c). *W.E.B. Du Bois's Historic Lecture: "The Sufferings of Black Americans, Socialism, and the Arrogance of U.S. Capitalism"* [Compact Disc]. Durham, NC: Black Historic CD Series.

———. (2001). *The Negro.* Mineola, NY: Dover.

———. (2002). *Du Bois on Education* (Eugene F. Provenzo, Jr., Ed.). Walnut Creek: Altamira.

———. (2004). *The Social Theory of W.E.B. Du Bois* (Phil Zuckerman, Ed.). Thousand Oaks: Sage.

———. (2005). *The Illustrated Souls of Black Folk* (Eugene F. Provenzo, Jr., Ed.). Boulder, CO: Paradigm Publishers.

———. (2007). *The Suppression of the African Slave Trade to the United States of America, 1638–1870.* New York: Oxford University Press.

Du Bois, W.E.B. and Washington, Booker T. (1970). *The Negro in the South.* New York: University Books.

du Cille, Ann. (1994). "The Occult of True Black Womanhood: Critical Demeanor and Black Feminist Studies." *Signs* 19 (3), 591–629.

Duffy, Patricia A. (1997). "Philadelphia Stories: Studying W.E.B. Du Bois's Portrait of Family Life and the Impact of Changing Economics." *American Sociological Association.*

Dunleavy, Patrick. (1993). "The State." In Robert E. Goodin and Philip Pettit (Eds.), *A Companion to Contemporary Political Philosophy* (pp. 611-621). Malden, MA: Blackwell.

Dunn, Frederick D. (1991). "African American Philosophy and Philosophies of Education: Their Roots, Aims and Relevance for the 21st Century." Ph.D. dissertation, Columbia University Teacher's College.

During, Simon. (1987). "Postmodernism or Postcolonialism Today," *Textual Practice* 1 (1), 32–47.

Durr, Marlese. (2001). *The New Politics of Race: From Du Bois to the 21st Century.* Westport, CT: Greenwood.

Dussel, Enrique. (1976). *History and the Theology of Liberation: A Latin American Perspective.* Maryknoll, NY: Orbis Books.

———. (1978). *Ethics and the Theology of Liberation.* Maryknoll, NY: Orbis.

———. (1985). *Philosophy of Liberation.* Maryknoll, NY: Orbis.

———. (1988). *Ethics and Community.* Maryknoll, NY: Orbis.

———. (1995). *The Invention of the Americas: Eclipse of the "Other" and the Myth of Modernity.* New York: Continuum.

———. (1996). *The Underside of Modernity: Apel, Ricoeur, Rorty, Taylor, and the Philosophy of Liberation* (Eduardo Mendieta, Ed.). New York: Prometheus.

———. (2003). *Beyond Philosophy: Ethics, History, Marxism, and Liberation Theology* (Eduardo Mendieta, Ed). Lanham, MD: Rowman and Littlefield.

Dworkin, Ronald M. (1977). *Taking Rights Seriously.* Cambridge: Harvard University Press.

Dykstra, Robert R. (1993). *Bright Radical Star: Black Freedom and White Supremacy on the Hawkeye Frontier.* Cambridge: Harvard University Press.

Dyson, Michael Eric. (2005). *Is Bill Cosby Right?, or Has the Black Middle Class Lost Its Mind.* New York: Basic/Civitas.

Early, Gerald. (Ed.). (1993). *Lure and Loathing: Essays on Race, Identity, and the Ambivalence of Assimilation.* New York: Viking/Penguin.

Echeruo, Michael J.C. (1992). "Edward W. Blyden, W.E.B. Du Bois, and the 'Color Complex'." *Journal of Modern African Studies* 30 (4), 669–84.

Edelin, Ramona Hoage. (1981). "The Philsophical Foundations and Implications of William Edward Burghardt Du Bois's Social Ethic." Ph.D. dissertation, Boston University Graduate School.

Edwards, Barrington Steven. (2001). "W.E.B. Du Bois: Empirical Social Research and the Challenge to Race, 1868–1910." Ph.D. dissertation, Harvard University.

Edwards, Brent Hayes. (2001). "One More Time: W.E.B. Du Bois as 'Ladies Man'." *Transition* 11 (89), 88–118.

Efrat, Edgar S. (1967). "Incipient Pan-Africanism: W.E.B. Du Bois and the Early Days." *Australian Journal of Politics & History* 13 (3), 382–93.

Egerton, George W. (1978). *Great Britain and the Creation of the League of Nations: Strategy, Politics, and International Organization, 1914–1919.* Chapel Hill, NC: University of North Carolina Press.

Eisenstein, Zillah. (Ed.). (1979). *Capitalist Patriarchy and the Case for Socialist Feminism.* New York: Monthly Review Press.

Ekpo, Denis. (1995). "Toward a Post-Africanism: Contemporary African Thought and Postmodernism." *Textual Practice* 9 (1), 121–35.

Elliott, Anthony. (2003). *Critical Vision: New Directions in Social Theory.* Lanham, MD: Rowman and Littlefield.

Ellis, Mark. (1992). "'Closing Ranks' and 'Seeking Honors': W.E.B. Du Bois in World War I." *Journal of American History* 79, 96–124.

——. (1995). "W.E.B. Du Bois and the Formation of Black Opinion in World War I: A Commentary on "the Damnable Dilemma." *Journal of American History* 81 (4), 1584–591.

Ellison, Christopher. (1993). "Religious Involvement and Self-Perception among Black Americans." *Social Forces* 71 (4), 1071–1155.

Ellison, Ralph. (1980). *Invisible Man.* New York: Vintage Books.

English, Parker, and Kalumba, Kibujjo M. (Eds.). (1996). *African Philosophy: A Classical Approach.* Upper Saddle River, NJ: Prentice Hall.

Engs, Robert F. (1999). *Educating the Disfranchised and Disinherited: Samuel Chapman Armstrong and Hampton Institute, 1839-1893.* Knoxville: University of Tennessee Press.

Erskine, Noel Leo. (1981). *Decolonizing Theology: A Caribbean Perspective.* Marynoll, NY: Orbis.

Esedebe, P. Olisanwuche. (1994). *Pan-Africanism: The Idea and Movement, 1776–1991.* Washington, D.C.: Howard University Press.

Essed, Philomena, and Goldberg, David Theo. (Eds.). (2001). *Race Critical Theories: Texts and Contexts.* Malden: Blackwell.

Eustace, Linda A., and Obadele, Imari A. (2000). *Eight Women Leaders of the Reparations Movement, USA.* Baton Rouge: Malcolm Generation, Inc.

Evans, Curtis. (2007). "W.E.B. Du Bois: Interpreting Religion and the Problem of *The Negro Church.*" *Journal of the American Academy of Religion* 75 (2), 268–97.

Everage, James H. (1979). "W.E.B. Du Bois, A Pioneer in American Sociology: *The Philadelphia Negro* Revisited." *Southern Sociological Society.*

Eze, Emmanuel Chukwudi. (Ed.). (1997a). *African Philosophy: An Anthology.* Malden, MA: Blackwell.

——. (Ed.). (1997b). *(Post) Colonial African Philosophy: A Critical Reader.* Malden, MA: Blackwell.

——. (Ed.). (1997c). *Race and the Enlightenment: A Reader.* Malden, MA: Blackwell.

——. (2001). *Achieving Our Humanity: The Idea of the Post-Racial Future.* New York: Routledge.

Fanon, Frantz. (1965). *A Dying Colonialism* New York: Grove.

——. (1967). *Black Skin, White Masks.* New York: Grove.

——. (1968). *The Wretched of the Earth.* New York: Grove.

——. (1969). *Toward the African Revolution.* New York: Grove.

——. (2001). "The Lived Experience of the Black." In Robert Bernasconi (Ed.), *Race* (pp. 184–202). Malden, MA: Blackwell.

Fargania, Sondra. (1995). *The Social Reconstruction of the Feminine Character.* Lanham, MD: Rowman and Littlefield.

Feagin, Joe R. (2000). *Racist America: Roots, Current Realities, and Future Repara-tions*. New York: Routledge.

Fegerson, Gerard. (1987). "Race, Science, and Medicine in the Late Nineteenth Cen-tury: W.E.B. Du Bois and the Health and Physique of the Negro American." M.A. thesis, Yale University, New Haven, CT.

Fehrenbacher, Don E. (1970). *Manifest Destiny and the Coming of the Civil War.* New York: Appleton/Century/Crofts.

Fenn, Richard K., (Ed.). (2001). *The Blackwell Companion to Sociology of Religion.* Malden, MA: Blackwell.

Ferber, Abby L. (1998). *White Man Falling: Race, Gender, and White Supremacy.* Lanham, MD: Rowman and Littlefield.

———. (Ed.). 2004. *Home-Grown Hate: Gender and Organized Racism.* New York: Routledge.

Ferguson, Ann. (1986). "Motherhood and Sexuality: Some Feminist Questions." *Hy-patia* 1 (2), 87–102.

———. (1998). "Socialism." In Alison M. Jaggar, and Iris Marion Young (Eds.), *A Companion to Feminist Philosophy* (pp. 520–40). Malden, MA: Blackwell.

Ferguson, Kathy E. (1980). *Self, Society, and Womankind: The Dialectic of Libera-tion.* Westport, CT: Greenwood.

Fierce, Milfred C. (1991). *Africana Studies Outside the United States: Africa, Brazil, and the Caribbean.* Ithaca, NY: Cornell University Press.

Fitchue, M. Anthony. (1996–1997). "Locke and Du Bois: Two Major Black Voices Muzzled by Philanthropic Organizations." *Journal of Blacks in Higher Education* 14, 111–16.

Fitzpatrick, Sheila. (1982). *The Russian Revolution, 1917–1932.* New York: Oxford University Press.

Flank, Lenny. (2007). *Hegemony and Counter-Hegemony: Marxism, Capitalism, and Their Relation to Sexism, Racism, Nationalism, and Authoritarianism.* Saint Pe-tersburg, FL: Red and Black Publishers.

Fletcher, Diorita C. (1973). "W.E.B. Du Bois's Arraignment and Indictment of White Civilization." *Black World* 22 (May), 16–23.

Floyd-Thomas, Stacey M. (2006a). *Mining the Motherlode: Methods in Womanist Ethics.* Cleveland, Ohio: Pilgrim Press.

———. (Eds.). (2006b). *Deeper Shades of Purple: Womanism in Religion and Society.* New York: New York University Press.

Foley, Barbara. (2003). *Spectres of 1919: Class and Nation in the Making of the New Negro.* Urbana: University of Illinois Press.

Foner, Philip S. (1964). *Frederick Douglass.* New York: Citadel.

———. (1976). *Organized Labor and the Black Worker, 1619–1973.* New York: Inter-national Publishers.

———. (1977). *American Socialism and Black Americans: From the Age of Jackson to World War II.* Westport, CT: Greenwood Press.

———. (1992). "Introduction to *Frederick Douglass on Women's Rights.*" In Philip S. Foner (Ed.), *Frederick Douglass on Women's Rights* (pp. 3–48). New York: Da Capo.

Foner, Philip S., and Allen, James S. (Eds.). (1987). *American Communism and Black Americans: A Documentary History, 1919–1929*. Philadelphia: Temple University Press.

Foner, Philip S., and Lewis, Ronald L. (Eds.). (1989). *Black Workers: A Documentary History from Colonial Times to the Present*. Philadelphia: Temple University Press.

Foner, Philip S., and Shapiro, Herbert. (Eds.). (1991). *American Communism and Black Americans: A Documentary History, 1930–1934*. Philadelphia: Temple University Press.

Fontenot, Chester. (Ed.). (2001). *W.E.B. Du Bois & Race: Essays Celebrating the Centennial Publication of The Souls of Black Folk*. Macon: Mercer University.

Ford, Nick Aaron. (1973). *Black Studies: Threat or Challenge*. New York: Kennikat.

Ford, Richard Thompson. (1995). "The Boundaries of Race: Political Geography in Legal Analysis." In Crenshaw, Gotanda, Peller and Thomas (Eds.), *Critical Race Theory* (pp. 449–64). New York: New Press.

Forman, James. (1997). "Manifesto to the White Christian Churches and Jewish Synagogues in the United States of America and All Other Racist Institutions." In William Van Deburg (Ed.), *Modern Black Nationalism: From Marcus Garvey to Louis Farrakhan* (pp. 183–87). New York: New York University Press.

Forney, Craig Allen. (2002). "W. E. B. Du Bois: The Spirituality of a Weary Traveler." Ph.D. dissertation, University of Chicago.

Forrester, Duncan B. (1988). *Theology and Politics*. New York: Blackwell.

Forster, Charles David, Jr. (2003). "'Spiritual Strivings': The Value of Race and the Rise of Black Consciousness in the Thought of W. E. B. Du Bois." Ph. D. dissertation, University of California, Los Angeles.

Fossett, Judith Jackson, and Tucker, Jeffrey A. (Eds.). (1997). *Race Consciousness: African American Studies for the New Century*. New York: New York University Press.

Foucault, Michel. (1977a). *Language, Counter-Memory, Practice: Selected Essays and Interviews by Michel Foucault* (Donald F. Bouchard, Ed.). Ithaca: Cornell University Press.

——. (1977b). *Power/Knowledge: Selected Interviews and Other Writings, 1972–1977* (Colin Gordon, Ed.). New York: Pantheon.

——. (1984). *The Foucault Reader* (Paul Rabinow, Ed.). New York: Pantheon.

——. (1988). *Politics, Philosophy, Culture: Interviews and Other Writings, 1977–1984* (Lawrence D. Kritzman, Ed.). New York: Routledge.

——. (1997). *The Essential Works of Michel Foucault, 1954–1984, Volume 1–Ethics: Subjectivity and Truth* (Paul Rabinow, Ed.). New York: New Press.

——. (1998). *The Essential Works of Michel Foucault, 1954-1984, Volume 2–Aesthetics, Method, and Epistemology* (Paul Rabinow, Ed.). New York: New Press.

——. (2000). *The Essential Works of Michel Foucault, 1954-1984, Volume 3–Power* (Paul Rabinow, Ed.). New York: New Press.

Franklin, John Hope. (2001). "Horowitz's diatribe contains historical inaccuracies." *Duke Chronicle* (29 March). Available on-line at: www.chronicle.duke.edu/vnews/display.v/ART/2001/03/29/3d768902b56be?in_archive=1 (Accessed on 15 January 2003).

Franklin, John Hope, and Meier, August. (Eds.). (1982). *Black Leaders of the Twenti-eth Century*. Chicago: University of Chicago Press.

Franklin, Robert Michael. (1990). *Liberating Visions: Human Fulfillment and Social Justice in African American Thought*. Minneapolis, MN: Fortress Press.

Franklin, V.P. (1995). "The Autobiographical Legacy of W.E.B. Du Bois." In V.P. Franklin, *Living Our Stories, Telling Our Truths: Autobiography and the Making of the African American Intellectual Tradition*. New York: Scribner.

Frantz, Nevin R., Jr. (1997). "The Contributions of Booker T. Washington and W.E.B. Du Bois in the Development of Vocational Education." *Journal of Industrial Teacher Education* 34 (4), 87–91.

Fraser, Nancy. (1989). *Unruly Practices: Power, Discourse and Gender in Contemporary Social Theory*. Minneapolis: University of Minnesota Press.

———. (1991). "What's Critical About Critical Theory?: The Case of Habermas and Gender." In David Ingram and Julia Simon-Ingram (Eds.), *Critical Theory: The Essential Readings* (pp. 357–87). New York: Paragon House.

———. (1996). "Multiculturalism and Gender Equity: The US 'Difference' Debates Revisited." *Constellations* 3.

———. (1997). *Justice Interruptions: Critical Reflections on the "Postsocialist" Condition*. New York: Routledge.

———. (1998). "Another Pragmatism: Alain Locke, Critical 'Race' Theory, and the Politics of Culture." In Morris Dickstein (Ed.), *The Revival of Pragmatism: New Essays on Social Thought, Law, and Culture* (pp. 157–75). Duke University Press.

Frazier, E. Franklin. (1939). *The Negro Family in the United States*. Chicago: University of Chicago Press.

———. (1949). *The Negro in the United States*. New York: Macmillan.

———. (1951). *The Integration of the Negro into American Society*. Washington, D.C.: Howard University Press.

———. (1957). *Race and Culture Contacts in the Modern World*. New York: Knopf.

———. (1962). *The Black Bourgeoisie: The Rise of a New Middle Class in the United States*. New York: Collier.

———. (1968). *On Race Relations: Selected Writings* (G. Franklin Edwards, Ed.). Chicago: University of Chicago Press.

———. (1974). *The Negro Church in America*. New York: Schocken.

———. (1998). "The Failure of the Negro Intellectual." In Joyce A. Ladner (Ed.), *The Death of White Sociology: Essays on Race and Culture* (pp. 52–66). Baltimore: Black Classic Press.

Fredrickson, George. (1981). *White Supremacy: A Comparative Study in American and South African History*. New York: Oxford University Press.

———. (1987). *The Black Image in the White Mind: The Debate on Afro-American Character and Destiny, 1817–1914*. Hanover, NH: Wesleyan University Press.

Freedman, Martin Neil. (1975). "The Rhetorical Adaptation of Social Movement Leaders: Booker T. Washington and W.E.B. Du Bois." Ph.D. dissertation, Purdue University, Lafayette, IN.

Freire, Paulo. (1975). *Miscellaneous Writings by Paulo Freire*. Berkeley: University of California Press.

———. (1976). *Education: The Practice of Freedom.* London: Writers and Readers Publishing.

———. (1978). *Pedagogy in Process: The Letters to Guinea-Bissau.* New York: Seabury Press.

———. (1985). *The Politics of Education: Culture, Power, and Liberation.* South Hadley, MA: Bergin and Garvey Publishers.

———. (1987). *Literacy: Reading the Word and the World.* South Hadley, MA: Bergin and Garvey Publishers.

———. (1989). *Learning to Question: A Pedagogy of Liberation.* New York: Continuum.

———. (1993). *Pedagogy of the Oppressed.* New York: Conitnuum.

———. (1994). *Pedagogy of Hope: Reliving Pedagogy of the Oppressed.* New York: Continuum.

———. (1996a). *Education for Critical Consciousness.* New York: Continuum.

———. (1996b). *Letters to Cristina: Reflections on My Life and Work.* New York: Routledge.

———. (1997). *Pedagogy of the Heart.* New York: Continuum.

———. (1998a). *The Paulo Freire Reader* (Ana Maria Araujo Freire and Donaldo Macedo, Eds). New York: Continuum.

———. (1998b). *Pedadgogy of Freedom: Ethics, Democracy, and Civic Courage.* Lanham, MD: Rowman and Littlefield.

———. (2000). *Cultural Action for Freedom.* Cambridge: Harvard University Press.

———. (2004). *Pedagogy of Indignation.* Boulder, CO: Paradigm Publishers.

———. (2005). *Teachers as Cultural Workers: Letters to Those Who Dare to Teach.* Boulder, CO: Paradigm Publishers.

———. (2007). *Daring to Dream: Toward a Pedagogy of the Unfinished.* Boulder, CO: Paradigm Publishers.

Freire, Paulo, and Fraser, James W. (Eds.). (1997). *Mentoring the Mentor: Critical Dialogue with Paulo Freire.* New York: Peter Lang.

Freundlieb, Dieter, Hudson, Wayne, and Rundell, John F. (Eds.), (2004). *Critical Theory After Habermas.* Boston: Brill.

Frey, Raymond G., and Wellman, Christopher Heath. (Eds.). (2003). *A Companion to Applied Ethics.* Malden: Blackwell.

Friedman, George. (1980). *The Political Philosophy of the Frankfurt School.* Ithaca, NY: Cornell University Press.

Fritz, Jan M. (1990). "In Pursuit of Justice: W.E.B. Du Bois." *Clinical Sociology Review* 8, 15–26.

Fromm, Erich. (1947). *Man for Himself.* New York: Holt, Rinehart & Winston.

———. (1955). *The Sane Society.* New York: Holt, Rinehart & Winston.

———. (1970). *The Crisis of Psychoanalysis.* New York: Holt, Rinehart & Winston.

Frye, Charles A. (1978). *Towards a Philosophy of Black Studies.* San Francisco: R & E Research Associates.

Fulop, Timothy, and Raboteau, Albert J. (Eds.). (1996). *African American Religion: Interpretive Essays in History and Culture.* New York: Routledge.

Funk, Rainer. (1982). *Erich Fromm: The Courage To Be Human.* New York: Continuum.

Gabbidon, Shaun L. (1996). "The Criminological Writings of W.E.B. Du Bois: A Historical Analysis." Ph.D. dissertation, Indiana University of Pennsylvania.

———. (2000). "An Early American Crime Poll by W.E.B. Du Bois." *Western Journal of Black Studies* 24 (3), 167–74.

———. (2001). "W.E.B. Du Bois: Pioneering American Criminologist." *Journal of Black Studies* 31 (5), 581–99.

Gaines, Kevin K. (1996). *Uplifting the Race: Black Leadership, Politics, and Culture in the Twentieth Century.* Chapel Hill: University of North Carolina Press.

Gaines, Stanley O., Jr. (1996). "Perspectives of Du Bois and Fanon on the Psychology of Oppression." In Lewis R. Gordon, T. Denean Sharley-Whiting, and Renee T. White (Eds.), *Fanon: A Critical Reader* (pp. 24–34). Cambridge, MA: Blackwell.

Gaines, Stanley O., Jr., and Reed, Edward S. (1994). "Two Social Psychologies of Prejudice: Gordon W. Allport, W.E.B. Du Bois, and the Legacy of Booker T. Washington." *Journal of Black Psychology* 20 (1), 8–28.

Gamble, Sarah. (Ed.). (2002). *The Routledge Companion to Feminism and Postfeminism.* New York: Routledge.

Gandhi, Leela. (1998). *Postcolonial Theory: A Critical Introduction.* Edinburgh: Edinburgh University Press.

Gardiner, James J., and Roberts, J. Deotis. (Eds.). (1971). *Quest for a Black Theology.* Philadelphia: Pilgrim Press.

Garry, Ann, and Pearsall, Marilyn. (Eds.). (1996). *Women, Knowledge, and Reality: Explorations in Feminist Philosophy.* New York: Routledge.

Gatens, Moira. (1991). *Feminism and Philosophy: Perspectives on Difference and Equality.* Indianapolis: Indiana University Press.

Gates, Henry Louis, Jr. (Ed.). (1990). *Reading Black/Reading Feminist: A Critical Anthology.* New York: Meridian.

———. (1996). "W.E.B. Du Bois and 'The Talented Tenth'." In Henry Louis Gates, Jr., and Cornel West, *The Future of the Race* (pp. 115–32). New York: Alfred A. Knopf.

———. (2000). "W.E.B. Du Bois and the Encyclopedia Africana, 1909–1963." *Annals of the American Academy of Political and Social Science* 568 (March), 203–19.

Gates, Henry Louis, Jr., and West, Cornel. (1996). *The Future of the Race.* New York: Alfred A. Knopf.

Gates, Henry Louis, Jr., and West, Cornel. (1996). *The Future of the Race.* New York: Alfred A. Knopf.

Gatewood, William B. (1994). "W.E.B. Du Bois: Elitist as Racial Radical." *Georgia Historical Quarterly* 78 (2), 306–27.

Gbadegesin, Segun. (1991a). *African Philosophy: Traditional Yoruba Philosophy and Contemporary African Realities.* New York: Peter Lang.

———. (1996). "Kinship of the Dispossessed: Du Bois, Nkrumah, and the Foundations of Pan-Africanism." In Bernard W. Bell, Emily R. Grosholz, and James B. Stewart (Eds.), *W.E.B. Du Bois: On Race and Culture* (pp. 219–42). New York: Routledge.

Geggus, David P. (2002). *Haitian Revolutionary Studies.* Bloomington: Indiana University Press.

Geiss, Imanuel. (1974). *The Pan-African Movement: A History of Pan-Africanism in America, Europe, and Africa.* New York: Holmes & Meier.

Gershoni, Yekutiel. (1995). "Contributions of W.E.B. Du Bois to Pan-Africanism." *Journal of Third World Studies* 12 (2), 440–43.

Geuss, Raymond (1981). *The Idea of a Critical Theory: Habermas and the Frankfurt School.* Cambridge: Cambridge University Press.

Gibson, Lovie Nancy. (1977). "Du Bois's Propaganda Literature: An Outgrowth of His Sociological Studies." Ph.D. dissertation, State University of New York-Buffalo.

Giddings, Paula. (1984). *When and Where I Enter: The Impact of Black Women on Race and Sex in America.* New York: Quill.

Gilkes, Cheryl Townsend. (1996). "The Margin as the Center of a Theory of History: African American Women, Social Change, and the Sociology of W.E.B. Du Bois." In Bernard W. Bell, Emily R. Grosholz, and James B. Stewart (Eds.), *W.E.B. Du Bois: On Race and Culture* (pp. 111–41). New York: Routledge.

———. (2001). *If It Wasn't for the Women: Black Women's Experience and Womanist Culture in Church and Community.* Maryknoll, NY: Orbis.

Gillman, Susan, and Weinbaum, Alys E. (Eds.). (2007). *Next to the Color-Line: Gender, Sexuality, and W.E.B. Du Bois.* Minneapolis, MN: University of Minnesota Press.

Gilman, Charelotte P. (1908). "A Suggestion on the Negro Problem." *American Journal of Sociology* 14, 78–85.

Gilmore, Glenda E. (1996). *Gender and Jim Crow: Women and the Politics of White Supremacy in North Carolina, 1896–1920.* Chapel Hill, NC: University of North Carolina Press.

———. (2008). *Defying Dixie: The Radical Roots of Civil Rights, 1919–1950.* New York: Norton.

Gilmore, Glenda, Dailey, Jane, and Simon, Bryant. (Eds.). (2000). *Jumpin' Jim Crow: Southern Politics from Civil War to Civil Rights.* Princeton: Princeton University Press.

Gilroy, Paul. (1987). *There Ain't No Black in the Union Jack.* New York: Routledge.

———. (1993a). *The Black Atlantic: Modernity and Double Consciousness.* Cambridge: Harvard University Press.

———. (1993b). *Small Acts: Thoughts on the Politics of Black Cultures.* New York: Serpent's Tail.

———. (2000). *Against Race: Imagining Political Culture Beyond the Color Line.* Cambridge: Harvard University Press.

Gipson, Carolyn Renee. (1971). "Intellectual Dilemmas in the Novels of W.E.B. Du Bois." Ph.D. dissertation, University of Michigan, Ann Arbor.

Giroux, Henry. (1981). *Ideology, Culture and the Process of Schooling.* Philadelphia: Temple University Press.

———. (1983a). *Theory and Resistance in Education.* Westport, CT: Bergin and Garvey.

———. (1983b). *Critical Theory and Educational Practice.* Sydney: Deakin University Press.

———. (1988). *Teachers as Intellectuals: Toward a Critical Pedagogy of Learning.* Westport, CT: Bergin and Garvey.

——. (1990). *Curriculum Discourse as Postmodernist Critical Practice.* Sydney: Deakin University Press.

——. (Ed.). (1991). *Postmodernism, Feminism and Critical Politics: Rethinking Educational Boundaries.* Albany: State University of New York Press.

——. (1992). *Border Crossings: Cultural Workers and the Politics of Education.* New York: Routledge.

——. (1993). *Living Dangerously: Multiculturalism and the Politics of Culture.* New York: Lang Publishing.

——. (1994). *Disturbing Pleasures: Learning Popular Culture.* New York: Routledge.

——. (1996). *Fugitive Cultures: Race, Violence, and Youth.* New York: Routledge.

——. (1997). *Pedagogy and the Politics of Hope: Theory, Culture, and Schooling.* New York: Westview/Harper-Collins.

——. (1998). *Channel Surfing: Racism, the Media, and the Destruction of Today's Youth.* New York: St. Martin's Press.

——. (1999). *The Mouse That Roared: Disney and the End of Innocence.* Lanham, MD: Rowman and Littlefield.

——. (2000). *Impure Acts: The Practical Politics of Cultural Studies.* New York: Routledge.

——. (2001). *Stealing Innocence: Corporate Culture's War on Children.* New York: St. Martin's Press.

——. (2002). *Breaking into the Movies: Film and the Culture.* Malden, MA: Blackwell.

——. (2003a). *Public Spaces/Private Lives: Democracy Beyond 9/11.* Boulder, CO: Rowman and Littlefield.

——. (2003b). *The Abandoned Generation: Democracy Beyond the Culture of Fear.* New York: Palgrave Macmillan.

——. (2004). *The Terror of Neoliberalism: Authoritarianism and the Eclipse of Democracy.* Boulder, CO: Paradigm Publishers.

——. (2005a). *Against the New Authoritarianism: Politics After Abu Ghraib.* New York: Arbeiter Ring.

——. (2005b). *Schooling and the Struggle for Public Life: Democracy's Promise and Education's Challenge.* Boulder, CO: Paradigm Publishers.

——. (2006a). *The Henry Giroux Reader* (Christopher Robbins, Ed.). Boulder, CO: Paradigm Publishers.

——. (2006b). *Beyond the Spectacle of Terrorism: Global Uncertainty and the Challenge of the New Media.* Boulder, CO: Paradigm Publishers.

——. (2006c). *America on the Edge: Henry Giroux on Politics, Culture, and Education.* New York: Palgrave Macmillan.

——. (2006d). *Stormy Weather: Katrina and the Politics of Disposability.* Boulder, CO: Paradigm Publishers.

——. (2007). *The University in Chains: Confronting the Military-Industrial-Academic Complex.* Boulder, CO: Paradigm Publishers.

Giroux, Henry, and Aronowitz, Stanley. (1991). *Postmodern Education: Politics, Culture, and Social Criticism.* Minneapolis: University of Minesota Press.

Giroux, Henry, and Aronowitz, Stanley. (1994). *Education Under Seige: The Conservative, Liberal, and Radical Debate Over Schooling.* Westport, CT: Bergin and Garvey.

Giroux, Henry, Castells, Manuel, Flecha, Ramon, Freire, Paulo, Macedo, Donald, and Willis, Paul). (1999). *Critical Education in the New Information Age*. Lanham, MD: Rowman and Littlefield.

Giroux, Henry, and Giroux, Susan. (2004). *Taking Back Higher Education: Race, Youth, and the Crisis of Democracy in the Post Civil Rights Era*. New York: Palgrave.

Giroux, Henry, and McLaren, Peter. (1989). *Critical Pedagogy, the State, and the Struggle for Culture*. Albany, NY: State University of New York Press.

Giroux, Henry, and McLaren, Peter. (1994). *Between Borders: Pedagogy and Politics in Cultural Studies*. New York: Routledge.

Giroux, Henry, McLaren, Peter, Lankshear, and Cole, Mike. (1996). *Counternarratives: Cultural Studies and Critical Pedagogies in Postmodern Spaces*. New York: Routledge.

Giroux, Henry, and Myrsiades, Kostas. (Eds.). (2001). *Beyond the Corporate University: Pedagogy, Culture, and Literary Studies in the New Millennium*. Lanham, MD: Rowman and Littlefield.

Giroux, Henry, and David Purpel. (Eds.). (1983). *The Hidden Curriculum and Moral Education: Deception or Discovery?* New York: McCutchan Publishing.

Giroux, Henry, and Shannon, Patrick. (Eds.). (1997). *Cultural Studies and Education: Towards a Perfomative Practice*. New York: Routledge.

Giroux, Henry, and Simon, Roger. (Eds.). (1989). *Popular Culture, Schooling, and Everyday Life*. Westport, CT: Bergin and Garvey.

Glascoe, Myrtle G. (1996). "W.E.B. Du Bois: His Evolving Theory of Education." *Research in Race & Ethnic Relations* 9, 171–88.

Glaude, Eddie S., Jr. (2000). *Exodus!: Religion, Race, and Nation in Early Nineteenth-Century Black America*. Chicago: University of Chicago Press.

———. (Ed). (2002). *Is It Nation Time?: Contemporary Essays on Black Power and Black Nationalism*. Chicago: University of Chicago Press.

Godshalk, David F. (2005). *Veiled Visions: The 1906 Atlanta Race Riot and the Reshaping of American Race Relations*. Chapel Hill, NC: University of North Carolina Press.

Goldberg, David Theo. (1987). "Raking the Field of the Discourse of Racism." *Journal of Black Studies* 18, 58–71.

———. (Ed.). (1990). *Anatomy of Racism*. Minneapolis: University of Minnesota Press.

———. (1993). *Racist Culture: Philosophy and the Politics of Meaning*. Cambridge: Blackwell.

———. (Ed.). (1994). *Multiculturalism: A Critical Reader*. Cambridge: Blackwell.

———. (1997). *Racial Subjects: Writing on Race in America*. New York: Routledge.

———. (2000). "Heterogeneity and Hybridity: Colonial Legacy, Postcolonial Heresy." In Henry Schwarz and Sangeeta Ray (Eds.), *A Companion to Postcolonial Studies* (pp. 72–86). Malden, MA: Blackwell.

———. (2001). *The Racial State*. Malden, MA: Blackwell.

Goldberg, David Theo, Musheno, Michael, and Bower, Lisa. (Eds.). (2001). *Between Law and Culture: Relocating Legal Studies*. Minneapolis, MN: University of Minnesota Press.

Goldberg, David Theo, and Quayson, Ato. (Eds.). (1999). *Relocating Postcolonialism: A Critical Reader.* Malden, MA: Blackwell.

Goldberg, David Theo, and Solomos, John. (Eds.). (2002). *A Companion to Racial and Ethnic Studies.* Malden: Blackwell.

Golden, L. Hanga, and Milikan, Ov. (1966). "William E.B. Du Bois: Scientist and Public Figure." *Journal of Human Relations* 14, 156–68.

Goldman, Anita Haya. (1994). "Negotiating Claims of Race and Rights: Du Bois, Emerson, and the Critique of Liberal Nationalism." *Massachusetts Review* 35 (Spring-Summer), 169–201.

Goldstein, Stanley L. (1972). "The Influence of Marxism on the Educational Philosophy of W.E.B. Du Bois." Ph.D. dissertation, University of Texas, Austin.

Gomez, Michael A. (2005). *Black Cresent: The Experience and Legacy of African Muslims in the Americas.* New York: Cambridge University Press.

Goodin, Patrick. (2002). "Du Bois and Appiah: The Politics of Race and Racial Identity." In Robert E. Birt (Ed.), *The Quest for Community and Identity: Critical Essays in Africana Social Philosophy* (pp. 73–83). Lanham, MD: Rowman and Littlefield.

Goodin, Robert E., and Pettit, Philip. (Eds.). (1993). *A Companion to Contemporary Political Philosophy.* Malden, MA: Blackwell.

Goodin, Robert E., and Pettit, Philip. (Eds.) (1997). *Contemporary Political Philosophy: An Anthology.* Cambridge: Blackwell.

Gooding-Williams, Robert. (1987). "Philosophy of History and Social Critique in *The Souls of Black Folk.*" *Social Science Information* 26, 99–114.

———. (1991). "Evading Narrative Myth, Evading Prophetic Pragmatism: A Review of Cornel West's *The American Evasion of Philosophy.*" *American Philosophical Association Newsletter of the Black Experience* 90 (3), 12–16.

———. (1991-92). "Evading Narrative Myth, Evading Prophetic Pragmatism: Cornel West's *The American Evasion of Philosophy.*" *Massachusetts Review* 32 (December), 517–42.

———. (1994). "Du Bois's Counter-Sublime." *Massachusetts Review* 35 (Spring–Summer), 203–24.

———. (1996). "Outlaw, Appiah, and Du Bois's 'The Conservation of Races'." In Bernard W. Bell, Emily R. Grosholz, and James B. Stewart (Eds.), *W.E.B. Du Bois: On Race and Culture* (pp. 39-56). New York: Routledge.

———. (2005). *Look, a Negro!: Philosophical Essays on Race, Culture and Politics.* New York: Routledge.

Gordon, Lewis R. (1993). "Racism as a Form of Bad Faith." *APA Newsletter on Philosophy and the Black Experience* 92 (2), 6–8.

———. (1995a). *Bad Faith and Anti-Black Racism.* Atlantic Highlands, NJ: Humanities Press.

———. (1995b). *Fanon and the Crisis of the European Sciences: An Essay on Philosophy and the Human Sciences.* New York: Routledge.

———. (Ed.). (1997a). *Existence in Black: An Anthology of Black Existential Philosophy.* New York: Routledge.

———. (1997b). *Her Majesty's Other Children: Sketches of Racism From A Neocolonial Age*. Lanham, MD: Rowman and Littlefield.

———. (1998). "African American Philosophy: Theory, Politics, and Pedagogy." *Philosophy of Education Yearbook: 1998* (On-line article). Available at: www.ed.uiuc .edu/EPS/PES-Yearbook/1998/gordon.htm (17 October 2001).

———. (1999). "A Short History of the 'Critical' in Critical Race Theory." *APA Newsletter on Philosophy and the Black Experience* 98 (2), 23–26.

———. (2000a). *Existentia Africana: Understanding Africana Existential Thought*. New York: Routledge.

———. (2000b). "What Does It Mean to Be a Problem?: W.E.B. Du Bois on the Study of Black Folk." In Lewis R. Gordon, *Existentia Africana: Understanding Africana Existential Thought* (pp. 62–95). New York: Routledge.

———. (2000c). "Du Bois's Humanistic Philosophy of Human Sciences." *Annals of the American Academy of Political and Social Science* 568 (March), 265–80.

———. (2002). "Sartrean Bad Faith and Anti-Black Racism." Julie K. Ward and Tommy L. Lott (Eds), *Philosophers on Race: Critical Essays* (pp. 241–59). Malden: Blackwell.

———. (2006a). *Disciplinary Decadence: Living Thought in Trying Times*. Boulder, CO: Paradigm Publishers.

———. (2006b). "African American Philosophy, Race, and the Geography of Reason." In Lewis R. Gordon and Jane Anna Gordon (Eds.), *Not Only the Master's Tools: African American Studies in Theory and Practice* (p. 3–50). Boulder, CO: Paradigm.

———. (2008). *An Introduction to Africana Philosophy*. Cambridge: Cambridge University Press.

Gordon, Lewis R., and Gordon, Jane Anna. (Eds). (2006a). *A Companion to African American Studies*. Malden, MA: Blackwell.

Gordon, Lewis R., and Gordon, Jane Anna. (Eds.). (2006b). *Not Only the Master's Tools: African American Studies in Theory and Practice*. Boulder, CO: Paradigm.

Gordon, Lewis R., and Martinez, Jacquelin M. (Eds.). (2008). *Communicating Differences: Essays in Phenomenology and Communicative Praxis*. Lanham, MD: Rowman and Littelfield.

Gordon, Lewis R., Sharley-Whiting, T. Denean, and White, Renee T. (Eds.). (1996). *Fanon: A Critical Reader*. Cambridge: Blackwell.

Gordon, Lewis, and White, Renee T. (Eds.). (2008). *Black Texts and Textuality: Constructing and Deconstructing Blackness*. Lanham, MD: Rowman and Littlefield.

Gorman, William. (1950). "W.E.B. Du Bois and His Work." *Fourth International* 2, 80–85.

Gotanda, Neil. (1995). "A Critique of 'Our Constitution is Color-Blind'." In Kimberle Crenshaw, Neil Gotanda, Gary Peller, and Kendall Thomas (Eds.), *Critical Race Theory: The Key Writings That Formed the Movement* (pp. 257–75). New York: New Press.

Gottlieb, Roger S. (Ed.). (1989). *An Anthology of Western Marxism: From Lukács and Gramsci to Socialist-Feminism*. New York: Oxford University Press.

——. (1992). *Marxism, 1844–1990: Origins, Betrayal, Rebirth.* New York: Routledge.

Gouldner, Alvin W. (1980). *The Two Marxisms: Contradictions and Anomalies in the Development of Theory.* New York: Seabury.

Graham, Shirley. (1976). *His Day Is Marching On: A Memoir of W.E.B. Du Bois.* Chicago: Johnson.

Gramsci, Antonio. (1967). *The Modern Prince and Other Writings* (Louis Marks, Ed.). New York: International.

——. (1971). *Selections from the Prison Notebooks of Antonio Gramsci* (Quintin Hoare and Geoffrey Nowell-Smith, Eds.). New York: International.

——. (1975). *History, Philosophy, and Culture in the Young Gramsci* (Pedro Cavalcanti and Paul Piccone, Eds.). St. Louis: Telos Press.

——. (1977). *Selections from the Political Writings, 1910–1920* (Quintin Hoare, Ed.). New York: International.

——. (1978). *Selections from the Political Writings, 1921–1926* (Quintin Hoare, Ed.). New York: International.

——. (1985). *Selections from the Cultural Writings* (David Forgacs and Geoffrey Nowell-Smith, Eds.). Cambridge: Harvard University Press.

——. (1992). *Prison Notebooks* (Volume 1, Joseph A. Buttigieg, Ed.). New York: Columbia University Press.

——. (1994a). *Antonio Gramsci: Pre-Prison Writings* (Richard Bellamy, Ed). New York: Cambridge University Press.

——. (1994b). *Letters from Prison* (2 Volumes, Frank Rosengarten, Ed.). New York: Columbia University Press.

——. (1995a). *Antonio Gramsci: Further Selections from the Prison Notebooks* (Derek Boothman, Ed). Minneapolis: University of Minnesota Press.

——. (1995b). *The Southern Question* (Pasquale Vericchio, Ed.). West Lafayette, IN: Bordighera.

——. (1996). *Prison Notebooks* (Volume 2, Joseph A. Buttigieg, Ed.). New York: Columbia University Press.

——. (2000). *The Antonio Gramsci Reader: Selected Writings, 1916–1935* (David, Forgacs, Ed.). New York: New York University Press.

Grant, Jacquelyn. (1989). *White Women's Christ and Black Women's Jesus: Feminist Christology and Womanist Response.* Atlanta: Scholars Press.

Greco, Rose Dorothy. (1984). "The Educational Views of Booker T. Washington and W.E.B. Du Bois: A Critical Comparison." Ph.D. dissertation, Loyola University of Chicago.

Green Dan S. (1973). "The Truth Shall Make Ye Free: The Sociology of W.E.B. Du Bois." Ph.D. dissertation, University of Massachusetts.

——. (1977). "W.E.B. Du Bois's Talented Tenth: A Strategy for Racial Advancement." *Journal of Negro Education* 46 (3), 358–66.

Green, Dan S. and Driver, Edwin D. (1976). "W.E.B. Du Bois: A Case in the Sociology of Sociological Negation." *Phylon* 37 (4), 308–33.

Green, Dan S., and Smith, Earl. (1983). "W.E.B. Du Bois and the Concepts of Race and Class." *Phylon* 44, 262–72.

Green, Lisa J. (2002). *African American English: A Linguistic Introduction.* New York: Cambridge University Press.

Gregg, Robert. (1998). "Giant Steps: W.E.B. Du Bois and the Historical Enterprise." In Michael B. Katz and Thomas J. Sugrue (Eds.), *W.E.B. Du Bois, Race, and the City: The Philadelphia Negro and Its Legacy* (pp. 77–100). Philadelphia: University of Pennsylvania Press.

Griffin, Farah Jasmine. (2000). "Black Feminists and W.E.B. Du Bois: Respectability, Protection, and Beyond." *Annals of the American Academy of Political and Social Science* 568 (March), 28–40.

Grigsby, Daryl R. (1987). *For the People: Black Socialists in the United States, Africa, and the Caribbean.* San Diego: Asante Publications.

Grimshaw, Jean. (1986). *Philosophy and Feminist Thinking.* Minneapolis, MN: University of Minnesota Press.

Grosholz, Emily R. (1996). "Nature and Culture in *The Souls of Black Folk* and *Quest of The Silver Fleece.*" In Bernard W. Bell, Emily R. Grosholz, and James B. Stewart (Eds.), *W.E.B. Du Bois: On Race and Culture* (pp. 177–92). New York: Routledge.

Guess, Raymond. (1981). *The Idea of Critical Theory.* Cambridge: Cambridge University Press.

Guettel, Charnie. (1974). *Marxism and Feminism.* Toronto: Women's Educational Press.

Guevara, Ernesto "Che." (1968). *Venceremos!: The Speeches and Writings of Che Guevara* (John Gerassi, Ed.). New York: Macmillan.

Guiner, Lani. (1995). "Groups, Representation, and Race-Consciousness Districting: A Case of the Emperor's Clothes." In Kimberle Crenshaw, Neil Gotanda, Gary Peller, and Kendall Thomas (Eds.), *Critical Race Theory: The Key Writings That Formed the Movement* (pp. 205–34). New York: New Press.

Gunaratnam, Yasmin. (2003). *Researching Race and Ethnicity: Methods, Knowledge, and Power.* Thousand Oaks, CA: Sage.

Gustav, Saron. (1955). *The Jews in South Africa: A History.* Cape Town: Oxford University Press.

Gutiérrez, Gustavo. (1983). *The Power of the Poor in History: Selected Writings of Gustavo Gutierrez.* Maryknoll, NY: Orbis.

———. (1988). *A Theology of Liberation: History, Politics, and Salvation.* Maryknoll, NY: Orbis.

———. (1994). *Las Casas: In Search of the Poor of Jesus Christ.* Maryknoll, NY: Orbis.

———. (1996). *Essential Writings of Gustavo Gutiérrez* (James B. Nickoloff, Ed.). Maryknoll, NY: Orbis.

———. (1999). "The Task and Content of Liberation Theology." In Christopher Rowland (Ed.), *The Cambridge Companion to Liberation Theology* (pp. 19–38). New York: Cambridge University Press.

Gutman, Amy (Ed.). (1994). *Multiculturalism.* Princeton: Princeton University Press.

Guy-Sheftall, Beverly. (1990). *Daughters of Sorrow: Attitudes Toward Black Women, 1880–1920.* Brooklyn, NY: Carlson.

——. (Ed.). (1995). *Words of Fire: An Anthology of African American Feminist Thought*. New York: The Free Press.

Guzman, Jessie P. (1961). "W.E.B. Du Bois—The Historian." *Journal of Negro Education* 30, 377–85.

Gyekye, Kwame. (1995). *An Essay on African Philosophical Thought: The Akan Conceptual Scheme*. Philadelphia: Temple University Press.

——. (1996). *African Cultural Values: An Introduction*. Elkins Park, PA: Sankofa Publishing.

——. (1997). *Tradition and Modernity: Philosophical Reflections on the African Experience*. New York: Oxford University Press.

Habermas, Jurgen. (1984). *Theory of Communicative Action* (Volume 1). Boston: Beacon.

——. (1986a). *Theory and Practice*. Cambridge: Polity Press.

——. (1986b). *Knowledge and Human Interests*. Cambridge: Polity Press.

——. (1986c). *Toward a Rational Society*. Cambridge: Polity Press.

——. (1987a). *Theory of Communicative Action* (Volume 2). Boston: Beacon.

——. (1987b). *The Philosophical Discourse on Modernity*. Cambridge: MIT Press.

——. (1988). *On the Logic of the Social Sciences*. Cambridge: MIT Press.

——. (1989a). *The Structural Transformation of the Public Sphere*. Cambridge: MIT Press.

——. (1989b.) *On Society and Politics: A Reader* (Steven Seidman, Ed.). Boston: Beacon.

——. (1990). *Moral Consciousness and Communicative Action*. Cambridge: MIT Press.

——. (1992a). *Autonomy and Solidarity* (Peter Dews, Ed.). London: Verso.

——. (1992b). *Postmetaphysical Thinking*. Cambridge: Polity Press.

——. (1993). *Justification and Application*. Cambridge: Polity Press.

——. (1994). *The Past as Future*. Lincoln: University of Nebraska Press.

——. (1995). *Between Facts and Norms: Contributions to a Discourse Theory of Law and Democracy*. Cambridge: MIT Press.

——. (1996). *The Habermas Reader* (William Outhwaite, Ed.). Malden, MA: Blackwell.

——. (1998). *On the Pragmatics of Communication* (Maeve Cooke, Ed.). Cambridge: MIT Press.

——. (2000). *On the Pragmatics of Social Interaction: Preliminary Studies in the Theory of Communicative Action*. Cambridge: MIT Press.

Hackney, James R., Jr. (1998). "Derrick Bell's Re-Sounding: W.E.B. Du Bois, Modernism, and Critical Race Scholarship." *Law & Social Inquiry* 23 (1), 141–64.

Hahn, Steven. (2003). *A Nation Under Our Feet: Black Political Struggles in the Rural South, From Slavery to the Great Migration*. Cambridge: Belknap/Havard University Press.

Haines, Herbert M. (1988). *Black Radicals and the Civil Rights Mainstream, 1954–1970*. Knoxville: University of Tennessee Press.

Hakim, Ida. (Ed). (1994). *Reparations, the Cure for America's Race Problem: A Collaborative Effort in Reparations Advocacy by the Founding Members of C.U.R.E.* Hampton, VA: U.B. & U.S. Communication Systems.

———. (Ed.). (2005).*The Debtors: Whites Respond to the Call for Black Reparations.* Hampton, VA: U.B. & U.S. Communication Systems.

Hale, Grace E. (1998). *Making Whiteness: The Culture of Segregation in the South, 1890–1940.* New York: Pantheon.

Hall, Perry A. (1999). *In the Vineyard: Working in African American Studies.* Knoxville: University of Tennessee Press.

Hall, Stuart. (1996). *Stuart Hall: Critical Dialogues in Cultural Studies* (David Morley and Kuan-Hsing Chen, Eds.). New York: Routledge.

Hall, William S. (1975). *Culture and Language: The Black American Experience.* Washington, D.C.: Hemisphere Publishing.

Hames-Garcia, Michael. (2001). "Can Queer Theory Be Critical Theory." In William S. Wilkerson and Jeffrey Paris (Eds.), *New Critical Theory: Essays on Liberation* (pp. 201–22). Lanham, MD: Rowman and Littlefield Publishers.

Hamilton, Malcolm B. (2001). *The Sociology of Religion: Theoretical and Comparative Perspectives.* New York: Routledge.

———. (1998). *Sociology and the World's Religions.* New York: St. Martin's Press.

Hamilton, Virginia. (1972). *W.E.B. Du Bois: A Biography.* New York: Crowell.

Hammond, Evelynn M. (1997). "Toward A Genealogy of Black Female Sexuality: The Problematic of Silence." In M. Jacqui Alexander and Chandra Talpade Mohanty (Eds.), *Feminist Genealogies, Colonial Legacies, Democratic Futures* (pp. 170–81). New York: Routledge.

Hanrahan, Nancy W. (2000). *Difference in Time: A Critical Theory of Culture.* Westport, CT: Praeger.

Hansberry, William Leo. (1970). "W.E.B. Du Bois's Influence on African History." In John Henrik Clarke, Esther Jackson, Ernest Kaiser, and J.H. O'Dell (Eds.), *Black Titan: W.E.B. Du Bois* (pp. 98–114). Boston: Beacon.

Hansen, Emmanuel. (1977). *Frantz Fanon: Social and Political Thought.* Columbus, OH: Ohio State University Press.

Hansen, Jonathan M. (1997). "Fighting Words: The Transnational Patriotism of Eugene V. Debs, Jane Addams, and W.E.B. Du Bois." Ph.D. dissertation, Boston University.

Hansen, Karen V., and Philipson, Ilene J. (Ed.). (1990). *Women, Class, and the Feminist Imagination: A Socialist-Feminist Reader.* Philadelphia: Temple University Press.

Harding, Vincent. (1970). "W.E.B. Du Bois and the Black Messianic Vision." In John Henrik Clarke, Esther Jackson, Ernest Kaiser, and J.H. O'Dell (Eds.), *Black Titan: W.E.B. Du Bois* (pp. 52–68). Boston: Beacon.

———. (1981). *There Is A River: The Black Struggle for Freedom in America.* New York: Harcourt Brace Jovanovich.

Hare, Nathan. (1969). "W.E. Burghardt Du Bois: An Appreciation." In W.E.B. Du Bois, *The Souls of Black Folk.* New York: New American Library.

———. (1972). "The Battle of Black Studies." *Black Scholar* 3 (9), 32–37.

———. (1998). "The Challenge of a Black Scholar." In Joyce A. Ladner (Ed.), *The Death of White Sociology: Essays on Race and Culture* (pp. 67–80). Baltimore: Black Classic Press.

Harlan, Louis R. (1971). "The Secret Life of Booker T. Washington." *Journal of Southern History* 37, 393–416.

———. (1972). *Booker T. Washington: The Making of a Black Leader, 1856–1901*. New York: Oxford University Press.

———. (1979). "Booker T. Washington and the *Voice of the Negro*, 1904–1907. *Journal of Southern History* 45, 45–62.

———. (1982). "Booker T. Washington and the Politics of Accommodation." In John Hope Franklin and August Meier (Eds.), *Black Leaders of the Twentieth Century* (pp. 1–18). Chicago: University of Illinois Press.

———. (1983). *Booker T. Washington: The Wizard of Tuskegee, 1901–1915*. New York: Oxford University Press.

———. (1988). *Booker T. Washington in Perspective: Essays of Louis R. Harlan* (Raymond W. Smock, Ed.). Jackson: University Press of Mississippi.

Harlan, Louis R., and Smock, Raymond W. (Eds.). (1972–1989). *The Booker T. Washington Papers* (Volumes 1–14). Urbana: University of Chicago Press.

Harris, Cheryl I. (1995). "Whiteness as Property." In Kimberle Crenshaw, Neil Gotanda, Gary Peller, and Kendall Thomas (Eds.), *Critical Race Theory: The Key Writings That Formed the Movement* (pp. 276–91). New York: New Press.

Harris, Fredrick C. (1999). *Something Within: Religion in African American Political Activism*. New York: Oxford University Press.

Harris, James H. (1987). *Black Ministers and Laity in the Urban Church: An Analysis of Political and Social Expectations*. Lanham, MD: University of America Press.

Harris, Joseph E. (Ed). (1993). *Global Dimensions of the African Diaspora*. Washington, D.C.: Howard University Press.

Harris, Leonard. (Ed.). (1983). *Philosophy Born of Struggle: An Anthology of Afro-American Philosophy from 1917*. Dubuque, IA: Kendall/Hunt.

———. (Ed.). (1989). *The Philosophy of Alain Locke: Harlem Renaissance and Beyond*. Philadelphia: Temple University Press.

———. (Ed.). (1999a). *The Critical Pragmatism of Alain Locke: A Reader on Value, Theory, Aesthetics, Community, Culture, Race, and Education*. Lanham, MD: Rowman and Littlefield.

———. (Ed.). (1999b). *Racism: Key Concepts in Critical Theory*. Amherst, NY: Humanity Books.

Harris, Robert, Hine, Darlene Clark, and McKay, Nellie. (Eds.). (1990). *Black Studies in the Academy*. New York: The Ford Foundation.

Harris, Thomas E. (1993). *Analysis of the Clash Over the Issues Between Booker T. Washington and W.E.B. Du Bois*. New York: Garland.

Harris, Trudier. (1982). *From Mammies to Militants: Domestics in Black American Literature*. Philadelphia: Temple University Press.

Harrison, Faye V. (1992). "The Du Boisian Legacy in Anthropology." *Critique of Anthropology* 12 (3), 239–60.

Hartmann, Heidi I. (1981). "The Unhappy Marriage of Marxism and Feminism: Towards A More Progressive Union." In Lydia Sargent (Ed.), *Women and Revolution: A Discussion of the Unhappy Marriage of Marxism and Feminism* (pp. 1–41). Boston: South End.

Harvey, Jennifer. (2007). *Whiteness and Morality: Pursuing Racial Justice Through Reparations and Sovereignty.* New York: Palgrave Macmillan.

Haskins, James. (1993). *The Psychology of Black Language.* New York: Hippocrene.

Hattery, Angela J., and Smith, Earl. (2005). "William Edward Burghardt Du Bois and the Concepts of Race, Class, and Gender." *Sociation Today* 3 (1). Online at: www.ncsociology.org/sociationtoday/v31/smith.htm (Accessed on 23 February 2005).

Hawkins, Hugh. (1974). *Booker T. Washington and His Critics: Black Leadership in Crisis.* Lexington, MA: Heath.

Hayes, Diana L. (1996). *And Still We Rise: An Introduction to Black Liberation Theology.* New York: Paulist Press.

Hayes, Floyd W. (Ed.). (2000). *A Turbulent Voyage: Readings in African American Studies.* Lanham, MD: Rowman and Littlefield Publishers.

Haywood, Harry. (1934). *The Road Negro Liberation.* New York: Workers' Library Publishing.

———. (1948). *Negro Liberation.* New York: International Publishers.

———. (1978). *Black Bolshevik: Autobiography of an Afro-American Communist.* Chicago: Lake View Press.

Held, David. (1980). *Introduction to Critical Theory: Horkheimer to Habermas.* Berkeley: University of California Press.

Henderson, Lenneal J., Jr. (1970). "W.E.B. Du Bois, Black Scholar, and Prophet." *Black Scholar* 1, 48–57.

Henderson, Vivian W. (1974). *Race, Economics, and Public Policy: With Reflection on W.E.B. Du Bois.* Atlanta: Atlanta University Press.

———. (1976). "Race, Economics, and Public Policy with Reflections on W.E.B. Du Bois." *Phylon* 37 (1), 1–11.

Hennelly, Alfred T. (1995). *Liberation Theologies: The Global Pursuit of Justice.* Mystic, CT: Twenty-Third Publications.

Hennessey, Alistair. (Ed.). (1992). *Intellectuals in the Twentieth-Century Caribbean* (2 Volumes). London: Macmillan, Caribbean.

Hennessey, Rosemary, and Ingraham, Chrys. (Eds.). (1997). *Materialist Feminism: A Reader in Class, Difference, and Women's Lives.* New York: Routledge.

Henry, Charles P. (2007). *Long Overdue: The Politics of Racial Reparations.* New York: New York University Press.

Henry, Paget. (2000). *Caliban's Reason: Introducing Afro-Caribbean Philosophy.* New York: Routledge.

Herrman, Louis. (1935). *A History of Jews in South Africa from the Earliest Times to 1895.* London: Gollancz.

Henton, Jennifer E. (2001). "Twain, Du Bois, Toomer, and Hurston: Reading American Literature and Reading Race." Ph.D. dissertation, University of Delaware.

Higbee, Mark David. (1993). "W.E.B. Du Bois, F.B. Ransom, the Madam Walker Company, and Black Business Leadership in the 1930's." *Indiana Magazine of History* 89, 101–24.

———. (1995a). "W.E.B. Du Bois and the Problems of the Twentieth Century: Race, History, and Literature in Du Bois's Political Thought, 1903–1940." Ph.D. dissertation, Columbia University.

——. (1995b). "Du Bois: The First Half Century." *Science & Society* 59 (1), 82–87.

Higginbotham, Evelyn Brooks. (1989). "Beyond the Sound of Silence: Afro-American Women in History." *Gender & History* 1 (1), 50–67.

——. (1993). *Righteous Discontent: The Women's Movement in the Black Baptist Church, 1880–1920.* Cambridge: Harvard University Press.

Higginbotham, A. Leon, Jr. (1978). *In the Matter of Color: Race and the American Legal Process—The Colonial Period.* New York: Oxford University Press.

——. (1996). *Shades of Freedom: Racial Politics and Presumptions of the American Legal Process.* New York: Oxford University Press.

Hill Patricia L. (1978). "American Popular Response to W.E.B. Du Bois's *The Souls of Black Folk.*" *Western Journal of Black Studies* 2 (1), 54–59.

Hindess, Barry. (1993). "Marxism." In Robert E. Goodin and Philip Pettit (Eds.), *A Companion to Contemporary Political Philosophy* (pp. 312–33). Malden, MA: Blackwell.

Hine, Darlene Clark. (Ed.). (1990). *Black Women in the United States 1619–1989* (Volumes 1–16). Brooklyn: Carlson.

——. (1994). *Culture, Consciousness, and Community: The Making of an African American Women's History.* Greenville, NC: East Carolina University.

Hine, Darlene Clark, Brown, Elsa Barkley, and Teborg-Penn, Rosalyn. (Eds.). (1993). *Black Women in America: An Historical Encyclopedia* (2 Volumes). Brooklyn: Carlson.

Hine, Darlene Clark, King, Wilma, and Reed, Linda. (Eds.). (1995). *We Specialize in the Wholly Impossible: A Reader in Black Women's History.* Brooklyn: Carlson.

Hine, Darlene Clark, and Thompson, Kathleen. (1998). *A Shining Thread of Hope: The History of Black Women in America.* New York: Broadway Books.

Hine, Darlene Clark, and Jenkins, Earnestine. (Ed.). (1999). *A Question of Manhood: A Reader in U.S. Black Men's History and Masculinity* (Volume 1). Bloomington: Indiana University Press.

——. (Ed.). (2001). *A Question of Manhood: A Reader in U.S. Black Men's History and Masculinity* (Volume 2). Bloomington: Indiana University Press.

Hine, Darlene Clark, Hine, William C., and Harrold, Stanley. (2002). *The African American Odyssey* (2nd Edition). Upper Saddle River, NJ: Prentice Hall.

Hirschberg, Haim Z. (1974). *A History of Jews in North Africa.* Leiden: Brill.

Holloway, Jonathan S. (2002). *Confronting the Veil: Abram Harris, Jr., E. Franklin Frazier, and Ralph Bunch, 1919-1941.* Chapel Hill, NC: University of North Carolina Press.

Holloway, Jonathan S., and Keppel, Ben. (Eds.). (2007). *Black Scholars on the Line: Race, Social Science, and American Thought in the Twentieth Century.* Notre Dame, IN: University of Notre Dame Press.

Holloway, Joseph E. (Ed.). (1991). *Africanisms in American Culture.* Bloomington: Indiana University Press.

——. (1997). *The African Heritage of American English.* Bloomington: Indiana University Press.

Holmes, Eugene C. (1970). "W.E.B. Du Bois: Philosopher." In John Henrik Clarke, Esther Jackson, Ernest Kaiser, and J.H. O'Dell (Eds.), *Black Titan: W.E.B. Du Bois* (pp. 76–81). Boston: Beacon.

Holmstrom, Nancy C.L. (2002). *The Socialist Feminist Project: A Contemporary Reader in Theory and Politics.* New York: Monthly Review.

Holt, Thomas C. (1982). "The Lonely Warrior: Ida B. Wells-Barnett and the Struggle for Black Leadership." In John Hope Franklin and August Meier (Eds.), *Black Leaders of the Twentieth Century* (pp. 39–62). Chicago: University of Illinois Press.

———. (1990). "The Political Uses of Alienation: W.E.B. Du Bois on Politics, Race, and Culture, 1903–1940." *American Quarterly* 42 (2), 301–23.

———. (1998). "W.E.B. Du Bois's Archaeology of Race: Re-Reading "The Conservation of Races." In Michael B. Katz and Thomas J. Sugrue (Eds.), *W.E.B. Du Bois, Race, and the City: The Philadelphia Negro and Its Legacy* (pp. 61–76). Philadelphia: University of Pennsylvania Press.

———. (2002). *The Problem of Race in the 21st Century.* Cambridge: Harvard University Press.

Honneth, Axel. (1991). *The Critique of Power: Reflective Stage in a Critical Social Theory.* Cambridge: MIT Press.

Hood, Robert E. (1990). *Must God Remain Greek?: Afro-Cultures and God-Talk.* Minneapolis, MN: Fortress Press.

hooks, bell. (1981). *Ain't I A Woman: Black Women and Feminism.* Boston: South End.

———. (1984). *Feminist Theory: From Margin to Center.* Boston: South End.

———. (1989). *Talking Back: Thinking Feminist, Thinking Black.* Boston: South End.

———. (1990). *Yearning: Race, Gender, and Cultural Politics.* Boston: South End.

———. (1991). *Black Looks: Race and Representation.* Boston: South End.

———. (1994a). *Teaching to Transgress: Education as the Practice of Freedom.* Boston: South End.

———. (1994b). *Outlaw Culture: Resisting Representation.* New York: Routledge.

———. (1995). *Killing Rage: Ending Racism.* New York: Henry Holt.

———. (2000a). *Where We Stand: Class Matters.* New York: Routledge.

———. (2000b). *Feminism is for Everybody: Passionate Politics.* New York: Routledge.

———. (2003a). *Teaching Community: A Pedagogy of Hope.* New York: Routledge.

———. (2003b). *Rock My Soul: Black People and Self-Esteem.* New York: Atria.

———. (2004a). *The Will to Change: Men, Masculinity, and Love.* New York: Atria.

———. (2004b). *We Real Cool: Black Men and Masculinity.* New York: Routledge.

Hopkins, Dwight N. (1989). *Black Theology USA and South Africa: Politics, Culture, and Liberation.* Maryknoll, NY: Orbis.

———. (1993). *Shoes That Fit Our Feet: Sources for a Constructive Theology.* Maryknoll, NY: Orbis.

———. (1999a). *Introducing Black Theology of Liberation.* Maryknoll, NY: Orbis.

———. (Ed.). (1999b). *Black Faith and Public Talk: Critical Essays on James H. Cone's Black Theology and Black Power.* Maryknoll, NY: Orbis.

———. (2000). *Down, Up, and Over: Slave Religion and Black Theology.* Minneapolis, MN: Fortress Press.

———. (2003). *Heart and Head: Black Theology—Past, Present, and Future.* New York: Palgrave Macmillan.

———. (2005). *Being Human: Race, Culture, and Religion.* Minneapolis, MN: Fortress Press.

Hopkins, Dwight N., and Cummings, George C.L. (Eds.). (1991). *Cut Loose Your Stammering Tongue: Black Theology in the Slave Narratives.* Maryknoll, NY: Orbis.

Hopkins, Dwight N., and Davaney, Sheila G. (Eds.). (1996). *Changing Conversations: Religious Reflection and Cultural Analysis.* New York: Routledge.

Hopkins, Dwight N., Dolamo, Ramathate, and Tepedino, Ana Maria. (Eds.) (2003). *Global Voices for Gender Justice.* Cleveland, OH: Pilgrims Press.

Hopkins, Dwight N., Batstone, David, and Lorentzen, Lois A. (Eds.). (2001). *Religions/Globalizations: Theories and Cases.* Durham, NC: Duke University Press.

Hopkins, Kevin. (2001). "Forgive U.S. Our Debts?: Righting the Wrongs of Slavery." *Georgetown Law Journal* 89 (8), 2531–56.

Hord, Fred Lee, and Lee, Johnathan Scott. (Eds.). (1995). *I Am Because We Are: Readings in Black Philosophy.* Amherst: University of Massachusetts Press.

Horkheimer, Max. (1972). *Critical Theory.* New York: Continuum.

———. (1974a). *Eclipse of Reason.* New York: Continuum.

———. (1974b). *Critique of Instrumental Reason.* New York: Continuum.

———. (1978). *Dawn and Decline: Notes, 1926–1931 and 1950–1969.* New York: Continuum.

Horkheimer, Max, and Adorno, Theodor W. (1995). *Dialectic of Enlightenment.* New York: Continuum.

Horne, Gerald. (1986). *Black and Red: W.E.B. Du Bois and the Afro-American Response to the Cold War, 1944–1963.* Albany: State University of New York Press.

———. (2000). *Race Woman: The Lives of Shirley Graham Du Bois.* New York: New York University Press.

Hornsman, Reginald. (1986). *Race and Manifest Destiny: Origins of American Racial Anglo-Saxonism.* Cambridge, MA: Harvard University Press.

Horowitz, David. (2001). *Uncivil Wars: The Controversy over Reparations for Slavery.* New York: Encounter.

Horsman, Reginald. (1981). *Race and Manifest Destiny: The Origins of American Racial Anglo-Saxonism.* Cambridge: Harvard University Press.

Horton, Robin. (1993). *Patterns of Thought in Africa and the West: Essays on Magic, Religion, and Science.* Cambridge: Cambridge University Press.

Hountondji, Paulin J. (1996). *African Philosophy: Myth and Reality.* Indianapolis: Indiana University Press.

How, Alan. (2003). *Critical Theory.* New York: Palgrave Macmillan.

Howard, Dick. (1972). *The Development of the Marxian Dialectic.* Carbondale and Edwardsville, IL: Southern Illinois University Press.

———. (1988). *The Marxian Legacy.* Minneapolis: University of Minnesota Press.

Howard, Dick, and Klare, Karl E. (Eds.). (1972). *The Unknown Dimension: European Marxism Since Lenin.* New York: Basic Books.

Hudson-Weems, Clenora. (1989). "Cultural and Agenda Conflicts in Academia: Critical Issues for Africana Women's Studies." *Western Journal of Black Studies* 13 (4), 185–89.

———. (1992). "Africana Womanism." *Voice: The Caribbean International Magazine* 37–38, 46.

———. (1995). *Africana Womanism: Reclaiming Ourselves*. Boston: Bedford.

———. (1997). "Africana Womanism and the Critical Need for Africana Theory and Thought." *Western Journal of Black Studies* 21 (2), 79–84.

———. (1998a). "Africana Womanism: An Historical, Global Perspective for Women of African Descent." In Patricia Liggins Hill (Ed.), *Call and Response: The Riverside Anthology of the African American Literary Tradition* (pp. 1811–15). Boston: Houghton Mifflin.

———. (1998b). "Africana Womanism, Black Feminism, African Feminism, Womanism." In Obioma Nnaemeka (Ed.), *Sisterhood, Feminisms, and Power: From Africa to the Diaspora* (pp. 149–62). Trenton, NJ: Africa World Press.

———. (1998c). "Self-Naming and Self-Defining: An Agenda for Survival." In Obioma Nnaemeka (Ed.), *Sisterhood, Feminisms, and Power: From Africa to the Diaspora* (pp. 449–52). Trenton, NJ: Africa World Press.

———. (2000). "Africana Womanism: An Overview." In Delores Aldridge and Carlene Young (Eds.), *Out of the Revolution: The Development of Africana Studies* (pp. 205–17). Lanham, MD: Lexington Books.

———. (2001a). "Africana Womanism, Black Feminism, African Feminism, Womanism." In William Nelson, Jr., (Ed.), *Black Studies: From the Pyramids to Pan-Africanism and Beyond*. New York: McGraw-Hill.

———. (2001b). "Africana Womanism: Entering the New Millennium." In Jemadari Kamara and T. Menelik Van Der Meer (Eds.), *State of the Race, Creating Our 21st Century: Where Do We Go From Here*. Amherst: University of Massachusetts Press.

———. (2004). *Africana Womanist Literary Theory*. Trenton, NJ: Africa World Press.

———. (Ed). (2007). *Contemporary Africana Theory, Thought, and Action: A Guide to Africana Studies*. Trenton, NJ: Africa World Press.

Hufford, D. (1997). "The Religious Thought of W.E.B. Du Bois." *Journal of Religious Thought* 53/54 (2/1), 73–94.

Huggins, Nathan Irvin. (1971). *The Harlem Renaissance*. New York: Oxford University Press.

———. (Ed.). (1995). *Voices from the Harlem Renaissance*. New York: Oxford University Press.

Hughes, G. (1968). Reparations for Blacks. *New York University Law Review* 43, 1063–74.

Hughes, Langston. (1962). *Fight for Freedom: The Story of the NAACP*. New York: Norton.

Hull, Gloria T., Scott, Patricia Bell, and Smith, Barbara. (Eds.). (1982). *All the Women Are White, All the Blacks Are Men, But Some of Us Are Brave: Black Women's Studies*. New York: The Feminist Press at CUNY.

Humm, Maggie. (Ed.). (1992). *Modern Feminisms: Political, Literary, Cultural*. New York: Columbia University Press.

Hunter, Jehron. (1996). "Du Bois Revisited." *Black Issues in Higher Education* 13 (5), 14.

Huntington, Patricia. (2001). "Challenging the Colonial Contract: The Zapatistas' Insurgent Imagination." In William S. Wilkerson and Jeffrey Paris (Eds.), *New Crit-

ical Theory: Essays on Liberation (pp. 105–34). Lanham, MD: Rowman and Littlefield Publishers.

Hunton, W. Alphaeus. (1970). "W.E.B. Du Bois: The Meaning of His Life." In John Henrik Clarke, Esther Jackson, Ernest Kaiser, and J.H. O'Dell (Eds.), *Black Titan: W.E.B. Du Bois* (pp. 131–37). Boston: Beacon.

Hutchinson, George. (1995). *Harlem Renaissance in Black and White*. Cambridge, MA: Harvard University Press.

———. (Ed.). (2007). *The Companion to the Harlem Renaissance*. New York: Cambridge University Press.

Hutchinson, Louise D. (1981). *Anna Julia Cooper: A Voice from the South*. Washington, D.C.: Anacostia Neighborhood Museum and Smithsonian Press.

———. (1993). "Anna Julia Haywood Cooper." In Darlene Clark Hine, Elsa Barkley Brown, and Rosalyn Teborg-Penn (Eds.), *Black Women in America: An Historical Encyclopedia* (Volume 1, pp. 275–80). Brooklyn: Carlson.

Hwang, Hae-Sung. (1988). "Booker T. Washington and W.E.B. Du Bois: A Study in Race Leadership, 1895–1915." Ph.D. dissertation, University of Hawaii.

Idowu, E. Bolaji. (1975). *African Traditional Religions*. Maryknoll, NY: Orbis.

Ijere, Martin O. (1974). "W.E.B. Du Bois and Marcus Garvey as Pan-Africanists: A Study in Contrasts." *Presence Africaine* 79, 188–206.

Imbo, Samuel Oluoch. (1998). *An Introduction to African Philosophy*. Lanham, MD: Rowman and Littlefield.

Ingram, David. (1990). *Critical Theory and Philosophy*. New York: Paragon House.

———. (1995). *Reason, History, and Politics: The Communitarian Grounds of Legitimation in the Modern Age*. Albany, NY: State University of New York Press.

Ingram, David, and Simon-Ingram, Julia. (Eds.). (1992). *Critical Theory: The Essential Readings*. New York: Paragon House.

Irele, F. Abiola. (1990). *The African Experience in Literature and Ideology*. Indianapolis: Indiana University Press.

———. (2001). *The African Imagination: Literature in Africa and the Black Diaspora*. New York: Oxford University Press.

Irele, F. Abiola, and Gikandi, Simon. (Eds.). (2004). *The Cambridge History of African and Caribbean Literature*. Cambridge: Cambridge University Press.

Jack, Robert L. (1943). *History of the National Association for the Advancement of Colored People*. Boston: Meador.

Jackson, Helen. (1993). *A Century of Dishonor: A Sketch of the United States Government's Dealings with Some of the Indian Tribes*. New York: Indian Head Books.

Jackson, Stevi. (Ed.). (1993). *Women's Studies: Essential Readings*. New York: New York University Press.

Jackson, Stevi, and Scott, Sue. (Eds.). (2001). *Gender: A Sociological Reader*. New York: Routledge.

Jacoby, Russell. (1981). *Dialectic of Defeat: Contours of Western Marxism*. Cambridge: Cambridge University Press.

Jafri, Naqi Husain. (2004). *Critical Theory: Perspectives from Asia*. New Delhi: Jamia Millia Islamia University Press.

Jaggar, Alison M. (1983). *Feminist Politics and Human Nature*. Totowa, NJ: Rowman and Allanheld.

Jaggar, Alison M., and Young, Iris Marion. (Eds.). (1998). *A Companion to Feminist Philosophy*. Malden, MA: Blackwell.

James, C.L.R. (1963). *The Black Jacobins: Toussaint L'Ouverture and the San Domingo Revolution*. New York: Vintage Books.

———. (1977). *The Future in the Present: Selected Writings*. London: Allison and Busby.

———. (1980). *Spheres of Existence: Selected Writings*. London: Allison and Busby.

———. (1984). *At the Rendezvous of Victory: Selected Writings*. London: Allison and Busby.

———. (1992). *The C.L.R. James Reader* (Anna Grimshaw, Ed.). Cambridge: Blackwell.

———. (1994). *C.L.R. James and Revolutionary Marxism: Selected Writings of C.L.R. James, 1939–1949* (Scott McLemee and Paul Le Blanc, Eds.). Atlantic Highlands, NJ: Humanities Press.

———. (1995). *A History of Pan-African Revolt*. Chicago: Charles H. Kerr Publishing.

———. (1996). *C.L.R. James on the "Negro Question"* (Scott McLemee, Ed.). Jackson, MS: University of Mississippi Press.

———. (1999). *Marxism for Our Times: C.L.R. James on Revolutionary Organization* (Martin Glaberman, Ed.). Jackson, MS: University of Mississippi Press.

James, Joy A. (1996a). *Resisting State Violence: Radicalism, Gender, and Race in U.S. Culture*. Minneapolis, MN: University of Minnesota Press.

———. (1996b). "The Profeminist Politics of W.E.B. Du Bois, with Respects to Anna Julia Cooper and Ida B. Wells Barnett." In Bernard W. Bell, Emily R. Grosholz, and James B. Stewart (Eds.), *W.E.B. Du Bois: On Race and Culture* (pp. 141–61). New York: Routledge.

———. (1997). *Transcending the Talented Tenth: Black Leaders and American Intellectuals*. New York: Routledge.

———. (1999). *Shadow Boxing: Representations of Black Feminist Politics*. New York: St. Martin's Press.

———. (2000). "The Future of Black Studies: Political Communities and the 'Talented Tenth'." In Manning Marable (Ed.), *Dispatches from the Ebony Tower: Intellectuals Confront the African American Experience* (pp. 153–57). New York: Columbia University Press.

James, Joy A., and Sharpley-Whiting, T. Denean. (Eds.). (2000). *The Black Feminist Reader*. Malden, MA: Blackwell.

James, Stanlie, and Busia, Abena. (Eds.). (1993). *Theorizing Black Feminism: The Visionary Pragmatism of Black Women*. New York: Routledge.

James, Winston. (1998). *Holding Aloft the Banner of Ethiopia: Caribbean Radicalism in Early Twentieth-Century America*. New York: Verso.

Jameson, Fredric. (1971). *Marxism and Form: Twentieth-Century Dialectical Theories of Literature*. Princeton, NJ: Princeton University Press.

———. (1975). "Notes Toward a Marxist Cultural Politics." *Minnesota Review* 5, 35–39.

———. (1979a). "Marxism and Historicism." *New Literary History* 11, 41–73.

——. (1979b). "Marxism and Teaching." *New Political Science* 2/3, 31–36.

——. (1979c). "Reification and Utopia in Mass Culture." *Social Text* 1, 130–48.

——. (1990). *Late Marxism: Adorno, or, The Persistence of the Dialectic*. London: Verso.

——. (1991). *Postmodernism, or, The Cultural Logic of Late Capitalism*. Durham: Duke University Press.

JanMohamed, Adul R. (1983). *Manichean Aesthetics: The Politics of Literature in Colonial Africa*. Amherst: University of Massachusetts Press.

Jardine, Alice, and Smith, Paul. (Eds.). (1987). *Men in Feminism*. New York: Methuen.

Jay, Martin. (1984). *Marxism and Totality: The Adventures of a Concept from Lukács to Habermas*. Berkeley: University of California Press.

——. (1996). *The Dialectical Imagination: A History of the Frankfurt School and the Institute of Social Research, 1923–1950*. Berkeley: University of California Press.

Jefferson, Paul. (1996). "Present at the Creation: Rethinking Du Bois's Practice Theory." *Research in Race & Ethnic Relations* 9, 127–69.

Jeffries, Judson L. (2002). *Huey P. Newton: The Radical Theorist*. Jackson: University Press of Mississippi.

Jennings, Francis. (1976). *The Invasion of America: Indians, Colonialism, and the Cant of Conquest*. New York: Norton.

Jennings, Patricia K. (1998). "The Lions and the Canon: The Formative Contributions of W.E.B. Du Bois and Frantz Fanon to Social Theory." *American Sociological Association*.

Jewell, Joseph O. (2007). *Race, Social Reform, and the Making of a Middle Class: The American Missionary Association and Black Atlanta, 1870–1900*. Lanham, MD: Rowman and Littlefield.

Johnson, Adolph, Jr. (1976). "A History and Interpretation of the William Edward Burghardt Du Bois-Booker Taliaferro Washington Higher Education Controversy." Ph.D. dissertation, University of Southern California, Los Angeles.

Johnson, Arthur L. (1949). "The Social Theories of W.E.B. Du Bois." M.A. thesis, Atlanta University, Atlanta, GA.

Johnson, Cedric. (2007). *Revolutionaries to Race Leaders: Black Power and the Making of African American Politics*. Minneapolis, MN: University of Minnesota Press.

Johnson, Dennis L. (1995). "In the Hush of Great Barrington: One Writer's Search for W.E.B. Du Bois." *The Georgia Review* 49 (3), 581.

Johnson, E. Patrick, and Henderson, Mae G. (Eds.). (2005). *Black Queer Studies: A Critical Anthology*. Durham, NC: Duke University Press.

Johnson, Karen A. (2000). *Uplifting the Women and the Race: The Educational Philosophies and Social Activism of Anna Julia Cooper and Nannie Helen Burroughs*. New York: Garland.

Johnson, Paul E. (Ed.). (1994). *African American Christianity: Essays in History*. Berkeley: University of California Press.

Johnson, Vernon, and Lyne, Bill. (Eds.). (2002). *Walkin' the Talk: An Anthology of African American Studies*. Prentice Hall.

Johnstone, Ronald L. (1997). *Religion in Society: A Sociology of Religion.* Upper Saddle River, NJ: Prentice-Hall.

Johnson-Feelings, Dianne. (Ed.). (1996). *The Best of the Brownies Book.* New York: Oxford University Press.

Jonas, Gilbert. (2005). *Freedom's Sword: The NAACP and the Struggle Against Racism in America, 1909–1969.* New York. Routledge.

Jones, Atlas Jack. (1976). "The Sociology of W.E.B. Du Bois." *Black Sociologists* 6 (1), 4–15.

Jones, Charles E. (Ed.). (1998). *The Black Panther Party (Reconsidered).* Baltimore: Black Classic Press.

Jones, Gail. (1997). "W.E.B. Du Bois and the Language of the Color-Line." In Judith Jackson Fossett and Jeffrey A. Tucker (Eds.), *Race Consciousness: African American Studies for the New Century* (pp. 19–35). New York: New York University Press.

Jones, Jacqueline. (1985). *Labor of Love, Labor of Sorrow: Black Women, Work and the Family from Slavery to the Present.* New York: Basic Books.

———. (1998). "'Lifework' and Its Limits: The Problem of Labor in *The Philadelphia Negro.*" In Michael B. Katz and Thomas J. Sugrue (Eds.), *W.E.B. Du Bois, Race, and the City: The Philadelphia Negro and Its Legacy* (pp. 103–26). Philadelphia: University of Pennsylvania Press.

Jones, William R. (1973). *Is God A White Racist?: A Preamble to Black Theology.* Boston: Beacon.

Jordan, Winthrop D. (1968). *White Over Black: American Attitudes Toward the Negro, 1550–1812.* Chapel Hill, NC: University of North Carolina Press.

Joseph, Peniel E. (2006a). *Waiting 'Til the Midnight Hour: A Narrative of Black Power in America.* New York: Henry Holt.

———. (Ed.). (2006b). *Black Power Movement: Rethinking the Civil Rights-Black Power Era.* New York: Routledge.

Juan, E. San, Jr. (2000). *Beyond Postcolonial Theory.* New York: Palgrave Macmillan.

Judy, Ronald T. (1994). "The New Black Aesthetic and W.E.B. Du Bois, or Hephaestus Limping." *Massachusetts Review* 35 (2), 249–82.

———. (Eds.). (2000a). *Sociologically Hesitant: Thinking with W.E.B. Du Bois.* Durham, NC: Duke University Press.

———. (2000b). "Introduction: On W.E.B. Du Bois and Hyperbolic Thinking." *Boundary 2* 27 (3), 1–35.

Juguo, Zhang. (2001). *W.E.B. Du Bois: Quest for the Abolition of the Color Line.* New York: Routledge.

Kahn, Jonathon Samuel. (2003). "The Religious Imagination of W. E. B. Du Bois." Ph.D. dissertation, Columbia University, New York.

Kaiser, Ernest. (1970). "Cultural Contributions of Dr. Du Bois." In John Henrik Clarke, Esther Jackson, Ernest Kaiser, and J.H. O'Dell (Eds.), *Black Titan: W.E.B. Du Bois* (pp. 69–75). Boston: Beacon.

Kaplan, Jeffrey, and Bjorgo, Tore. (Eds.). (1998). *Nation and Race: The Developing Euro-American Racist Subculture.* Boston: Northeastern University Press.

Karenga, Maulana. (1988). "Black Studies and the Problematic of Paradigm: The Philosophical Dimension," *Journal of Black Studies* 18 (4), 395–414.

——. (1997). "African Culture and the Ongoing Quest for Excellence: Dialogue, Principles, Practice." *The Black Collegian* (February), 160–63.

——. (1999). *Odu Ifa: The Ethical Teachings*. Los Angeles: University of Sankore Press.

——. (2001). "Mission, Meaning and Methodology in Africana Studies: Critical Reflections from a Kawaida Framework." *Black Studies Journal* 3, 54–74.

——. (2002). *Introduction to Black Studies* (3rd Edition). Los Angeles: University of Sankore Press.

——. (2003). "Du Bois and the Question of the Color Line: Race and Class in the Age of Globalization." *Socialism and Democracy* 17, 1 (33), 141–60. Available online at: www.sdonline.org/33/maulana_karenga.htm (Accessed on 23 February 2003).

——. (2004). *Maat, The Moral Ideal in Ancient Egypt: A Study in Classical African Ethics*. New York: Routledge.

——. (2008). *Kawaida and Questions of Life and Struggle: African American, Pan-African, and Global Issues*. Los Angeles: University of Sankore of Press.

Katz, Michael B. (2000). "Race, Poverty, and Welfare: Du Bois's Legacy for Policy." *Annals of the American Academy of Political and Social Science* 568 (March), 111–27.

Katz, Michael B., and Sugrue, Thomas J. (Eds.). (1998). *W.E.B. Du Bois, Race, and the City: The Philadelphia Negro and Its Legacy*. Philadelphia: University of Pennsylvania Press.

Katznelson, Ira. (1999). "Du Bois's Century." *Social Science History* 23 (4), 459–74.

Kauffman, Linda S. (Ed.). (1993). *American Feminist Thought at Century's End*. Cambridge: Blackwell.

Kautzsch, Alexander. (2002). *The Historical Evolution of Earlier African American English: An Empirical Comparison of Early Sources*. Berlin and New York: Mouton de Gruyter.

Kee, Alistair. (1990). *Marx and the Failure of Liberation Theology*. Philadelphia: Trinity Press International.

Keene, Jennifer D. (2001). "W.E.B. Du Bois and the Wounded World: Seeking Meaning in the First World War for African Americans." *Peace & Change* 26 (2), 135–52.

Keita, Lansana. (1991). "Contemporary African Philosophy: The Search for a Method." In Tsenay Serequeberhan (Ed.), *African Philosophy: The Essential Readings* (pp. 132–55). New York: Paragon House.

Keita, Maghan. (2000). *Race and the Writing of History: Riddle of the Sphinx*. New York: Oxford University Press.

Kelley, Robin D.G. (1990). *Hammer and Hoe: Alabama Communists During the Great Depression*. Chapel Hill, NC: University of North Carolina Press.

——. (1994). *Race Rebels: Culture, Politics, and the Black Working Class*. New York: The Free Press.

——. (1997a). *Yo' Mama's Disfunktional: Fighting the Culture Wars in Urban America*. Boston: Beacon.

———. (1997b). "Looking B(L)ackward: African American Studies in the Age of Identity Politics." In Judith Jackson Fossett and Jeffrey A. Tucker (Eds.), *Race Consciousness: African American Studies for the New Century* (pp. 1–17). New York: New York University Press.

———. (2002). *Freedom Dreams: The Black Radical Imagination.* Boston: Beacon.

Kellner, Douglas. (1984). *Herbert Marcuse and the Crisis of Marxism.* Berkeley: University of California Press.

———. (1989). *Critical Theory, Marxism, and Modernity.* Baltimore: Johns Hopkins University Press.

———. (1990a). "The Postmodern Turn in Social Theory: Positions, Problems, and Prospects." In George Ritzer (Ed.), *The Frontiers of Social Theory: The New Syntheses* (pp. 255–86). New York: Columbia University Press.

———. (1990b). "Critical Theory and Ideology Critique." In Ronald Roblin (Ed.), *Critical Theory and Aesthetics* (pp. 85–123). Lewistown: Edwin Mellen Press.

———. (1990c). "Critical Theory and the Crisis of Social Theory." *Sociological Perspectives* 33 (1), 11–33.

———. (1992). "Erich Fromm, Feminism, and the Frankfurt School." In Michael Kessler and Rainer Funk (Eds.), *Erich Fromm und die Frankfurter Schule* (pp. 111–30). Tubingen: Francke Verlag.

———. (1993). "Critical Theory and Social Theory: Current Debates and Challenges." *Theory, Culture, and Society* 10 (2), 43–61.

———. (1995). "The Obsolescence of Marxism?" Bernard Magnus and Stephen Cullenberg (Eds.), *Whither Marxism?: Global Crises in International Perspective* (pp. 3–30). New York: Routledge.

Kellogg, Charles Flint. (1967). *NAACP: History of the National Association for the Advancement of Colored People.* Baltimore: Johns Hopkins University Press.

Kelly, Michael. (1982). *Modern French Marxism.* Baltimore: John Hopkins University Press.

———. (Ed.). (1990). *Hermeneutics and Critical Theory in Ethic and Politics.* Cambridge: MIT Press.

Kemp, Sandra, and Squires, Judith. (Eds.). (1997). *Feminisms.* New York: Oxford University Press.

Kershaw, Terry. (1989). "The Emerging Paradigm in Black Studies." *Western Journal of Black Studies* 13 (1), 45–51.

———. (1992). "Toward A Black Studies Paradigm: An Assessment and Some Directions." *Journal of Black Studies* 22 (4), 477–93.

———. (2003). "The Black Studies Paradigm: The Making of Scholar Activists." In James L. Conyers (Ed.), *Afrocentricity and the Academy* (pp. 27–36). Jefferson, NC: McFarland & Co.

Killian, Lewis M. (1999). "Generals, the Talented Tenth, and Affirmative Action." *Society* 36 (6/242), 33–40.

Kilson, Martin. (1973). "Reflections on Structure and Content in Black Studies." *Journal of Black Studies* 1 (3), 197–214.

————. (2000a). "Black Studies Revisited." In Manning Marable (Ed.), *Dispatches from the Ebony Tower: Intellectuals Confront the African American Experience* (pp. 171–76). New York: Columbia University Press.

————. (2000b). "The Washington and Du Bois Leadership Paradigms Reconsidered." *Annals of the American Academy of Political and Social Science* 568 (March), 298–313.

Kimbrough, Marvin Gordon. (1974). "W.E.B. Du Bois as Editor of *The Crisis.*" Ph.D. dissertation, University of Texas, Austin.

King, Deborah K. (1995). "Multiple Jeopardy, Multiple Consciousness: The Contest of Black Feminist Ideology." In Beverly Guy-Sheftall (Ed.), *Words of Fire: An Anthology of African American Feminist Thought* (pp. 294–318). New York: Free Press.

King, Desmond. (1995). *Separate and Unequal: Black American and the U.S. Federal Government.* Oxford: Claredon.

King, Martin Luther, Jr. (1970). "Honoring Dr. Du Bois." In Philip S. Foner (Ed.), *W.E.B. Du Bois Speaks: Speeches and Addresses, 1890–1919* (pp. 20–29). New York: Pathfinder.

Kiros, Teodros. (2004). "Frantz Fanon (1925–1961)." In Kwasi Wiredu (Ed.), *A Companion to African Philosophy* (pp. 216–24). Malden: Blackwell.

Kochuthara, Thomas. (1993). *Theology of Liberation and Ideology Critique: A Study of the Praxis of Liberation in the Light of Critical Theory.* New Delhi: Intercultural Publications.

Kohlenbach, Margarete, and Geuss, Raymond. (Eds.). (2005) *The Early Frankfurt School and Religion.* New York: Palgrave Macmillan.

Kolakowski, Leszek. (1978a). *Main Currents of Marxism: I. The Founders.* New York: Oxford University Press.

————. (1978b). *Main Currents of Marxism: II. The Golden Age.* New York: Oxford University Press.

————. (1978c). *Main Currents of Marxism: III. The Breakdown.* New York: Oxford University Press.

Kolm, Serge-Christophe. (1993). "Distributive Justice." In Robert E. Goodin and Philip Pettit (Eds.), *A Companion to Contemporary Political Philosophy* (pp. 438–61). Malden: Blackwell.

Kopano, Baruti N., and Williams, Yohuru R. (Eds.). (2004). *Treading Our Ways: Selected Topics in Africana Studies.* Dubuque, IA: Kendall/Hunt Publishing.

Kornweibel, Theodore. (1998). *Seeing Red: Federal Campaigns Against Black Militancy.* Bloomington: Indiana University Press.

————. (2002). *"Investigate Everything": Federal Efforts to Compel Black Loyalty During World War I.* Bloomington: Indiana University Press.

Kostelanetz, Richard. (1985). "Fictions for a Negro Politics: The Neglected Novels of W.E.B. Du Bois." In William L. Andrews (Ed.), *Critical Essays on W.E.B. Du Bois* (pp. 173–93). Boston: G.K. Hall.

————. (1991). *Politics of the African American Novel: James Weldon Johnson, W.E.B. Du Bois, Richard Wright, and Ralph Ellison.* Westport, CT: Greenwood.

Kourany, Janet A., Sterba, James P., and Tong, Rosemarie. (Eds.). (1999). *Feminist Philosophies: Problems, Theories, and Applications* (2nd Edition). Englewood, NJ: Prentice Hall.

Kramarae, Cheris, and Spender, Dale. (Eds.). (2000). *The Routledge International Encyclopedia of Women: Global Women's Issues and Knowledge* (Volumes 1–4). New York: Routledge.

Krell, David Farrell. (2000). "The Bodies of Black Folk: From Kant and Hegel to Du Bois and Baldwin." *Boundary 2* 27 (3), 103–34.

Kuhn, Annette, and Wolpe, Ann Marie. (Eds.). (1978). *Feminism and Marxism: Women and Modes of Production.* Boston: Routledge & Kegan.

Kunnie, Julian. (1994). *Models of Black Theology: Issues in Class, Culture, and Gender.* Valley Forge, PA: Trinity Press.

Kwame, Safro. (Ed.). (1995). *Readings in African Philosophy: An Akan Collection.* New York: University Press of America.

Kymlicka, Will. (1997). "Justice and Minority Rights." In Robert E. Goodin and Philip Pettit (Eds.), *Contemporary Political Philosophy: An Anthology* (pp. 366–88). Cambridge: Blackwell.

Labov, William. (1972). *Language in the Inner City: Studies in the Black English Vernacular.* Philadelphia: University of Pennsylvania Press.

Laclau, Ernesto, and Mouffe, Chantal. (1985). *Hegemony and Socialist Strategy: Toward a Radical Democratic Politics.* New York: Verso.

——. (1987). "Post-Marxism Without Apologies." *New Left Review* 166, 79–106.

Lacy, Karyn R. (2007). *Blue-Chip Black: Race, Class, and Status in the New Black Middle Class.* Berkeley: Universiry of California Press.

Lacy, Leslie Alexander. (1970). *Cheer the Lonesome Traveler: The Life of W.E.B. Du Bois.* New York: Dial.

Ladner, Joyce A. (Ed.). (1998). *The Death of White Sociology: Essays on Race and Culture.* Baltimore: Black Classic Press.

Ladson-Billings, Gloria. (1994). *The Dreamkeepers: Successful Teachers of African American Children.* San Fracisco: Jossey-Bass.

——. (2001). *Crossing Over Canaan: The Journey of New Teachers in Diverse Classrooms.* San Fracisco: Jossey-Bass.

——. (Ed.). (2003). *Critical Race Theory Perspectives on the Social Studies: The Profession, Policies, and Curriculum.* Charlotte, NC: Information Age Publishing.

——. (2005a). *Beyond the Big House: African American Educators on Teacher Education.* New York: Teachers College Press.

——. (Ed). (2005b). *Culturally Relevent Teaching.* Philadelphia, PA: Lawrence Erlbaum.

Ladson-Billings, Gloria, and Fecho, Bob. (Eds.). (2003). *"Is This English?": Race, Language, and Culture in the Classroom.* New York: Teachers College Press.

Ladson-Billings, Gloria, and Tate, William F. (Eds.). (2006). *Education Research in the Public Interest: Social Justice, Action, and Policy.* New York: Teachers College Press.

Lafollette, Hugh. (Ed.). (1999). *Blackwell Guide to Ethical Theory.* Malden: Blackwell.

———. (Ed.). (2003). *Oxford Handbook of Practical Ethics.* New York: Oxford University Press.

Lakeland, Paul. (1990). *Theology and Critical Theory.* Nashville: Abingdon Press.

Lancaster, Roger N., and di Leonardo, Micaela. (Eds.). (1997). *The Gender and Sexuality Reader.* New York: Routledge.

Landry, Bart. (1987). *The New Black Middle Class.* Berkeley: University of California Press.

Lanehart, Sonja L. (Ed.). (2001). *Sociocultural and Historical Contexts of African American English.* Amsterdam: John Benjamins Publishing.

Lang, Jesse Michael. (1992). *Anticipations of the Booker T. Washington-W.E.B. Du Bois Dialectic in the Writings of Frances E.W. Harper, Ida B. Wells, and Anna Julia Cooper.* M.A. thesis, Georgetown University.

Lange, Werner J. (1982). "W.E.B. Du Bois, Franz Boas and the Rise of Anti-racism in American Anthropology." *North Central Sociological Association.*

Langley, J. Ayodele. (1973). *Pan-Africanism and Nationalism in West Africa, 1900–1945: A Study in Ideology and Social Classes.* New York: Oxford University Press.

———. (1979). *Ideologies of Liberation in Black Africa, 1856–1970.* London: Collings Publishing Group.

Lanternari, Vittorio. (1963). *The Religions of the Oppressed.* New York: Knopf.

Larue, H.C. (1971). "W.E.B. Du Bois and the Pragmatic Method of Truth." *Journal of Human Relations* 19, 76–83.

Lash, John S. (1957). "Thought, Research, Action: Dr. Du Bois and History." *Phylon* 18, 184–85.

Lawson, Bill E. (Ed.). (1992). *The Underclass Question.* Philadelphia: Temple University Press.

Lawson, Bill E., and Kirkland, Frank M. (Eds.). (1999). *Fredrick Douglass: A Critical Reader.* Malden: Blackwell.

Lazerow, Jama, and Williams, Yohuru. (Eds.). (2006). *In Search of the Black Panther Party: New Perspectives on a Revolutionary Movement.* Durham, NC: Duke University Press.

Lecky, Robert S., and Wright, H.E. (1969). *Black Manifesto: Religion, Racism, and Reparations.* New York: Sheed and Ward.

Lee, James Kyung-Jin. (2002). "Where the Talented Tenth Meets the Model Minority." *Novel: A Forum on Fiction* 35 (2/3), 231–57.

Lee, Jayne Chong–Soon. (1995). "Navigating the Topology of Race." In Kimberle Crenshaw, Neil Gotanda, Gary Peller , and Kendall Thomas (Eds.), *Critical Race Theory: The Key Writings That Formed the Movement* (pp. 441–48). New York: New Press.

Lee, Lenetta Raysha. (2000). "Whose Images: An Africological Study of the *Brownies Book* Series." Ph. D. dissertation, Temple University, Philadelphia.

Lee, Maurice. (1999). "Du Bois the Novelist: White Influence, Black Spirit, and *The Quest of the Silver Fleece.*" *African American Review* 33 (3), 389–400.

Lemelle, Sidney J., and Kelley, Robin D.G. (Eds.). (1994). *Imagining Home: Class, Culture, and Nationalism in the African Diaspora.* New York: Verso.

Lemert, Charles C. (1994). "A Classic from the Veil: Du Bois's *Souls of Black Folk*." *Sociological Quarterly* 35 (3), 383–96.

———. (2000a). "The Race of Time: Du Bois and Reconstruction." *Boundary 2* 27 (3), 215–48.

———. (2000b). "W.E.B. Du Bois." In George Ritzer (Ed.), *The Blackwell Companion to Major Social Theorists* (pp. 345–67). Malden: Blackwell.

Lemons, Gary L. (1997). "To be Black, Male and 'Feminist' — Making Womanist Space for Black Men." *International Journal of Sociology and Social Policy* 17, 37–53.

———. (2001). "'When and Where [We] Enter': In Search of a Feminist Forefather—Reclaiming the Womanist Legacy of W.E.B. Du Bois." In Rudolph P. Byrd and Beverly Guy-Sheftall (Eds.), *Traps: African American Men on Gender and Sexuality* (pp. 71–89). Indianapolis: Indiana University Press.

Lengermann, Patricia M., and Niebrugge-Brantley, Jil. (Eds.). (2007). *The Women Founders: Sociology and Social Theory, 1830–1930: A Text/Reader.* Long Grove, IL: Waveland Press.

Lenin, Vladimir I. (1975). *The Lenin Anthology* (Robert C. Tucker, Ed.). New York: Norton.

———. (1987). *The Essential Works of Lenin: "What is to be Done?" and Other Writings.* Mineola, NY: Dover.

Leonhard, Wolfgang. (1971). *Three Faces of Marxism.* New York: Holt, Rinehart & Winston.

Lerner, Gerda. (Ed.). (1972). *Black Women in White America: A Documentary History.* New York: Vintage.

Lester, Julius. (1971). "Introduction to *The Seventh Son*." In Julius Lester (Ed.), *The Seventh Son: The Thought and Writings of W.E.B. Du Bois* (Volume 1, pp. 1–153). New York: Vintage Books.

Lewis, David Levering. (1989). *When Harlem Was In Vogue.* New York: Oxford University Press.

———. (1993). *W.E.B. Du Bois: Biography of a Race, 1868–1919.* New York: Henry Holt.

———. (Ed.). (1994). *The Portable Harlem Renaissance Reader.* New York: Viking.

———. (2000). *W.E.B. Du Bois: The Fight for Equality and the American Century, 1919–1963.* New York: Henry Holt.

Lichtheim, George. (1965). *Marxism.* New York: Praeger.

———. (1966). *Marxism in Modern France.* New York: Columbia University Press.

Lichtman, Richard. (1993). *Essays in Critical Social Theory: Toward a Marxist Critique of Liberal Ideology.* New York: Peter Lang.

Lincoln, C. Eric. (Ed.). (1974). *The Black Experience in Religion.* Garden City, NY: Anchor Press.

———. (1984). *Race, Religion, and the Continuing American Dilemma.* New York: Hill & Wang.

———. (1993). "The Du Boisian Dubiety and the American Dilemma: Two Levels of Lure and Loathing." In Gerald Early (Ed.), *Lure and Loathing: Essays on Race, Identity, and the Ambivalence of Assimilation* (pp. 194–206). New York: Viking/Penguin.

Lincoln, C. Eric, and Mamiya, Lawrence H. (1990). *The Black Church in the African American Experience*. Durham, NC: Duke University Press.

Linnemann, Russell J. (Ed.). (1982). *Alain Locke: Reflections on a Modern Renaissance Man*. Baton Rouge, LA: Louisiana State University.

Liss, Julia. (1998). "Diasporic Identities: The Science and Politics of Race in the Work of Franz Boas and W.E.B. Du Bois, 1894–1919." *Cultural Anthropology: Journal of the Society for Cultural Anthropology* 13 (2), 127–66.

Litwack, Leon. (1961). *North of Slavery: The Negro in the Free States, 1790–1860*. Chicago: University of Chicago Press.

———. (1979). *Been in the Storm So Long: The Aftermath of Slavery*. New York: Knopf.

———. (1998). *Trouble in Mind: Black Southerners in the Age of Jim Crow*. New York: Knopf.

Litwack, Leon, and Meier, August. (Eds.). (1988). *Black Leaders of the Nineteenth Century*. Chicago: University of Illinois Press.

Lloyd, Genevieve. (1984). *The Man of Reason: "Male" and "Female" in Western Philosophy*. Minneapolis, MN: University of Minnesota.

Lloyd, Sheila Renee. (1999). "Plots on an Alternative Map: Emplotments of Pan-Africanism in the Writings of W.E.B. Du Bois, Langston Hughes, and Alice Walker." Ph.D. dissertation, Cornell University, Ithaca.

Locke, Alain L. (Ed.). (1968). *The New Negro*. New York: Antheneum.

———. (1983a). "The New Negro." In Leonard Harris (Ed.), *Philosophy Born of Struggle: An Anthology of Afro-American Philosophy from 1917* (pp. 242–51). Dubuque, IA: Kendall/Hunt.

———. (1983b). *The Critical Temper of Alain Locke: A Selection of His Essay on Art and Culture* (Jeffrey C. Stewart, Ed.). New York: Garland Publishing.

———. (1989). *The Philosophy of Alain Locke: Harlem Renaissance and Beyond* (Leonard Harris, Ed.). Philadelphia: Temple University Press.

———. (1992). *Race Contacts and Interracial Relations: Lectures on the Theory and Practice of Race* (Jeffrey C. Stewart, Ed.). Washington, D.C.: Howard University Press.

Loewberg, Bert James, and Bogin, Ruth. (Eds.). (1976). *Black Women in Nineteenth Century American Life: Their Words, Their Thoughts, Their Feelings*. University Park, PA: Pennsylvania State University Press.

Logan, Rayford W. (1940). *The Attitude of the Southern White Press Toward Negro Suffrage, 1932–1940*. Washington, D.C.: Howard University Press.

———. (Ed.). (1944). *What the Negro Wants*. Chapel Hill, NC: University of North Carolina Press.

———. (1954). *The Negro in American Life and Thought: The Nadir, 1877–1901*. New York: Dail Press.

———. (1967). *The American Negro: Old World Background and New World Experience*. Boston: Houghton-Mifflin.

———. (1965). *The Betrayal of the Negro: From Rutherford B. Hayes to Woodrow Wilson*. New York: Collier.

———. (Ed.). (1971). *W.E.B. Du Bois: A Profile*. New York: Hill & Wang.

Loomba, Ania. (1998). *Colonialism/Postcolonialism*. New York: Routledge.

Lopez, Ian F.H. (1995). "The Social Construction of Race." In Delgado (Ed.), *Critical Race Theory* (pp. 191–203). Philadelphia: Temple University Press.

———. (1996). *White by Law: The Legal Construction of Race.* New York: New York University Press.

Lorde, Audre. (1984). *Sister Outsider: Essays and Speeches by Audre Lorde.* Freedom, CA: The Crossing Press Feminist Series.

———. (1988). *A Burst of Light: Essays by Audre Lorde.* Ithaca, NY: Firebrand.

———. (1996). *The Audre Lorde Compendium: Essays, Speeches, and Journals.* London: Pandora.

———. (2004). *Conversations with Audre Lorde* (Joan Wylie Hall, Ed.). Jackson: University Press of Mississippi.

Lott, Tommy L. (1997). "Du Bois on the Invention of Race." In John P. Pittman (Ed.), *African American Perspectives and Philosophical Traditions* (pp. 166–87). New York: Routledge.

———. (Ed.). (1998). *Subjugation and Bondage: Critical Essays on Slavery and Social Philosophy.* Lanham, MD: Rowman and Littlefield.

———. (1999). *The Invention of Race: Black Culture and the Politics of Representation.* Malden: Blackwell.

———. (2000). "Du Bois and Locke on the Scientific Study of the Negro." *Boundary 2* 27 (3), 135–52.

———. (2001). "Du Bois's Anthropological Notion of Race." In Robert Bernasconi (Ed.), *Race* (pp. 59–83). Malden: Blackwell.

———. (Ed). (2002). *African American Philosophy: Selected Readings.* Upper Saddle River, NJ: Prentice Hall.

Lott, Tommy L., and Pittman, John P. (Eds.). (2003). *A Companion to African American Philosophy.* Malden: Blackwell.

Lovell, Terry. (1996). "Feminist Social Theory." In Barry S. Turner (Ed.). (1996). *The Blackwell Companion to Social Theory* (pp. 307–39). Malden: Blackwell.

Lucal, Betsy. (1996). "Race, Class, and Gender in the Work of W.E.B. Du Bois: An Exploratory Study." *Research in Race & Ethnic Relations* 9, 191–210.

Luke, Carmen. (Eds.). (1996). *Feminisms and Pedagogies of Everyday Life.* Albany, NY: State University of New York Press.

Luke, Carmen, and Gore, Jennifer. (Eds.). (1992). *Feminisms and Critical Pedagogy.* New York: Routledge.

Lumumba, Chokwe, Obadele, Imari A., and Tafia, Nkechi. (1993). *Reparations Yes!: The Legal and Political Reasons Why New Afrikans—Black People in the United States—Should Be Paid for Enslavement of Our Ancestors and for War Against Us After Slavery* (3rd Edition). Baton Rouge, LA: House of Songhay.

Lyotard, Jean-Francois. (1984). *The Postmodern Condition.* Minneapolis: University of Minnesota Press.

Macey, David. (2000). *Frantz Fanon: A Biography.* New York: Picador.

MacMullan, Terrance A. (2002). "Dewey and Du Bois: The Meaning of Race and Whiteness." Ph.D. dissertation, University of Oregon.

Magnus, Bernard, and Cullenberg, Stephen. (Eds.). (1995). *Whither Marxism?: Global Crises in International Perspective.* New York: Routledge.

Magubane, Bernard Makhosezwe. (1987). *The Ties that Bind: African American Consciousness of Africa.* Trenton, NJ: African World Press.

Makang, Jean-Marie. (1993). "The Problem of Democratic Inclusion in the Light of the Racial Question: W.E.B. Du Bois and the Emancipation of Democracy." Ph.D. dissertation, Boston College.

Makoni, Sinfree. (Ed.). (2003). *Black Linguistics: Language, Society, and Politics in Africa and the Americas.* New York: Routledge.

Mansbridge, Jane J., and Okin, Susan Mollier. (1993). "Feminism." In Robert E. Goodin, and Philip Pettit (Eds.), *A Companion to Contemporary Political Philosophy* (pp. 269–90). Malden: Blackwell.

Marable, Manning. (1982). "Alain Locke, W.E.B. Du Bois, and the Crisis of Black Education During the Great Depression." In Russell J. Linnemann (Ed.), *Alain Locke: Reflections on a Modern Renaissance Man* (pp. 63–76). Baton Rouge, LA: Louisiana State University.

———. (1983). *How Capitalism Underdeveloped Black America.* Boston: South End.

———. (1983/84). "Peace and Black Liberation: The Contributions of W.E.B. Du Bois." *Science & Society* 47, 385–405.

———. (1985a). *Black American Politics: From the Washington Marches to Jesse Jackson.* London: Verso.

———. (1985b). "The Black Faith of W.E.B. Du Bois: Sociocultural and Political Dimensions of Black Religion." *Southern Quarterly* 23 (Spring), 15–33.

———. (1985c). "W.E.B. Du Bois and the Struggle Against Racism." *Black Scholar* 16 (May-June), 43–44, 46–47.

———. (1986). *W.E.B. Du Bois: Black Radical Democrat.* Boston: Twayne.

———. (1987). *African and Carribean Politics: From Kwame Nkrumah to Maurice Bishop.* London and New York: Verso.

———. (1991). *Race, Reform, and Rebellion: The Second Reconstruction in Black America, 1945–1990.* Jackson, MS: University Press of Mississippi.

———. (1992). *The Crisis of Color and Democracy: Essays on Race, Class and Power.* Monroe, ME: Common Courage Press.

———. (1993). *Blackwater: Historical Studies in Race, Class Consciousness, and Revolution.* Niwot, CO: University Press of Colorado.

———. (1995). *Beyond Black and White: Transforming African American Politics.* New York and London: Verso.

———. (1996). *Speaking Truth to Power: Essays on Race, Resistance and Radicalism.* Boulder, CO: Westview.

———. (1997). *Black Liberation in Conservative America.* Boston: South End.

———. (1998). *Black Leadership.* New York: Columbia University Press.

———. (Ed.). (2000). *Dispatches from the Ebony Towers: Intellectuals Confront the African American Experience.* New York: Columbia University Press.

———. (2002). *The Great Wells of Democracy: The Meaning of Race in American Life.* New York: Basic/Civitas.

———. (Ed). (2005). *The New Black Renaissance: The Souls Anthology of Critical African American Studies.* Boulder, CO: Paradigm Publishers.

———. (2006). *Living Black History: How Re-Imagining the African American Past Can Remake America's Racial Future.* New York: Basic/Civitas.

Marable, Manning and Mullings, Leith. (Eds.). (2000). *Let Nobody Turn Us Around: Voices of Resistance, Reform, and Renewal—An African American Anthology.* Lanham, MD: Rowman and Littlefield.

Marcus, Judith, and Tar, Zoltan. (Eds.). (1984). *The Foundations of the Frankfurt School of Social Research.* New York: Transaction Books.

Marcuse, Herbert. (1958). *Soviet Marxism.* New York: Columbia University Press.

———. (1960). *Reason and Revolution.* Boston: Beacon.

———. (1964). *One-Dimensional Man: Studies in the Ideology of Advanced Industrial Society.* Boston: Beacon.

———. (1965a). "Socialism in the Developed Countries." *International Socialist Journal* 2 (8), 139–51.

———. (1965b). "Socialist Humanism?" In Erich Fromm (Ed.), *Socialist Humanism* (pp. 107–17). New York: Doubleday.

———. (1965c). "Repressive Tolerance." In Robert Paul Wolff, Barrington Moore, Jr., and Herbert Marcuse, *A Critique of Pure Tolerance* (pp. 81–118). Boston: Beacon.

———. (1966). *Eros and Civilization.* Boston: Beacon.

———. (1967). "The Obsolescence of Marxism." In Nikolaus Lobkowicz (Ed.), *Marxism in the Western World* (pp. 409–417). Notre Dame: University of Notre Dame Press.

———. (1968). *Negations: Essays in Critical Theory.* Boston: Beacon.

———. (1969). *An Essay on Liberation.* Boston: Beacon.

———. (1970a). *Five Lectures: Psychoanalysis, Politics, and Utopia.* Boston: Beacon.

———. (1970b). "Marxism and the New Humanity: An Unfinished Revolution." In John C. Raines and Thomas Dean (Eds.), *Marxism and Radical Religion: Essays Toward a Revolutionary Humanism* (pp. 3–10). Philadelphia: Temple University Press.

———. (1971). "Dear Angela." *Ramparts* 9, 22.

———. (1972a). *Counter-Revolution and Revolt.* Boston: Beacon.

———. (1972b). *From Luther to Popper.* London: Verso.

———. (1973). *Studies in Critical Philosophy.* Boston: Beacon.

———. (1974). "Marxism and Feminism." *Women's Studies* 2 (3), 279–88.

———. (1976a). "On the Problem of the Dialectic" (Part 1). *Telos* 27, 12–24.

———. (1976b). "On the Problem of the Dialectic" (Part 2). *Telos* 27, 12–39.

———. (1978a). *The Aesthetic Dimension: Toward a Critique of Marxist Aesthetics.* Beacon: Boston.

———. (1978b). "BBC Interview: Marcuse and the Frankfurt School." In Bryan Magee (Ed.), *Man of Ideas* (pp. 62–73). London: BBC Publishing.

———. (1978c). "Theory and Politics: A Discussion." *Telos* 38, 124–53.

———. (1979a). "The Reification of the Proletariat." *Canadian Journal of Philosophy and Social Theory* 3 (1), 20–23.

———. (1979b). "The Failure of the New Left?" *New German Critique* 18, 3–11.

———. (1997a). *Technology, War and Fascism: The Collected Papers of Herbert Marcuse* (Volume 1, Douglas Kellner, Ed.). New York: Routledge.

———. (1997b). "A Note on Dialectic." In Andrew Arato and Eike Gebhardt (Eds.), *The Essential Frankfurt School Reader* (pp. 444–51). New York: Continuum.

———. (2001). *Towards a Critical Theory of Society: The Collected Papers of Herbert Marcuse* (Volume 2, Douglas Kellner, Ed.). New York: Routledge.

———. (2004). *The New Left and the 1960's: The Collected Papers of Herbert Marcuse* (Volume 3, Douglass Kellner, Ed.). New York: Routledge.

———. (2005). *Heideggerian Marxism.* (Richard Wolin and John Abromeit, Eds.). Lincoln: University of Nebraska Press.

———. (2007a). *Art and Liberation: The Collected Papers of Herbert Marcuse* (Volume 4, Douglass Kellner, Ed.). New York: Routledge.

———. (2007b). *The Essential Marcuse: Selected Writings of Philosopher and Social Critic Herbert Marcuse* (Andrew Feenberg and William Leiss, Eds.). Boston: Beacon.

Marsh, James L. (1995). *Critique, Action, and Liberation.* Albany, NY: State University of New York Press.

———. (1998). *Post-Cartesian Meditations.* New York: Fordham University Press.

———. (1999). *Process, Praxis, and Transcendence.* Albany, NY: State University of New York Press.

———. (2001). "Toward a New Critical Theory." In William S. Wilkerson and Jeffrey Paris (Eds.), *New Critical Theory: Essays on Liberation* (pp. 49–64). Lanham, MD: Rowman and Littlefield.

Marsh-Lockett, Carol P. (1997). "Womanism." In William L. Andrews, Frances Smith Foster, and Trudier Harris (Eds.), *The Oxford Companion to African American Literature* (pp. 784–85). New York: Oxford University Press.

Marshall, Jessica. (1994). " 'Counsels of Despair': W.E.B. Du Bois, Robert E. Park, and the Establishment of American Race Sociology." Ph.D. dissertation, Harvard University.

Martin, Gloria. (1986). *Socialist Feminism: The First Decade, 1966–1976.* Seattle, WA: Freedom Socialist Publications.

Martin, Michael T, and Yaquinto, Marilyn. (Eds.). (2007). *Redress for Historical Injustices in the United States: On Reparations for Slavery, Jim Crow, and Their Legacies.* Durham, NC: Duke University Press.

Martin, Michael, and Yeakey, Lamont. (1982). "Pan-African and Asian Solidarity: A Central Theme in W.E.B. Du Bois's Conception of Racial Stratification and Struggle on a World Scale." *Phylon* 43, 202–17.

Martin, Waldo E., Jr. (1984). *The Mind of Frederick Douglass.* Chapell Hill, NC: University of North Carolina Press.

———. (1990). "Images of Frederick Douglass in the Afro-American Mind: The Recent Black Freedom Struggle." In Eric J. Sundquist (Ed.), *Frederick Douglass: New Literary and Historical Essays* (pp. 271–86). New York: Cambridge University Press.

———. (2005). *No Coward Soldiers: Black Cultural Politics in Post-War America.* Cambridge: Harvard University Press.

Marx, Anthony W. (1998). *Making Race and Nation: A Comparison of the United States, South Africa, and Brazil.* New York: Cambridge University Press.

Marx, Karl. (1964). *Early Writings* (Tom B. Bottomore, Ed.). New York: McGraw-Hill.

——. (1968). *Karl Marx on Colonialism and Modernization: His Dispatches and Other Writings on China, India, Mexico, the Middle East and North Africa* (Shlomo Avineri, Ed.). Garden City, NY: Doubleday.

——. (1971). *Early Texts* (David McLellan, Ed.). New York: Barnes & Nobles.

——. (1974). *Karl Marx on Religion* (Saul Padover, Ed.). New York: McGraw-Hill.

——. (1975). *Karl Marx: Texts on Method* (Terrell Carver, Ed.). New York: Barnes & Nobles.

——. (1976a). *Political Writings, Volume 1: The Revolution of 1848* (David Fernbach, Ed.). New York: Random House.

——. (1976b). *Political Writings, Volume 2: Surveys from Exile* (David Fernbach, Ed.). New York: Random House.

——. (1976c). *Political Writings, Volume 3: The First International and After* (David Fernbach, Ed.). New York: Random House.

——. (1984). *Karl Marx: Selected Writings in Sociology and Social Philosophy* (Tom Bottomore and Maximilien Rubel, Eds.). New York: McGraw-Hill.

——. (1994). *Marx: Early Political Writings* (Joseph O'Malley, Ed.). New York: Cambridge University Press.

——. (1996). *Marx: Later Political Writings* (Terrell Carver, Ed.). New York: Cambridge University Press.

——. (2002). *Marx on Religion* (John Raines, Ed.). Philadelphia: Temple University Press.

Marx, Karl, and Engels, Friedrich. (1964). *On Religion.* New York: Schocken.

——. (1972). *On Colonialism.* New York: International.

——. (1978). *The Marx-Engels Reader* (2nd Edition, Robert C. Tucker, Ed.). New York: Norton.

——. (1989). *Marx & Engels: The Basic Writings on Politics and Philosophy* (Lewis S. Feuer, Ed.). New York: Anchor.

——. (2008). *Karl Marx and Friedrich Engels on Religion.* Mineola, NY: Dover.

Massey, Douglas S., and Denton, Nancy A. (1993). *American Apartheid: Segregation and the Making of the Underclass.* Cambridge: Harvard University Press.

Massiah, Louis. (Director). (1995). *W.E.B. Du Bois: A Biography in Four Voices* [Documentary]. San Francisco: California Newsreel.

Masolo, Dismas A. (1994). *African Philosophy in Search of Identity.* Indianapolis: Indiana University Press.

Matsuda, Mari. (1995). "Looking to the Bottom: Critical Legal Studies and Reparations." In Kimberle Crenshaw, Neil Gotanda, Gary Peller, and Kendall Thomas (Eds.), *Critical Race Theory: The Key Writings That Formed the Movement* (pp. 63–79). New York: New Press.

Matustik, Martin J. Beck. (1998). *Specters of Liberation: Great Refusals in the New World Order.* Albany, NY: State University of New York Press.

Mawasha, Abram L. (1982). *Language in Black Education: The Politics of Language in a Multi-lingual Situation.* Pietersburg: University of the North Press.

Mazrui, Ali A. (1967). *Towards a Pax Africana: A Study of Ideology and Ambition.* Chicago: University of Chicago Press.

———. (1974). *World Culture and the Black Experience.* Seattle: University of Washington Press.

———. (1975). *The Political Sociology of the English Language: An African Perspective.* The Hague: Mouton.

———. (1978). *Political Values and the Educated Class in Africa.* Berkeley: University of California Press.

———. (1980). *The African Condition: A Political Diagnosis.* New York: Cambridge University Press.

———. (1986). *The Africans: A Triple Heritage.* Boston: Little Brown.

———. (1993). *Africa since 1935.* Berkeley: University of California Press.

———. (1998). *The Power of Babel: Language and Governance in the African Experience.* Chicago: University of Chicago Press.

———. (2002a). *Black Reparations in the Era of Globalization*: Binghamton, NY: Institute of Global Culture Publications, Binghamton University.

———. (2002b). *Africa and Other Civilizations: Conquest and Counter-Conquest.* Trenton, NJ: Africa World Press.

———. (2002c). *Africanity Re-defined.* Trenton, NJ: Africa World Press.

———. (2004). *Power, Politics, and the African Condition.* Trenton, NJ: Africa World Press.

Mazrui, Ali A., Okpewho, Isidore, and Davies, Carole Boyce. (Eds.). (1999). *The African Diaspora: African Origins and New World Identites.* Bloomington: Indiana University Press.

Mbiti, John S. (1975). *Introduction to African Religion.* London: Heinemann.

———. (1989). *African Religions and Philosophy.* London: Heinemann.

McCarthy, Thomas. (1991). *Ideal and Illusion: On Reconstruction and Deconstruction in Contemporary Critical Theory.* Cambridge: MIT Press.

McCarthy, Thomas, and Hoy, David Couzens. (1994). *Critical Theory.* Cambridge: Blackwell.

McCartney, John T. (1992). *Black Power Ideologies: An Essay in African American Political Thought.* Philadelphia: Temple University Press.

McClintock, Anne. (1992). "The Angel of Progress: Pitfalls of the Term 'Postcolonial'." *Social Text* 31/32, 84–98.

———. (1995). *Imperial Leather: Race, Gender, and Sexuality in the Colonial Context.* New York: Routledge.

McCollester, Charles. (1973). "The Political Thought of Amilcar Cabral." *Monthly Review* (March), 10–21.

McCulloch, Jock. (1983). *In the Twilight of Revolution: The Political Theory of Amilcar Cabral.* London and Boston: Routledge and Kegan Paul.

McDaniel, Antonio. (1998). "*The Philadelphia Negro*, Then and Now: Implications for Empirical Research." In Michael B. Katz and Thomas J. Sugrue (Eds.), *W.E.B. Du Bois, Race, and the City: The Philadelphia Negro and Its Legacy* (pp. 155–94). Philadelphia: University of Pennsylvania Press.

McFeely, William S. (1991). *Frederick Douglass.* New York: Norton.

McGary, Howard, and Bill Lawson. (1992). *Between Slavery and Freedom: Philosophy and American Slavery.* Indianapolis: Indiana University Press.

McGary, Howard. (1974). "Reparations and Inverse Discrimination." *Dialogue* 17 (1), 4–17.

———. (1977-78). "Justice and Reparations." *Philosophical Forum* 9 (2-3), 250–63.

———. (1984). "Reparations, Self-Respect, and Public Policy." *The Journal* 1, 15–26.

———. (1986). "Morality and Collective Liability." *Journal of Value Inquiry* 20, 157–65.

———. (1999). *Race and Social Justice*. Malden, MA: Blackwell.

McGee, B.R. (1998). "Speaking About the Other: W.E.B. Du Bois Responds to the Klan." *Communications Abstracts* 21, 6.

McGill, Ralph. (1965). "W.E.B. Du Bois." *Atlantic Monthly* (November), 78–81.

McGovern, Arthur. (1989). *Liberation Theology and Its Critics: Toward an Assessment*. Maryknoll, NY: Orbis.

McGuire, Robert Grayson, III. (1974). "Continuity in Black Political Protest: The Thought of Booker T. Washington, W.E.B. Du Bois, Marcus Garvey, Joseph B. Danquah, and Kwame Nkrumah." Ph.D. dissertation, Columbia University, New York.

McKay, Nellie Y. (1985). "W.E.B. Du Bois: The Black Woman in His Writings — Selected Fictional and Autobiographical Portraits." In William L. Andrews (Ed.), *Critical Essays on W.E.B. Du Bois* (pp. 230–52). Boston: G.K. Hall.

———. (1990). "The Souls of Black Women Folk in the Writings of W.E.B. Du Bois." In Henry Louis Gates, Jr. (Ed.), *Reading Black/Reading Feminist: A Critical Anthology* (pp. 227–43). New York: Meridian.

McLaren, Peter. (1995). *Critical Pedagogy and Predatory Culture*. New York: Routledge.

———. (1997). *Revolutionary Multiculturalism: Pedagogies of Dissent for the New Millennium*. Boulder, CO: Westview.

———. (1998). "The Pedagogy of Che Guevara: Critical Pedagogy and Globalization Thirty Years After Che." *Cultural Circles* 3, 28–103.

———. (1999a). *School as Ritual Performance*. Boulder, CO: Rowman and Littlefield.

———. (1999b). "Revolutionary Leadership and Pedagogical Praxis: Revisiting the Legacy of Che Guevara." *International Journal of Leadership in Education* 2 (3), 269–92.

———. (2000a). *Che Guevara, Paulo Freire, and the Pedagogy of Revolution*. Lanham, MD: Rowman and Littlefield.

———. (2000b). "Paulo Freire's Pedagogy of Possibility." In Peter McLaren, Robert Bahruth, Stan Steiner, and Mark Krank (Eds.), *Freirean Pedagogy, Praxis, and Possibilities: Projects for the New Millennium* (pp. 1–22). New York: Falmer Press.

———. (2002). *Life in Schools: An Introduction to Critical Pedagogy in the Foundations of Education*. New York: Longman.

———. (2005a). *Capitalists and Conquerors: A Critical Pedagogy Against Empire*. Boulder, CO: Rowman and Littlefield.

———. (2005b). *Red Seminars: Radical Excursions into Educational Theory, Cultural Politics, and Pedagogy*. Cresskill, NJ: Hampton Press.

———. (2006). *Rage and Hope: Interviews with Peter McLaren on War, Imperialism, and Critical Pedagogy*. New York: Peter Lang.

McLaren, Peter, Bahruth, Robert, Steiner, Stan, and Krank, Mark. (Eds.). (2000). *Freirean Pedagogy, Praxis, and Possibilities: Projects for the New Millennium.* New York: Falmer Press.

McLaren, Peter, and Farahmandur, Ramin. (2005). *Teaching Against Global Capitalism and the New Imperialism: A Critical Pedagogy.* Boulder, CO: Rowman and Littlefield.

McLaren, Peter, Fischman, Gustavo, Sunker, Heinz, and Lankshear, Colin. (Eds). (2005). *Critical Theories, Radical Pedagogies, and Global Conflicts.* Lanham, MD: Rowman and Littlefield.

McLaren, Peter, and Giarelli, Jim. (Eds.). (1995). *Critical Theory and Educational Research.* Albany, NY: State University of New York Press.

McLaren, Peter, Hill, Dave, Cole, Mike, and Rikowski, Glenn. (2002). *Marxism Against Postmodernism in Educational Theory.* Lanham, MD: Lexington Books.

McLaren, Peter, and Kincheloe, Joe L. (Eds.). (2007). *Critical Pedagogies: Where Are We Now?* New York: Peter Lang.

McLaren, Peter, and Lankshear, Colin. (Eds.). (1994). *Politics of Liberation: Paths from Freire.* New York: Routledge.

McLaren, Peter, and Leonard, Peter. (Eds.). (1993). *Paulo Freire: A Critical Encounter.* New York: Routledge.

McLaren, Peter, and Sleeter, Christine. (Eds.). *Multiculturalism Education, Critical Pedagogy, and the Politics of Difference.* Albany, NY: State University of New York Press.

McMurry, Linda O. (1998). *To Keep the Waters Troubled: The Life of Ida B. Wells.* New York: Oxford University Press.

McNann, Carole, and Kim, Seung-Kyung. (Eds.). (2002). *Feminist Theory Reader: Local and Global Perspectives.* New York: Routledge.

McPhail, Mark L. (2002). *The Rhetoric of Racism Revisited: Reparations or Separation?* Lanham, MD: Rowman and Littlefield.

Meade, Homer Lee, II. (1987). "W.E.B. Du Bois and His Place in the Discussion of Racism." Ph.D. dissertation, University of Massachusetts.

Meehan, Johanna. (Ed.). (1995). *Feminists Read Habermas: Gendering the Subject of Discourse.* New York: Routledge.

Meeks, Brian. (1993). *Caribbean Revolutions and Revolutionary Theory: An Assessment of Cuba, Nicaragua, and Grenada.* London: Macmillan.

———. (1996). *Radical Caribbean: From Black Power to Abu Bakar.* Kingston, Jamaica: University of West Indies Press.

———. (2000). *Narratives of Resistances: Jamaica, Trinidad and the Caribbean.* Kingston, Jamaica: University of West Indies Press.

Meeks, Brian, and Lindahl, Folke. (Eds.). (2001). *New Caribbean Thought: A Reader.* Kingston, Jamaica: University of West Indies Press.

Meier, August. (1954). "Booker T. Washington and the Rise of the NAACP." *Crisis* 60 (February).

———. (1959). "From 'Conservative' to 'Radical': The Ideological Development of W.E.B. Du Bois, 1885-1905." *Crisis* 75 (February), 527–36.

———. (1963). *Negro Thought in America, 1880-1915: Racial Ideologies in the Age of Booker T. Washington.* Ann Arbor: University of Michigan Press.

———. (1969). *The Making of Black America: Essays in Negro Life and History*. New York: Atheneum.

———. (1976). *From Plantation to Ghetto: An Interpretive History of American Negroes*. New York: Hill and Wang.

Meier, August, and Bracey, John H. (1993). "The NAACP as a Reform Movement, 1909–1965: "To Reach the Conscience of America." *Journal of Southern History* 59 (1), 3–30.

Meier, August, and Rudwick, Elliott. (1976). *Along the Color-Line: Explorations in the Black Experience*. Urbana: University of Illinois Press.

———. (Eds.). (1986). *Black History and the Historical Profession, 1915–1980*. Urbana: University of Illinois Press.

Mendelssohn, Sidney. (1920). *The Jews of Africa, Especially in the Sixteenth and Seventeenth Centuries*. New York: Dutton.

Mendieta, Eduardo. (Ed.). (2003). *Latin American Philosophy: Currents, Issues, Debates*. Bloomington: Indiana University Press.

———. (Ed.). (2005). *The Frankfurt School on Religion: Key Writings by the Major Thinkers*. New York: Routledge.

———. (2007). *Global Fragments: Globalizations, Latinamericanisms, and Crtiical Theory*. Albany, NY: State University of New York Press.

Mercer, Kobena. (1994). *Welcome to the Jungle: New Positions in Black Cultural Studies*. New York: Routledge.

Meulenbelt, Anja. (Ed.). (1984). *A Creative Tension: Explorations in Socialist Feminism*. London: Pluto Press.

Meyer, Arthur S. (1999). "W.E.B. Du Bois and the Open Forum: Human Relations in a 'Difficult Industrial District'." *Journal of Negro History* 84 (2), 192–212.

Meyers, Diana Tietjens. (Ed.). (1997). *Feminist Social Thought: A Reader*. New York: Routledge.

Mezu, S. Okechukwu, Mezu, Rose Ure, and Bell, Bernard W. (1999). *Black Nationalists: Reconsidering Du Bois, Garvey, Booker T. and Nkrumah*. Randallstown: Black Academy Press.

Michelson, Melissa R. (2002). "The Black Reparation Movement: Public Opinion and Congressional Policy Making." *Journal of Black Studies* 32 (5), 574–87.

Mielke, David Nathaniel. (1977). "W.E.B. Du Bois: An Educational Critique." Ph.D. dissertation, University of Tennessee, Knoxville.

Mignolo, Walter. (2005). *The Idea of Latin America*. Malden, MA: Blackwell.

———. (2003). *The Darker Side of the Renaissance: Literacy, Territoriality, and Colonization*. Ann Arbor: University of Michigan Press.

———. (2000). *Local Histories/Global Designs: Coloniality, Subaltern Knowledges, and Border Thinking*. Princeton: Princeton University Press.

Milbank, John. (1990). *Theology and Social Theory: Beyond Secular Reason*. Cambridge: Blackwell.

Miles, Kevin T. (2003). "'One Far Off Divine Event': 'Race' and a Future History in Du Bois." In Robert Bernasconi (Ed.) *Race and Racism in Continental Philosophy* (pp. 19–31). Bloomington, IN: Indiana University Press.

Miller, Jon, and Kumar, Rahul. (Eds.). (2007). *Reparations: Interdisciplinary Inquiries*. New York: Oxford.

Miller, Robert J. (2006). *Native America, Discovered and Conquered: Thomas Jefferson, Lewis & Clark, and Manifest Destiny.* Westport, CT: Praeger.

Miller, Sally M. (Ed.). (1981). *Flawed Liberation: Socialism and Feminism.* Westport, CT: Greenwood.

Milligan, Nancy Muller. (1985). "W.E.B. Du Bois's American Pragmatism." *Journal of American Culture* 8 (2), 31–37.

Mills, Charles W. (1987). "Race and Class: Conflicting or Reconcilable Paradigms?" *Social and Economic Studies* 36 (2), 69–108.

———. (1997). *The Racial Contract.* Ithaca: Cornell University Press.

———. (1998). *Blackness Visible: Essays on Philosophy and Race.* Ithaca: Cornell University Press.

———. (1999). "The Racial Polity." In Susan E. Babbitt and Sue Campbell (Eds.), *Racism and Philosophy* (pp. 13–31, [endnotes] 255–57). Ithaca: Cornel University Press.

———. (2000). "Race and the Social Contract Tradition." *Social Identities: A Journal for the Study of Race, Nation and Culture* 6 (4), 441–62.

———. (2001). "White Supremacy and Racial Justice." In James Sterba (Ed.), *Social and Political Philosophy: Contemporary Perspectives* (pp. 321–37). New York: Routledge.

———. (2003). *From Class to Race: Essays in White Marxism and Black Radicalism.* Lanham, MD: Rowman and Littlefield.

Mills, Patricia. (1987). *Women, Nature and Psyche.* New Haven: Yale University Press.

Mishra, V. and Hodge, B. (1991). "What is Post(-)colonialism?" *Textual Practice* 5 (3), 399–415.

Mitchell, Ella Pearson. (1993). "Du Bois's Dilemma and African American Adaptiveness." In Gerald Early (Ed.), *Lure and Loathing: Essays on Race, Identity, and the Ambivalence of Assimilation* (pp. 264–73). New York: Viking/Penguin.

Mitchell, Henry H. (1975). *Black Belief: Folk Beliefs of Blacks in America and West Africa.* New York: Harper and Row.

———. (2004). *Black Church Beginnings: The Long-Hidden Realities of the First Years.* Grand Rapids, MI: Eerdmans.

Mitchem, Stephanie Y. (2002). *Introducing Womanist Theology.* Maryknoll, NY: Orbis.

Mixon, Gregory. (2005). *The Atlanta Riot: Race, Class, and Violence in a New South City.* Gainsville, FL: University Press of Florida.

Mizruchi, Susan. (1996). "Neighbors, Strangers, and Corpses: Death and Sympathy in the Early Writings of W.E.B. Du Bois." In Robert Newman (Ed.), *Centuries' Ends, Narrative Means.* Stanford: Stanford University Press.

Mohanty, Chandra Talpade. (1991). *Third World Women and the Politics of Feminism.* Bloomington, IN: Indiana University Press.

———. (2003). *Feminism Without Borders: Decolonizing Theory, Praticing Solidarity.* Durham, NC: Duke University Press.

Monteiro, Anthony. (2000). "Being an African in the World: The Du Boisian Epistemology." *Annals of the American Academy of Political and Social Science* 568 (March), 220–34.

———. (1994). "The Scientific and Revolutionary Legacy of W.E.B. Du Bois." *Political Affairs* 73 (2), 1–19.

Moon, Henry Lee. (1968). "The Leadership of W.E.B. Du Bois." *Crisis* 75, 51–57.

Moore, Jack B. (1981). *W.E.B. Du Bois*. Boston: Twayne.

Moore, Jacqueline M. (2003). *Booker T. Washington, W.E.B. Du Bois, and the Struggle for Racial Uplift*. Wilmington, DE: Scholarly Resources.

Moore, Percy L. (1996). "W.E.B. Du Bois: A Critical Study of His Philosophy of Education and its Relevance for Three Contemporary Issues in Education of Significance to African Americans." Ph.D. dissertation, Wayne State University.

Moore, Richard B. (1970). "Du Bois and Pan-Africa." In John Henrik Clarke, Esther Jackson, Ernest Kaiser, and J.H. O'Dell (Eds.), *Black Titan: W.E.B. Du Bois* (pp. 187–212). Boston: Beacon.

Moore-Gilbert, Bart. (1997). *Postcolonial Theory: Contexts, Practices, Politics*. London Verso.

Morrison, Hugh James. (2000). "The Evolution of a Reform Plan: W.E.B. Du Bois's Sociological Research, 1896–1910." Ph.D. dissertation, Queen's University at Kingston, Canada.

Morrison, Michael A. (1997). *Slavery and the American West: The Eclipse of Manifest Destiny and the Coming of the Civil War*. Chapel Hill, NC: University of North Carolina.

Morrison, Toni. (1990). *Playing in the Dark: Whiteness and the Literary Imagination*. Cambridge: Harvard University Press.

Morrow, Raymond A. (1994). *Critical Theory and Methodology* (with David D. Brown). Thousands Oaks, CA: Sage.

Morton, Patricia. (1991). *Disfigured Images: The Historical Assault on Afro-American Women*. New York: Praeger.

Moses, Wilson Jeremiah. (1975). "The Poetic of Ethiopianism: W.E.B. Du Bois and Literary Black Nationalism." *American Literature* 47 (November), 411–27.

———. (1978). *The Golden Age of Black Nationalism, 1850–1925*. New York: Oxford University Press.

———. (1990). "Sexual Anxieties of the Black Bourgeoisie in Victorian America: The Cultural Context of W.E.B. Du Bois's First Novel." In Wilson Jeremiah Moses, *The Wings of Ethiopia: Studies in African American Life and Letters*. Ames, IA: Iowa State University Press.

———. (1993a). "W.E.B. Du Bois's 'The Conservation of Races' and Its Context: Idealism, Conservatism, and Hero Worship." *Massachusetts Review* 34 (Summer), 275–94.

———. (1993b). " Du Bois's *Dark Princess* and the Heroic Uncle Tom." In Wilson Jeremiah Moses, *Black Messiahs and Uncle Toms: Social and Literary Manipulations of a Religious Myth*. University Park, PA: Pennsylvania State University Press.

———. (1996). "Culture, Civilization, and the Decline of the West: The Afrocentricism of W.E.B. Du Bois." In Bernard W. Bell, Emily R. Grosholz, and James B. Stewart (Eds.), *W.E.B. Du Bois: On Race and Culture* (pp. 243–60). New York: Routledge.

———. (1998). "W.E.B. Du Bois and Antimodernism." In Wilson Jeremiah Moses, *Afrotopia: The Roots of African American Popular History* (pp. 136–68). New York: Cambridge University Press.

———. (2004). *Creative Conflict in African American Thought: Frederick Douglass, Alexander Crummell, Booker T. Washington, W.E.B. Du Bois, and Marcus Garvey.* New York: Cambridge University Press.

Mosley, Albert. G. (Ed.). (1995). *African Philosophy: Selected Readings.* Englewood Cliffs, NJ: Prentice Hall.

———. (2003). "Affirmative Action As a Form of Reparation." *University of Memphis Law Review* 33 (2), 353–65.

Moss, Alfred A. (1981). *The American Negro Academy: Voice of the Talented Tenth.* Baton Rouge, LA: Louisiana State University Press.

Moss, Richard Lawrence. (1975). "Ethnographic Perspectives and Literary Strategies in the Early Writings of W.E.B. Du Bois." Ph.D. dissertation, State University of New York, Buffalo.

Mosse, George L. (1978). *Toward a Final Solution: A History of European Racism.* London: Dent & Sons.

Mostern, Kenneth. (1996). "Three Theories of the Race of W.E.B. Du Bois." *Cultural Critique* 34 (Fall), 27–63.

———. (2000). "Postcolonialism after W.E.B. Du Bois." *Rethinking Marxism* 12 (2), 61–80.

Moten, Fred. (2003). *In the Break: The Aesthetics of the Black Radical Tradition.* Minneapolis: University of Minnesota Press.

Mtima, Lateef. (1999). "African American Economic Empowerment Strategies for the New Millennium: Revisiting the Washington-Du Bois Dialectic. *Howard Law Journal* 42 (3), 391.

Mudimbe, V.Y. (1988). *The Invention of Africa: Gnosis, Philosophy, and the Order of Knowledge.* Indianapolis: Indiana University Press.

———. (1994). *The Idea of Africa.* Indianapolis: Indiana University Press.

Mullaney, Marie Marmo. (1983). *Revolutionary Women: Gender and the Socialist Revolutionary Role.* New York: Praeger.

Mullen, Bill V. (1999). *Popular Fronts: Chicago and African American Cultural Politics.* Urbana: University of Illinois Press.

———. (2004). *Afro-Orientalism.* Minneapolis: University of Minnesota Press.

Mullen, Bill V., and Smethurst, James. (Eds.). (2003). *Left of the Color-Line: Race, Radicalism, and Twentieth Century Literature of the United States.* Chapel Hill, NC: University of North Carolina Press.

Munford, Clarence J. (1996). *Race and Reparations: A Black Perspective for the Twenty-First Century.* Trenton, NJ: Africa World Press.

Murdock, Deroy. (2002). "Should the U.S. Pay Reparations for Slavery?" *Vital Speeches of the Day* 68 (16), 404–06.

Murphy, Joseph M. (1994). *Working the Spirit: Ceremonies of the African Diaspora.* Boston: Beacon.

Murphy, Larry, Melton, J. Gordon, and Ward, Gary L. (Eds.). (1993). *Encyclopedia of African American Religions.* New York: Garland.

Murray, Hugh. (1987). "Du Bois and the Cold War." *Journal of Ethnic Studies* 15 (3), 115–24.

Muse, Benjamin. (1968). *The Black Revolution: From Nonviolence to Black Power, 1963-1967.* Bloomington, IN: Indiana University Press.

Muzorewa, Gwinyai H. (1985). *The Origins and Development of African Theology.* Maryknoll, NY: Orbis.

Nagl-Docekal, Herta. (1998). "Modern Moral and Political Philosophy." In Alison M. Jaggar and Iris Marion Young (Eds.), *A Companion to Feminist Philosophy* (pp. 58–65). Malden, MA: Blackwell.

Naison, Mark. (1983). *Communists in Harlem During the Depression.* Urbana: University of Illinois Press.

Namasaka, Boaz Nalika. (1971). "William E. B. Du Bois and Thorstein Veblen: Intellectual Activists of Progressivism, A Comparative Study, 1900–1930." Ph.D. dissertation, Claremont Graduate School and University Center, Claremont, CA.

Neal, Larry. (1989). *Visions of a Liberated Future: Black Arts Movements Writings.* New York: Thunder's Mouth Press.

Neal, Terry Ray. (1984). "W.E.B. Du Bois's Contributions to the Sociology of Education." Ph.D. dissertation, University of Cincinnati.

Nealon, Jeffrey T., and Irr, Caren. (Eds.). (2002). *Rethinking the Frankfurt School: Alternative Legacies of Cultural Critique.* Albany, NY: State University of New York Press.

Nelsen, Hart M., and Nelsen, Anne K. (Eds.). (1975). *The Black Church in the Sixties.* Lexington, KY: University of Kentucky Press.

Nelsen, Hart M., Yokley, Raythat L., and Nelsen, Anne K. (Eds.). (1971). *The Black Church in America.* New York: Basic Books.

Nelson, Cary, and Grossberg, Lawrence. (Eds.). (1988). *Marxism and the Interpretation of Culture.* Chicago: University of Illinois Press.

Nelson, Truman. (1958). "W.E.B. Du Bois: Prophet in Limbo." *Nation* (January 25), 76–79.

———. (1970). "W.E.B. Du Bois as a Prophet." In John Henrik Clarke, Esther Jackson, Ernest Kaiser, and J.H. O'Dell (Eds.), *Black Titan: W.E.B. Du Bois* (pp. 138–51). Boston: Beacon.

Nesbitt, Francis Njubi. (2004). *Race for Sanctions: African Americans Against Apartheid, 1946–1994.* Bloomington: Indiana University Press.

Newman, Louise M. (1999). *White Women's Rights: The Racial Origins of Feminism in the United States.* New York: Oxford University Press.

Newsome, Elaine Mitchell. (1971). "W.E.B. Du Bois's 'Figure in the Carpet': A Cyclical Pattern in the Belletristic Prose." Ph.D. dissertation, University of North Carolina, Chapel Hill.

Neyland, James. (1992). *W.E.B. Du Bois.* Los Angeles, CA: Melrose Square Publishing.

Nicholson, Linda J. (Ed.). (1990). *Feminism/Postmodernism.* New York: Routledge.

Nickel, James W. (1973). "Should Reparations be to Groups or Individuals?" *Analysis* 34 (5), 37–51.

Nickson, Victor and Aiyetoro, Adjoa, Mataka, Laini. (2002). *Black Reparations: American Slavery & Its Vestiges.* Washington, D.C.: National Coalition of Blacks for Reparations in America.

Nikopoulos, Konstantina H. (2003). "W. E. B. Du Bois, Martin Luther King, Jr., and the FBI's Historic Abuse of the Civil Rights of Two Leaders of the Civil Rights Movement." M.A. thesis, University of Houston, Clear Lake.

Ngũgĩ wa Thiong'o. (1972). *Homecoming: Essays on African and Caribbean Literature, Culture, and Politics.* New York: Lawrence Hill.

———. (1983). *Barrel of a Pen: Resistance to Repression in Neocolonial Kenya.* Trenton, NJ: Africa World Press.

———. (1986). *Decolonizing the Mind: The Politics of Language in African Literature.* Portsmouth, NH: James Currey/ Heinemann.

———. (1993). *Moving the Center: The Struggle for Cultural Freedoms.* Portsmouth, NH: James Currey/Heinemann.

———. (1997). *Writers in Politics: A Re-Engagement with Issues of Literature and Society.* Portsmouth, NH: James Currey/EAEP/Heinemann.

Nkrumah, Kwame. (1962). *Towards Colonial Freedom.* London: Panaf Books.

———. (1964). *Consciencism: Philosophy and Ideology for Decolonization.* New York: Monthly Review Press.

———. (1965). *Neo-Colonialism: The Last Stage of Imperialism.* London: Panaf Books.

———. (1968). *The Handbook of Revolutionary Warfare.* New York: International.

———. (1970a). *Africa Must Unite.* New York: International.

———. (1970b). *Class Struggle in Africa.* New York: International.

———. (1973a). *Revolutionary Path.* London: Panaf Books.

———. (1973b). *The Struggle Continues.* London: Panaf Books.

Nnaemeka, Obioma. (Ed.). (1998). *Sisterhood, Feminisms, and Power: From Africa to the Diaspora.* Trenton, NJ: Africa World Press.

Noble, Jeanne. (1978). *Beautiful, Also, Are the Souls of My Black Sisters: A History of the Black Woman in America.* Englewood Cliffs, NJ: Prentice-Hall.

Nolen, Claude H. (1967). *The Negro's Image in the South: The Anatomy of White Supremacy.* Lexington, KY: University of Kentucky Press.

Nonini, Donald. (1992). "Du Bois and Radical Theory and Practice." *Critique of Anthropology* 12 (3), 292–318.

Norment, Nathaniel, Jr. (2007a). *An Introduction to African American Studies: The Discipline and Its Dimensions.* Durham, NC: Carolina Academic Press.

———. (Ed.). (2007b). *The African American Studies Reader.* Durham, NC: Carolina Academic Press.

Novick, Michael. (1995). *White Lies, White Power: The Fight Against White Supremacy and Reactionary Violence.* Monroe, ME: Common Courage Press.

Nozick, Robert. (1975). *Anarchy, State, Utopia.* New York: Basic Books.

———. (1997). "Distributive Justice." In Robert E. Goodin and Philip Pettit (Eds.), *Contemporary Political Philosophy: An Anthology* (pp. 203–46). Cambridge: Blackwell.

Nwankwo, Henry C. (1989). "The Educational Philosophy of W.E.B. Du Bois: A Nigerian Interpretation." Ph.D. dissertation, East Texas State University.

Nye, Andrea. (1988). *Feminist Theory and the Philosophies of Man.* New York: Croom Helm.

Nyerere, Julius Kambarage. (1966). *Freedom and Unity/Uhura na Umoja: A Selection From Writings and Speeches, 1952-1965.* New York: Oxford University Press.

———. (1968). *Freedom and Socialism/Uhuru na Ujamaa: A Selection from Writings and Speeches, 1965–1967.* New York: Oxford University Press.

———. (1973). *Freedom and Development/Uhuru na Maendeleo: A Selection from Writings and Speeches.* New York: Oxford University Press.

Oatts, Terry O'Neal. (2003). "W. E. B. Du Bois and Critical Race Theory: Toward a Du Boisian Philosophy of Education." Ed.D. dissertation, Georgia Southern University.

———. (2006). *W.E.B. Du Bois and Critical Race Theory: Toward a Du Boisian Philosophy of Education.* Sydney: Exceptional Publications.

Obadele, Imari A. (1975). *Foundations of the Black Nation.* Detroit: House of Songhay.

———. (1997). "An Act to Stimulate Economic Growth in the United States and Compensate, in Part, for the Grievous Wrongs of Slavery and the Unjust Enrichment Which Accrued to the United States Therefrom." In William Van Deburg (Ed.), *Modern Black Nationalism: From Marcus Garvey to Louis Farrakhan* (pp. 334–41). New York: New York University Press.

Obenga, Theophile. (1990). *Origine Commune de L'Egyptien Ancien, Du Copte et des Langues Negro-Africaines Modernes: Introduction a la Linguistique Historique Africaine.* Paris: LHarmattan.

———. (1992). *Ancient Egypt and Black Africa: A Handbook for the Study of Ancient Egypt in Philosophy, Linguistics and Gender Relations* (Amon Saba Saakana, Ed.). London: Karnak House.

———. (1993). *La Philodophie Africaine de la Periode Pharaonique, 2780–330 Avant Notre Ere.* Paris: L'Harmattan.

———. (1995). *A Lost Tradition: African Philosophy in World History.* Philadelphia, PA: Source Editions.

O'Dea, Thomas F. (1966). *The Sociology of Religion.* Englewood Cliffs, NJ: Prentice-Hall.

O'Dell, Jack H. (1970). "Du Bois and 'The Social Evolution of the Black South'." In John Henrik Clarke, Esther Jackson, Ernest Kaiser, and J.H. O'Dell (Eds.), *Black Titan: W.E.B. Du Bois* (pp. 152–63). Boston: Beacon.

Ofari, Earl. (1970). "W.E.B. Du Bois and Black Power." *Black World* 19 (August), 26–28.

Ogbar, Jeffrey O.G. (2004). *Black Power: Radical Politics and African American Identity.* Baltimore: Johns Hopkins University Press.

Ogletree, Charles. (2003). "Reparations for the Children of Slaves: Litigating the Issues." *University of Memphis Law Review* 33 (2), 245–64.

Ogunmodede, Francis I. (2001). *Of History and Historiography in African Philosophy.* Ibadan, Nigeria: Hope Publications.

———. (Ed.). (2004). *African Philosophy Down the Ages: 10, 000 B.C. to the Present.* Ibadan, Nigeria: Hope Publications.

Ohadike, Don C. (2007). *Sacred Drums of Liberation: Religions and Music of Resistance in Africa and Diaspora.* Trenton, NJ: Africa World Press.

Okediji, Moyo. (1998). "On Reparations Exodus and Embodiment." *African Arts* 31 (2), 8–10.

Okere, Theophilus. (1971). "Can There Be an African Philosophy?: A Heremeneutical Investigation with Special Reference to Igbo Culture." Ph.D. dissertation, Louvain University.

———. (1991). *African Philosophy: A Historico-Hermeneutical Investigation of the Conditions of Its Possibility*. Lanham, MD: University of America Press.

Okin, Susan Moller. (1992). *Women in Western Political Thought*. Princeton, NJ: Princeton University Press.

Okolo, Okondo. (1991). "Tradition and Destiny: Horizons of an African Philosophical Hermeneutics." In Tsenay Serequeberhan (Ed.), *African Philosophy: The Essential Readings* (pp. 201–11). New York: Paragon House.

Okoro, Martin Umachi. (1982). "W.E.B. Du Bois's Ideas on Education: Implications for Nigerian Education." Ph.D. dissertation, Loyola University of Chicago.

Okpewho, Isidore, Davies, Carole Boyce, and Mazrui, Ali. A. (Eds.). (1999). *The African Diaspora: African Origins and New World Identities*. Indianapolis: Indiana University Press.

Olaniyan, Tejumola. (1992). "Narrativing Postcoloniality: Responsibilities." *Public Culture* 5 (1), 47–55.

———. (2000). "Africa: Varied Colonial Legacies." In Henry Schwarz and Sangeeta Ray (Eds.), *A Companion to Postcolonial Studies* (pp. 269–81). Malden, MA: Blackwell.

Omi, Michael, and Winant, Howard. (1994). *Racial Formation in United States: From the 1960's to the 1990's*. New York: Routledge.

O'Neill, John. (Ed.). (1976). *On Critical Theory*. New York: Seabury Press.

Onyewuenyi, Innocent C. (1993). *The African Origin of Greek Philosophy: An Exercise in Afrocentricism*. Nsukka, Nigeria: University of Nigeria Press.

Osabu-Kle, Daniel Tetteh. (2000). "The African Reparation Cry: Rationale, Estimate, Prospects, and Strategies." *Journal of Black Studies* 30 (3), 331–50.

Ostrower, Gary B. (1979). *Collective Insecurity: The United States and the League of Nations During the Early Thirties*. Lewisburg, PA: Bucknell University Press.

Outlaw, Lucius. T., Jr. (1974). "Language and Consciousness: Foundations for a Hermeneutics of Black Culture." *Cultural Hermeneutics* 1 (February), 403–13.

———. (1983a). "Philosophy, Hermeneutics, Social-Political Theory: Critical Thought in the Interest of African American." In Leonard Harris (Ed.), *Philosophy Born of Struggle: An Anthology of Afro-American Philosophy from 1917* (pp. 60–88). Dubuque, IA: Kendall/Hunt.

———. (1983b). "Race and Class in the Theory and Practice of Emancipatory Social Transformation." In Leonard Harris (Ed.), *Philosophy Born of Struggle: An Anthology of Afro-American Philosophy from 1917* (pp. 117–29). Dubuque, IA: Kendall/Hunt.

———. (1983c). "Philosophy and Culture: Critical Hermeneutics and Social Transformation." In *Philosophy and Cultures: Proceedings of the 2nd Afro-Asian Philosophy Conference* (pp. 26–31). Nairobi, Kenya: Bookwise Limited.

———. (1983d). "Critical Theory in a Period of Radical Transformation." *Praxis International* 3 (2), 138–46.

——. (1987)."On Race and Class, or, On the Prospects of 'Rainbow Socialism'." In Marable, Manning, Mike Davis, Fred Pfeil, and Michael Sprinker (Eds.), *The Year Left 2: Toward a Rainbow Socialism—Essays on Race, Ethnicity, Class and Gender* (pp. 73–90). London: Verso.

——. (1990). "Toward a Critical Theory of 'Race'." In David Theo Goldberg (Ed.), *Anatomy of Racism* (pp. 58–82). Minneapolis: University of Minnesota Press.

——. (1992). "The Thought of W.E.B. Du Bois." *African Philosophy* 4 (1), 13–28.

——. (1995). "On W.E.B. Du Bois's 'The Conservation of Races'." In Linda A. Bell and David Blumenfeld (Eds.), *Overcoming Racism and Sexism* (pp. 79–102). Lanham, MD: Rowman and Littlefield.

——. (1996a). *On Race and Philosophy*. New York: Routledge.

——. (1996b). "'Conserve' Races?: In Defense of W.E.B. Du Bois." In Bernard W. Bell, Emily R. Grosholz, and James B. Stewart (Eds.), *W.E.B. Du Bois: On Race and Culture* (pp. 15–38). New York: Routledge.

——. (1997). "African, African American, Africana Philosophy." In John P. Pittman (Ed.), *African American Perspectives and Philosophical Traditions* (pp. 63–93). New York: Routledge.

——. (2000). "W.E.B. Du Bois on the Study of Social Problems." *Annals of the American Academy of Political and Social Science* 568 (March), 281–97.

——. (2001). "On Cornel West on W.E.B. Du Bois." In George Yancy (Ed.), *Cornel West: A Critical Reader*. Malden, MA: Blackwell.

——. (2005). *Critical Social Theory in the Interest of Black Folk*. Lanham, MD: Rowman and Littlefield.

Outwaite, William. (1987). *New Philosophies of Social Science: Realism, Hermeneutics, and Critical Theory*. New York: St. Martin's Press.

Owen, Chandler. (1973). "Du Bois on Revolution." In Theodore G. Vincent (Ed.), *Voices of a Black Nation: Political Journalism in the Harlem Renaissance* (pp. 88–92). Trenton, NJ: Africa World Press.

Packard, Jerrold M. (2003). *American Nightmare: The History of Jim Crow*. New York: St. Martin's Griffin.

Padmore, George. (1931). *The Life and Struggles of Negro Toilers*. London: R.I.L.U. Magazine.

——. (1936). *How Britain Rules Africa*. London: Wishart Books.

——. (1942). *The White Man's Duty: An Analysis of the Colonial Question in Light of the Atlantic Charter*. London: W.H. Allen.

——. (1945). *The Voice of Colored Labor*. Manchester: Panaf.

——. (1946). *How Russia Transformed Her Colonial Empire: A Challenge to the Imperialist Powers*. London: Dennis Dobson.

——. (1949). *Africa: Britain's Third Empire*. London: Dennis Dobson.

——. (1953). *The Gold Coast Revolution: The Struggle of an African People from Slavery to Freedom*. London: Dennis Dobson.

——. (1956). *Pan-Africanism or Communism?: The Coming Struggle for Africa*. London: Dennis Dobson.

——. (1972). *Africa and World Peace*. London: Cass.

Painter, Nell Irvin. (1993). "Sojourner Truth." In Darlene Clark Hine, Elsa Barkley Brown, and Rosalyn Teborg-Penn (Eds.), *Black Women in America: An Historical Encyclopedia* (Volume 2, pp. 1172–76). Brooklyn: Carlson.

———. (1996). *Sojourner Truth: A Life, A Symbol*. New York: Norton.

Parascandola, Louis J. (Ed.). (2005). *Look For Me All Around You: Anglophone Caribbean Immigrants in the Harlem Renaissance*. Detroit: Wayne State University.

Parker, Laurence, Deyhle, Donna, and Villenas, Sofia. (Eds.). (1999). *Race Is, Race Isn't: Critical Race Theory and Qualitative Studies in Education*. Boulder, CO: Westview.

Parry, Benita. (1987). "Problems in Current Theories of Colonial Discourse." *Oxford Literary Review* 9 (1), 2–12.

———. (2004). *Postcolonial Studies: A Materialist Critique*. New York: Routledge.

Paschal, Andrew G. (1971). "The Spirit of W.E.B. Du Bois." *Black Scholar* 20 (February), 38–50.

Pateman, Carole. (1988). *The Sexual Contract*. Stanford: Stanford University Press.

———. (1989). *The Disorder of Women: Democracy, Feminism, and Political Theory*. Stanford: Stanford University Press.

Pattillo-McCoy, Mary. (2000). *Black Picket Fences: Privilege and Peril Among the Black Middle Class*. Chicago: University of Chicago Press.

Pauley, Garth E. (2000). "W.E.B. Du Bois on Woman Suffrage: A Critical Analysis of His Crisis Writings." *Journal of Black Studies* 30 (3), 383–410.

Payne, James Chris, II. (1973). "A Content Analysis of Speeches and Written Documents of Six Black Spokesmen: Frederick Douglass, Booker T. Washington, Marcus Garvey, W.E.B. Du Bois, Martin Luther King, Jr. and Malcolm X." Ph.D. dissertation, Florida State University, Tallahassee.

Paynter, Robert. (1992). "W.E.B. Du Bois and the Material World of African Americans in Great Barrington, Massachusetts." *Critique of Anthropology* 12 (3), 277–91.

Pearsall, Marilyn. (Ed.). (1986). *Women and Values: Readings in Recent Feminist Philosophy*. Belmont, CA: Wadsworth.

Peebles-Wilkins, Wilma, and Aracelis, Fran. (1990). "Two Outstanding Women in Social Welfare History: Mary Church Terrell and Ida B. Wells." *Affilia* 5 (Winter), 87–95.

Peeks, Edward. (1971). *The Long Struggle for Black Power*. New York: Scribner.

Peller, Gary. (1995). "Race-Consciousness." In Kimberle Crenshaw, Neil Gotanda, Gary Peller, and Kendall Thomas (Eds.), *Critical Race Theory: The Key Writings That Formed the Movement* (pp. 127–58). New York: New Press.

Pensky, Max. (Ed.). (2005). *Globalizing Critical Theory*. Lanham, MD: Rowman and Littlefield.

Perez, Emma. (1999). *The Decolonial Imaginary: Writing Chicanas into History*. Bloomington, IN: Indiana University Press.

Perkins, James W. (2004). *White Theology: Outing Supremacy in Modernity*. New York: Palgrave Macmillan.

Perkins, Linda M. (1981). "Black Women and Racial 'Uplift' Prior to Emancipation." In Filomina Chioma Steady (Ed.), *The Black Woman Cross-Culturally* (pp. 314–17). Cambridge: Schenkman.

——. (1997). "Women's Clubs." In William L. Andrews, Frances Smith Foster, and Trudier Harris (Eds.), *The Oxford Companion to African American Literature* (pp. 787–88). New York: Oxford University Press.

Peters, Michael, Olssen, Mark, and Lankshear, Colin. (Eds.). (2003). *Futures of Critical Theory: Dreams of Difference.* Lanham, MD: Rowman and Littlefield.

Peterson, Charles F. (2000). "Du Bois, Fanon, and Cabral and the Margins of Colonized Elite Leadership." Ph.D. dissertation, Binghamton University.

——. (2007). *Du Bois, Fanon, Cabral: The Margins of Elite Anti-Colonial Leadership.* Lanham, MD: Lexington Books.

Peterson, Dale. (1994). "Notes from the Underworld: Dostoyevsky, Du Bois and the Discovery of Ethnic Soul." *Massachusetts Review* 35 (Summer), 225–47.

Peterson, Michael L., and Van Arragon, Raymond J. (Eds.). (2004). *Contemporary Debates in Philosophy of Religion.* Malden, MA: Blackwell.

Phillips, L.W. (1995). "W.E.B. Du Bois and Soviet Communism: *The Black Flame* as Social Realism." *South Atlantic Quarterly* 94 (3), 837–63.

Pieterse, Jan Nederveen. (1992). *White on Black: Images of Africa and Blacks in Western Popular Culture.* New Haven, CT: Yale University Press.

Pinkney, Alphonso. (1976). *Red, Black, and Green: Black Nationalism in the United States.* Cambridge: Cambridge University Press.

Pinn, Anne H., and Pinn, Anthony B. (2002). *Fortress Introduction to Black Church History.* Minneapolis, MN: Fortress Press.

Pinn, Anthony B. (1995). *Why, Lord?: Suffering and Evil in Black Theology.* New York: Continuum.

——. (1998). *Varieties of African American Religious Experience.* Minneapolis, MN: Fortress Press.

——. (Ed.). (2001). *By These Hands: A Documentary History of African American Humanism.* New York: New York University Press.

——. (2002a). *The Black Church in the Post-Civil Rights Era.* Maryknoll, NY: Orbis.

——. (Ed). (2002b). *Moral Evil and Redemptive Suffering: A History of Theodicy in African American Religious Thought.* Gainesville, FL: University Press of Florida.

——. (2003). *Terror and Triumph: The Nature of Black Religion.* Minneapolis, MN: Fortress Press.

——. (2004). *African American Humanist Principles: Living and Thinking Like the Children of Nimrod.* New York: Palgrave Macmillan.

——. (2006). *The African American Religious Experience in America.* Westport, CT: Greenwood.

Pinn, Anthony B., and Hopkins, Dwight N. (Eds.). (2004). *Loving the Body: Black Religious Studies and the Erotic.* New York: Palgrave Macmillan.

Pinn, Anthony B., and Valentin, Benjamin. (Eds.). (2001). *The Ties that Bind: African American and Hispanic American/Latino/a Theology in Dialogue.* New York: Continuum.

Pittman, John P. (Ed.). (1992-93). "African American Perspectives and Philosophical Traditions." (Special Triple Issue). *The Philosophical Forum* 24, 1–3.

———. (Ed.). (1997). *African American Perspectives and Philosophical Traditions*. New York: Routledge.

Pitts, Walter F., Jr. (1993). *Old Ship of Zion: The Afro-Baptist Ritual in the African Diaspora*. New York: Oxford University Press.

Platt, Anthony M. (1991). *E. Franklin Frazier Reconsidered*. New Brunswick, NJ: Rutgers University Press.

Pobi-Asamani, Kwadwo O. (1993). *W.E.B. Du Bois: An Exploration of His Contributions to Pan-Africanism*. San Bernardino, CA: Borgo Press.

Pohlman, Marcus. (2003). *African American Political Thought* (6 Volumes). New York: Routledge.

Poliakov, Leon. (1974). *The Aryan Myth*. New York: Basic Books.

Pollard, Alton B. (1993). "The Last Great Battle of the West: W.E.B. Du Bois and the Struggle for African America's Soul." In Gerald Early (Ed.), *Lure and Loathing: Essays on Race, Identity, and the Ambivalence of Assimilation* (pp. 41–54). New York: Viking/Penguin.

Poplack, Shana. (Ed.). (2000). *The History of African American English*. Malden: Blackwell.

———. (2001). *African American English in the Diaspora*. Malden: Blackwell.

Posnock, Ross. (1995). "The Distinction of Du Bois: Aesthetics, Pragmatism, Politics." *American Literary History* 7 (3), 500–24.

———. (1997). "How Does it Feel to Be a Problem?: Du Bois, Fanon, and the 'Impossible Life' of the Black Intellectual." *Critical Inquiry* 23 (2), 323–49.

———. (1998). *Color and Culture: Black Writers and the Making of the Modern Intellectual*. Cambridge: Harvard University Press.

Poster, Mark. (1975). *Existential Marxism in Postwar France: From Sartre to Althusser*. Princeton: Princeton University Press.

Prakash, Gyan. (Ed.). (1995). *After Colonialism: Imperial Histories and Postcolonial Displacements*. Princeton, NJ: Princeton University Press.

Prashad, Vijay. (2000). *The Karma of Brown Folk*. Minneapolis, MN: University of Minnesota.

———. (2001). *Everybody Was Kung Fu Fighting: Afro-Asian Connections and the Myth of Cultural Purity*. Boston: Beacon Press.

Price-Spratley, Townsand. (1996). "Negotiating Legacies: Audre Lorde, W.E.B. Du Bois, Marlon Riggs, and Me." *Harvard Educational Review* 66 (2), 216–30.

Pugh, Wesley C. (1974). "The Inflated Controversy: Du Bois vs. Washington." *Crisis* 81 (April), 132–33.

Pulido, Laura. (2006). *Black, Brown, Yellow, and Left: Radical Activism in Los Angeles*. Berkeley: University of California Press.

Pulitano, Elvira. (2003). *Toward a Native American Critical Theory*. Lincoln: University of Nebraska Press.

Puri, Shalini. (2004). *The Caribbean Postcolonial: Social Equality, Post-Nationalism, and Cultural Hybridity*. New York: Palgrave Macmillan.

Quainoo, Vanessa Wynder. (1993). *"The Souls of Black Folk*: In Consideration of W.E.B. Du Bois and the Exigency of an African American Philosophy of Rhetoric." Ph.D. dissertation, University of Massachusetts.

Quarles, Benjamin. (1966). "Frederick Douglass, Bridge-Builder in Human Relations." *Negro History Bulletin* 29 (5), 103–24.

———. (1991). *Black Abolitionists.* New York: Da Capo.

———. (1997). *Frederick Douglass.* New York: Da Capo.

Quayson, Ato. (2000a). *Postcolonialism: Theory, Practice or Process?* Malden: Polity.

———. (2000b). "Postcolonialism and Postmodernism." In Henry Schwarz and Sangeeta Ray (Eds.), *A Companion to Postcolonial Studies* (pp. 87–111). Malden: Blackwell.

Quinn, Philip L., and Taliaferro, Charles. (Eds.). (1999). *A Companion to Philosophy of Religion.* Malden, MA: Blackwell.

Rabaka, Reiland. (2001). "Africana Critical Theory: From W.E.B. Du Bois and C.L.R. James's Discourse on Domination and Liberation to Frantz Fanon and Amilcar Cabral's Dialectics of Decolonization." Ph.D. dissertation, Temple University, Philadelphia, PA.

———. (2002). "Malcolm X and/as Critical Theory: Philosophy, Radical Politics, and the African American Search for Social Justice." *Journal of Black Studies* 33 (2), 145–65.

———. (2003a). "I Found Myself in His Words: Reflections on the Centennial of W.E.B. Du Bois's *The Souls of Black Folk." Newark Reads Du Bois Newsletter.* Newark, NJ: Institute on Ethnicity, Culture, and the Modern Experience, Rutgers University–Newark. Available at: andromeda.rutgers.edu/~history/DuBois /rabaka.html [23 February 2003].

———. (2003b). "W.E.B. Du Bois's Evolving Africana Philosophy of Education." *Journal of Black Studies* 33 (4), 399–449.

———. (2003c). "'Deliberately Using the Word *Colonial* in a Much Broader Sense': W.E.B. Du Bois's Concept of 'Semi-Colonialism' as Critique of and Contribution to Postcolonialism." *Jouvert: A Journal of Postcolonial Studies* 7 (2), 1–32. Available online at: social.chass.ncsu.edu/jouvert/index.htm (23 February 2003).

———. (2003d). "W.E.B. Du Bois and 'The Damnation of Women': An Essay on Africana Anti-Sexist Critical Social Theory." *Journal of African American Studies* 7 (2), 39–62.

———. (2003e). "W.E.B. Du Bois and/as Africana Critical Theory: Pan-Africanism, Critical Marxism, and Male-Feminism." In James L. Conyers (Ed.), *Afrocentricity and the Academy* (pp. 67–112). Jefferson, NC: McFarland & Co.

———. (2004). "The Souls of Black Female Folk: W.E.B. Du Bois and Africana Anti-Sexist Critical Social Theory." *Africalogical Perspectives* 1 (2), 100–41.

———. (2005a). "W.E.B. Du Bois and Decolonization: Pan-Africanism, Postcolonialism, and Radical Politics." In James L. Conyers (Ed.), *W.E.B. Du Bois, Marcus Garvey, and Pan-Africanism* (pp. 123–54). Lewistown, NY: Mellen Press.

——. (2005b). "W.E.B. Du Bois's Theory of the Talented Tenth." In Molefi K. Asante and Ama Mazama (Eds.), *The Encyclopedia of Black Studies* (pp. 443–45). Thousand Oaks, CA: Sage.

——. (2005c). "Booker T. Washington's Philosophy of Accommodationism." In Molefi K. Asante and Ama Mazama (Eds.), *The Encyclopedia of Black Studies* (pp. 1–3). Thousand Oaks, CA: Sage.

——. (2005d). "African Worldview Theory." In Molefi K. Asante and Ama Mazama (Eds.), *The Encyclopedia of Black Studies* (pp. 56–57). Thousand Oaks, CA: Sage.

——. (2006a). "Africana Critical Theory of Contemporary Society: Ruminations on Radical Politics, Social Theory, and Africana Philosophy." In Molefi K. Asante and Maulana Karenga (Eds.), *The Handbook of Black Studies* (pp.130–52). Thousand Oaks, CA: Sage.

——. (2006b). "The Souls of Black Radical Folk: W.E.B. Du Bois, Critical Social Theory, and the State of Africana Studies." *Journal of Black Studies* 36 (5), 732–63.

——. (2006c). "W.E.B. Du Bois's 'The Comet' and Contributions to Critical Race Theory: An Essay on Black Radical Politics and Anti-Racist Social Ethics." *Ethnic Studies Review: Journal of the National Association of Ethnic Studies* 29 (1), 34–57.

——. (2006d). "The Souls of White Folk: W.E.B. Du Bois's Critique of White Supremacy and Contributions to Critical White Studies (Part I)." *Ethnic Studies Review: Journal of the National Association for Ethnic Studies* 29 (2), 1–19.

——. (2007a). *W.E.B. Du Bois and the Problems of the Twenty-First Century: An Essay on Africana Critical Theory.* Lanham, MD: Lexington Books.

——. (2007b). "The Souls of White Folk: W.E.B. Du Bois's Critique of White Supremacy and Contributions to Critical White Studies (Part II)." *Journal of African American Studies* 11 (1), 1–15.

——. (2008a). "Malcolm X and Africana Critical Theory: Rethinking Revolutionary Black Nationalism, Black Radicalism, and Black Marxism." In James L. Conyers and Andrew P. Smallwood (Eds.), *Malcolm X: A Historical Reader* (pp. 281–98). Durham, NC: Carolina Academic Press.

——. (2008b). "The Prophet of Problems: W.E.B. Du Bois, Philosophy of Religion, Sociology of Religion, and Black Liberation Theology—A Critical Review of Edward J. Blum's *W.E.B. Du Bois: American Prophet.*" *Journal of Southern Religion.*

——. (2009). *Africana Critical Theory: Reconstructing the Black Radical Tradition from W.E.B. Du Bois to Amilcar Cabral.* Lanham, MD: Lexington Books.

Raboteau, Albert J. (1978). *Slave Religion: The "Invisible Institution" in the Antebellum South.* New York: Oxford University Press.

——. (1995). *A Fire in the Bones: Reflections on African American Religious History.* Boston: Beacon.

——. (1999). *Canaan Land: A Religious History of African Americans.* New York: Oxford University Press.

Rajan, Gita, and Mohanran, Radhika. (Eds.). (1995). *Postcolonial Discourse and Changing Cultural Context: Theory and Criticism.* Westport, CT: Greenwood.

Rajan, Rajeswari. (1993). *Real and Imagined Women: Gender, Culture and Postcolonialism.* New York: Routledge.

Rampersad, Arnold. (1989). "Slavery and the Literary Imagination: Du Bois's *The Souls of Black Folk*." In Deborah E. McDowell and Arnold Rampersad (Eds.), *Slavery and the Literary Imagination: Selected Papers from the English Institute, 1987*. Baltimore: Johns Hopkins University Press.

———. (1990). *The Art and Imagination of W.E.B. Du Bois*. New York: Schocken.

———. (1996a). "Du Bois's Passage to India—*Dark Princess*." In Bernard W. Bell, Emily R. Grosholz, and James B. Stewart (Eds.), *W.E.B. Du Bois: On Race and Culture*. (pp. 161–76). New York: Routledge.

———. (1996b). "W.E.B. Du Bois, Race, and the Making of American Studies." In Bernard W. Bell, Emily R. Grosholz, and James B. Stewart (Eds.), *W.E.B. Du Bois: On Race and Culture* (pp. 289–305). New York: Routledge.

Randall, Margaret. (1992). *Gathering Rage: The Failure of Twentieth Century Revolutions to Develop a Feminist Agenda*. New York: Monthly Review.

Randolph, A. Philip, and Owen, Chandler. (1971). "Du Bois Fails as a Theorist." In August Meier, Elliott Rudwick, and Francis L. Broderick (Eds.), *Black Protest Thought in the Twentieth Century* (pp. 91–94). New York: MacMillan.

———. (1973). "Du Bois on Revolution: A Reply." In Theodore G. Vincent (Ed.), *Voices of a Black Nation: Political Journalism in the Harlem Renaissance* (pp. 88–92). Trenton, NJ: Africa World Press.

Ransby, Barbara. (2003). *Ella Baker and the Black Freedom Movement: A Radical Democratic Vision*. Chapel Hill, NC: University of North Carolina Press.

Rasmussen, David M. (Ed.). (1999). *The Handbook of Critical Theory*. Malden: Blackwell.

Rasmussen, David M., and Swindal, James. (Eds.). (2004). *Critical Theory* (4 Volumes). Thousand Oaks, CA: Sage.

Rath, Richard Cullen. (1997). "Echo and Narcissus: The Afrocentric Pragmatism of W.E.B. Du Bois." *Journal of American History* 84 (2), 461–95.

Rattansi, Ali. (1997). "Postcolonialism and Its Discontents." *Economy and Society* 26 (4), 480–500.

Rawls, Anne Warfield. (2000). "'Race' as an Interaction Order Phenomenon: W.E.B. Du Bois's 'Double-Consciousness' Thesis Revisited." *Sociological Theory* 18 (2), 241–74.

Rawls, John. (1971). *A Theory of Justice*. Cambridge: Harvard University Press.

———. (1997). "Justice as Fairness." In Robert E. Goodin and Philip Pettit (Eds.), *Contemporary Political Philosophy: An Anthology* (pp. 187–202). Cambridge: Blackwell.

Ray, Benjamin C. (2000). *African Religions: Symbol, Ritual, and Community*. Upper Saddle, NJ: Prentice Hall.

Ray, Larry. (1993). *Rethinking Critical Theory: Emancipation in the Age of Global Social Movements*. Thousand Oaks, CA: Sage.

Recht, J.J. (1971). "From W.E.B. Du Bois to Marcus Garvey: Shadows and Lights." *Revue Francaise d'Etudes Politiques Africaines* 62 (February), 40–59.

Reddie, Anthony G. (2003). *Nobodies to Somebodies: A Pratical Theology for Education and Liberation*. London: Epsworth.

———. (2005). *Acting in Solidarity: Reflections in Critical Christianity.* London: Darton, Longman, and Todd.

———. (2006a). *Black Theology in Transatlantic Dialogue.* New York: Palgrave Macmillan.

———. (2006b). *Dramatizing Theologies: A Participative Approach.* London: Equinox.

———. (2008). *Working Against the Grain: Black Theology in the Twenty-First Century.* London: Equinox.

Reddie, Anthony G., and Jagessar, Michael N. (Eds.). (2007). *Black Theology in Britain: A Reader.* London: Equinox.

Redding, J. Saunders. (1949). "Portrait of W.E.B. Du Bois." *American Scholar* 18, 93–96.

———. (1970). "*The Souls of Black Folk*: Du Bois's Masterpiece Lives On." In John Henrik Clarke, Esther Jackson, Ernest Kaiser, and J.H. O'Dell (Eds.), *Black Titan: W.E.B. Du Bois* (pp. 47–51). Boston: Beacon.

———. (1979). "The Correspondence of W.E.B. Du Bois: A Review Article." *Phylon* 40 (June), 119–22.

Reed, Adolph L., Jr. (1975). "The Political Philosophy of Pan-Africanism: A Study of the Writings of Du Bois, Garvey, Nkrumah, and Padmore and Their Legacy." M.A. thesis, Atlanta University, Atlanta, GA.

———. (1985). "W.E.B. Du Bois: A Perspective on the Bases of His Political Thought." *Political Theory* 13 (August), 431–56.

———. (1986). "Pan-Africanism as Black Liberation: Du Bois and Garvey." In W. Ofuatey-Kudjoe (Ed.), *Pan-Africanism: New Directions in Strategy.* Lanham, MD: University of America Press.

———. (1992). "Du Bois's 'Double-Consciousness': Race and Gender in Progressive Era American Thought." *Studies in American Political Development* 6, 132–37.

———. (1997). *W.E.B. Du Bois and American Political Thought: Fabianism and the Color Line.* New York: Oxford University Press.

———. (2000). "The Case Against Reparations." *Progressive* 64, 15–17.

Reed, Ishmael. (2000). "Eminent Contrarian: A Portrait of Public a Public Intellectual, W.E.B. Du Bois." *Village Voice Literary Supplement* (October-November), 146.

Reedom, John Anthony. (1977). "Du Bois and Washington: Opposite or Similar—An Evaluation of the Philosophies of Du Bois and Washington." *Southwestern Sociological Association.*

Reimer, A. James. (Ed.). (1992). *The Influence of the Frankfurt School on Contemporary Theology: Critical Theory and the Future of Religion.* Lewiston, NY: Mellen Press.

Reiss, Edward. (1997). *Marx: A Clear Guide.* London: Pluto Press.

Rhoads, John K. (1991). *Critical Issues in Social Theory.* University Park, PA: Pennsylvania State University.

Richards, Paul. (1970). "W.E.B. Du Bois and American Social History: Evolution of a Marxist." *Radical America* 5 (November), 43–87.

Riches, Cromwell A. (1933). *The Unanimity Rule and the League of Nations.* Baltimore, MD: Johns Hopkins University Press.

Rickford, John R. (1987). *Dimensions of a Creole Continuum: History, Texts, Linguistic Analysis of Guyanese Creole.* Stanford: Stanford University Press.

———. (1999). *African American Vernacular English: Features, Evolution, Educational Implications.* Malden: Blackwell.

———. (2000). *Spoken Soul: The Story of Black English.* New York: Wiley.

Rickford, John R., Mufwene, Salikoko S., Bailey, Guy, and Baugh, John. (Eds.). (1998). *African American English.* New York: Routledge.

Riggs, Marcia Y. (1994). *Awake, Arise, and Act: A Womanist Call for Black Liberation.* Cleveland, OH: Pilgrim Press.

Roach, Ronald. (2001). "Moving Towards Reparations: The Resurgence of the Reparations Movements is Taking Shape with Black Leaders and Intellectuals in the United States." *Black Issues in Higher* (November 8), 6–9.

Roberts, J. Deotis. (2003). *Black Religion, Black Theology: The Collected Essays of J. Deotis Roberts* (David Emmanuel Goatley, Ed.). Harrisburg, PA: Trinity Press.

Roberts, Marie M., and Mizuta, Tamae. (Eds.). (1993). *The Reformers: Socialist Feminism.* New York: Routledge.

Roberts, Richard H. (2002). *Religion, Theology, and the Human Sciences.* New York: Cambridge University Press.

Robinson, Armstead, Foster, Craig C., and Ogilvie, Donald L. (Eds.). (1969). *Black Studies in the University: A Symposium.* New York: Bantam.

Robinson, Cedric J. (1977). "A Critique of W.E.B. Du Bois's *Black Reconstruction.*" *Black Scholar* 8 (7), 44–50.

———. (1980). *The Terms of Order: Political Science and the Myth of Leadership.* Albany, NY: State University of New York Press.

———. (1990). "Du Bois and Black Sovereignty: The Case of Liberia." *Race & Class* 32 (2), 39–50.

———. (1994). "W.E.B. Du Bois and Black Sovereignty." In Sidney Lemelle and Robin D.G. Kelley (Eds.), *Imagining Home: Class, Culture, and Nationalism in the African Diaspora* (pp. 145–57). New York: Verso.

———. (1997). *Black Movements in America.* New York: Routledge.

———. (2000). *Black Marxism: The Making of the Black Radical Tradition.* Chapel Hill: University of North Carolina.

———. (2001). *An Anthropology of Marxism.* Aldershot: Ashgate.

Robinson, Dean E. (2001). *Black Nationalism in American Politics and Thought.* New York: Cambridge University Press.

Robinson, Randall. (2000). *The Debt: What America Owes Blacks.* New York: Dutton.

———. (2002). *The Reckoning: What Blacks Owe to Each Other.* New York: Dutton.

Rodgers-Rose, La Frances. (Ed.). (1980). *The Black Woman.* Beverly Hills: Sage.

Rodney, Walter. (1972). *How Europe Underdeveloped Africa.* Washington, D.C.: Howard University Press.

———. (1981). *Marx in the Liberation of Africa.* Georgetown, Guyana: People's Progressive Party Press.

———. (1990). *Walter Rodney Speaks.* Trenton, NJ: Africa World Press.

Roediger, David R. (1994). *Towards the Abolition of Whiteness: Essays on Race, Politics, and Working Class History.* New York: Verso.

———. (1999). *The Wages of Whiteness: Race and the Making of the American Working Class*. New York: Verso.

Rogers, Ben F. (1955). "W.E.B. Du Bois, Marcus Garvey, and Pan-Africa." *Journal of Negro History* 40 (April), 154–65.

Rogers, Mary F. (Ed.). (1998). *Contemporary Feminist Theory: A Text/Reader*. New York: McGraw-Hill.

Rojas, Fabio. (2007). *From Black Power to Black Studies: How a Radical Social Movement Became an Academic Discipline*. Baltimore: Johns Hopkins University Press.

Romero, Patricia W. (1976). "W.E.B. Du Bois, Pan-Africanists, and Africa, 1963–1973." *Journal of Black Studies* 6 (4), 321–36.

Roof, Maria. (1996). "W.E.B. Du Bois, Isabel Allende, and the Empowerment of Third World Women." *CLA Journal* 39 (4), 401–17.

Rooks, Noliwe M. (2006). *White Money/Black Power: The Surprising History of African American Studies and the Crisis of Race in Higher Education*. Boston: Beacon Press.

Rosenau, Pauline Marie. (1992). *Postmodernism and the Social Sciences*. Princeton: Princeton University Press.

Rosenberg, Jonathan. (2000). "The Global Editor: Du Bois and *The Crisis*." *The New Crisis* 107 (4), 15.

Ross, R. (Ed.). (1982). *Racism and Colonialism*. Leyden: Martinus Nijhoff.

Roth, Benita. (2003). *Separate Roads to Feminism: Black, Chicana and White Feminist Movements in America's Second Wave*. New York: Cambridge University Press.

Rowbotham, Sheila. (1973). *Woman's Consciousness, Man's World*. Harmondsworth: Penguin.

———. (1979). *Beyond the Fragments: Feminism and the Making of Socialism*. London: Merlin.

Rowland, Christopher. (Ed.). (1999). *The Cambridge Companion to Liberation Theology*. New York: Cambridge University Press.

Royster, Jacqueline Jones. (1997). *Southern Horrors and Other Writings: The Anti-Lynching Campaign of Ida B. Wells, 1892–1930*. Boston: Bedford.

Rucker, Walter. (2002). "'A Negro Nation Within the Nation': W.E.B. Du Bois and the Creation of a Revolutionary Pan-Africanist Tradition, 1903–1947." *Black Scholar* 32 (3/4), 37–46.

Ruddick, Sara. (1999). "Maternal Thinking as a Feminist Standpoint." In Janet A. Kourany, James P. Sterba, and Rosemarie Tong (Eds.), *Feminist Philosophies: Problems, Theories, and Applications* (2nd Edition, pp. 404–14). Englewood, NJ: Prentice Hall.

Rudwick, Elliott M. (1956). "W.E.B. Du Bois: A Study in Minority Group Leadership." Ph.D. dissertation, University of Pennsylvania.

———. (1957a). "The Niagara Movement." *Journal of Negro History* 42 (July), 177–200.

———. (1957b). "The National Negro Committee Conference of 1909." *Phylon* 18 (4), 413–19.

———. (1957c). "W.E.B. Du Bois and the Atlanta University Studies on the Negro." *Journal of Negro Education* 26 (4), 466–76.

———. (1958a). "W.E.B. Du Bois: In the Role of *Crisis* Editor." *Journal of Negro History* 18 (July), 214–40.

———. (1958b). "Du Bois's Last Year as *Crisis* Editor." *Journal of Negro Education* 27 (4), 426–33.

———. (1959a). "Du Bois versus Garvey: Race Propagandists at War." *Journal of Negro Education* 28 (Fall), 421–29.

———. (1959b). "W.E.B. Du Bois and the Universal Races Congress of 1911." *Phylon* 20 (4), 372–78.

———. (1960a). *W.E.B. Du Bois: A Study in Minority Group Leadership.* Philadelphia: University of Pennsylvania.

———. (1960b). "Booker T. Washington's Relations with the National Association for the Advancement of Colored People." *Journal of Negro Education* 29 (2), 134–44.

———. (1968). *W.E.B. Du Bois: Propagandists of the Negro Protest.* New York: Antheneum.

———. (1969). "Notes on a Forgotten Black Sociologists: W.E.B. Du Bois and the Sociological Profession." *American Sociologist* 4 (4), 303–36.

———. (1974). "W.E.B. Du Bois as Sociologists." In James E. Blackwell and Morris Janowitz (Eds.), *Black Sociologists: Historical and Contemporary Perspectives.* (pp. 25–55). Chicago: University of Chicago Press.

———. (1982a). *W.E.B. Du Bois: Voice of the Black Movement.* Urbana: University of Illinois Press.

———. (1982b). "W.E.B. Du Bois: Protagonist of the Afro-American Protest." In John Hope Franklin and August Meier (Eds.), *Black Leaders of the Twentieth Century* (pp. 63–84). Chicago: University of Illinois Press.

Rutledge, Rebecka Rychelle. (2001). "Metahpors of Mediation: Race and Nation in Black Atlantic Literature—W.E.B. Du Bois, Ralph Ellison, Edourd Glissant, and Olaudah Equiano." Ph. D. dissertation, Washington University.

Sadar, Ziauddin. (1998). *Postmodernism and the Other: The New Imperialism of Western Culture.* London: Pluto Press.

Said, E.W. (1999). "Traveling Theory Reconsidered." In Nigel C. Gibson (Ed.), *Rethinking Fanon* (pp. 197–214). Amherst, NY: Humanity Books.

———. (2000). "Traveling Theory." In Moustafa Bayoumi and Andrew Rubin (Eds.), *The Edward Said Reader* (pp. 195–217). New York: Vintage.

Salem, Dorothy. (1990). *To Better Our World: Black Women in Organized Reform, 1890–1920.* Brooklyn, NY: Carlson.

———. (1993). "National Association of Colored Women." In Darlene Clark Hine, Elsa Barkley Brown, and Rosalyn Teborg-Penn (Eds.), *Black Women in America: An Historical Encyclopedia* (Volume 2, pp. 842–51). Brooklyn: Carlson.

Salzberger, Ronald P., and Turck, Mary C. (Eds.). (2004). *Reparations for Slavery: A Reader.* Lanham, MD: Rowman and Littlefield.

Sanchez, Lisa. (1991). "W.E.B. Du Bois: Clinical Sociologist." *Sociological Practice Association/ISA Working Group in Clinical Sociology.*

Sandoval, Chela. (2000). *Methodology of the Oppressed.* Minneapolis: University of Minnesota Press.

Sargent, Lydia. (Ed.). (1981). *Women and Revolution: A Discussion of the Unhappy Marriage of Marxism and Feminism.* Boston: South End.

Savage, Barbara Dianne. (2000). "W.E.B. Du Bois and 'The Negro Church'." *Annals of the American Academy of Political and Social Science* 568 (March), 249–53.

Sawyer, Mary R. (1994). *Black Ecumenism: Implementing the Demands of Justice.* Valley Forge, PA: Trinity Press International.

Sayers, Sean, and Osborne, Peter. (Eds.). (1990). *Socialism, Feminism, and Philosophy: A Radical Philosophy Reader.* New York: Routledge.

Schafer, Alex R. (2001). "W.E.B. Du Bois, German Social Thought, and the Racial Divide in American Progressivism, 1892–1909." *Journal of American History* 88 (3), 925–49.

Schechter, Patricia A. (2001). *Ida B. Wells-Barnett and American Reform, 1880–1930.* Chapel Hill, NC: University of North Carolina Press.

Schedler, George. (1998). *Racist Symbols and Reparations: Philosophical Reflections on Vestiges of the American Civil War.* Lanhma, MD: Rowman and Littlefield.

Schindler, Ronald J. (1998). *The Frankfurt School Critique of Capitalist Culture: A Critical Theory for Post-Democratic Society and Its Re-Education.* Brookfield, VT: Ashgate.

Schneider, Paul Ryan. (1998). "Inventing the Public Intellectual: Ralph Waldo Emerson, W.E.B. Du Bois, and the Cultural Politics of Representing Men." Ph.D. dissertation, Duke University.

Schor, Joel. (1977). *Henry Highland Garnet: A Voice of Black Radicalism in the Nineteenth Century.* Westport: Greenwood Press.

Schrager, Cynthia D. (1996). "Both Sides of the Veil: Race, Science, and Mysticism in W.E.B. Du Bois." *American Quarterly* 48 (4), 551.

Schrecker, Ellen. (1998). *Many are the Crimes: McCarthyism in America.* Boston: Little Brown.

Schuchter, Arnold. Reparations. (1970). *The Black Manifesto and its Challenge to White America.* Philadelphia: Lippincott.

Schultz, Mark. (2005). *The Rural Face of White Supremacy.* Urbana, IL: University of Illinois Press.

Schwarz, Henry and Ray, Sangeeta. (Eds.). (2000). *A Companion to Postcolonial Studies.* Malden, MA: Blackwell.

Scott, Jacqueline, and Franklin, A. Todd. (Eds.). (2006). *Critical Affinities: Nietzsche and African American Thought.* Albany, NY: State University of New York.

Segundo, Juan Luis. (1976). *Liberation of Theology.* Maryknoll, NY: Orbis Books.

Seibert, Rudolf. (1985). *The Critical Theory of Religion and the Frankfurt School: From The Universal Pragmatic to Political Theology.* New York: Mounton.

———. (1989). *From Critical Theory to Communicative Political Theology: Universal Solidarity.* New York: Lang.

Seidman, Steven. (1994). *Contested Knowledge: Social Theory in the Postmodern Era.* Oxford: Blackwell.

Seidman, Steven, and Wagner, David. (Eds.). (1992). *Postmodernism and Social Theory*. Oxford: Blackwell.

Self, Peter. (1993). "Socialism." In Robert E. Goodin and Philip Pettit (Eds.), *A Companion to Contemporary Political Philosophy* (pp. 333–65). Malden, MA: Blackwell.

Sénghor, Leopold S. (1995). "On Negrohood: Psychology of the African Negro." In Albert Mosley (Ed.), *African Philosophy: Selected Readings* (pp. 116–27). Englewood Cliffs, NJ: Prentice Hall.

Serequeberhan, Tsenay. (1990). "Karl Marx and African Emancipatory Thought: A Critique of Marx's Euro-Centric Metaphysics." *Praxis International* 10 (1/2), 161–81.

———. (Ed.). (1991). *African Philosophy: The Essential Readings*. New York: Paragon House.

———. (1994). *The Hermeneutics of African Philosophy: Horizon and Discourse*. New York: Routledge.

———. (1997). "The Critique of Eurocentrism and the Practice of African Philosophy." In Emmanuel C. Eze (Ed.), *(Post)Colonial African Philosophy: A Critical Reader* (pp. 141–61). Malden, MA: Blackwell.

———. (1998). "Africanity at the End of the Twentieth Century," *African Philosophy* 11 (1), 13–21.

———. (2000). *Our Heritage: The Past in the Present of African American and African Existence*. Lanham, MD: Rowman and Littlefield.

———. (2003). "The African Anti-Colonial Struggle: An Effort at Reclaiming History." *Philosophia Africana* 6 (1), 47–58.

———. (2007). *Contested Memory: The Icon of the Occidental Tradition*. Trenton, NJ: Africa World Press.

Sernett, Milton C. (Ed). (1999). *African American Religious History: A Documentary Witness*. Durham, NC: Duke University Press.

Serota, Arthur. (1996). *Ending Apartheid in America: The Need for a Black Political Party and Reparations Now*: Evanston, IL: Troubadour Press.

Sevitch, Benjamin. (2002). "W.E.B. Du Bois and Jews: A Lifetime of Opposing Anti-Semitism." *Journal of African American History* 87, 323–38.

Shapiro, Herbert. (1988). *White Violence and Black Response: From Reconstruction to Montgomery*. Amherst: University of Massachusetts Press.

Shiach, Morag. (Ed.). (1999). *Feminism and Cultural Studies*. New York: Oxford University Press.

Shipley, W. Maurice. (1972). "Reaching Back to Glory: Comparative Sketches in the Dreams of W.B. Yeats and W.E.B. Du Bois." *Crisis* 83, 195–98.

Shobat, Ella. (1993). "Notes on the 'Post-Colonial'." *Social Text* 31/32, 99–113.

Shuford, John. (2001). "Four Du Boisian Contributions to Critical Race Theory." *Transactions of the Charles S. Peirce Society* 37 (3), 301–37.

Sica, Alan. (Ed.). (1998). *What Is Social Theory?: The Philosophical Debates*. Malden, MA: Blackwell.

Siemerling, Winfried. (2001). "W.E.B. Du Bois, Hegel, and the Staging of Alterity." *Callaloo* 24, (1), 325–33.

Simms, Rupe. (2000). *The Politics of Accommodation and Resistance in the Black Church: A Gramscian Analysis.* Lewiston, NY: Mellen Press.

Simpson, George E. (1978). *Black Religions in the New World.* New York: Columbia University Press.

Simpson, Lorenzo C. (2003). "Critical Theory, Aesthetics, and Black Modernity." In Tommy L. Lott and John P. Pitman (Eds.), *A Companion to African American Philosophy* (pp. 386–98). Malden, MA: Blackwell Publishers.

Singer, Peter. (Ed.). (1993). *A Companion to Ethics.* Malden, MA: Blackwell.

Singh, Amritjit, and Schimdt, Peter. (Eds.). (2000). *Postcolonial Theory and the United States: Race, Ethnicity and Literature.* Jackson: University Press of Mississippi.

Singh, Nikhil P. (2004). *Black Is A Country: Race and the Unfinished Struggle for Democracy.* Cambridge: Havard Univerity Press.

Singleton, Harry H., III. (2002). *Black Theology and Ideology: De-ideological Dimensions in the Theology of James H. Cone.* Collegeville, MN: Liturgical Press.

Sivanandan, Ambalavaner. (1990). *Communities of Resistance: Writings on Black Struggles for Socialism.* New York: Verso.

Skinner, Quentin. (1997). "The State." In Robert E. Goodin and Philip Pettit (Eds.), *Contemporary Political Philosophy: An Anthology* (pp. 3–26). Cambridge: Blackwell.

Slaughter, Jane, and Kern, Robert. (Eds.). (1981). *European Women on the Left: Socialism, Feminism, and the Problems Faced by Political Women, 1880 to the Present.* Westport, CT: Greenwood.

Sloan, Ella Faye. (2003). "W. E. B. Du Bois's 'Talented Tenth': A Pioneering Conception of Transformational Leadership." Ed.D. dissertation, University of San Diego.

Smart, Barry. (1992). *Modern Conditions, Postmodern Controversies.* London: Routledge.

———. (1993). *Postmodernity.* New York: Routledge.

Smerdlow, Amy, and Lessinger, Hanna. (Eds.). (1983). *Class, Race, and Sex: The Dynamics of Control.* Boston: G.K. Hall.

Smith, Andrea. (2005). *Conquest: Sexual Violence and American Indian Genocide.* Boston: South End.

Smith, Barbara. (Ed.). (1983). *Home Girls: A Black Feminist Anthology.* New York: Kitchen Table Press.

———. (1998). *The Truth that Never Hurts: Writings on Race, Gender, and Freedom.* New Brunswick, NJ: Rutgers University Press.

Smith, Christian. (1991). *The Emergence of Liberation Theology: Radical Religion and Social Movement Theory.* Chicago: University of Chicago Press.

Smith, Dorothy E. (1977). *Feminism and Marxism: A Place to Begin, A Way To Go.* Vancouver: New Star Books.

Smith, Eddie Calvin. (1975). "Educational Themes in the Published Work of W.E.B. Du Bois, 1883–1960: Implications for African American Educators." Ph.D. dissertation, University of Wisconsin–Milwaukee.

Smith, John David. (1980). "Du Bois and Phillips: Symbolic Antagonists of the Progressive Era." *Centennial Review* 24 (1), 88–102.

Smith, Linda Tuhiwai. (1999). *Decolonizing Methodologies: Research and Indigenous Peoples.* Dunedin: University of Otago Press.

Smith, Robert C. (2003). "Imari Obadele: The Father of the Modern Reparations Movement." *Africana: Gateway to the Black World.* Available on-line at: www.africana.com/articles/daily/index_20000601.asp (Accessed on 19 June 2003).

Smith, Tony. (1993). *Dialectical Social Theory and Its Critics: From Hegel to Analytical Marxism and Postmodernism.* Albany, NY: State University of New York Press.

Smitherman, Geneva. (1975). *Black Language and Culture: Sounds of Soul.* New York: Harper and Row.

———. (1986). *Talkin' and Testifyin: The Language of Black America.* Detroit: Wayne State University Press.

———. (2000). *Talkin' That Talk: Language, Culture and Education in African America.* New York: Routledge.

Sobel, Mechal. (1979). *Trabelin' On: The Slave Journey to an Afro-Baptist Faith.* Westport, CT: Greenwood.

Speck, Beatrice F. (1974). "W.E.B. Du Bois: A Historiographical Study." Ph.D. dissertation, Texas Christian University.

Spencer, Samuel R. (1955). *Booker T. Washington and the Negro's Place in American Life.* Boston: Little Brown.

Springer, Kimberly. (Ed.). (1999). *Still Lifting, Still Climbing: Contemporary African American Women's Activism.* New York: New York University Press.

———. (2005). *Living for the Revolution: Black Feminist Organizations, 1968–1980.* Durham, NC: Duke University Press.

Stannard, David E. (1992). *American Holocaust: Columbus and the Conquest of the New World.* New York: Oxford University Press.

Steady, Filomina Chioma. (Ed.). (1981). *The Black Woman Cross-Culturally.* Cambridge: Schenkman.

———. (1987). "African Feminism: A Worldwide Perspective." In Rosalyn Terborg-Penn, Sharon Harley, and Andrea Benton Rushing (Eds.), *Women in Africa and the African Diaspora* (pp. 3-24). Washington, D.C.: Howard University Press.

Stein, Judith. (2001). "The Difficult Doctor Du Bois." *Reviews in American History* 29 (2), 247–54.

Stephan, Nancy Leys. (1982). *The Idea of Race in Science: Great Britain, 1800–1960.* New York: MacMillan.

———. (1990). "Race and Gender: The Role of Analogy in Science." In David Theo Goldberg (Ed.), *Anatomy of Racism* (pp. 38–57). Minneapolis: University of Minnesota Press.

Stephanson, Anders. (1996). *Manifest Destiny: American Expansion and the Empire of Right.* New York: Hill and Wang.

Stephens, Ronald J. (2003). "Narrating Acts of Reisistance: Explorations of Untold Heroic and Horrific Battle Stories Surrounding Robert Franklin Williams' Residance in Lake County, Michigan." *Journal of Black Studies* 33 (5), 675–703.

———. (2004). "Garveryism in Idlewild, Michigan, 1927-1936." *Journal of Black Studies* 34 (4), 462–88.

Stepto, Robert B. (1985). "The Quest of the Weary Traveler: W.E.B. Du Bois's *The Souls of Black Folk.*" In William L. Andrews (Ed.), *Critical Essays on W.E.B. Du Bois* (pp. 139–72). Boston: G.K. Hall.

Sterba, James P. (Ed.). (1998). *Ethics.* Malden: Blackwell.

———. (Ed.). (1999). *Feminism and Its Critics.* Lanham: Rowman and Littlefield.

———. (Ed.). (2000). *Controversies in Feminism.* Lanham: Rowman and Littlefield.

Sterling, Dorothy. (1965). *Lift Every Voice: The Lives of Booker T. Washington, W.E.B. Du Bois, Mary Church Terrell, and James Weldon Johnson.* Garden City, NY: Doubleday.

———. (1979). *Black Foremothers: Three Lives.* Old Westbury, NY: Feminist Press.

———. (Ed.). (1984). *We Are Your Sisters: Black Women in the Nineteenth Century.* New York: Norton.

Stewart, James B. (1976). "Black Studies and Black People in the Future." *Black Books Bulletin* 4 (2), 20–25.

———. (1979). "Introducing Black Studies: A Critical Examination of Some Textual Materials." *Umoja* 3 (1), 5–17.

———. (1981). "Alternative Models of Black Studies." *Umoja* 5 (3), 17–39.

———. (1983). "The Psychic Duality of Afro-Americans in the Novels of W.E.B. Du Bois." *Phylon* 44 (2), 93–107.

———. (1984). "The Legacy of W.E.B. Du Bois for Contemporary Black Studies." *Journal of Negro Education* 53 (Summer), 296–311.

———. (1992). "Reaching for Higher Ground: Toward an Understanding of Black/Africana Studies." *The Afrocentric Scholar* 1 (1), 1–63.

———. (1996a). "In Search of a Theory of Human History: W.E.B. Du Bois's Theory of Social and Cultural Dynamics." In Bernard W. Bell, Emily R. Grosholz, and James B. Stewart (Eds.), *W.E.B. Du Bois: On Race and Culture* (pp. 261–88). New York: Routledge.

———. (1996b). "Africana Studies: New Directions for the Twenty-First Century." *International Journal of Black Studies* 4 (1&2), 1–21.

———. (1999). "Deciphering the Thought of W.E.B. Du Bois: A Thematic Approach." In James L. Conyers (Ed.), *Black American Intellectualism and Culture: A Social Study of African American Social and Political Thought* (pp. 57–84). Stamford, CT: JAI Press.

———. (2004). *Flight: In Search of Vision.* Trenton, NJ: Africa World Press.

Stewart, James, Hare, Bruce, Young, Alfred, and Aldridge, Delores. (2003). "The State of Africana Studies." *International Journal of Africana Studies* 8 (1), 1–26.

Stewart, Maria W. (1987a). *Maria W. Stewart, America's First Black Woman Political Writer: Essays and Speeches* (Marilyn Richardson, Ed.). Indianapolis: Indiana University Press.

———. (1987b). *Meditations From the Pen of Mrs. Maria Stewart. In Maria W. Stewart, America's First Black Woman Political Writer: Essays and Speeches.* (Marilyn Richardson, Ed.). Indianapolis: Indiana University Press.

Stewart-Cain, Karen LaVerne. (2003). "W. E. B. DuBois: The Neglected American Sociologist. A Study in Race-Biased Exclusion from the Academy." Ph.D. dissertation, Union Institute and University.

Stirk, Peter M.R. (2000). *Critical Theory, Politics and Society*. London: Pinter Press.

Stuart, Jack. (1997). "A Note on William English Walling and His 'Cousin' W.E.B. Du Bois." *Journal of Negro History* 82 (2), 270–75.

Stuckey, Sterling. (1987). *Slave Culture: Nationalist Theory and the Foundations of Black America*. New York: Oxford University Press.

———. (1994). *Going Through the Storm: The Influence of African American Art in History*. New York: Oxford University Press.

Sullivan, Shannon. (2003). "Remembering the Gift: W.E.B. Du Bois on the Unconscious and Economic Operations of Racism." *Transactions of the Charles S. Peirce Society* 39 (2), 205–25.

Summers, Martin A. (2004). *Manliness and Its Discontents: The Black Middle Class and the Transformation of Masculinity, 1900–1930*. Chapel Hill, NC: University of North Carolina Press.

Sumner, Claude. (1985). *Classical Ethiopian Philosophy*. Addis Ababa, Ethiopia: Addis Ababa University Press.

Sumner, Claude, and Wolde, Samuel. (Eds). (2002). *Perspectives in African Philosophy: An Anthology on the Problematics of an African Philosophy*. Addis Ababa: Addis Ababa University Press.

Sumpter, Richard David. (1973). "A Critical Study of the Educational Thought of W.E.B. Du Bois." Ph.D. dissertation, Peabody College for Teacher of Vanderbilt University.

———. (2000). "W.E.B. Du Bois on Education: Its Socialistic Foundation." *Journal of Thought* 35 (1), 61–87.

———. (2001). "W.E.B. Du Bois: Reflections on Democracy." *Journal of Thought* 36 (2), 25–32.

Sundquist, Eric J. (Ed.). (1990). *Frederick Douglass: New Literary and Historical Essays*. New York: Cambridge University Press.

———. (1993). *To Wake the Nations: Race in the Making of American Literature*. Cambridge: Harvard University Press.

———. (1996). "W.E.B. Du Bois and the Autobiography of Race." In W.E.B. Du Bois, *The Oxford W.E.B. Du Bois Reader* (Eric Sundquist, Ed., pp. 3–36). New York: Oxford University Press.

Sutcliffe, David, and Wong, Ansel. (Eds.). (1986). *The Language of the Black Experience: Cultural Expression Through Word and Sound in the Caribbean and Black Britian*. New York: Blackwell.

Táíwò, Olúfémi. (1999a). "Cabral." In Robert L. Arrington (Ed.), *A Companion to the Philosophers* (pp. 5–12). Malden: Blackwell.

———. (1999b). "Fanon." In Robert L. Arrington (Ed.), *A Companion to the Philosophers* (pp. 13–19). Malden: Blackwell.

Talbot, Edith A. (1904). *Samuel Chapman Armstrong: A Biographical Study*. New York: Doubleday.

Taylor, Carl McDonald. (1971). "W.E.B. Du Bois: The Rhetoric of Redefinition." Ph.D. dissertation, University of Oregon.

Taylor, Carol M. (1981). "W.E.B. Du Bois's Challenge to Scientific Racism." *Journal of Black Studies* 11 (June), 449–60.

Taylor, Clarence. (2002). *Black Religious Intellectuals: The Fight for Equality from Jim Crow to the Twenty-First Century*. New York: Routledge.

Taylor, Paul C. (2000). "Appiah's Uncompleted Argument: W.E.B. Du Bois and the Reality of Race." *Social Theory and Practice* 26 (1), 103–28.

Taylor, Robert, Thornton, Michael, and Chatters, Linda. (1987). "Black Americans' Perceptions of the Sociohistorical Role of the Church." *Journal of Black Studies* 18 (2), 128–38.

Teele, James E. (Eds.). (2002). *E. Franklin Frazier and the Black Bourgeoisie*. Columbia, MO: University of Missouri Press.

Terborg-Penn, Rosalyn, Harley, Sharon, and Rushing, Andrea Benton. (Eds.). (1987). *Women in Africa and the African Diaspora*. Washington, D.C.: Howard University Press.

Tewari, Shruti Bhawana. (2002). "A Revolution of the Colored Races: Merging of African and Indian Thought in the Novels of W. E. B. Du Bois." M.A. thesis, Michigan State University.

Theoharis, Jeanna, and Woodard, Komozi. (Eds.). (2003). *Freedom North: Black Freedom Struggles Outside the South, 1940–1980*. New York: Palgrave Macmillan.

Therborn, Goran. (1996). "Critical Theory and the Legacy of Twentieth-Century Marxism." In Barry S. Turner (Ed.), (1996). *The Blackwell Companion to Social Theory* (pp. 53–82). Malden, MA: Blackwell.

Thiam, Awa. (1978). *Black Sister, Speak Out: Feminism and Oppression in Black Africa*. London: Pluto Press.

Thomas, Darryl C. (Ed.). (2005). *Cedric Robinson and the Black Radical Tradition*. *Race & Class* 47 (2).

Thomas, Douglas E. (1998). *The Rise of Black Empowerment Theology in America: Remembering an Era*. Philadelphia, PA: Guidinglight Books.

Thompson, Janna. (2002). *Taking Responsibility for the Past: Reparation and Historical Injustice*. Cambridge: Polity.

Thompson, John B. (1990). *Ideology and Modern Culture: Critical Social Theory in the Era of Mass Communication*. Palo Alto, CA: Stanford University Press.

Thompson, Robert Dee, Jr. (1997). "A Socio-Biography of Shirley Graham-Du Bois: A Life in the Struggle." Ph.D. dissertation, University of California, Santa Cruz.

Thompson, Vincent Bakpetu. (1969). *Africa and Unity: The Evolution of Pan-Africanism* London: Longman.

———. (1987). *The Making of the African Diasporain the Americas, 1441–1900*. New York: Longman.

Tiffin, Helen. (1988). "Post-colonialism, Post-modernism and the Rehabilitation of Post-colonial History." *Journal of Commonwealth Literatures* 23 (1), 169–81.

Tolnay, Stewart E. (1995). *A Festival of Violence: An Analysis of Southern Lynchings, 1882–1930*. Urbana: University of Illinois Press.

Tomisawa, Rieko. (2003). "The Crisis of Democracy in a Pluralistic Society: A Genealogy of W. E. B. Du Bois's Double Consciousness." Ph.D. dissertation, Michigan State University.

Torpey, John C. (2006). *Making Whole What Has Been Smashed: On Reparations Politics*. Cambridge: Harvard University Press.

Townes, Emilie M. (1993). *Womanist Justice, Womanist Hope.* Atlanta: Scholars Press.

———. (1995). *In a Blaze of Glory: Womanist Spirituality as Social Witness.* Nashville, TN: Abingdon.

———. (2006). *Womanist Ethics and the Cultural Production of Evil.* New York: Palgrave Macmillan.

Townsend, Kim. (1996). "'Manhood' at Harvard: W.E.B. Du Bois." *Raritan* 15 (4), 70–82.

Travis, Toni Michelle C. (1996). "Double Consciousness and the Politics of the Elite." *Research in Race and Ethnic Relations* 9, 91–123.

Tuana, Nancy. (1992). *Woman and the History of Philosophy.* New York: Paragon House.

Tuana, Nancy, and Tong, Rosmarie. (Eds.). (1995). *Feminism & Philosophy: Essential Readings in Theory, Reinterpretation, and Application.* Boulder, CO: Westview.

Turner, Barry S. (Ed.). (1996). *The Blackwell Companion to Social Theory.* Malden, MA: Blackwell.

Turner, Bryan S. (1997). *Religion and Social Theory.* Newbury Park, CA: Sage.

Turner, Darwin W. (1974). "W.E.B. Du Bois and the Theory of a Black Aesthetic." *Studies in the Literary Imagination* 7, 1–21.

Turner, James. (Ed.). (1984). *The Next Decade: Theoretical and Research Issues in Africana Studies.* Ithaca, NY: Africana Studies and Research Center, Cornell University.

Turner, James, and McGann, Charles S. (1980). "Black Studies as an Integral Tradition in African American Intellectual History." *Journal of Negro Education* 49, 52–59.

Turner, M. Rick. (2000). "What's Happening to Our Talented Tenth?" *Black Issues in Higher Education* 17 (21), 152.

Tursi, Renee. (2000). "The Force of Habit at the Turn of the Century: William James, Henry James, Edith Wharton, and W.E.B. Du Bois." Ph.D. dissertation, Columbia University, New York.

Tushnet, Mark. (1987). "The Politics of Equality in Constitutional Law: The Equal Protection Clause, Dr. Du Bois, and Charles Hamilton Houston." *Journal of American History* 74 (3), 884–903.

Tuttle, William M. (Ed.). (1957). *W.E.B. Du Bois.* Boston: Beacon.

———. (Ed.). (1973). *W.E.B. Du Bois: Essays and Explorations.* Englewood Cliffs, NJ: Prentice-Hall.

———. (1974). "W.E.B. Du Bois's Confrontation with White Liberalism During the Progressive Era." *Phylon* 35 (3), 241–58.

Twine, Frances W., and Blee, Kathleen M. (Eds.). (2001). *Feminism and Anti-Racism: International Struggles for Justice.* New York: New York University Press.

Tye, Larry. (2004). *Rising from the Rails: Pullman Porters and the Making of the Black Middle Class.* New York: Henry Holt.

Tyner, James. (2006). *Geography of Malcolm X: Black Radicalism and the Remaking of American Space.* New York: Routledge.

Tyner, Jarvis. (1997). "From the Talented Tenth to the Communist Party: The Evolution of W.E.B. Du Bois." *Political Affairs* 76 (2), 5–9.

Urban, Wayne J. (1997). "W.E.B. Du Bois." *History of Education Quarterly* 37 (4), 441–44.

Valdes, Francisco, Culp, Jerome M., and Harris, Angela P. (Eds.). (2002). *Crossraods, Directions, and a New Critical Race Theory.* Philadelphia, PA: Temple University Press.

Van Deburg, William. (1992). *New Day in Babylon: The Black Power Movement and American Culture, 1965–1975.* Chicago: University of Chicago Press.

———. (1997a). *Black Camelot: African American Culture Heroes in Their Times, 1960–1980.* Chicago: University of Chicago Press.

———. (Ed.). (1997b). *Modern Black Nationalism: From Marcus Garvey to Louis Farrakhan.* New York: New York University Press.

Vann Woodard, C. (1974). *The Strange Career of Jim Crow* (3rd Edition). New York: Oxford University Press.

Vaz, Kim Marie. (Ed.). (1995). *Black Women in America.* Thousand Oaks, CA: Sage.

Vedun, Vincene. (1993). "If the Shoe Fits Wear It: An Analysis of Reparations for African Americans." *Tulane Law Review* 67 (3), 597–668.

Velikova, R. (2000). "W.E.B. Du Bois vs. 'the Sons of the Fathers': A Reading of *The Souls of Black Folk* in the Context of American Nationalism." *African American Review* 34 (3), 431–42.

Verney, Kevern. (2001). *The Art of the Possible: Booker T. Washington and Black Leadership in the United States, 1881–1925.* New York: Routledge.

Vincent, Theodore G. (1973). *Voices of a Black Nation: Political Journalism in the Harlem Renaissance.* Trenton, NJ: Africa World Press.

Vivian, John Donald. (1997). "The Making of a Radical: W.E.B. Du Bois's Turn to the Left." M.A. thesis, Florida Atlantic University.

Vogel, Lise. (1983). *Marxism and the Oppression of Women: Towards a Unitary Theory.* New Brunswick: Rutgers University Press.

Von Eschen, Penny M. (1997). *Race Against Empire: Black Americans and Anticolonialism, 1937–1957.* Ithaca, NY: Cornell University Press.

Walden, Daniel. (1963a). "NAACP Mourns the Passing of Dr. Du Bois, A Founder." *Crisis* 70 (October).

———. (1963b). "W.E.B. Du Bois: Pioneer Reconstruction Historian." *Negro History Bulletin* 26, 159–60, 164.

———. (1966). "W.E.B. Du Bois's Essential Years: The Link from Douglass to the Present." *Journal of Human Relations* 14, 28–41.

———. (1977). "W.E.B. Du Bois: A Renaissance Man in the Harlem Renaissance." *Minority Voices* 2 (1), 11–20.

Walker, David. (1993). *David Walker's Appeal in Four Articles.* Baltimore, MD: Black Classic Press.

Walker, S. Jay. (1975). "Du Bois's Uses of History: On Nat Turner and John Brown." *Black World* 24 (February), 4–11.

Walker, Theodore, Jr. (1991). *Empower the People: Social Ethics for the African American Church.* Maryknoll, NY: Orbis.

Wallace, Michele. (1990a). *Black Macho and the Myth of the Superwoman.* New York: Verso.

——. (1990b). *Invisibility Blues: From Pop to Theory.* New York: Verso.

Walters, Ronald W. (1993). *Pan-Africanism in the African Diaspora: An Analysis of Modern Afrocentric Political Movement.* Detroit: Wayne State University Press.

Walton, Sidney. (1969). *The Black Curriculum: Developing Programs in Afro-American Studies.* East Palo Alto: Black Liberation Publishers.

Ward, Julie K., and Lott, Tommy L. (Eds). (2002). *Philosophers on Race: Critical Essays.* Malden: Blackwell.

Ware, Vron. (1992). *Beyond the Pale: White Women, Racism, and History.* New York: Verso.

Warren, Kenneth W. (2000). "An Inevitable Drift?: Oligarchy, Du Bois, and the Politics of Race between the Wars." *Boundary 2* 27 (3), 153–69.

Warren, Nagueyalti. (1984). "The Contributions of W.E.B. Du Bois to Afro-American Studies in Higher Education." Ph.D. dissertation, University of Mississippi.

Washington, Booker T. (1896). *Daily Resolves.* New York: E.P. Dutton.

——. (1899). *The Future of the American Negro.* Boston: Small and Maynard.

——. (1900a). *The Story of My Life and Work.* Cincinnati: W.H. Ferguson Publishing.

——. (1900b). *A New Negro for a New Century: An Accurate and Up-to-Date Record of the Upward Struggles of the Negro Race.* Chicago: American Publishing House.

——. (1900c). *Sowing and Reaping.* Boston: L.C. Page Publishing.

——. (1900d). *The Education of the Negro.* Albany, NY: J.B. Lyon Publishing.

——. (1901). *Up from Slavery: An Autobiography.* New York: Doubleday.

——. (1902). *Character-Building.* New York: Doubleday.

——. (1904). *Working with the Hands: Being a Sequel to Up from Slavery, Covering the Authors Experiences in Industrial Training at Tuskegee.* New York: Doubleday.

——. (1906a). *Putting the Most into Life.* New York: Crowell.

——. (1906b). *Tuskegee and Its People: Their Ideals and Achievements.* New York: Appleton.

——. (1907). *Frederick Douglass.* Philadelphia: G.W. Jacobs and Company.

——. (1909). *The Story of the Negro: The Rise of the Race from Slavery.* New York: Doubleday.

——. (1911). *My Larger Education.* New York: Doubleday, Page & Co.

——. (1912). *The Man Farthest Down: A Record of Observation and Study in Europe.* New Brunswick, NJ: Transaction.

——. (1913). *The Story of Slavery.* Dansville, NY: F.A. Owen Publishing.

——. (1932). *Selected Speeches of Booker T. Washington.* (E. Davidson Washington, Ed.). Garden City, NY: Doubleday, Doran & Co.

——. (1972-1989). *The Booker T. Washington Papers* (14 Volumes, Louis R. Harlan, Ed.). Urbana: University of Illinois Press.

——. (1996). *Up From Slavery: Authoritative Text, Contexts, and Composition History and Criticism* (William L. Andrews, Ed.). New York: Norton.

——. (2003). *Up from Slavery: With Related Documents* (W. Fitzhugh, Ed.). Boston: Bedford/St. Martin's.

Washington, Johnny. (1986). *Alain Locke and Philosophy: A Quest for Cultural Pluralism*. New York: Greenwood Press.

——. (1994). *A Journey Into the Philosophy of Alain Locke*. New York: Greenwood Press.

Washington, Joseph R., Jr. (1964). *Black Religion: Blacks and Christianity in the United States*. Boston: Beacon.

Washington, Mary Helen. (Ed.). (1987). *Invented Lives: Narratives of Black Women, 1860–1960*. Garden City, NY: Anchor.

Waters, Kristin, and Conaway, Carol B. (Eds.). (2007). *Black Women's Intellectual Traditions: Speaking Their Minds*. Burlington, VT: University of Vermont Press.

Watson, Steven. (1995). *The Harlem Renaissance: Hub of African American Culture, 1920–1930*. New York: Pantheon.

Watts, Eric King. (1995). "Reconstituting 'The Message': An Exploration of Double Consciousness in Rap Artistry." Ph.D. dissertation, Northwestern University.

——. (2001). "Cultivating a Black Public Voice: W.E.B. Du Bois and "The Criteria of Negro Art." *Rhetoric & Public Affairs* 4 (2), 181–201.

Weate, Jeremy. (2001). "Fanon, Merleau-Ponty and the Difference of Phenomenology." In Robert Bernasconi (Ed.), *Race* (pp. 169–83). Malden, MA: Blackwell.

Weatherford-Jacobs, Odesa Maria. (2002). "Hegel and Du Bois: A Study of the Influence of G. W. F. Hegel on the Early Writings of W. E. B. Du Bois." Ph.D. dissertation, Saint Louis University.

Weber, Max. (1963). *The Sociology of Religion* (Hans H. Gerth and C. Wright Mills, Eds.). New York: Oxford University Press.

Weiler, Kathleen. (1994). "Freire and Feminist Pedagogy of Difference." In Peter McLaren and Colin Lankshear (Eds.), *Politics of Liberation: Paths from Freire* (pp. 12–40). New York: Routledge.

——. (Ed.). (2001). *Feminist Engagements: Reading, Resisting, and Revisioning Male Theorists in Education and Cultural Studies*. New York: Routledge.

Weinbaum, Alys Eve. (2001). "Reproducing Racial Globality: W.E.B. Du Bois and the Sexual Politics of Black Internationalism." *Social Text* 19 (2), 15–41.

Weinbaum, Batya. (1978). *The Curious Courtship of Women's Liberation and Socialism*. Boston: South End.

Wellmer, Albrecht. (1974). *The Critical Theory of Society*. New York: Seabury.

Wells, Ida B. (1969). *On Lynchings*. New York: Arno Press.

——. (1970). *Crusade for Justice: The Autobiography of Ida B. Wells* (Alfreda Duster, Ed.). Chicago: University of Chicago Press.

——. (1991). *The Selected Works of Ida B. Wells-Barnett* (Trudier Harris, Ed.). New York: Oxford University Press.

——. (1993). *A Red Record: Lynchings in the U.S.* Salem, NH: Ayer & Co.

——. (1995). *The Memphis Dairy of Ida B. Wells* (Miriam Decosta-Willis, Ed.). Boston: Beacon.

Werbner, Richard P. (Ed.). (2002). *Postcolonial Subjectivities in Africa*. London: Zed.

Wesley, Charles H. (1965). "W.E.B. Du Bois: Historian." *Freedomways* 5, 59–72.

——. (1984). *The History of the National Association of Colored Women's Clubs: A Legacy of Service.* Washington, D.C.: National Association of Colored Women.

West, Cornel. (1982). *Prophesy Deliverance! An Afro-American Revolutionary Christianity.* Philadelphia: Westminister.

——. (1988a). *Prophetic Fragments.* Grand Rapids: Eerdmans.

——. (1988b). "Marxist Theory and the Specificity of Afro-American Oppression." In Cary Nelson and Lawrence Grossberg (Eds.), *Marxism and the Interpretation of Culture* (pp. 17–34). Chicago: University of Illinois Press.

——. (1989). "W.E.B. Du Bois: The Jamesian Organic Intellectual." In *The American Evasion of Philosophy: A Genealogy of Pragmatism.* Madison: University of Wisconsin Press.

——. (1993a). *Keeping Faith: Philosophy and Race in America.* New York: Routledge.

——. (1993b). *Race Matters.* New York: Random House.

——. (1993c). *Beyond Eurocentrism and Multiculturalism, Volume One: Prophetic Thought in Postmodern Times.* Monroe, ME: Common Courage.

——. (1993d). *Beyond Eurocentrism and Multiculturalism, Volume Two: Prophetic Reflections: Notes on Race and Power in America.* Monroe, ME: Common Courage.

——. (1996). "Black Strivings in a Twilight Civilization." In Henry Louis Gates, Jr. and Cornel West, *The Future of the Race* (pp. 53–114). New York: Alfred A. Knopf.

——. (Ed.). (1999). *The Cornel West Reader.* New York: Civitas.

——. (2004). *Democracy Matters: Winning the Fight Against Imperialism.* New York: Penguin.

West, Cornel, and Glaude, Eddie S., Jr. (Eds.). (2003). *African American Religious Thought: An Anthology.* Louisville: Westminster John Knox Press.

West, Michael R. (2005). *The Education of Booker T. Washington: American Democracy and the Idea of Race Relations.* New York: Columbia University Press.

Westley, Robert. (1998). "Many Billions Gone: Is It Time to Reconsider the Case for Black Reparations?" *Boston College Law Review* (December), 429–76.

White, Deborah Gray. (1999). *Too Heavy A Load: Black Women in Defense of Themselves, 1894–1994.* New York: Norton.

White, E. Frances. (1984). "Listening to the Voices of Black Feminism." *Radical America* 18 (2–3), 7–25.

——. (1995). "Africa On My Mind: Gender, Counter Discourse and African American Nationalism." In Beverly Guy-Sheftall (Ed.), *Words of Fire: An Anthology of African American Feminist Thought* (pp. 504–24). New York: The Free Press.

Whitten, Norman E., Jr., and Torres, Arlene. (Eds.). (1998). *Blackness in Latin America and the Caribbean: Social Dynamics and Cultural Transformations* (2 volumes). Indianapolis: Indiana University Press.

Wiatrowski-Phillips, Lily. (1995). "W.E.B. Du Bois and Soviet Communism: *The Black Flame* as Socialist Realism." *Southern Atlantic Quarterly* 94 (3), 837–75.

Wiggerhaus, Rolf. (1995). *The Frankfurt School: Its History, Theories, and Political Significance.* Cambridge: MIT Press.

Wilder, Craig S. (2001). *In the Company of Black Men: The African Influence on African American Culture in New York City.* New York: New York University.

Wilkerson, William S., and Paris, Jeffrey. (Eds.). (2001). *New Critical Theory: Essays on Liberation.* Lanham, MD: Rowman & Littlefield.

Willet, Cynthia. (2001). "The Mother Wit of Justice: Eros and Hubris in the African American Context." In William S. Wilkerson and Jeffrey Paris (Eds.), *New Critical Theory: Essays on Liberation* (pp. 223–48). Lanham, MD: Rowman and Littlefield Publishers.

Williams, Delores S. (1993). *Sisters in the Wilderness: The Challenge of Womanist God-talk.* Maryknoll, NY: Orbis.

Williams, Eric E. (1942). *The Negro in the Caribbean.* New York: Haskell House.

———. (1955). *The Case for Party Politics in Trinidad and Tobago.* Port of Spain: People's National Movement Publishing.

———. 1961). *Massa Day Done: A Masterpiece of Political and Sociological Analysis.* Port of Spain: People's National Movement Publishing.

———. (1962). *History of the People of Trinidad and Tobago.* Port of Spain: People's National Movement Publishing.

———. (1963). *Documents of West Indian History.* Port of Spain: People's National Movement Publishing.

———. (1964). *British Historians and the West Indies.* Port of Spain: People's National Movement Publishing.

———. (1965). *Reflections on the Caribbean Economic Community: A Series of Seven Articles.* Port of Spain: People's National Movement Publishing.

———. (1966). *Capitalism and Slavery.* New York: Capricorn Books.

———. (1969). *Britain and the West Indies.* London: University of Essex Press.

———. (1970). *From Columbus to Castro: The History of the Caribbean, 1492–1969.* London: Deutsch.

———. (1993). *Eric E. Williams Speaks: Essays on Colonialism and Independence.* Wellesley, MA: University of Massachusetts Press.

Williams, Patrick, and Chrisman, Laura. (Eds.). (1994). *Colonial Discourse and Postcolonial Theory: A Reader.* London: Harvester Wheatsheaf.

Williams, Randall. (2001). *W.E.B. Du Bois: A Scholar's Courageous Life.* Montgomery: New South.

Williams, Robert C. (1983). "W.E.B. Du Bois: Afro-American Philosopher of Social Reality." In Leonard Harris (Ed.), *Philosophy Born of Struggle: An Anthology of Afro-American Philosophy from 1917* (pp. 11–20). Dubuque, IA: Kendall/Hunt.

Williams, Shirley. (1990). "Some Implications of Womanist Theory." In Henry Louis Gates, Jr., (Ed.), *Reading Black/Reading Feminist: A Critical Anthology* (pp. 68–75). New York: Meridian.

Wilmore, Gayraud S. (1983). *Black Religion and Black Radicalism: An Interpretation of the Religious History of Afro-American People.* Maryknoll, NY: Orbis.

———. (Ed.). (1989). *African American Religious Studies: An Interdisciplinary Anthology.* Durham, NC: Duke University Press.

Wilson, Bobby M. (2002). "Critically Understanding Race-Connected Practices: A Reading of W.E.B. Du Bois and Richard Wright." *The Professional Geographer* 54 (1), 31–41.

Wilson, Kirt H. (1999). "Toward a Discursive Theory of Racial Identity: *The Souls of Black Folk* as a Response to Nineteenth-Century Biological Determinism." *Western Journal of Communication* 63 (2), 193–216.

Winant, Howard. (2001). *Racial Conditions: Politics, Theory, Comparisons.* Minneapolis, MN: University of Minnesota Press.

Winbush, Raymond A. (2003). *Should America Pay?: Slavery and the Debate on Reparations.* New York: HarperCollins.

Wing, Adrien Katherine. (Ed.). (1997). *Critical Race Feminism: A Reader.* New York: New York University Press.

———. (Ed). (2000). *Global Critical Race Feminism: An International Reader.* New York: New York University Press.

Wintz, Cary D. (1996). *African American Political Thought, 1890-1930: Washington, Du Bois, Garvey, and Randolph.* Armonk: M.E. Sharpe.

Wiredu, Kwasi. (1980). *Philosophy and an African Culture.* New York: Cambridge University Press.

———. (1991). "On Defining African Philosophy." In Tsenay Serequeberhan (Ed.), *African Philosophy: The Essential Readings* (pp. 87–110). New York: Paragon House.

———. (1995). *Conceptual Decolonization in African Philosophy: Four Essays.* Ibadan, Nigeria: Hope Publications.

———. (1996). *Cultural Universals and Particulars: An African Perspective.* Indianapolis: Indiana University Press.

———. (Ed.). (2004). *A Companion to African Philosophy.* Malden, MA: Blackwell.

Wolfram, Walt. (2002). *The Development of African American English.* Malden, MA: Blackwell.

Wolin, Richard. (1992). *The Terms of Cultural Criticism: The Frankfurt School, Existentialism, Postructuralism.* New York: Columbia University Press.

———. (1994). *Walter Benjamin: An Aesthetic of Redemption.* Berkeley: University of California Press.

———. (1995). *Labyrinths: Explorations on the Critical History of Ideas.* Amherst, MA: University of Massachusetts Press.

———. (2006). *The Frankfurt School Revisited: And Other Essays on Politics and Society.* New York: Routledge.

Wolters, Raymond. (2001). *Du Bois and His Rivals.* Columbia: University of Missouri Press.

Woodard, Frederic. (1976). "W.E.B. Du Bois: The Native Impulse—Notes toward an Ideological Biography, 1868-1897." Ph.D. dissertation, University of Iowa.

Woodard, Komozi. (1999). *A Nation within a Nation: Amiri Baraka (LeRoi Jones) and Black Power Politics.* Chapel Hill: University of North Carolina Press.

Woods, Jeff. (2004). *Black Struggle, Red Scare: Segregation and Anti-Communism in the South, 1948–1968.* Baton Rouge, LA: Louisiana State University Press.

Wormser, Richard. (2003). *The Rise and Fall of Jim Crow.* New York: St. Martin's Press.

Wortham, John M. (1997). "The Economic Ideologies of Booker T. Washington and W.E.B. Du Bois: 1895–1915." Ph.D. dissertation, Boston University.

Wortham, Robert A. (2005a). "The Early Sociological Legacy of W.E.B. Du Bois." In Anthony J. Blasi (Ed.), *Diverse Histories of American Sociology*. Boston: Brill.

———. (2005b). "Introduction to the Sociology of W.E.B. Du Bois." *Sociation Today* 3 (1). Online at: www.ncsociology.org/sociationtoday/v31/atlanta.htm (Accessed on 23 February 2005).

Wright, Earl. (2001). "The Atlanta Sociological Laboratory: America's First Model of Urban Sociological Research." *Southern Sociological Society*.

Wright, Richard A. (Ed.). (1984). *African Philosophy: An Introduction* (3rd Edition). Lanham, MD: University of America Press.

Wright, William. (1978). "Du Bois's Theory of Political Democracy." *Crisis* 85 (March), 85–89.

Wright, William D. (1985). "The Socialist Analysis of W.E.B. Du Bois." Ph.D. dissertation, State University of New York, Buffalo.

Yamamoto, Eric K. (1998). "Racial Reparations: Japanese American Redress and African American Claims." *Boston College Law Review* 40, 477–523.

Yancy, George. (Ed.). (1998). *African American Philosophers: 17 Conversations*. New York: Routledge.

———. (Ed.). (2001). *Cornel West: A Critical Reader*. Malden, MA: Blackwell.

———. (Ed.). (2004). *What White Looks Like: African American Philosophers on the Whiteness Question*. New York: Routledge.

———. (Ed.). (2005). *White on White/Black on Black*. Lanham, MD: Rowman and Littlefield.

Yee, Shirley J. (1992). *Black Women Abolitionists: A Study in Activism, 1828–1860*. Knoxville: University of Tennessee Press.

Yellin, Jean Fagan. (1973). "Du Bois's Crisis and Woman's Suffrage." *Massachusetts Review* 14 (2), 365–75.

Young, Henry J. (1977). *Major Black Religious Leaders, 1755–1940*. Nashville: Abingdon.

Young, Iris Marion. (1990). *Justice and the Politics of Difference*. Princeton: Princeton University Press.

Young, Jason R. (2007). *Rituals of Resistance: African Atlantic Religion in Kongo and the Low-Country South in the Era of Slavery*. Baton Rouge, LA: Louisiana State University Press.

Young, Josiah U. (1986). *Black and African Theologies: Siblings or Distant Cousins?* Maryknoll, NY: Orbis.

———. (1992). *A Pan-African Theology: Providence and the Legacies of the Ancestors*. Trenton, NJ: Africa World Press.

Young, Kenneth Ray, and Green, Dan S. (1972). "Harbinger to Nixon: W.E.B. Du Bois in China." *Negro History Bulletin* 35 (October).

Young, Robert Alexander. (1996). *The Ethiopian Manifesto*. In Wilson Jeremiah Moses (Ed.), *Classical Black Nationalism: From the American Revolution to Marcus Garvey*. New York: New York University Press.

Young, Robert J. (1995). *Colonial Desire: Hybridity in Theory, Culture and Race*. New York: Routledge.

———. (1999). *Postcolonialism: An Historical Introduction.* Malden, MA: Blackwell.

———. (2003). *Postcolonialism: A Very Short Introduction.* New York: Oxford University Press.

Yuan, Ji. (1998). "W.E.B. Du Bois and His Socialist Thought." Ph.D. dissertation, Temple University, Philadelphia.

———. (2000). *W.E.B. Du Bois and His Socialist Thought.* Lawrenceville: Africa World Press.

Zack, Naomi. (1993). *Race and Mixed Race.* Philadelphia: Temple University Press.

———. (Ed.). (1995). *American Mixed Race: The Culture of Microdiversity.* Lanham, MD: Rowman and Littlefield.

———. (1996). *Bachelors of Science: Seventeenth Century Identity, Then and Now.* Philadelphia: Temple University Press.

———. (Ed.). (1997). *Race/Sex: Their Sameness, Difference, and Interplay.* New York: Routledge.

———. (1998). *Thinking About Race.* Albany, NY: Wadsworth.

———. (Ed.). (2000). *Women of Color and Philosophy: A Critical Reader.* Malden, MA: Blackwell.

———. (2002). *Philosophy of Science and Race.* New York: Routledge.

———. (2005). *Inclusive Feminism: A Third Wave Theory of Women's Commonality.* Lanham, MD: Rowman and Littlefield.

Zack, Naomi, Shrage, Laurie, and Sartwell, Crispin. (Eds.). (1998). *Race, Class, Gender, and Sexuality: The Big Questions.* Cambridge: Blackwell.

Zahan, Dominique. (1979). *The Religion, Spirituality, and Thought of Traditional Africa.* Chicago: University of Chicago Press.

Zamir, Shamoon. (1994). " 'The Sorrow Songs'/'Song of Myself': Du Bois, the Crisis of Leadership, and Prophetic Imagination." In Werner Sollors and Maria Diedrich (Eds.), *The Black Columbiad: Defining Moments in African American Literature and Culture* (pp. 145–66). Cambridge, MA: Harvard University Press.

———. (1995). *Dark Voices: W.E.B. Du Bois and American Thought, 1888-1903.* Chicago: University of Chicago Press.

———. (Ed). (2008). *The Cambridge Companion to W.E.B. Du Bois.* Cambridge: Cambridge University Press.

Zegeye, Abebe, Harris, Leonard, and Maxted, Julia. (Eds.). (1991). *Exploitation and Exclusion: Race and Class in Contemporary US Society.* London: Hans Zell.

Zinn, Maxine Baca, and Dill, Bonnie Thornton. (Eds.). (1994). *Women of Color in U.S. Society.* Philadelphia: Temple University Press.

Zinn, Maxine Baca, Cannon, Lynn Weber, Higginbotham, Elizabeth, and Dill, Bonnie Thornton. (1986). "The Cost of Exclusionary Practices in Women's Studies." *Signs* 11 (2), 290–303.

Zuckerman, Phil. (2002). "The Sociology of Religion of W.E.B. Du Bois." *Sociology of Religion* 63 (2), 239–53.

———. (2003). *Invitation to the Sociology of Religion.* New York: Routledge.

————. (2004). "Introduction to the Social Theory of W.E.B. Du Bois". In Phil Zuck-
erman (Ed.), *The Social Theory of W.E.B. Du Bois* (pp. 1–17). Thousand Oaks:
Sage.
Zuckerman, Phil, Barnes, Sandra L., and Cady, Daniel. (2003). "*The Negro Church*:
An Introduction." In W.E.B. Du Bois (Ed.), *The Negro Church* (pp.vii–xxvi). Wal-
nut Creek: AltaMira.

Index

About the Author

Reiland Rabaka is an associate professor of Africana studies in the department of ethnic studies at the University of Colorado at Boulder, where he is also an affiliate professor of women and gender studies and a research fellow at the Center for Studies of Ethnicity and Race in America (CSERA). He is the author of *W.E.B. Du Bois and the Problems of the Twenty-First Century* and *Africana Critical Theory: Reconstructing the Black Radical Tradition from W.E.B. Du Bois to Amilcar Cabral*, both published by Lexington Books.